Albrecht Dürer's material world

Edited by
Edward H. Wouk and Jennifer Spinks

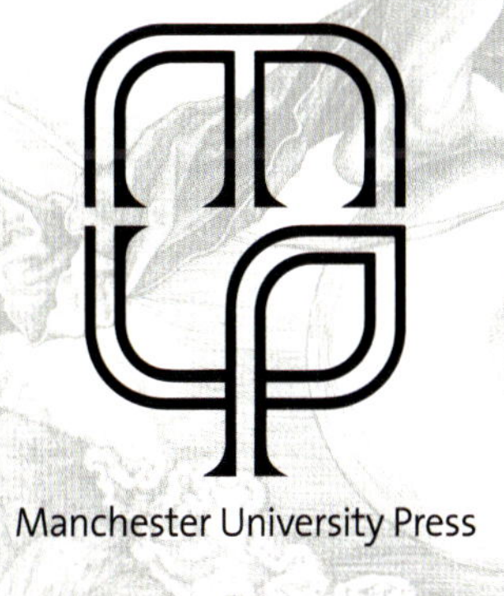

Manchester University Press

the **Whitworth**

Published by Manchester University Press
Oxford Road, Manchester M13 9PL

www.manchesteruniversitypress.co.uk

British Library Cataloguing-in-Publication Data

A catalogue record for this book is available from the British Library

ISBN 978 1 5261 6760 6   paperback

First published 2023

Albrecht Dürer's material world is published to coincide with the exhibition of the same name held at The Whitworth, The University of Manchester, 30 June 2023–10 March 2024.

Design: Alan J Ward
Printed in Great Britain by Bell & Bain Ltd, Glasgow

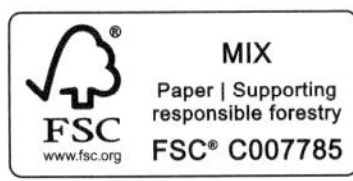

Contents

List of contributors

Matthew S. Champion, The University of Melbourne
Dagmar Eichberger, The University of Heidelberg
Holly Fletcher, The University of Manchester
Danielle Gravon, Minnesota State University Moorhead
Sasha Handley, The University of Manchester
Stefan Hanß, The University of Manchester
Imogen Holmes-Roe, The Whitworth
Larry Silver, The University of Pennsylvania
Jennifer Spinks, The University of Melbourne
Edward H. Wouk, The University of Manchester
Charles Zika, The University of Melbourne

Lenders to the exhibition

Albrecht Dürer's Material World, the Whitworth,
The University of Manchester, 30 June 2023–
10 March 2024. Curatorial team: Imogen Holmes-Roe,
Edward H. Wouk, Holly Fletcher, Sasha Handley,
Stefan Hanß and David Morris.

Ashmolean Museum, University of Oxford
The British Museum
Chetham's Library
Germanisches Nationalmuseum
The John Rylands Research Institute and Library
Manchester Art Gallery
Manchester Museum
The Museum of Medicine and Health
National Museums Scotland
The Royal Armouries Museum

Albrecht Dürer's material world
Foreword

Albrecht Dürer's material world represents a significant moment for the Whitworth. It is the first major exhibition of the gallery's outstanding collection of Dürer's woodcuts, etchings and engravings in over fifty years. It also brings a new perspective to the study of early modern prints and drawings by focusing on their relationship to a material world of art, design and manufacture in the increasingly globalised context of Dürer's Nuremberg and the regions he visited on his travels.

New research on Albrecht Dürer appears at a substantial rate. Important developments include Dürer as a collector and his connection to sculpture, and the technical and decorative processes of gold and silversmithing. However, his wider engagement with the material and sensory world around him has received surprisingly little attention, and links between material culture and Dürer research remain limited.

This exhibition and catalogue demonstrate the close collaborative relationship between the Whitworth and The University of Manchester's academic staff. The project draws on the expertise of a team of Manchester-based and international researchers who have been examining Dürer's art from the perspective of material culture studies for over five years. The team comprises established Dürer scholars, art historians, and historians of material culture: Manchester scholars Edward Wouk, Sasha Handley, Stefan Hanß and Whitworth Curator (Historic Fine Art) Imogen Holmes-Roe are joined by Australian and European researchers Jennifer Spinks, Matthew Champion, Dagmar Eichberger and Charles Zika. Together, they have created an exhibition that throws new light on Dürer's interface with the 'material Renaissance'.

The exhibition includes outstanding loans from national and international venues, which enable us to bring important historic objects from Dürer's own time to a regional gallery and audience. Ranging from Dürer's own designs for shoes to rare surviving examples of early modern German tiles, scientific instruments, armour and ornithological specimens, these loans provide unprecedented insight into the material world in which Dürer operated. We are particularly grateful to the British Museum, the Royal Armouries, National Museums Scotland, the Ashmolean Museum, University of Oxford, the Germanisches Nationalmuseum and Chetham's Library as well as our own University partners, The John Rylands Research Institute and Library, Manchester Museum and The Museum of Medicine and Health.

Albrecht Dürer's material world also presents new opportunities for widening access to collections. As a space for experimentation and learning, the exhibition serves as a bridge between the university and the people of the city. As a space to disseminate this new research, the exhibition serves as a lens to see afresh Dürer's artistic oeuvre.

Amy George
Interim Head of Collections
The Whitworth

Prof. John McAuliffe
Director
Creative Manchester

Acknowledgements

The editors wish to acknowledge the support of many individuals whose collaboration has helped bring this exhibition to fruition. Whitworth Curator (Historic Fine Art) Imogen Holmes-Roe has expertly and diligently shepherded this project from initial proposal to its final form as a spectacular exhibition, working closely with Dr Edward Wouk, from the Department of Art History and Cultural Practices, together with Dr Stefan Hanß and Professor Sasha Handley from the Department of History and David Morris, former Curator at the Whitworth, who has assisted with exhibition interpretation.

Much of the research motivating this exhibition stems from the project 'Albrecht Dürer's Material World – in Melbourne, Manchester and Nuremberg' (Australian Research Council Discovery Project DP210101623). The researchers on the project are all contributors to this volume: in addition to the academics listed above, they include Dr Matthew Champion, Professor Dagmar Eichberger, Associate Professor Jennifer Spinks and Professor Charles Zika. As our ideas began to crystallise into the form of this exhibition, we were joined by additional contributors whose essays round out this catalogue in important ways: Professor Larry Silver, Dr Holly Fletcher and Imogen Holmes-Roe. Our research assistants, Dr Danielle Gravon and Dr Hannah Spracklan-Holl, have aided in numerous ways, always with good humour.

In addition to Imogen Holmes-Roe, we are indebted to many other members of the Whitworth team, including former Director Alistair Hudson; from the Curatorial team Amy George, Poppy Bowers, Victoria Hartley and Hannah Vollam; and from the Collections Care team Ann French, Dan Hogger, Sarah Potter and Emma Brown, whose material knowledge has sharpened our understanding of the objects exhibited here. We are grateful to colleagues at lending institutions in Manchester, including Julianne Simpson of The John Rylands Research Institute and Library, Fergus Wilde of Chetham's Library, and our colleagues at Manchester Museum, Manchester Art Gallery and the Museum of Medicine and Health, The University of Manchester. Much of the excellent photography of these works has been produced by Michael Pollard.

We also express gratitude to our lending partners beyond Manchester: The Ashmolean Museum, National Museums Scotland, the Germanisches Nationalmuseum, The Royal Armouries Museum and especially the British Museum, whose generosity in loans have significantly enriched this exhibition.

We gratefully acknowledge the generous support of the Getty Foundation through The Paper Project initiative, and the Friends of the Whitworth who have made this exhibition and publication possible. Further funding support has come from the German History Society, the School of Arts, Languages and Cultures, The University of Manchester and The John Rylands Research Institute and Library.

Angela Roberts has copy-edited this volume with great care, and we wish to thank her together with the editorial team at Manchester University Press: Emma Brennan, Alun Richards, David Appleyard and Humairaa Dudhwala, and our designer Alan Ward, for their support and interest in this project.

Edward H. Wouk
Jennifer Spinks

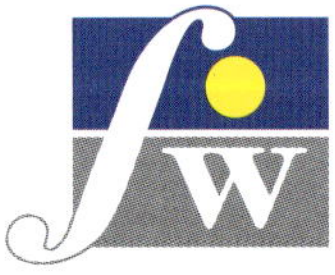

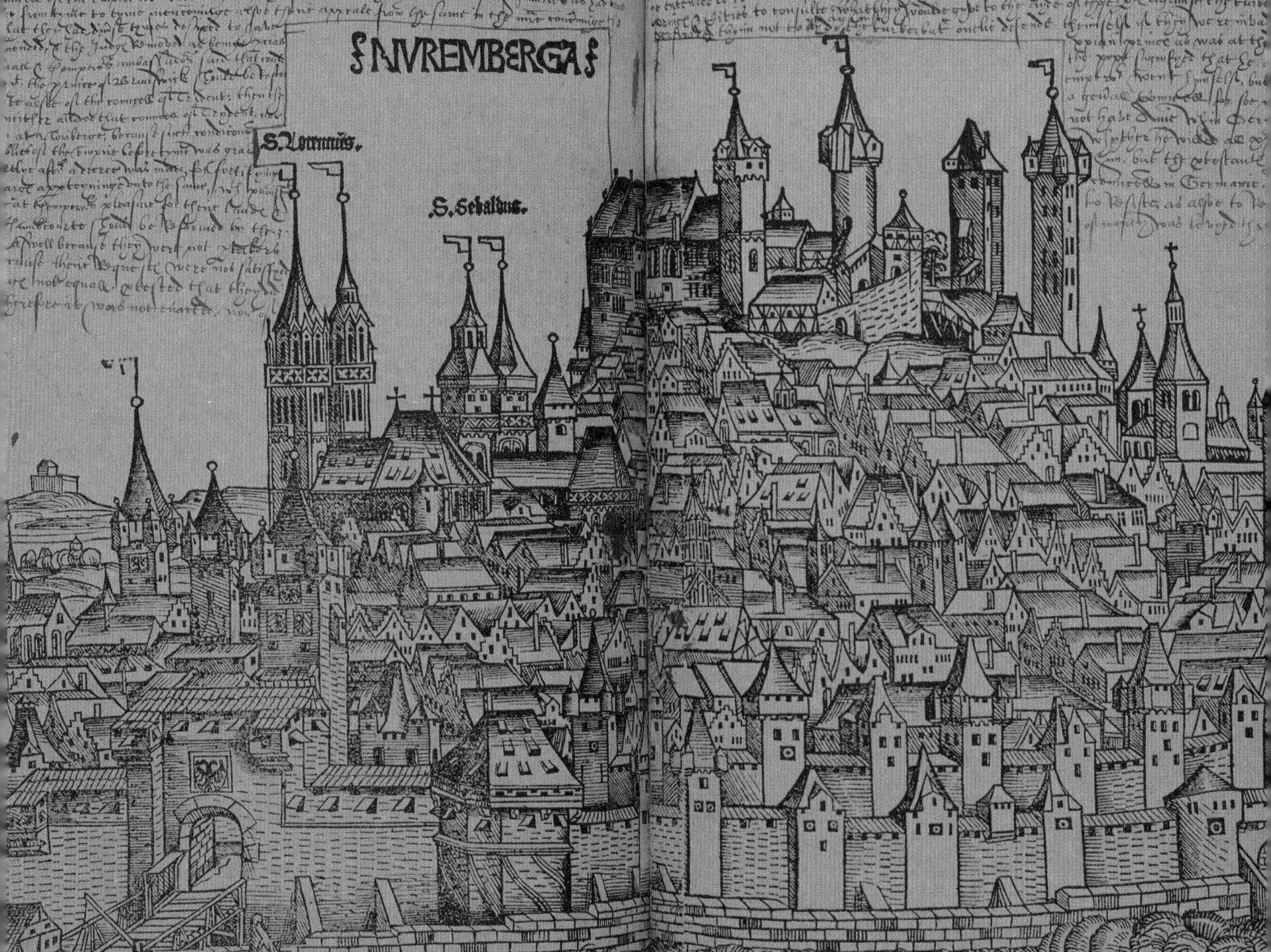

§ NVREMBERGA §

S. Laurencius.

S. Sebaldus.

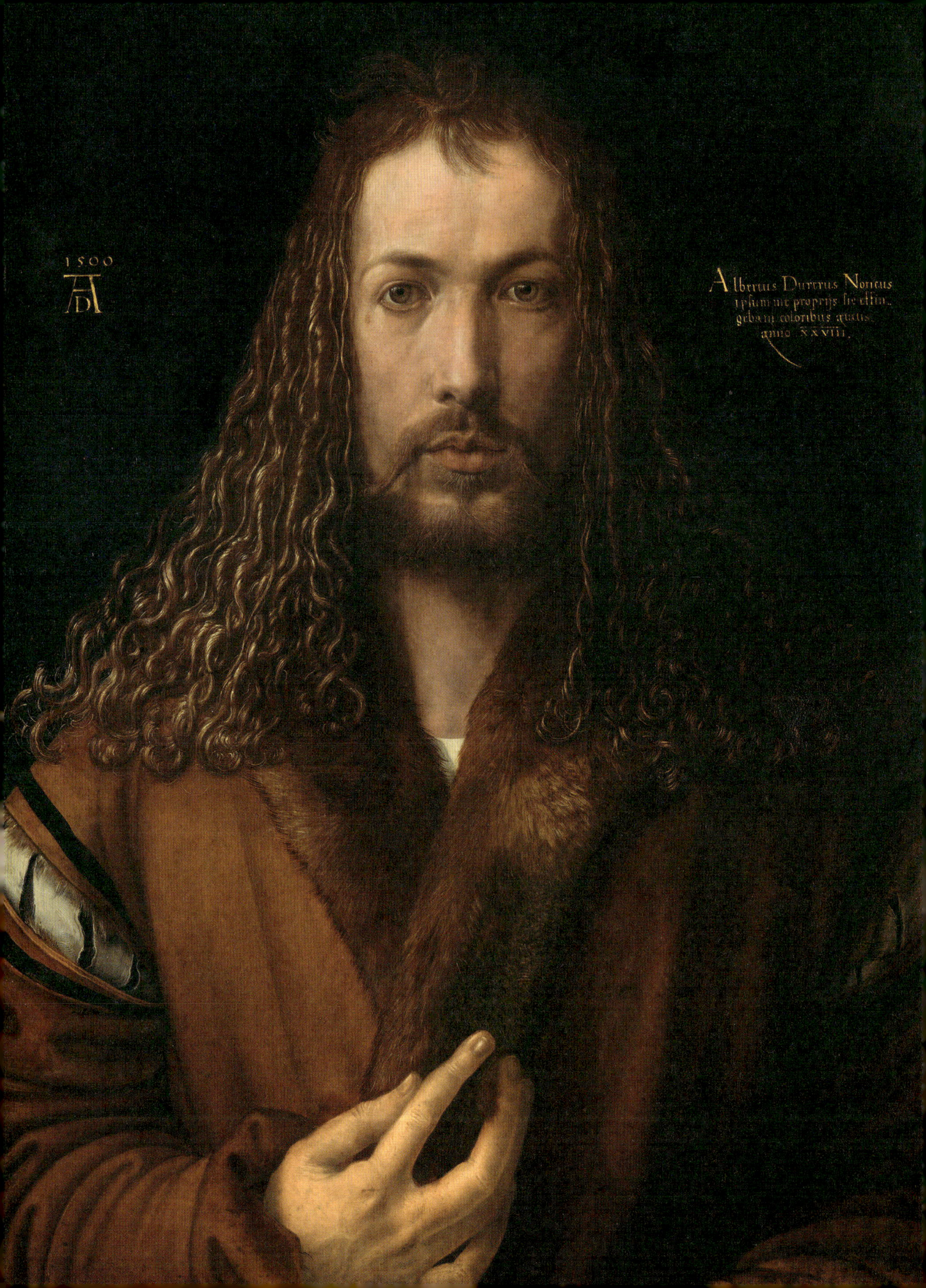

1500
AD
Albertus Durerus Noricus
ipsum me proprijs sic effin=
gebam coloribus aetatis
anno XXVIII.

[1] Introducing *Albrecht Dürer's material world*

Jennifer Spinks and Edward H. Wouk

Albrecht Dürer (1471–1528; Figure 1.1) was an intense observer of the worlds of manufacture, design and trade that fill his graphic art. *Albrecht Dürer's material world*, the first major exhibition of the Whitworth's outstanding Dürer collection in over half a century, juxtaposes examples of Dürer's woodcuts, etchings and engravings from the Whitworth's collection with a range of objects from Dürer's time.[1] It aims to highlight the ingenuity and skill with which this leading figure of Europe's print revolution represented the vast array of material objects that surrounded him, both in the vibrant manufacturing and consumer hub of Nuremberg – his home city – and the wider European world that he encountered on his travels and through networks of exchange.

During Dürer's lifetime, Europe witnessed a flourishing of material arts and consumer goods; from armour to measuring instruments, liturgical objects to books, hourglasses to the finest clothing. The exhibition brings together a team of scholars interested in what has come to be termed 'material culture'.[2] Historians, art historians and curators are increasingly turning to a wider array of material objects to expand knowledge of the past. These objects range from the luxurious to the mundane, and they reveal different facets of living in what has been dubbed a 'material Renaissance', when the production and ownership of consumer items accelerated.[3] This attention to materiality encompasses studies of global trade networks, the emotional lives of objects, and even projects recreating early modern workshop techniques.[4] Our focus on the types of objects that surrounded

Dürer provides new insights into the life of one of the most significant artists of the Renaissance. It also prompts us to look again at his groundbreaking prints, with a more detailed focus on how some of Dürer's most iconic images – in both technique and subject matter – were fostered by his innovative attention to the material world that surrounded him.[5]

A material biography

Materiality shaped Albrecht Dürer's world and he, in turn, advanced a radical approach to working with materials, redefining what constituted art and artistic practice in early modern Europe. The young Dürer joined his Hungarian father's successful goldsmithing studio as an apprentice before entering the workshop of Nuremberg's leading painter, Michael Wolgemut (1434–1519).[6] The tactile experience of using specialist metalworking tools gave Dürer skills that would prove invaluable when, in the mid-1490s, he turned to making prints independently.[7] From this time Dürer ran his own workshop with the assistance of his wife, Agnes Frey (1475–1539), securing increasingly prestigious painting commissions and producing prints, which he sold within Nuremberg and also, in an astute commercial move, via commissioned travelling salesmen after 1497. His early works included the groundbreaking *Book of Revelation* woodcuts from 1498, the first ever print cycle published as a book.[8]

Over the following decades, Dürer created an extraordinary body of paintings, drawings and prints. While his graphic work in particular has been examined from many angles, the lens of material culture pursued in this exhibition offers fresh insights into iconic images like the three spectacular engravings, later termed the *Meisterstiche* or master prints: *Saint Jerome in his Study* in 1514 (cat. 73), the saint surrounded by a range of

1.1 Albrecht Dürer, *Self-Portrait with Fur-Trimmed Robe*, 1500, painting on limewood, 67.1 x 48.9 cm. Bayerische Staatsgemaeldesammlungen © Photo SCALA, Florence.

lovingly depicted objects; *Knight, Death and the Devil* in 1513 (cat. 75), with its stunning armour and inventive demons; and the inscrutable *Melencolia* in 1514 (cat. 79), with its plethora of measuring instruments. Dürer's prints were crucial to developing his pan–European reputation for dazzling levels of detail, skilled handling of light and shade, precise cutting, and attention to the human body. His prints depicted religious scenes that were particularly focused on Christ and the Virgin Mary, Renaissance-inspired imagery that drew on classical antiquity, and scenes of daily life, ranging from bathhouses to peasant dancers. Dürer demonstrated a twinned fascination for the materiality of texture and depictions of objects – from cups to candlesticks to cannons – in many of his images. His stature as both an artist and a citizen of Nuremberg continued to grow. From 1512, he took on major commissions for the Holy Roman Emperor Maximilian I (1459–1519), including contributions to ambitious multi-sheet prints of processions and ornate, symbolic building facades. These large-scale woodcuts emphatically reminded viewers that prints, too, were material objects.

Travel was central to Dürer's development as an artist and contributed to his astute sensitivity to the diversity of art, the cultures of making and the patterns of consumption he encountered throughout central Europe and beyond. While undertaking the traditional *Wanderjahr* typical of young craftsmen, he likely encountered artworks in collections that increased his knowledge of developments in Netherlandish and northern art. On glistening panels, northern artists depicted objects, textures and interior spaces with unparalleled detail and luminosity.[9] He also encountered new developments in printmaking, which was beginning to find its footing as a medium for art. In Colmar, he sought an audience with Martin Schongauer (1440/53–91), and expressed his disappointment upon learning that the artist had recently died; Dürer must have been dazzled by Schongauer's extraordinary engravings such as this minute rendering of a censer (Figure 1.2), which elevates this liturgical furnishing from an autonomous object to a subject for contemplation. Over two trips to Italy – in 1494/5 and again in 1505/6 – he observed the remarkable array of goods available in trading ports

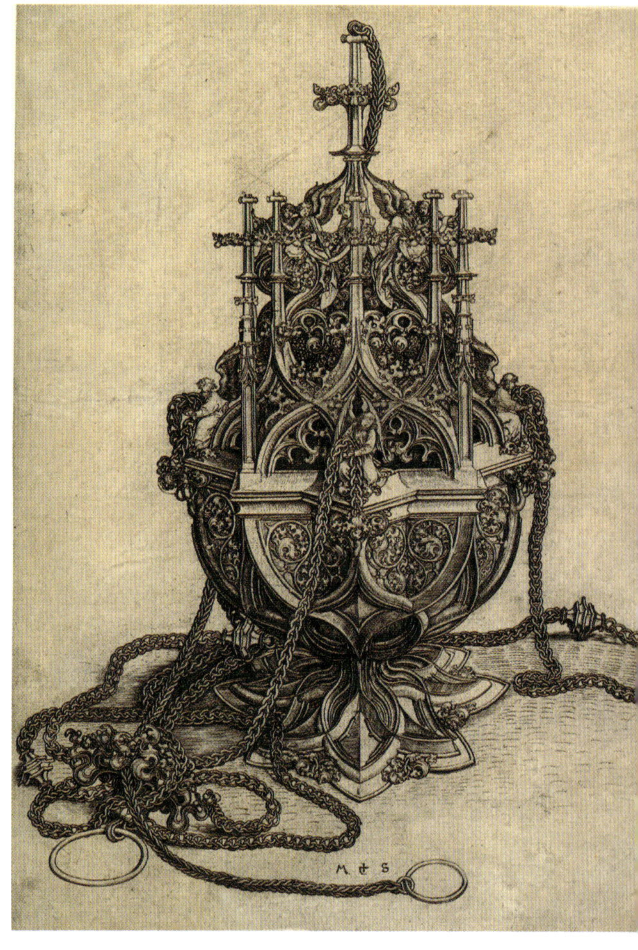

1.2 Martin Schongauer, *The Censer*, c. 1470–91, engraving, 489 x 363 mm.
New York, The Metropolitan Museum of Art, 26.41
© The Metropolitan Museum of Art.

and encountered exceptional painters like Jacopo Bellini (c. 1400–c. 1470), whose richly coloured work he rated above all others. In letters sent from Venice to his friend the Nuremberg humanist Willibald Pirckheimer (1470–1530), whom he later portrayed in an engraving (cat. 2), Dürer described the many objects – rings, rugs, feathers, clothes – that he purchased both for himself and as an agent for Pirckheimer, among others. Clothes in particular were fundamentally bound up with his sense of identity. His startlingly frontal self-portrait of 1500, for example, is Christlike, attesting to his piety and remarkable self-fashioning, but it also features a

    Albrecht Dürer's material world

sumptuous fur collar on which Dürer rests his fingers, the individual fibres appearing to spring out from the painting (Figure 1.1).[10]

In 1520–21, Dürer travelled to the Low Countries in hope of having his imperial pension reinstated by the new Holy Roman Emperor, Charles V (1500–1558), who was being crowned in Aachen. He kept detailed records in which objects and artworks proliferate, including notes about the value of his own prints.[11] But he was also dazzled by the entirely new things that he saw on this trip, from the carcass of a whale to Aztec featherwork and gold newly arrived from the Americas: 'amazing shields, curious costumes, bed coverings and every kind of spectacular things [sic] for all possible uses, more worth seeing than the usual prodigies'.[12] Dürer's health declined soon after this trip and he died in Nuremberg in 1528. His last major treatise, *Four Books on Human Proportion* (cat. 58), was published posthumously. Friends exhumed his body the day after his burial to secure final, relic-like objects that included a death mask and a lock of his famous curling hair.

The artist and the city

Dürer's home city of Nuremberg was the primary locus of his deep engagement with the material world. The Franconian city of over 25,000 inhabitants had long enjoyed favoured status. In 1424 Holy Roman Emperor Sigismund (1368–1437) made the city the repository of the imperial regalia – including crown and sceptre – and collection of relics, notably the Holy Lance which, according to tradition, pierced Christ's side at the Crucifixion. These were displayed at the annual *Heiltumsfest*, which doubled as a trade fair. By Dürer's time the city's success could be traced to several factors: its location at the heart of European trading networks; its strong ties to the Holy Roman Emperor; the patrician Council that directly oversaw artisanal work; and networks of craftworkers, artists and humanists engaged with the city's burgeoning arts and trades.[13]

In 1493 Dürer's godfather, Anton Koberger (1445–1513), published the *Nuremberg Chronicle*, a history of the world containing over 1,800 woodcuts, which became a landmark in the history of the printed book.[14]

Nuremberg's cityscape featured prominently in a double-page woodcut (cat. 1), reminding purchasers across Europe that the city was at the forefront of the printing revolution that had been set in motion by Johannes Gutenberg in Mainz in the 1450s. While a flurry of printing activity and the establishment of new workshops was a hallmark of Renaissance Nuremberg, the city had also been renowned since the fourteenth century for its metalwork. Enhanced particularly by innovations in luxury goldsmithing, armour-making, liturgical objects and even miniature screws for precision instruments, this reputation grew.[15]

In 1525, only a few years before Dürer's death in 1528, the Nuremberg council voted to accept the new Lutheran Reformation.[16] But for much of his life Nuremberg had been a city shaped by the sensuous material world of late medieval Catholic piety and the dynamism of skilled crafts. The large, sculpted *Pietà* displayed in this exhibition provides some sense of the colourful world of late medieval Catholic devotion (cat. 7). Rosaries, censers, candles and chalices all feature heavily in Dürer's art. In images such as *The Mass of Saint Gregory* (cat. 8), depicting an eighth-century miraculous apparition, he brought the objects of contemporary Catholic devotion into the space of the graphic imagination (see 'Objects of Devotion' by Charles Zika in this volume). Nonetheless, Dürer was deeply moved by Martin Luther's (1483–1546) call to reform from 1517. He produced portraits of Luther's close collaborator Philip Melanchthon (1497–1560; cat. 3) and of Friedrich the Wise (1463–1525; cat. 4), elector of Saxony and Luther's early protector. He even went so far as to record into his Netherlandish diary the prayer by Augustinian prior Jacob Probst (c. 1495–1562) for Luther's release from captivity.[17] But Dürer was only just becoming aware of the way in which the Reformation would fundamentally change the materiality of the Christian experience. That his prints played a role in a new spirituality, one that was focused on the individual encounter between a beholder and an image, is something art historians now acknowledge. His woodcuts, engravings and etchings, like the world of goods they represent, were both commodities and affective objects endowed with emotional values that surpass the monetary without negating its import.

Dürer's early critics posited that he initiated a new tradition of artmaking that focused on supreme technical skill and boundless creativity.[18] In their view, his art represented a union of virtuosity and theoretical knowledge that was largely unprecedented at the time, certainly north of the Alps. In addition to publishing treatises addressing the practice and theory of the visual arts, Dürer excelled through his mastery both of traditional media, such as painting and drawing, as well as the new media of print – woodcut, engraving and etching – which he strove to elevate to the level of art.[19] While a discourse on the arts in Italy measured artists' achievements in terms of the recovery of classical antiquity, the treatment of the body and the development of perspective, Dürer transformed the print revolution of his age into a revolution in art. Through the replicative technology of print, the meticulousness of his practice became available to new audiences – consumers of his art – and his fame increased.

Not only was Dürer's work in demand; portraits of him in medals and prints were already in circulation during his own lifetime and would play an important role in cultivating his celebrity. Erhard Schön (1491–1542) likely produced the woodcut *Portrait of Albrecht Dürer in Profile* (cat. 5) shortly after his death, although it is based on an earlier portrait medal struck by Mathes Gebel (c. 1500–74). It was printed in great quantities, with some impressions including a text by the *Meistersinger* Hans Sachs (1494–1576), recounting the artist's renown.[20] Lucas Kilian (1579–1637) in the dramatically lit *Portrait of Albrecht Dürer* (cat. 6), dated 1608, reveals the artist's cult-like status in the seventeenth century. The engraver based his work upon another artist's copy of Dürer's self-portrait in the *Feast of the Rose Garlands*, which the artist had painted for German merchants in Venice.[21]

One early commentator on Dürer's art was the Dutch scholar Erasmus of Rotterdam (c. 1466–1536), whose portrait Dürer famously recorded in a late print. Both Erasmus and Dürer recognised that the technologies of print were a precondition for their own success and celebrity.[22] Erasmus notably wrote that Dürer surpassed even the most famous painter of antiquity, Apelles, who relied on colour whereas Dürer was able to 'express absolutely anything in monochrome, that is with black lines only – shadows, light, reflections, emerging and receding forms, and even the different aspects of a single thing as they strike the eye of the spectator'.[23] Erasmus's comments highlight Dürer's consummate ability to manipulate copper, wood and ink – the materials of printmaking – to achieve unsurpassed visual effects.[24]

Dürer expertly marketed his prints, which were the source of his international success and celebrity. During his lifetime, other printmakers copied his work, most famously the Italian engraver Marcantonio Raimondi (1480–1534), whose engraved copy of Dürer's *Visitation* (cat. 55, 56) from the *Life of the Virgin* series testifies to his efforts to profit from the artist's renown. Dürer's likely attempt to suppress this early copyright infringement is a matter of art historical legend, one that highlights important concerns about originality, replication and multiplication.[25] But soon the challenge of copying Dürer itself became a privileged creative endeavour. In 1565, the Netherlandish engraver Hieronymus Wierix (1553–1619) remade Dürer's *Saint Jerome in his Study*. His was an astounding copy bearing both Dürer's monogram and Wierix's own name along with his age; he was only thirteen when he undertook this exercise in emulative virtuosity. Decades later, around the time of the so-called 'Dürer Renaissance' which flourished in Prague, Hieronymus Wierix's brother Johannes (1549–1620) engraved an exquisite copy of *Melencolia I* (cat. 80).[26] Later artists, including Francisco Goya (1744–1828), Käthe Kollwitz (1867–1945), Joseph Beuys (1921–86), Kiki Smith (b. 1954) and the collective Goldin+Senneby, have carried this tradition of response forward in a diversity of responses to Dürer's extraordinary prints.

Exhibiting Dürer's material world

Albrecht Dürer's material world invites visitors to enter three thematic spaces of creation and creativity in Renaissance Germany: the home, the workshop and the study. Artworks and objects in these three rooms expose aspects of Dürer's art and practice, including his examination of objects of daily domestic use, his involvement in economies of local manufacture and exchange, the microarchitectures of local craft and, finally, his attention to the furnishings and artefacts tied to cultures of natural and philosophical inquiry and learning. This exhibition's thematic approach draws upon recent work in the fields of material culture studies and digital microscopy to reconsider how a changing Renaissance material world, characterised by increasing globalisation, sparked artistic creativity

and innovation in the production of art and craft in Dürer's home town of Nuremberg and beyond. Microscopic analysis carried out in preparation for this exhibition is one means by which we have attempted to see Dürer's art with new eyes and to make visible his attention to detail and the tactile qualities of his materials. Microscopic enlargements of prints such as *Friedrich the Wise, Elector of Saxony* (cat. 4) reveal the artist's staggering skill in using his burin to render effects as varied as the glint of reflection in the elector's eye (Figure 1.3) and the artist's own celebrated 'AD' monogram – the widely recognised marking with which he signed and promoted much of his work (Figure 1.4).[27]

The exhibition also brings new perspectives to the history of collecting Dürer's art in the northwest of England and to the role that local collectors – many involved in trade, industry and design – played in amassing one of the country's most significant holdings of his graphic work. This catalogue explores the history of exhibiting Dürer's art in Manchester and presents essays by leading scholars examining individual Dürer prints in relation to their material contexts, focusing on cultures of making and consumption, on meaning and interpretation, and on context and legacy. A brief essay introduces the recently restored sculpture *Pietà* (cat. 7) from Dürer's Germany in the Whitworth's collection. The final portion of this catalogue comprises a brief introduction to the three conceptual spaces of the exhibition, each followed by a checklist of objects.

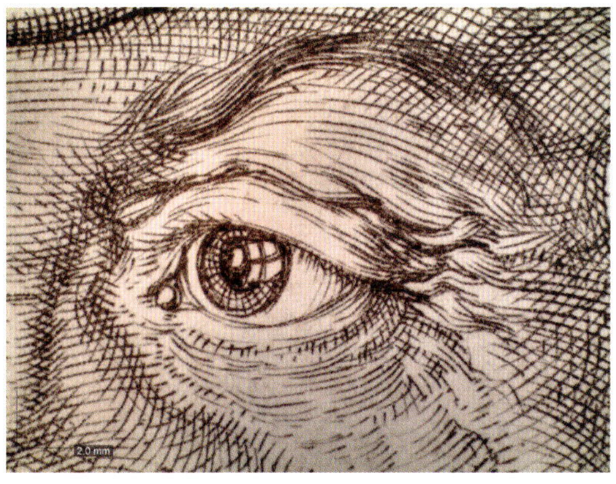

1.3 (cat. 4) Detail of Albrecht Dürer, *Friedrich the Wise*, showing the sitter's eye. Photograph taken with a Dino-Lite USB microscope, 18.3 magnification scale.

© The Whitworth, The University of Manchester. Photo: Stefan Hanß.

1.4 (cat. 4) Detail of Albrecht Dürer, *Friedrich the Wise*, showing the artist's monogram. Photograph taken with a Dino-Lite USB microscope, 18.3 magnification scale.

© The Whitworth, The University of Manchester. Photo: Stefan Hanß.

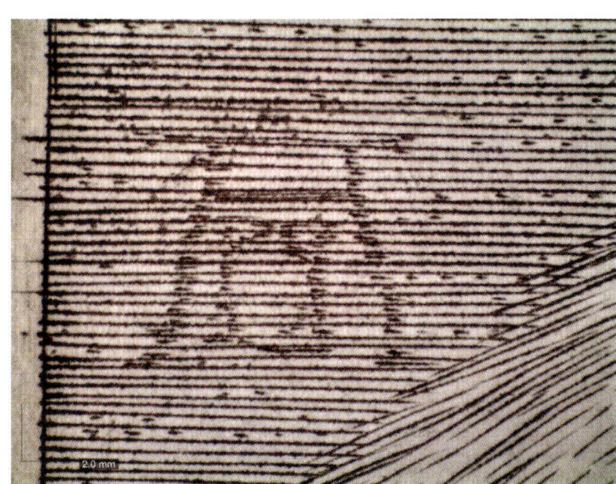

Notes

1   *Engravings and Woodcuts by Albrecht Dürer, 1471–1528*. The University of Manchester and Goethe-Institute of Manchester held a symposium to coincide with the exhibition; its proceedings were published in Levy and Dodwell, *Essays on Dürer*.

2   Gerritsen and Riello, eds, *Writing Material Culture History*; Harvey, ed., *History and Material Culture*.

3   O'Malley and Welch, eds, *The Material Renaissance*; Rublack, 'Matter in the Material Renaissance'.

4   Gerritsen and Riello, eds, *The Global Lives of Things*; Downes, Holloway and Randles, eds, *Feeling Things*; Smith, *From Lived Experience*.

5   This forms part of the interdisciplinary project 'Albrecht Dürer's Material World – in Nuremberg, Manchester and Melbourne', Australian Research Council DP210101623, 2021-2024. The project members are Matthew Champion, Dagmar Eichberger, Sasha Handley, Stefan Hanß, Jennifer Spinks, Edward H. Wouk and Charles Zika. For more information, see https://www.duerersmaterialworld.org.

6   The literature on Dürer is vast. Excellent recent general studies and edited volumes in English include Smith, *Dürer*; Hutchison, *Albrecht Dürer*; Silver and Smith, eds, *The Essential Dürer*; Eichberger and Zika, eds, *Dürer and his Culture*; the classic Panofsky, *Life and Art of Albrecht Dürer*; and Ashcroft, *Albrecht Dürer*, which presents Dürer in his own words in an accessible new edition. The standard reference work to Dürer's prints is now Schoch, Mende and Scherbaum, *Albrecht Dürer*. See also these important exhibition catalogues: Bartrum, *Dürer and his Legacy*; Baumbauer, Hirschfelder and Teget-Welz, eds, *Michael Wolgemut*; Metzger, ed., *Albrecht Dürer*; Sander, ed., *Albrecht Dürer*; van den Brink, ed., *Dürer war Hier*; published in a shortened English version as Foister and van den Brink, eds, *Dürer's Journeys*; Zdanowicz, ed., *Albrecht Dürer*. While art historians are familiar with his family heritage in goldsmithing, covered in some of these recent catalogues, other aspects of the crafted world of Renaissance Europe are less frequently brought into dialogue with Dürer's work.

7   Nuremberg traders had an interest in copper mining in Hungary, which may have helped to facilitate the elder Dürer's relocation to Nuremberg and his later interest in acquiring shares in the mine at Goldkronach. Hutchison, *Albrecht Dürer* 6, 11. See also Heuer, 'Evaporating Dürer'.

8   H.164-78.

9   Buck and Porras, *The Young Dürer*; Hess and Eser, eds, *The Early Dürer*.

10   Koerner, *The Moment of Self-Portraiture*; Sullivan, 'Alter Apelles'.

11   Griggs, 'Dürer's Diary of His Journey'; Remond, 'Distributing Dürer';

12   Ashworth, *Albrecht Dürer*, 1: 560.

13   Smith, *Nuremberg*; Gulden, 'An Ideal Neighbourhood'; Strauss, *Nuremberg*; Zika, 'Nuremberg'.

14   Rücker, *Hartmann Schedels Weltchronik*; Wilson, *Nuremberg Chronicle*.

15   Kahsnitz and Wixom, eds, *Gothic and Renaissance Art*, especially 20-2; Maué, Eser, Hauschke, and Stolzenberger, *Quasi Centrum Europæ*.

16   Schauerte, *Dürer als Zeitzeuge der Reformation*; Price, *Albrecht Dürer's Renaissance*.

17   Stumpel, 'Luther in Dürer's journal'. For the text of the prayer, see Ashworth, *Albrecht Dürer*, 1: 580-2.

18   Białostocki, *Dürer and his Critics* remains an important source.

19   Talbot, 'High art'.

20   Bartrum, *Dürer and his Legacy*, 86, no. 12.

21   *Ibid.*, 88, no. 18.

22   Hayum, 'Dürer's Portrait of Erasmus'.

23   For an alternate translation in its longer context, see Ashcroft, *Albrecht Dürer*, II, 859-60.

24   This line became the subject of the exhibition: Preising et al., *Albrecht Dürer: Apelles des Schwarz-Weiss*.

25   Pon, *Raphael, Dürer, and Marcantonio Raimondi*; Wouk, *Marcantonio Raimondi, Raphael and the Image Multiplied*.

26   Mauquoy-Hendrickx, *Les estampes des Wierix*, no. 1205; Hollstein Dutch and Flemish LXVII, 144, no. 2000. See also Clifton, 'Adriaen Huybrechts', 123, n. 2. Between the ages of twelve and seventeen, the Wiereix brothers produced no fewer than thirty copies after Dürer, and continued to do so until 1602, when Johannes engraved the *Melencolia I* (Mauquoy-Hendrickx, *Les estampes des Wierix*, no. 1576).

27   On the Dürer monogram, see, among others, Koerner, *The Moment of Self-Portraiture*, esp. 184-6.

Background: Catalogue 6 (detail), see p. 13.

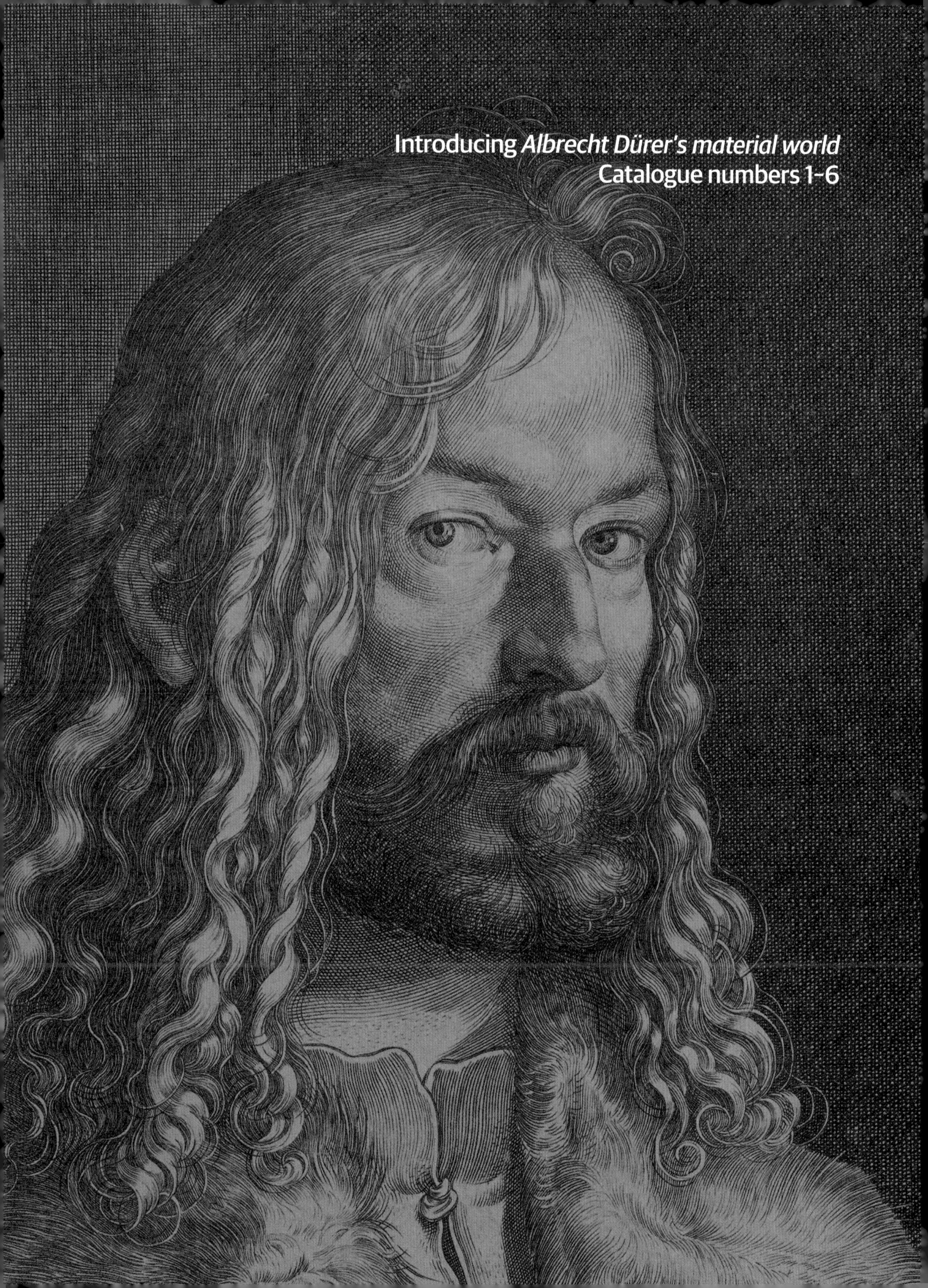
Introducing *Albrecht Dürer's material world*
Catalogue numbers 1–6

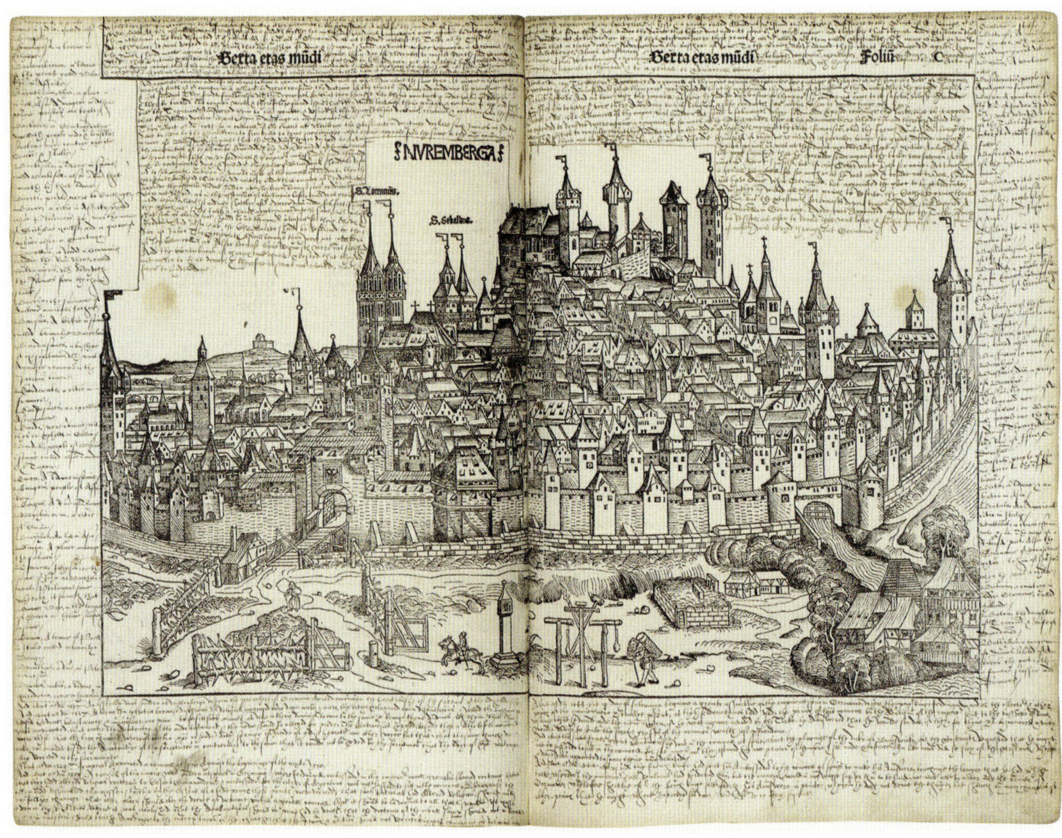

1
Michael Wolgemut and Wilhelm
Pleydenwurff
Nuremberg (*Nuremberga*) in Hartmann
Schedel, *Nuremberg Chronicle* (*Liber
Chronicarum*). Nuremberg: Anton
Koberger, 1493.

Woodcut, 390 x 580 mm

Chetham's Library, I.8.2. © Chetham's Library.
Photo: Michael Pollard.

> 2
Albrecht Dürer
Portrait of Willibald Pirckheimer, 1524.

Engraving, 183 x 116 mm, trimmed
Schoch, Mende and Scherbaum, *Albrecht Dürer*, I,
237–9, no. 99; B.VII.113.106; H.103

The Whitworth, The University of Manchester, P.4682.
Presented by Dr J. Barnes Burt in 1925.
© The Whitworth, The University of Manchester.
Photo: Michael Pollard.

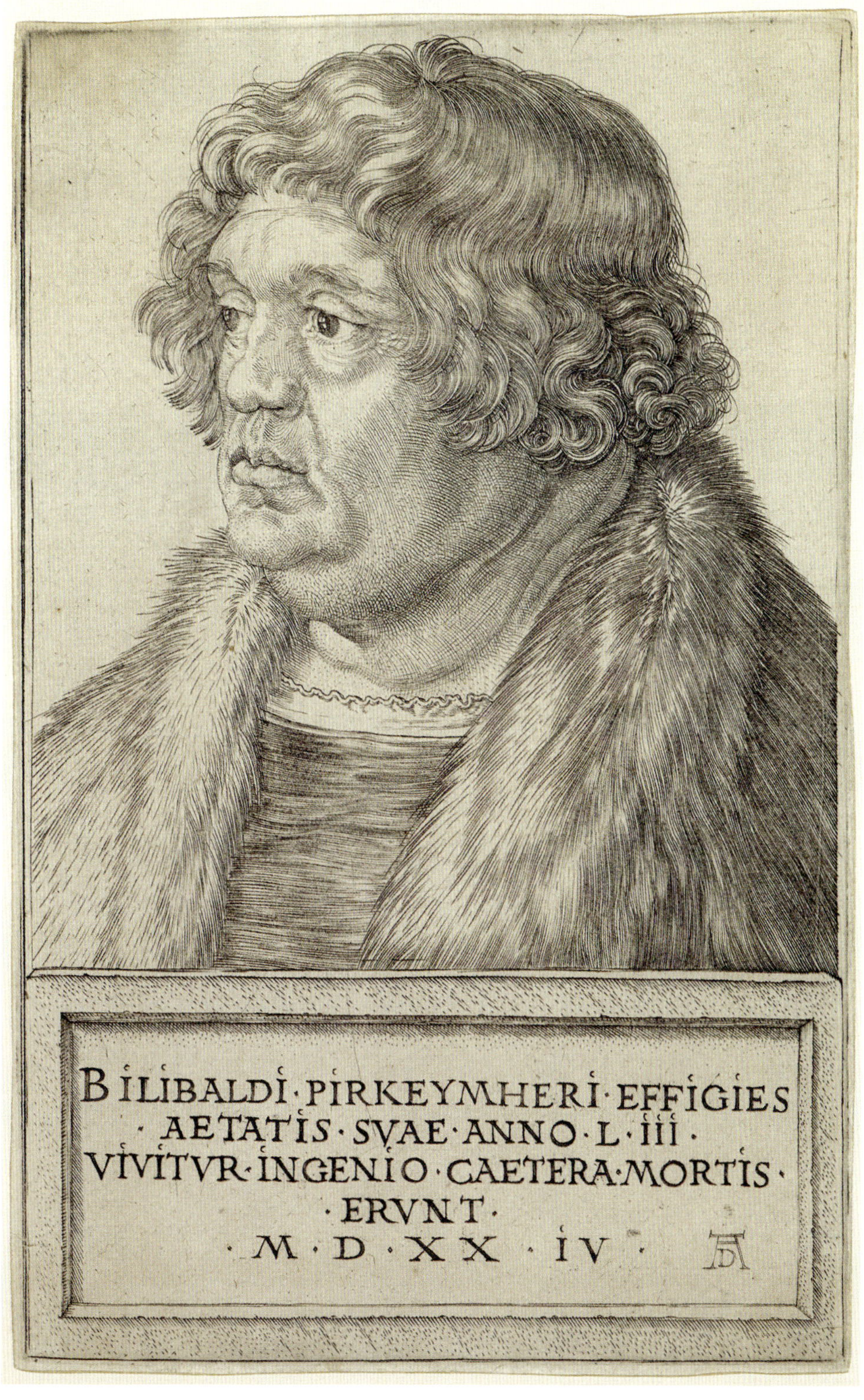

BILIBALDI · PIRKEYMHERI · EFFIGIES
· AETATIS · SVAE · ANNO · L · III ·
VIVITVR · INGENIO · CAETERA · MORTIS ·
· ERVNT ·
· M · D · XX · IV ·

Albrecht Dürer

Portrait of Philip Melanchthon, 1526.

Engraving, 175 x 129 mm, trimmed
Schoch, Mende and Scherbaum, *Albrecht Dürer*, I, 241–2, no. 101;
B.VII.112.105; H.104

The Whitworth, The University of Manchester, P.4684.
Presented by Dr J. Barnes Burt in 1925.
© The Whitworth, The University of Manchester. Photo: Michael Pollard.

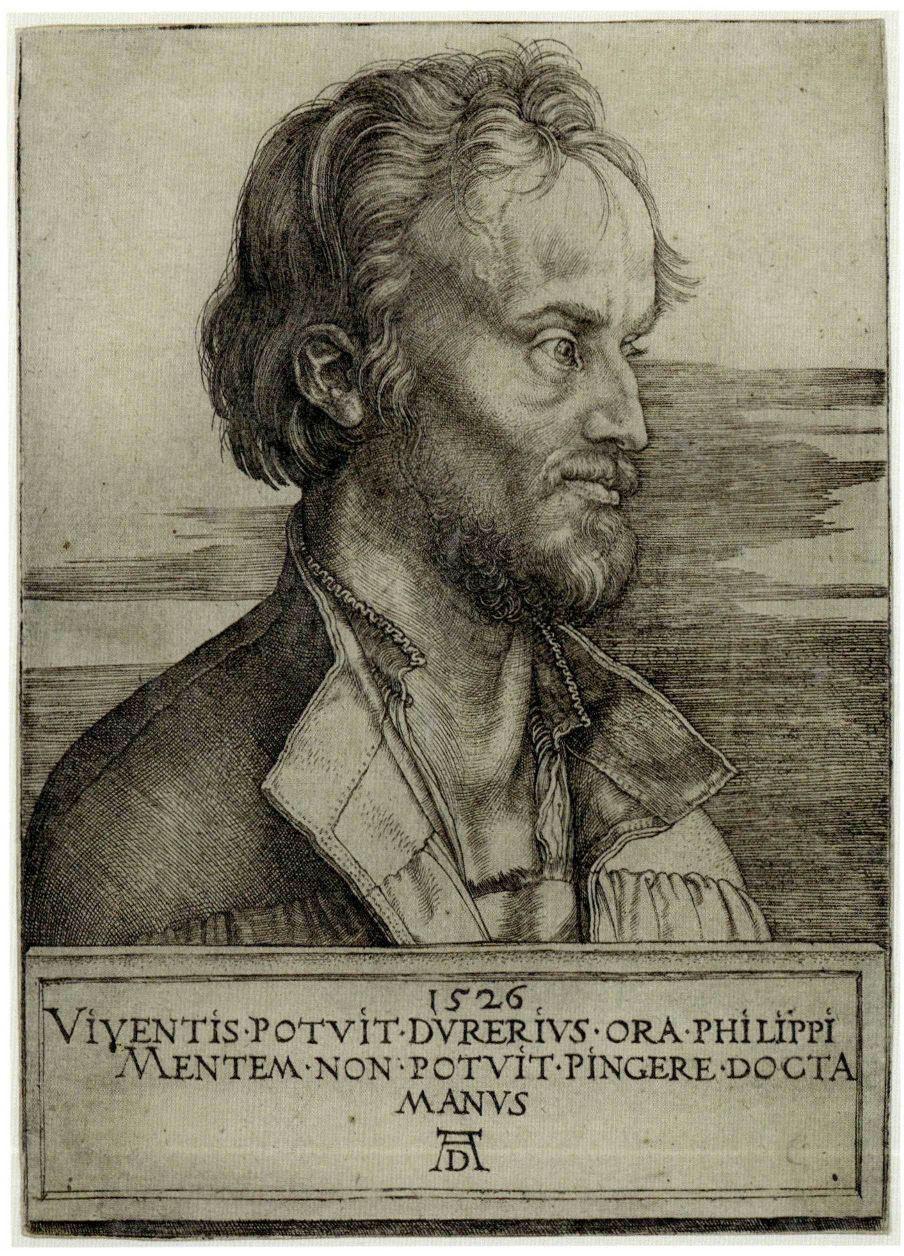

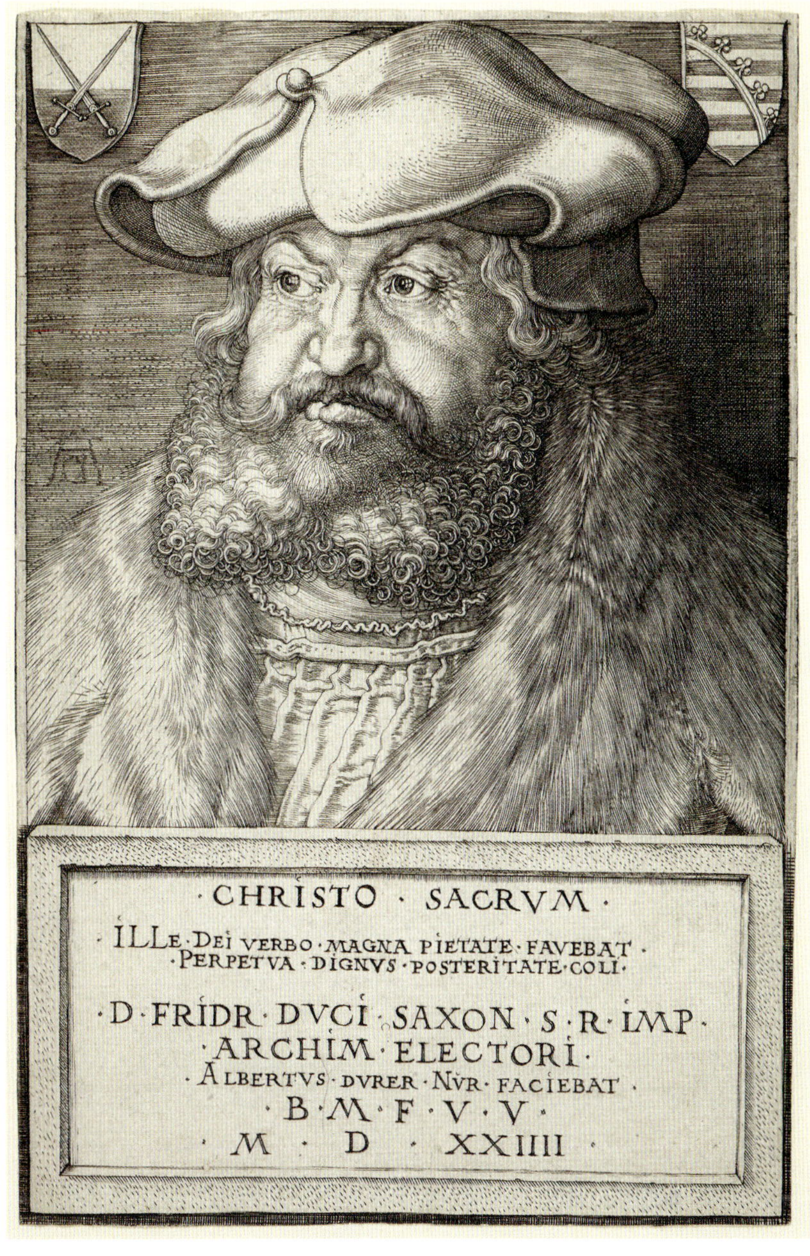

4

Albrecht Dürer

Friedrich the Wise, Elector of Saxony, 1524.

Engraving, 192 x 127 mm, trimmed
Schoch, Mende and Scherbaum, *Albrecht Dürer*, I, 236–7, no. 98;
B.VII.112.104; H.102

The Whitworth, The University of Manchester, P.3024.
Presented by George Thomas Clough in 1921.
© The Whitworth, The University of Manchester. Photo: Michael Pollard.

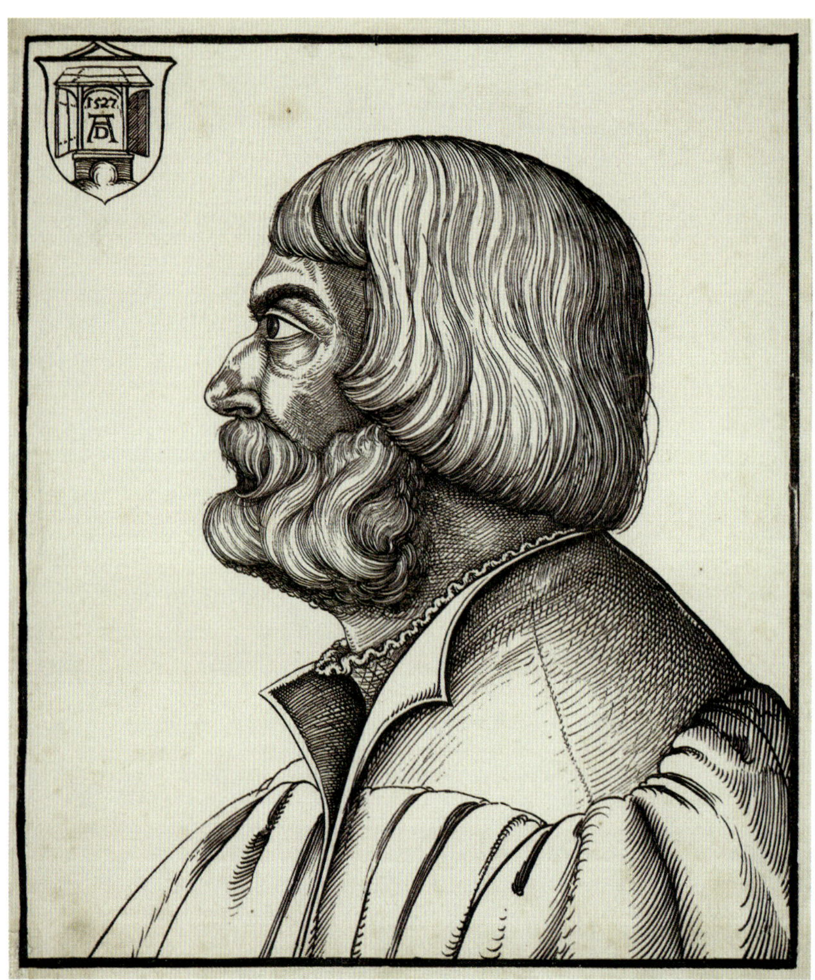

5
Erhard Schön
Portrait of Albrecht Dürer in Profile, c. 1528.

Woodcut, 309 x 266 mm
Hollstein German LXVIII.52-56.156/I

The Whitworth, The University of Manchester, P.4736.
Bequeathed by William Sharp Ogden in 1926.
© The Whitworth, The University of Manchester. Photo: Michael Pollard.

> 6
Lucas Kilian
Portrait of Albrecht Dürer, 1608.

Engraving, 275 x 204 mm
Hollstein German XVII.52.178

The Whitworth, The University of Manchester, P.3001.
Presented by George Thomas Clough in 1921.
© The Whitworth, The University of Manchester.
Photo: Michael Pollard.

PICTORVM ET CHALCOGRAPHOR. GERMANIÆ PRINCIPIS,
ALBERTI DVRERI GENVINA EFFIGIES.
C. S. C. M.
PRIVIL.

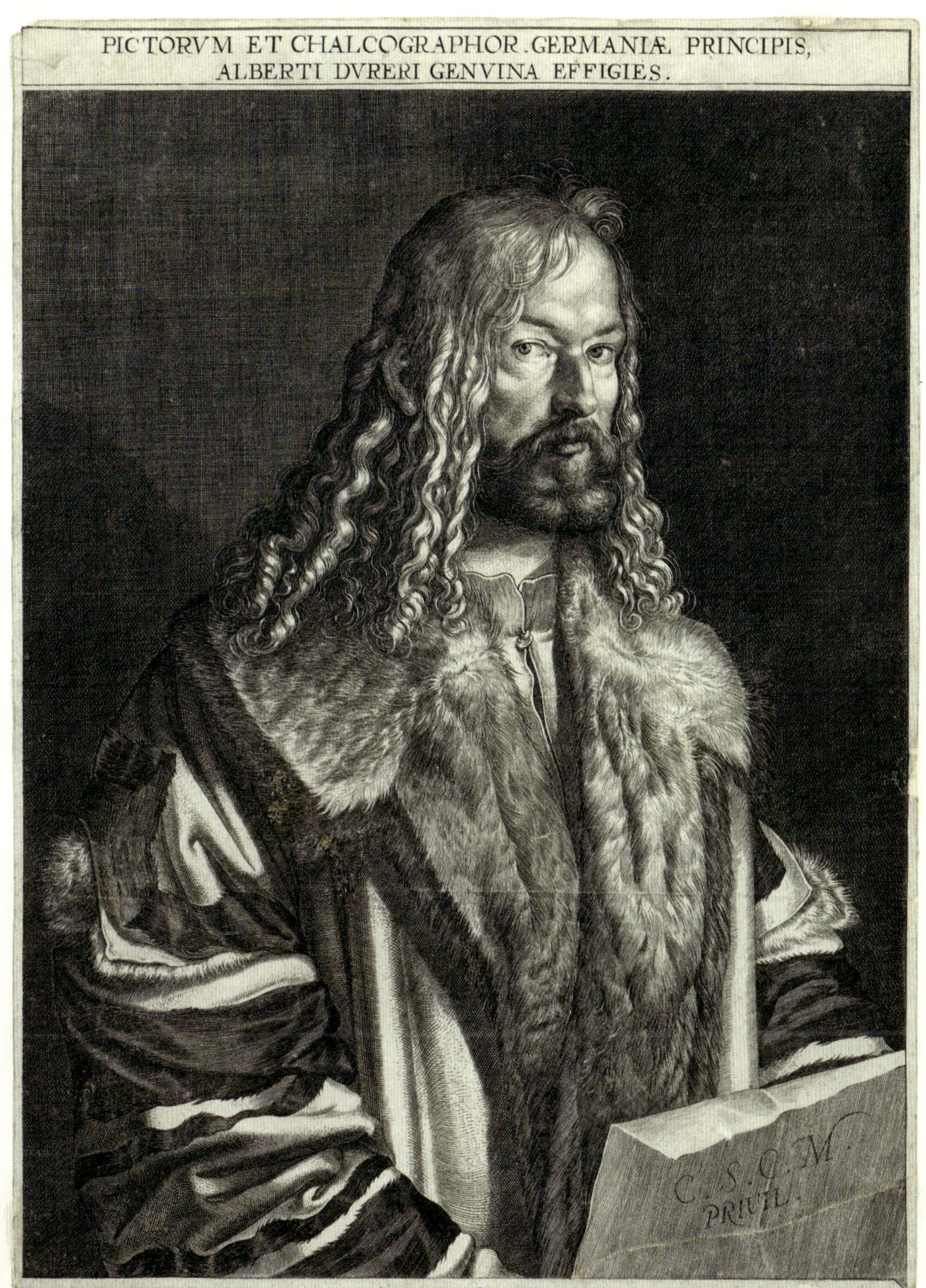

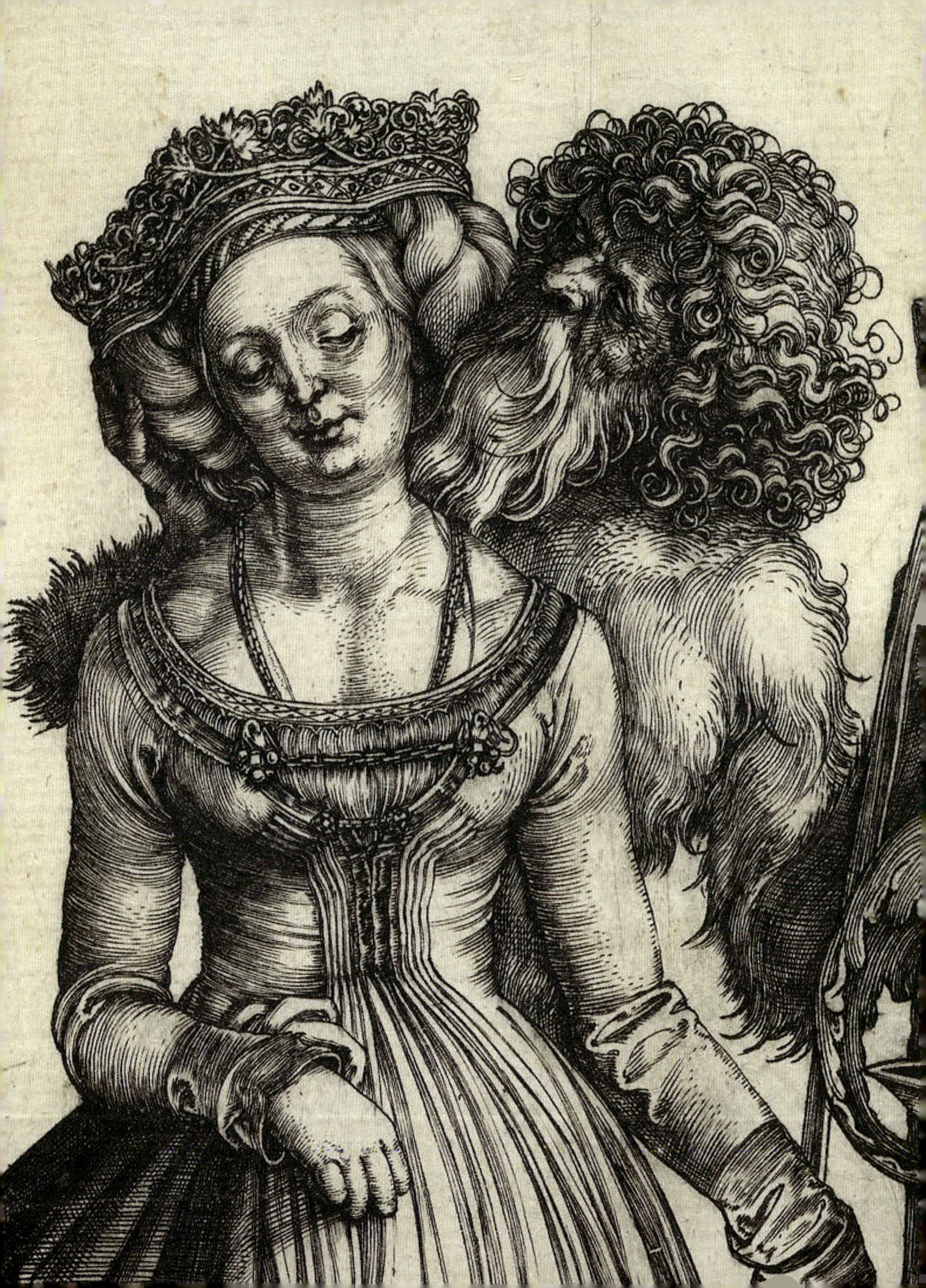

[2] The Thomas D. Barlow collection: A *fait accompli*

Imogen Holmes-Roe

On 24 November 1964, the *Guardian* published the obituary of Sir Thomas Dalmahoy Barlow GBE (1883–1964) (Figure 2.1). After listing Barlow's numerous business and financial interests, the announcement very briefly noted that 'He was a keen collector of pictures and an authority on the works of Dürer'.[1] Aware that this single line of praise in no way corresponded to Barlow's contribution to the fields of art and learning, Margaret Pilkington (1891–1974), formerly honorary director of the Whitworth (1936–59), felt compelled to write a *Letter to the Editor*. For Pilkington, Barlow's 'closest interests centred in art and scholarship'.[2] She explained that through his methodical and committed approach to selection, acquisition and comparison, Barlow's collection of woodcuts, engravings and illustrated books by Albrecht Dürer developed into 'one of the great collections of the world'.[3] Indeed, when shown to the public for the first time at Manchester Art Gallery in 1935, the gallery's curator Lawrence Haward (1878–1957) drew parallels between Barlow's collection and those of the Albertina and the British Museum.[4]

Barlow's father was the distinguished Royal physician Sir Thomas Barlow (1845–1945) and his paternal grandfather James (1821–87) was a textile manufacturer, philanthropist and former mayor of Bolton. Educated at Trinity College, Cambridge, Barlow entered his family's textile company Barlow and Jones, Cotton Spinners and Manufacturers of Edgworth, Bolton and Manchester where he created a name for himself as one of the leading figures in the textile industry.[5]

From the formation of his grandfather's company in the mid-nineteenth century, the Barlow family operated thriving and prosperous textile mills at a time when Manchester benefited from cheap cotton imported from the Southern slave-owning states

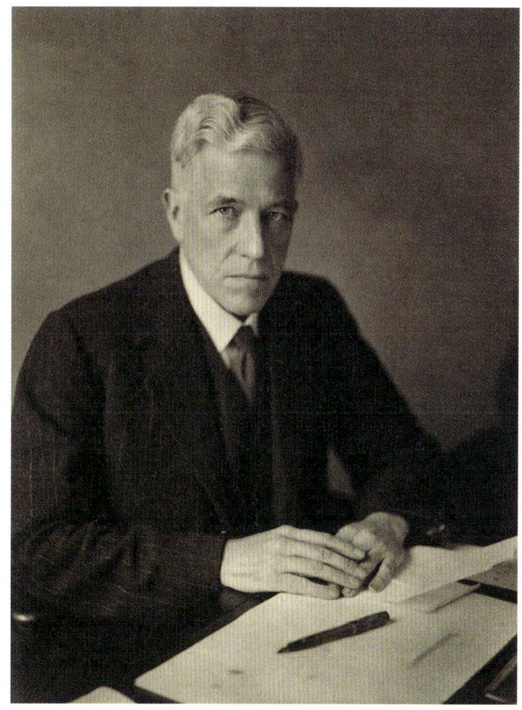

2.1 Walter Stoneman, *Sir Thomas ('Tommy') Dalmahoy Barlow*, October 1942, bromide print, 160 x 115 mm.

London, National Portrait Gallery, NPG x163895
© National Portrait Gallery, London.

of the United States, as well as from Egypt and the Indian subcontinent. Yet this period also coincided with James Barlow's active involvement in the British Abolitionist Movement. In 1863, the *Anti-Slavery Reporter* recorded the outcome of a meeting he chaired at which the following Parliamentary petition was motioned:

> Your petitioners view with deep regret the efforts of certain parties in this country to procure national

Figure 2.2 (detail).

recognition of the recently constituted Slaveholders' Confederacy, which is based on the execrable system of human bondage ... and they trust that British sanction will never be extended to a Confederacy that seeks to nationalize chattel Slavery, with its inseparable immoralities: your petitioners therefore earnestly and humbly pray your honourable House to reject all appeals.[6]

In common with his grandfather James and other industrial philanthropists of this time, Thomas Barlow used his position of privilege to convert personal prosperity into cultural capital. For thirty years he occupied the position of chairman of the Whitworth and was a founding member of the Friends of the Whitworth.[7] In recognition of his fifty years of service the gallery's lecture hall was named in his honour, and he was credited as a driving force behind the gallery becoming a part of The University of Manchester.[8]

During his lifetime, Barlow gifted 249 works to the Whitworth's fine art and textile collections, including etchings by Rembrandt (1606–69) and works by John Robert Cozens (1752–97) and Vincent Van Gogh (1853–90).[9] Barlow's longstanding association with the Whitworth placed him in a powerful position not only to shape the future of the gallery, but also the direction of its collecting. Shortly after his death, Margaret Pilkington wrote, 'The Whitworth owes the high standard maintained in its collections in no small measure to his knowledge and good taste'.[10]

No doubt fuelled by his father's own collecting of eighteenth- and early-nineteenth-century watercolours, Barlow had begun acquiring art, early books and manuscripts as a young boy. The work of Albrecht Dürer remained at the heart of his collecting, and for over half a century he meticulously sought out examples of the artist's work. He acquired his first Dürer print in 1904 and, taking advantage of the widespread sale of German print collections in response to the outbreak of the First World War, Barlow's collecting accelerated. In his recollection of this period, Barlow wrote that it provided 'unique opportunities for acquiring specially fine examples of Dürer's engravings and woodcuts – opportunities I realized should not be missed, on which I seized,

as far as I possibly could, and despite considerable competition'.[11]

During this period, Barlow was greatly assisted by Gustav Mayer (1873–1954), an authority on Dürer prints whose father Vincent (1831–1918) had developed a renowned print collection over a period of nearly thirty years. As a partner in one of the oldest commercial art galleries in the world, P. & D. Colnaghi & Co, Gustav facilitated Barlow in the acquisition of outstanding Dürer impressions from his late father's collection, which was sold in 1919. Amongst these works was the first edition of Dürer's *Treatise on Fortification* (1527) and fifteen engravings including a unique trial proof of the *Title Page of the Apocalypse* series.

Another significant acquisition by Vincent Mayer which merits mention was a group of prints from the collection of Dr August Sträter (1810–97), a well-connected collector, whose 132 Dürers were described as 'the pearls of the collection'.[12] When sold in 1898, the collection included the *The Rhinoceros*, which was subsequently acquired by Barlow.[13] During this same period, Barlow acquired three further engravings and thirty woodcuts from the disbanded collection of a wealthy German merchant named Paul Davidsohn (1839–1927?), who had acquired the entire body of work of Dürer, Rembrandt and Adriaen van Ostade (1610–85). Davidsohn's ambition of completeness, alongside his understanding of dates, numbers and collectors' marks, became an approach Barlow would emulate.[14]

Of equal if not greater significance was Barlow's acquisition of the collection of Professor Werner Weisbach (1873–1953). His impression of *Coat of Arms with a Skull* (Figure 2.2) was later described as 'One of the richest prints in the Barlow collection'.[15] This exceptional early impression, which merited mention in Meder's seminal catalogue of the artist's work, retains burr residue and was printed on paper containing the High Crown watermark, used for Dürer's prints dated between 1498 and 1525.[16]

2.2 Albrecht Dürer, *Coat of Arms with a Skull*, 1503, engraving, 220 x 158 mm, ex coll. Thomas Barlow.

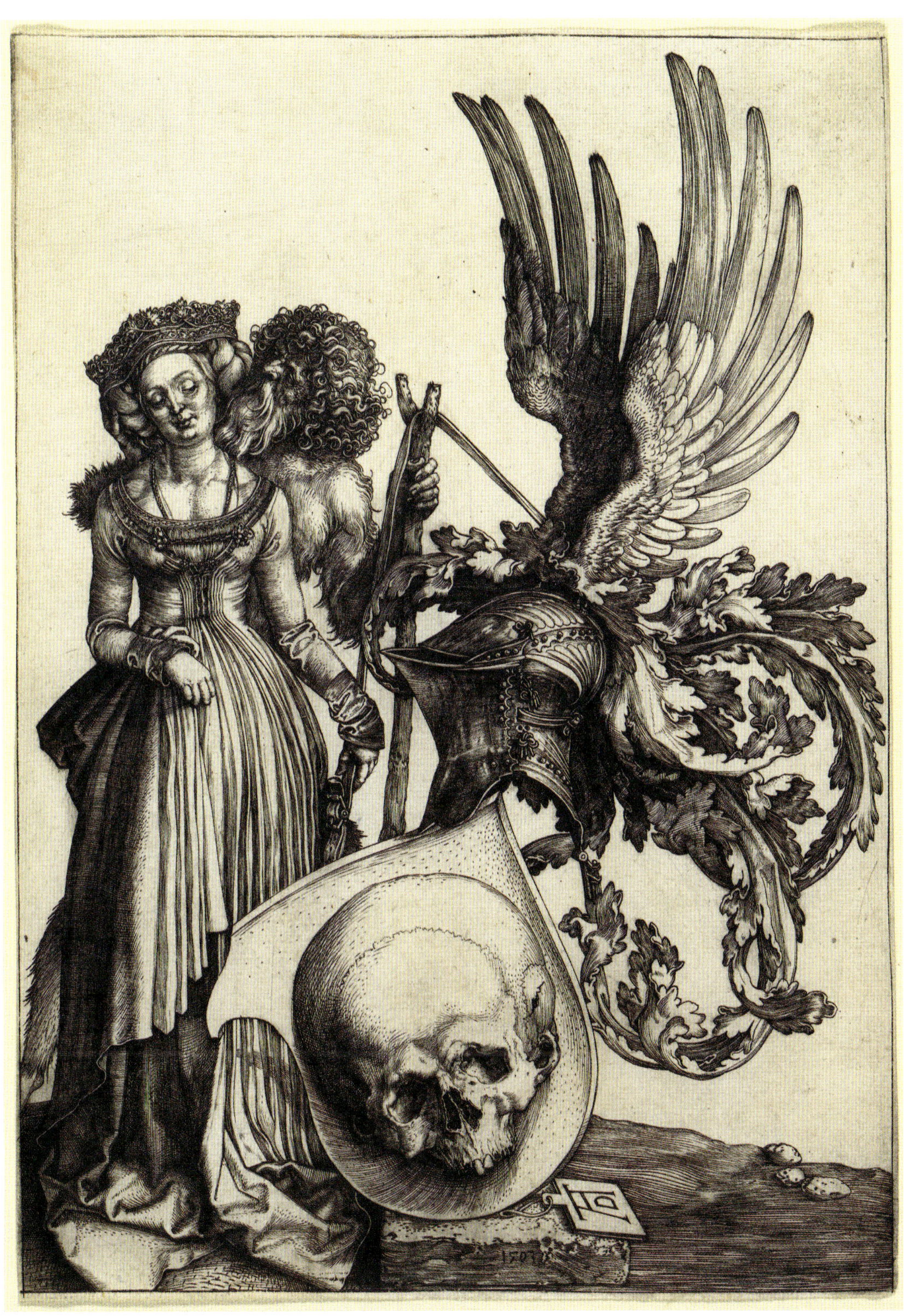

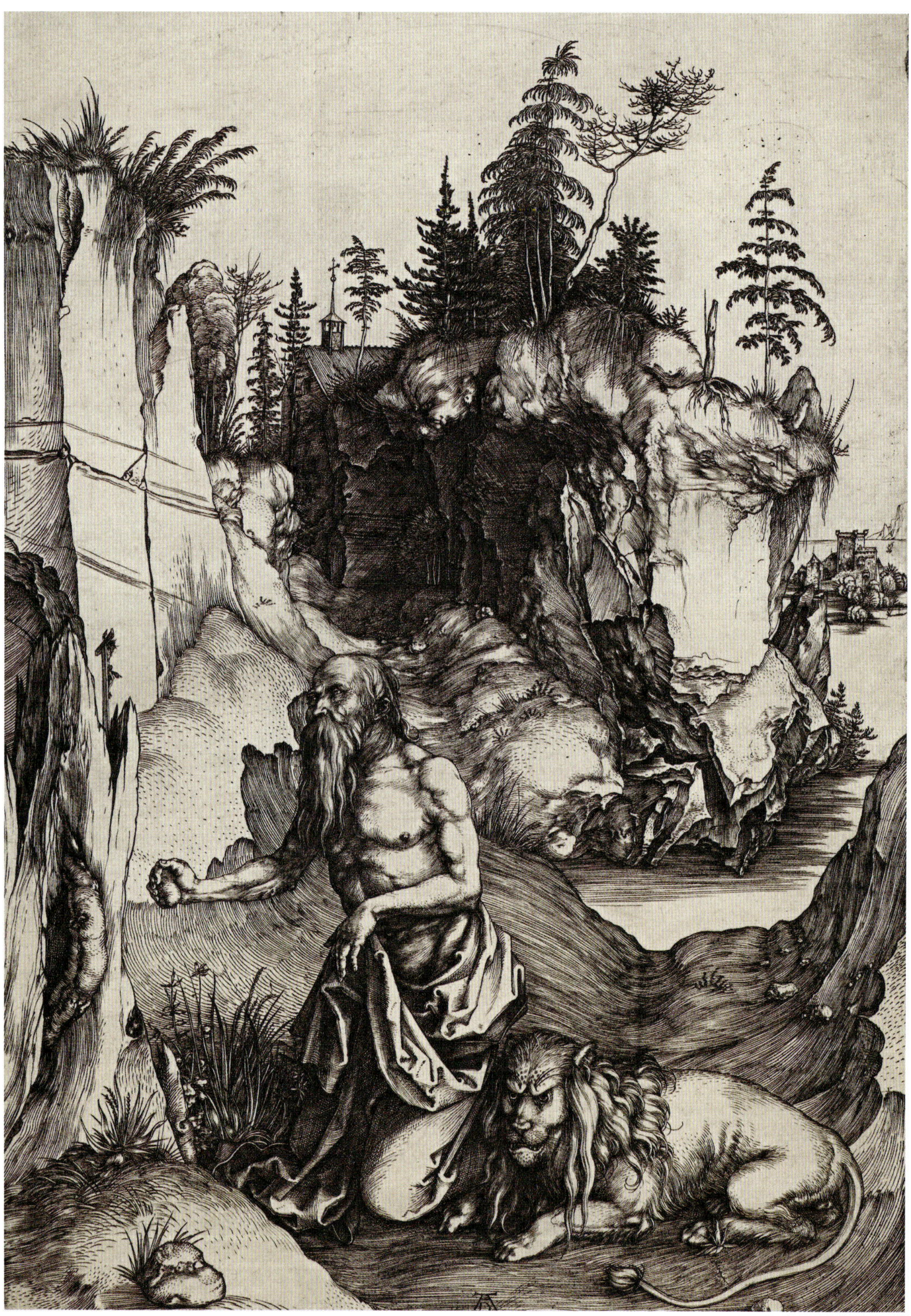

Rarity was also a major consideration in Barlow's collecting, as demonstrated by his purchase of first states of *Melencolia I* and *Adam and Eve Expelled from Paradise*, from the small woodcut Passion.[17] He also acquired a unique first state of *Saint Jerome Penitent in the Wilderness* (Figure 2.3), which he described as 'an early and brilliant impression'.[18] It has been suggested that within his collection there were impressions that were unlikely to ever appear on the open market again, including the woodcuts of *The Coat of Arms of Dürer*, *The Madonna on a Grassy Bank*, and the drypoint of *Saint Jerome by the Pollard Willow*.[19]

What is remarkable about Barlow's approach was his unwavering belief in the importance of the materiality of each individual impression. In 1935 he wrote: 'You cannot really get to know much about a subject unless you have the objects in your hands again and again and again.'[20] Wherever and whenever possible, he attempted not only to secure examples of every engraving and woodcut from Dürer's print oeuvre, but also the finest impressions available. Writing in 1956, he noted:

> Many of the prints in this collection have been exchanged by me – some of them several times – during the years in favour of finer impressions in my quest for that ultimate fully satisfactory impression that every careful print collector seeks of any print by any Master that interests him. I can now, therefore truly claim that the general quality of all my Dürer prints is exceptionally high throughout…and I must therefore regard the collection, now, as a *fait accompli*.[21]

The enduring reputation of Barlow's collection and his contribution to our understanding of Dürer cannot be understated. His monograph *Woodcuts and Engravings by Albert Dürer*, first published in 1926, was reissued as a paperback over eighty years later by Cambridge University Press, and it remains an important reference in the field.

2.3 Albrecht Dürer, *Saint Jerome Penitent in the Wilderness*, c. 1496, engraving, 310 x 225 mm, ex coll. Thomas Barlow.
Melbourne, National Gallery of Victoria, Felton Bequest, 1956. Inv. 3474-4 © National Gallery of Victoria, Melbourne.

As the Whitworth celebrates its first major exhibition of Dürer in over fifty years, an important question that cannot be overlooked is why an individual whose industrial and cultural interests were so deeply linked to Manchester chose Melbourne as the final home for his collection. As Barlow himself wrote, 'It will not be without many pangs that I part with this collection which has been my companion and the object of my constant studies over many years'.[22] One possible explanation may lie in the nature of Barlow's longstanding association and patronage of the Whitworth and the fact that, by this time, the gallery already possessed an important public collection of prints, certainly the finest in the north of England.

In 1921 the Whitworth received a substantial gift of early German and Italian prints from George Thomas Clough (1839–1928). The collection was formally recognised by the Whitworth Institute Council (now the Whitworth) both for its quality and uniqueness within Manchester's public collections.[23] By early 1922, a total of 256 prints from Clough's collection had been accepted by the Whitworth including seventy-one prints by Dürer, thirteen by Lucas van Leyden (1494–1533) and five by Martin Schongauer (c. 1440/53–91). When viewed together, Clough's collection was assembled with a strong didactic purpose.[24] This point was noted by Clough himself, who wrote that the works he collected, 'furnish the student with satisfactory evidence of progress made by the Master from immaturity to correctness in this side of draughtsmanship'.[25] The Clough collection was augmented by the William Sharp Ogden bequest of later old master prints in 1926.[26] Indeed, it was the growing collection of Continental European old master prints that propelled the opening of a permanent display in the Whitworth's first Print Room in 1927.

Barlow was deeply familiar with the Whitworth's already rich holdings of printed works. He was also determined that his collection of around 300 engravings, woodcuts and printed books remain together. These may be some of the factors that led Barlow to seek a home outside of the city, where his collection could make a larger impact and where it could be kept intact. When considering Barlow's motivations, moreover, it is equally important to revisit this period in the Whitworth's own history. From as early as 1905 the gallery was running at a deficit. By 1950, in his capacity as chairman, Barlow felt compelled to highlight the precarious financial position of the gallery:

> The balance showed us an undeviating record of gloom. The deficiency would have to be analysed but we had probably reached the depths to which we could sink ... if it were not for the voluntary work of Miss Pilkington and the assistance and gifts of some of our supporters, our position would be quite intolerable.[27]

As a result, negotiations began with The University of Manchester to take over ownership. Aided by Barlow, these negotiations were finally completed in 1958, providing the gallery with long-term stability, security and new opportunities for mutual collaboration.

Yet in the precarious period before this relationship with the University was formalised, Barlow had made his first visit to the print room of the National Gallery of Victoria where he had the opportunity to view three excellent impressions from Dürer's *Meisterstiche* prints: *Knight, Death and the Devil*, *Melencolia I* and *Saint Jerome in his Study*, which had been acquired from another British collector, Sir Francis Seymour Haden (1818–1910).[28] By this point the National Gallery of Victoria had already acquired a preparatory drawing and over 150 engravings and woodcuts by Dürer largely originating from the collections of the American metallurgist Robert Carl Sticht (1856–1922), the Australian artist, critic and collector Lionel Lindsay (1874–1961) and the Spanish Art Gallery in London. The collection included some fine impressions, notably the *Small Passion* woodcuts (purchased from Lindsay) and the *Engraved Passion* (acquired via the Spanish Gallery).[29] Yet few examples rivalled the standard attained by Barlow through his considered collecting.[30]

After initially gifting works by Thomas Gainsborough (1727–88) and J. M. W. Turner (1775–1851) to the National Gallery of Victoria in 1956, Barlow proposed to sell his Dürer collection to the Melbourne gallery for the greatly reduced sum of £45,000.[31] In his accompanying letter to the Felton Bequests' Committee he explained that 'there is no Gallery to which I should more like it to go than Melbourne's which I visited a few years ago, and where the collections very greatly impressed me by their variety and high standards'.[32] With purchase funds greater than those of the National and Tate galleries in London combined, the Felton Bequest transformed the collection of the National Gallery of Victoria, and it was prepared to acquire a collection of such international significance.[33] On 4 September 1956, Barlow's offer was unanimously accepted.

Shortly after his death in 1964, Margaret Pilkington asserted that the sale was motivated by Barlow's desire to support the Commonwealth countries by enabling them to have access to the same quality of publicly accessible collections as their European counterparts.[34] Having committed over half his life to the acquisition and research of Dürer's work, Barlow may have also been driven by the knowledge that when viewed alongside the National Gallery of Victoria's existing holdings his collection would allow for the serious comparative study of the artist's entire print oeuvre. It was a decision that positioned the National Gallery of Victoria alongside the world's greatest public Dürer collections. Yet the history of Barlow's collection remains bound to its origins in Manchester. It is a witness to the importance of art collecting in the northwest of England at the turn of the century and provides insights into the importance of philanthropy and the high status of German art in the United Kingdom before attitudes changed with the onset of the First World War.

Notes

1   'Sir Thomas Barlow', the *Guardian*, 5.

2   Pilkington, 'Letter to the Editor,' 8.

3   *Ibid.*

4   City of Manchester Art Galleries, *Albrecht Dürer Woodcuts and Engravings*, 3.

5   The Barlow family's association with the textile industry began in weaving before James Barlow formed Barlow and Jones, Cotton Spinners and Manufacturers of Edgworth, Bolton and Manchester. By 1964 the company had been acquired by the English Sewing Cotton Company Limited. A succession of mergers followed with the Calico Printers Association in 1968 (later English Calico), Tootal Ltd (1973) and finally the Coats Viyella Group in 1991.

6   British and Foreign Anti-Slavery Society, *The Anti-Slavery Reporter*, 167.

7   The inaugural meeting of the Friends of the Whitworth was chaired by Sir Thomas Barlow and was held at his residence on 27 November 1933.

8   Pilkington, 'Letter to the Editor', 8.

9   Sir Thomas Barlow and his family maintained a long association with the Whitworth gifting a total of 264 works to its collection.

10   Pilkington, 'Letter to the Editor', 8.

11   Cox, *A Search for a Collection*, 266.

12   Hoff, 'Thomas Barlow, Dürer Collector', 84.

13   This impression is now in the National Gallery of Victoria, Melbourne, inv. no. 3603-4. For further literature on this print, see Schoch, Mende and Scherbaum, *Albrecht Dürer*, II, 420–4; H.273.

14   Hoff, 'Thomas Barlow, Dürer Collector', 84.

15   Hoff, 'The Thomas D. Barlow Collection,', 15. For the print: Schoch, Mende and Scherbaum, *Albrecht Dürer*, I, 105–7, no. 37; H.98. The impression is now in the National Gallery of Victoria, Melbourne, inv. 3515-4.

16   Meder, *Dürer-Katalog*, 109, no. 98a.

17   Both of these impressions are now in the National Gallery of Victoria, Melbourne: *Melencolia I*, inv. no. 3486-4; *Adam and Eve Expelled from Paradise*, inv. no. 3528.2-4. For further literature on these prints, see, respectively, Schoch, Mende and Scherbaum, *Albrecht Dürer*, I, 179–84, no. 71; H.75, and Schoch, Mende and Scherbaum, *Albrecht Dürer*, II, 290–1, no. 188; H.127.

18   Barlow, *Woodcuts and Engravings by Albert Dürer*, 5. The impression is now in the National Gallery of Victoria, Melbourne, inv. 3474-4. For further literature on this print, see, Schoch, Mende and Scherbaum, *Albrecht Dürer*, I, 38–40, no. 6; H.57.

19   Hoff, 'The Thomas D. Barlow Collection', 15. These impressions are now in the National Gallery of Victoria, Melbourne: *The Coat of Arms of Dürer*, inv. no, 3617-4; *The Madonna on a Grassy Bank*, inv. no. 3566-4; *Saint Jerome by the Pollard Willow*, inv. no. 3472-4. For further literature on the prints, see Schoch, Mende and Scherbaum, *Albrecht Dürer*, II, 484–5, no. 258 (*The Coat of Arms of Albrecht Dürer*, H. 288); I, 103–4, no. 36 (*Virgin and Child on a Grassy Bank*, H.31); I, 158–60, no. 65 (*Saint Jerome Beside a Willow*, H.58).

20   Quoted in 'Engravings by Duerer', *Manchester Guardian*.

21   Quoted in Cox, *A Search for a Collection*, 266.

22   *Ibid.*, 267.

23   Morris, 'The Clough Collection of prints,' 168.

24   *Ibid.*, 174.

25   Clough, *Catalogue of the Clough Collection*, 3

26   In total the Willian Sharp Ogden bequest included over 3,000 prints.

27   Quoted in Dodwell, *The Whitworth Art Gallery*, 10.

28   These impressions are now in the National Gallery of Victoria, Melbourne: *Melencolia I*, inv. no. p.184./131; *Knight, Death and the Devil*, inv. no. p.184./14–1; *Saint Jerome in his Study*: inv no. p.184./12–1. For further literature on the prints, see Schoch, Mende and Scherbaum, *Albrecht Dürer*, I, 169–85, nos 69, 71, and 70 (H.74, H.75 and H.59), respectively.

29   These prints are now in the National Gallery of Victoria, Melbourne, with the following inv. nos respectively: *Small Passion*, 4754-3 - 4760-3, 4762-3 - 4764-3, 4768-3 - 4769-3, 4772-3 - 4775-3, 4779-3 - 4789-3; *Engraved Passion*, 2125.1-4 - 2125.16-4. For further literature on these prints, see, respectively, Schoch, Mende and Scherbaum, *Albrecht Dürer*, II, 286–344, nos 186–222; H.125–61; Schoch, Mende and Scherbaum, *Albrecht Dürer*, I, 125–52, nos 45–60; H.3–18.

30   Zdanowicz, *Albrecht Dürer*, x.

31   The purchase price was broken down in the following way: Engravings £23,200, Woodcuts £11,430, Books £10,450.

32   Quoted in Cox, *A Search for a Collection*, 267.

33   Inglis and Poynter state that between 1904 and 2004, more than 15,000 items were purchased with an estimated value today of approximately one and a half billion AUS dollars. See Inglis and Poynter, 'Desirable Things'.

34   Pilkington, 'Letter to the Editor', 8.

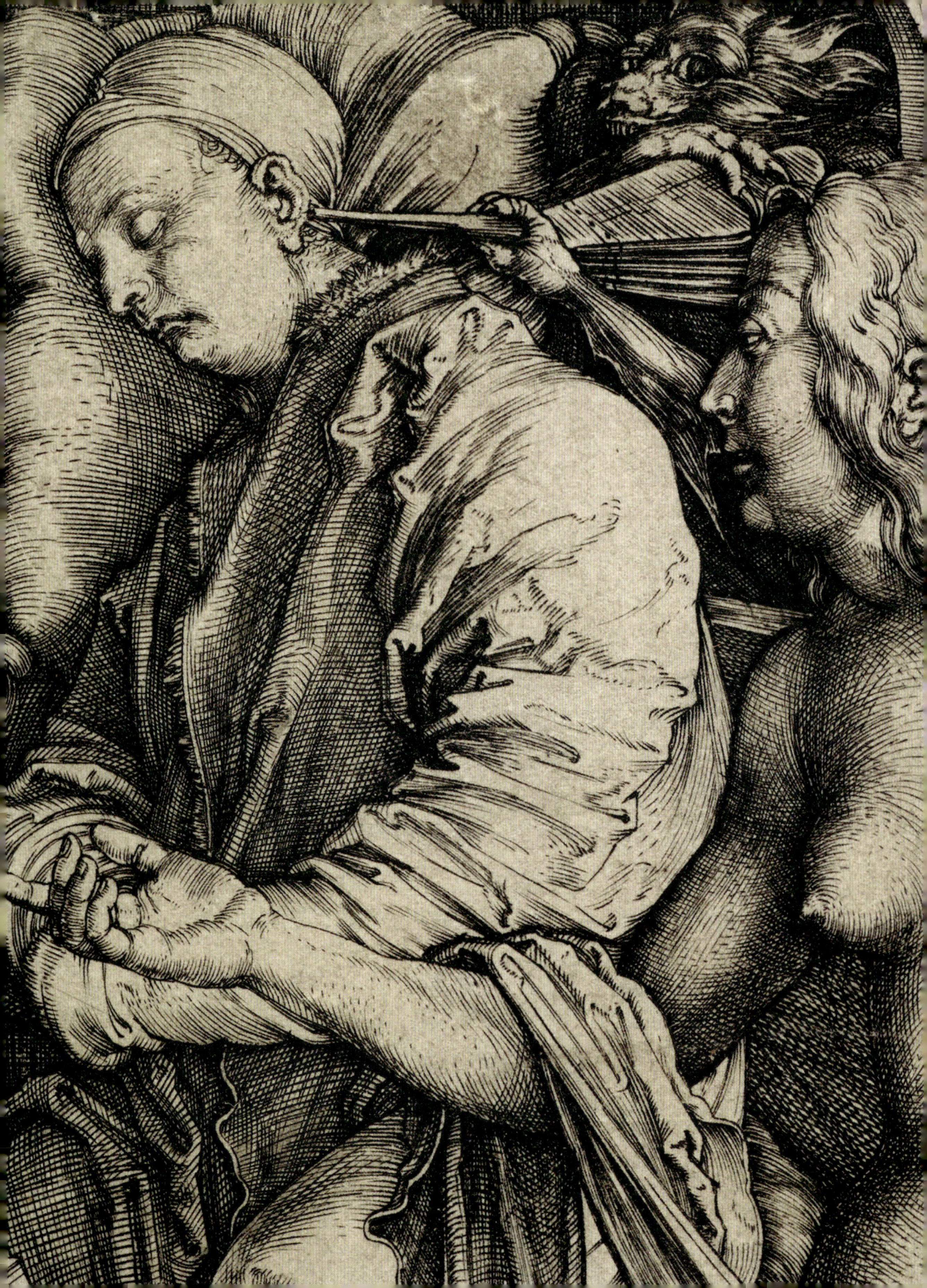

[3] Perilous possessions: *Kachelöfen* in Renaissance Nuremberg

Sasha Handley

How did material innovation shape the contours of daily life in Renaissance Nuremberg? This question is foregrounded in *The Temptation of the Idler* (Figure 3.1; cat. 10), one of Albrecht Dürer's earliest engravings. In Dürer's lifetime the households of all but the poorest participated in a consumer revolution. Homes became hubs for the display and use of new consumer goods: from fashionable clothes, decorative ceramics, glassware and candlesticks to elaborate chandeliers and finely crafted wooden chests. Expenditure on carefully commissioned and affordable ready-made domestic objects grew exponentially in these years, as did the spectrum of ornate and useful goods that flowed from the workshops of skilled artisans using cutting-edge technologies and materials that were sourced locally and that reached the cities of Northern Europe from across the globe.[1] We already know a great deal about the shopping behaviours of Renaissance men and women, especially in the iconic cities of northern Italy. But how did the citizens of Nuremberg experience this influx of consumer goods, and what difference did the day-to-day presence of such goods, and the technological innovations that underpinned them, make to Albrecht Dürer's work? I offer answers to these questions by combining close analysis of Dürer's *The Temptation of the Idler* with an examination of the material, thermal and aesthetic properties of Nuremberg's *Kachelöfen* (ceramic stoves). I argue that whilst *Kachelöfen* were undoubtedly a source of civic pride within the city, Dürer positions them as perilous possessions whose material components generated embodied effects that endangered the bodies and souls of those who sat near these powerful household objects. This assessment was likely the result of Dürer's own encounters with Nuremberg's *Kachelöfen*, as well as his close knowledge of stove manufacture and design.[2]

Produced in 1498, *The Temptation of the Idler* foregrounds a sleeping man wearing a linen nightcap and a fine fur-lined house cloak. He rests on a raised wooden bench padded by comfortable tasselled pillows in a *Stube* (living room). He sits beside a large warm *Kachelofen*, which was a high-status and novel domestic heating device popular in the homes of Albrecht Dürer's friends and neighbours. Tucked behind the sleeping man's pillows is the devil in flight, who is represented as a winged dragon-like figure with sharp talons. He clutches a large pair of bellows and is poised to insert them into the sleeper's ear to direct his lustful dream, which is depicted in the foreground of the engraving. Here, we encounter a Venus-like figure who symbolises sexual temptation and who is identified by Amor, the winged putto climbing on stilts at her side.

Dürer scholars have characterised this engraving as a depiction of sloth and thus one of the seven deadly sins.[3] There are of course numerous material and allegorical attributes of sloth represented in the work. The sleeper's head reclines not on one, but on two sumptuous, tasselled pillows, whose carefully observed soft folds suggest they were stuffed with expensive and comfortable bird feathers rather than straw.[4] The man's expensive fur-lined house cloak covers multiple layers of clothing that epitomise his wealth and place him in stark contrast to the figure of Saint Francis of Assisi (1181/2–1226), who shed his cloak and clothing to renounce his father's wealth and establish his virtue. The most flagrant evidence of sloth, however, is the representation of disorderly sleep. The man indulges in rest outside of his bed and outside of the 'seasonable' sleeping hours that were prescribed by a powerful combination of Christian ethics and medical advice in many parts of Renaissance Europe.

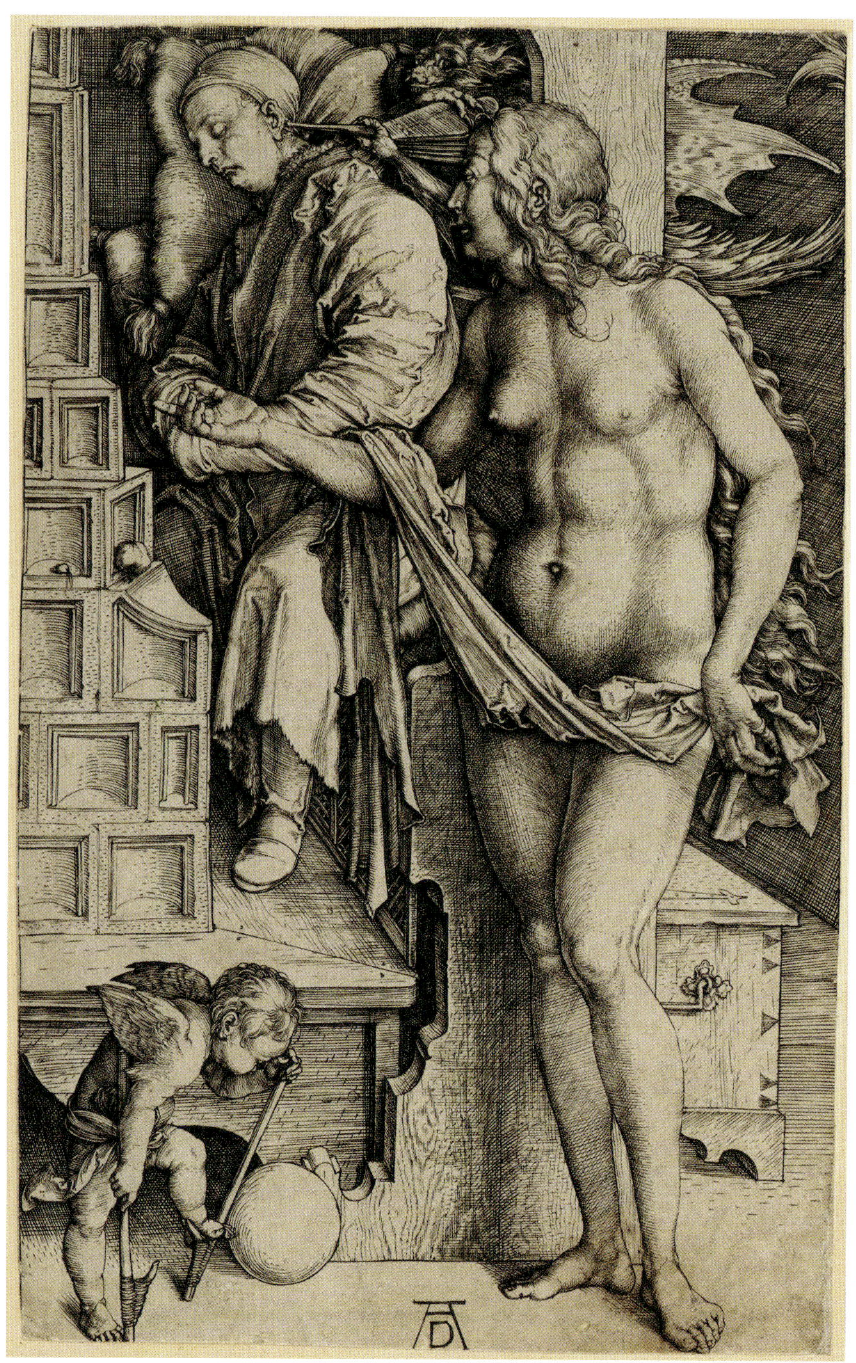

3.1 (cat. 10) Albrecht Dürer, *The Temptation of the Idler*
(*The Dream of the Doctor*), University of Oxford, 1498,
engraving, 185 x 117 mm.

Ashmolean Museum, University of Oxford, WA1863.2291
© Ashmolean Museum, University of Oxford.

Strengthening the interpretation of the engraving as a slothful scene is Dürer's association with the political satire *Das Narrenschiff*, or *The Ship of Fools* (cat. 11), by German humanist Sebastian Brant (1457–1521), first published in Basel in 1494. Inspired by an allegory from Book VI of Plato's *Republic*, Brant's text laid bare the pitfalls of governmental ineptitude and censured human folly in its various guises. Brant's masterpiece was highly illustrated and the young Albrecht Dürer, who spent time in Basel between 1492–94 developing his woodcut design skills, is associated with up to two-thirds (approximately 114) of the text's woodcuts.[5] Many of these woodcuts, which were also used in subsequent editions of the text, illustrate a literal or allegorical interpretation of human sin and vice. Sloth is here closely aligned with disorderly sleep and with *Kachelöfen*, creating a clear line of association with *The Temptation of the Idler*. In the book, Brant declared that 'Nobody is lazier than the man who sleeps by the oven' and elsewhere he set out the perils of sloth to body and soul:

> No one is fond of a sluggard in his house
> Any more than a hibernating mouse.
> To sleep by day and sleep by night,
> To sit by the stove is his delight.
> The Evil One quite soon takes heed
> And quickly sows his evil seed.[6]

A woodcut of a devil using bellows to attack a fool is a second shared pictorial theme between *The Ship of Fools* and *The Temptation of the Idler*. This devil appears in an outdoor, rather than an indoor setting, and in a chapter denouncing the sin of avarice as a sure way to the soul's ruin. There are nonetheless clear parallels between Dürer's earlier woodcut design and the devilish figure in his later engraving, not least his preoccupation with sin, moral culpability and the devil's threat. A final comparative woodcut image attributed to Dürer appears in the short moralising treatise, *Ein allerhailsamste Warnung vor der falschen Liebe diser Werlt* (A Most Salutary Warning of False Love in This World). The book, published by Peter Wagner (active 1483–1500) in Nuremberg c. 1489, emphasises the eternal torments of the condemned in hell. Dürer's accompanying woodcut is dominated by an airborne devil holding bellows who presides over a scene of torture and destruction.[7]

The Temptation of the Idler sits within a wider collection of visual meditations by Dürer in which the sin of sloth is exposed, along with its causes and consequences. What has drawn little attention to date, is the way that household objects create the essential conditions for the sinful act in Dürer's engraving. The presence of intense heat is key to the allegorical meaning of the work, and to the sleeping man's peril because the immersive heat represented in this scene foregrounds the material agency of the *Kachelofen* and of the devil's bellows, which were two very familiar objects in Nuremberg. The Venus figure in the foreground holds up her cloak and gestures towards the *Kachelofen* as if to identify the source of her power. Panofsky notes that the ring on her left hand symbolised her demonic nature so she appears to serve the devil's purpose by tempting the sleeping man into lustful thoughts, and she points towards the object that creates the material conditions for the devil's attack. The *Kachelofen* thus formed part of the 'social iconography' identified by Patricia Simons, in which common domestic objects, everyday activities and corporeal experiences shaped the contours of Renaissance art. Just as the spouts of cooking pots were conceived as phallic symbols by artists of the period, the increasing presence of *Kachelöfen* within many Nuremberg homes were incorporated into Dürer's creative process, and those of his followers, where they assumed similarly sexualised and potent meanings.[8] In Dürer's 1496 drawing *The Women's Bath* (*Frauenbad*), which was a blueprint for the later woodcut, a simpler *Kachelofen* with the same plain niche-style tiles as *The Temptation of the Idler* creates the thermal conditions for the bathers' fleshy, erotic poses. A fully clothed male onlooker clandestinely observes the naked women and children from behind a partially closed door.[9] The licentious potential of *Kachelöfen* that Dürer suggested was explored in even greater intensity by the Nuremberg-born brothers Barthel (1502–40) and Sebald Beham (1500–50), whose work was heavily influenced by Dürer. Sebald Beham's miniature engraving *Three Women in the Bath-House* (1548) is a reverse copy of his brother Barthel's earlier design. In this scene, the heat of the undecorated, tiled *Kachelofen* stokes the lust of three naked women, one of whom lifts her leg onto a wooden bench so that her genitals can be seen and caressed by her companions.[10] Another large, undecorated *Kachelofen* directs the scene of riotous debauchery in Barthel Beham's woodcut *Die Spinnstube* (1524) in which men and women are depicted asleep, engaged in illicit sexual encounters, thrusting a variety of objects in highly sexualised ways, and warming their backsides against the *Kachelofen*.[11]

Kachelöfen were understood then, at least in part, as perilous possessions.[12] The type of wooden bench on which the sleeping man reclines in *The Temptation of the Idler* was often en suite with *Kachelöfen*. By the mid-sixteenth century, it was proverbially known as 'the hell bench' because it was the hottest place within the household when the *Kachelofen* was lit. The Alsatian novelist and poet, Georg Wickram (1505–c.1555/60), described those who sat on the bench as lying 'hinder dem ofen in der hell' in his popular collection of stories and anecdotes, *Das Rollwagenbüchlin* (1555).[13] The engraving makes clear that the *Kachelofen* evokes intense heat in both a material and a metaphorical sense, lulling the man to sleep and rendering him vulnerable to the devil's assault.

Heat and virility in Renaissance medicine

If this image is approached through the lens of Renaissance medical knowledge, there is a very real sense in which the heat from the *Kachelöfen* assists the devil in activating the sleeping man's 'seed' or semen. Heat, both innate and externally generated, was one of the three principal characteristics associated with male sexual performance at this time, alongside the movement of their bodily fluids and their projective capacity. Male body heat accounted for the external projection of men's genitals and for ejaculation, which was triggered by an accumulation of hot semen. Simons has drawn attention to the way that domestic technologies shaped notions and metaphors of sexual activity in Renaissance art, so we can see the *Kachelofen*, an innovative domestic technology, being absorbed into this established lexicon in Dürer's print.

Another critical way in which the warmth of the *Kachelöfen* accelerates the sleeping man's descent into sloth is via the small, upturned fruit perched on the edge of one of its tiles. The fruit closely resembles a mandrake (*Mandragora officinarum*) or *Alraun* in German, and it was commonplace medical wisdom at this time to warm medicinal herbs on the *Kachelofen*.[14] The rounded fruits of the *Mandragora*, often referred to as 'love apples', are members of the nightshade family and they famously emit a sweet and intoxicating scent. The classical authorities of Hippocrates, Pliny the Elder and Dioscorides all described the heady fragrance of the plant's root and noted its capacity to elicit the passion of love. The fruit also had erotic connotations in biblical tradition.[15] In medieval medical culture, mandrakes were widely prescribed as love charms, and one contemporary Renaissance physician explained why when he characterised mandrake as a 'fragrant plant which affects the functioning of male sexual organs…and increases the desire of love-making'.[16] A second and highly pertinent quality of mandrake was the perceived ability of its fragrance to cause drowsiness, numb the senses or even trigger hallucinations. The power of the mandrake depicted by Dürer was, of course, heightened by the heat from the *Kachelofen* on which it sat, which would have intensified its intoxicating scent and embedded it more deeply into the sleeper's unguarded nostrils. This fruit was thus ideally suited to the scene's focus on licentious sexuality and demonic invasion.

The intense heat of Nuremberg's *Kachelöfen* was stoked by bellows, which appear in the devil's hands in Dürer's engraving, but which could be found in most of the city's homes, workshops, civic and sacred buildings at the turn of the sixteenth century.[17]

The records of two of Nuremberg's most important social foundations show that bellows were commonplace tools for the city's craftspeople. The Mendelsche and Landauer *Zwölfbrüderstiftungen* were almshouses that provided food and shelter for Nuremberg's elderly and impoverished craftsmen throughout the fifteenth and sixteenth centuries. They housed a maximum of twelve men at any one time and provided them with food, clothing and a private furnished room.[18] Both foundations kept detailed chronicles of their members and dedicated full-page portraits to each of them engaged in their trade. These *Hausbücher* reveal the widespread presence of bellows in many trade practices during and beyond Dürer's lifetime.[19] Bellows were essential tools for maintaining fires in Nuremberg's workshops and thus invaluable to blacksmiths, coppersmiths, wine-bottlers and goldsmiths, the latter being the trade in which Dürer himself was first trained by his father.

In iconographic terms, Renaissance artists drew strong parallels between the appearance and function of bellows and the physiology of male scrota. The wind chambers of bellows and men's testicles both inflated and deflated depending on the presence of hot air, known as *pneuma* or *spiritus*, and each of them stoked the intense heat from which productivity and fertility flowed.[20] Aristotelian physiology held that men's semen was produced when bodily fluids mixed with pneuma, and this hot air triggered penile projection and ejaculation. The material composition of bellows further strengthened their visual and linguistic association with male scrota.[21] The wind chambers of bellows originating in Nuremberg and elsewhere in Renaissance Europe were principally made of leather, which cracked and wrinkled over time and that bore a striking resemblance to deflated testicles. The devil's bellows in *The Temptation of the Idler* should thus be interpreted as a sexual prop. Inserted into the sleeper's ear, the bellows provide the air that mixed with the intense heat of the *Kachelofen* to stoke the sleeping man's pneuma and generate his semen, resulting in his licentious dream. His loosely draped cloak may even disguise an erection. The manufactured objects depicted in the engraving made it highly likely that the sleeper was engaged in, or about to engage in, the act of nocturnal emission. This interpretation is supported by influential medical wisdom at this time which held that the expulsion of male seed was the likely consequence of excessive body heat, and an effective way of cooling the body down.[22] Paying attention to the material form and embodied effects of the *Kachelofen* and bellows thus points to a fresh interpretative layer for *The Temptation of the Idler*, and one that positions Dürer as an astute observer of the complex world of consumer goods that enveloped him.

Most late medieval commentators on the subject of nocturnal emission agreed that the moral implications of this act depended on its root cause. As William F. Maclehose has observed, 'Discussions of demonically-induced nocturnal pollutions often emphasised the sleeper's passivity'.[23] Because of this passivity, and because the devil's power was widely acknowledged to peak at nighttime, sleepers could only be held morally accountable for seminal emission if they were 'guilty of some negligence which could have prevented the assault'.[24] The kind of negligence that might invite the devil's approach included acts of drunkenness, immoral living or neglect of prayer routines. Dürer's engraving invites us to consider whether disorderly slumber renders the sleeping man guilty of a venial sin. The presence of innovative and highly desirable consumer goods strongly supports this interpretation. The sleeping man is enrobed by an object of luxury, and he is enveloped by the heat of the fashionable and expensive *Kachelofen*, which has caused him to fall asleep in his *Stube*, rather than in his bed. The *Kachelofen* was certainly a desirable object but its introduction into the homes of many Nuremberg men and women elicited complex responses that stirred their owners' anxieties about their susceptibility to sloth and sin. These anxieties, as I will show, shaped the design and commission of *Kachelöfen* tiles.

Nuremberg's *Kachelöfen* trade

Kachelöfen, and the glazed ceramic tiles that decorated them, were sites of artistic creativity and of civic pride in Renaissance Nuremberg. Glazed earthenware tiles, some plain but others adorned with secular or religious motifs or with the arms of Nuremberg itself (cat. 12–14), were manufactured by highly skilled artisans for use within many of the city's well-appointed homes, which the one-time Nuremberg schoolmaster Johannes Cochlaeus (1479–1552) claimed were distinguished by their 'opulent household fitments' in his *Brevis Germaniae Descriptio* (1512).[25] Nuremberg's fame as a centre of tile manufacture stretched beyond the city's walls and led to a lively international trade in earthenware ceramics throughout the sixteenth and seventeenth centuries. A blue and white tin-glazed earthenware stove tile dated 1546 and believed to be from the Italian home of the Augsburg-based Langenmantel family, was manufactured in Nuremberg. Its painting of the cursing of Creusa by Medea bears the mark of German artist Bartholomäus Dill (1500–50), who may have trained alongside Albrecht Dürer in Nuremberg.[26] A polychrome tin-glazed stove tile dated 1580–1600 manufactured in Nuremberg features a full-length portrait of Elizabeth I (1533–1603) and was designed specifically for an English market.[27] These tiles are just two examples of Nuremberg's rich manufacturing history and the international reputation its *Haffners* (stove-fitters/ potters) enjoyed.

The city's most important charitable institutions, the Mendelsche and Landauer *Zwölfbrüderstiftungen*, were well known to Dürer, who designed stained glass windows and a painting of *The Adoration of the Holy Trinity* for the Landauschen's chapel. Both institutions kept meticulous records of their residents, dedicating full-page and brightly coloured portraits to each of them whilst engaged in their habitual craft. These records give direct evidence of Nuremberg's prominent *Kachelöfen*-tile manufacture. The second *Hausbuch* of the Mendelsche *Zwölfbrüderstiftungen*, for example, features a portrait of Hanß Presser (1534–1605), a *Haffner*, who entered the Mendelsche Haus in 1594, aged sixty (Figure 3.2). He is depicted barefoot and engaged in his craft.

Presser kneels over his moulding block to shape a pitcher of the kind that sits on his workshop shelves, bench and in the basket beside him. On the floor are two recently completed green-glazed moulded tiles of the kind that feature in Dürer's engraving. They sit alongside an unworked lump of clay and a two-handed cookie cutter. Presser's record is one of many pieces of evidence in the house books that pinpoints Nuremberg's craftspeople as expert *Kachelöfen*-tile producers at the time and that depict *Kachelöfen* in various domestic settings within the city. Landauer I, for example, includes the portrait of Pauly Mauser, a *Hausknecht* (house servant) of the institution's founder, Matthäus Landauer (d. 1516). Here, Mauser sweeps a floor in front of a large green glazed *Kachelofen*, which closely resembles the object

in Dürer's engraving (Figure 3.3). Mauser became a brother at the foundation in 1513 and his portrait dates to 1519. Further evidence of Nuremberg's tradition of 'Hafnerware' *Kachelofen* tiles can be found in the emergence of Paul Preuning's workshop in the 1540s, which was situated just outside of the city's Tiergarten Gate and mainly serviced a local market.[28]

Kachelöfen of this kind were ornamental and functional centrepieces in the homes of Nuremberg's patriciate, and of its craftspeople, physicians, theologians and merchants. Developed in the

3.2 Hanß Presser, *Haffner*, 1605, water- and tempera-colour on paper, 306 x 211 mm. Stadtbibliothek im Bildungscampus Nürnberg, *Die Hausbücher der Nürnberger Zwölfbrüderstiftungen*, Mendel II, fol. 71r.
© Stadtbibliothek Nürnberg.

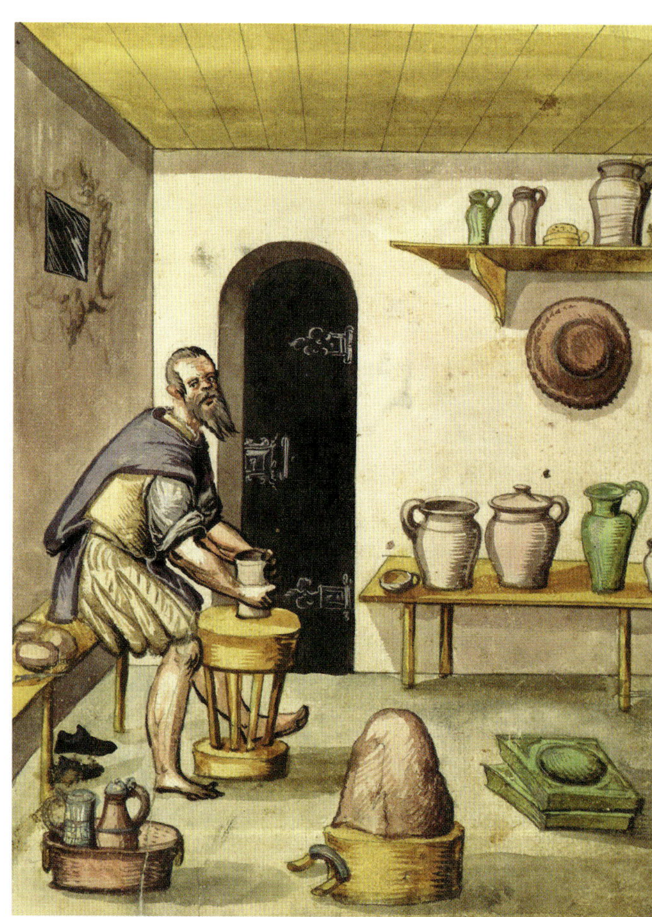

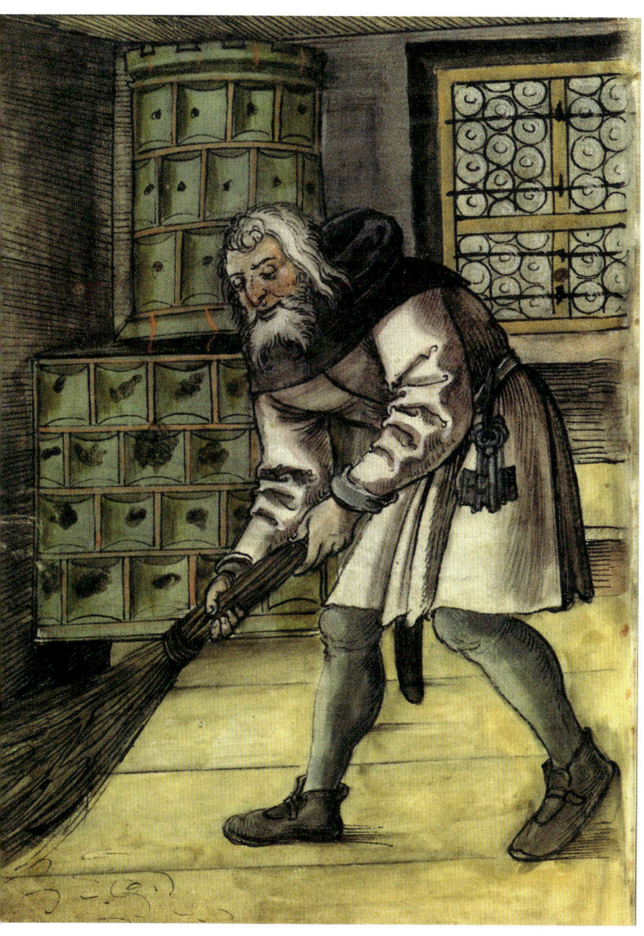

3.3 Pauly Mauser, *Haußknecht*, 1519, watercolour and black ink on parchment, 266 x 203 mm. Stadtbibliothek im Bildungscampus Nürnberg, *Die Hausbücher der Nürnberger Zwölfbrüderstiftungen*, Laudauer I, fol. 10v.

© Stadtbibliothek Nürnberg.

hot smoke and gas passed en route to the chimney. This, in turn, heated the tiles on the *Kachelofen*'s outer fascia. Smoke was expelled out of the chamber in which the *Kachelofen* was housed, by a pipe that led directly outside or into a separate, lower-status room. This expulsion was prized for allowing the air in the main chamber to remain untainted by noxious fumes that were deemed dangerous to health.[30] *Kachelöfen* frequently exceeded two metres in height, and so they often dominated the interior spaces in which they were installed.[31]

The emergence of *Kachelöfen* in domestic settings dates to the fourteenth century but it was during Europe's 'material Renaissance', which coincided with Dürer's engraving, that their visual and material qualities were transformed. From the mid-fifteenth century *Kachelöfen* gained new layers of symbolic meaning thanks to major technological innovations in ceramic manufacture. The invention of bright polychrome tin glazes, striking moulded relief tiles, decorative pipeclay figures, and the circulation of new design sources from cheap woodblock prints supercharged the visual and affective power of *Kachelöfen* tiles.[32]

The wider societal impacts of these material innovations have been most often discussed in relation to the iconography and propaganda strategies at play during Europe's religious reformations. Archaeologists, for example, track an important iconographic shift from pre-Reformation *Kachelöfen* tiles that commonly depicted the Virgin and Child and the martyred saints, to the contrasting visual style of tiles in Protestant homes that featured portraits of sovereigns, humanist figures, allegorical scenes and depictions of the life of Christ. Nowhere was this shift more striking than in the Wittenberg home of leading Protestant reformer Martin Luther (1483–1546), his residence from 1508–46.[33] Amongst the 4,000 tile fragments excavated from the garden of Luther's former home are the remnants of a discarded *Kachelofen*, dating to 1473, and those of its successor, dating to 1536. The dominant Catholic iconography of the Virgin and Child on the earlier tiles was later replaced by polychrome figures of biblical rulers, crests, coats of arms and a transposed print of the

thirteenth century in the eastern Alpine region, *Kachelöfen* had been installed in various parts of western, eastern and central Europe from the fourteenth century onwards.[29] *Kachelöfen* and earthenware tile manufacturing was largely based in the German lands, with important production centres in Wittenberg, Lower Saxony and Nuremberg. *Kachelöfen* had slight variations in form but typically comprised a rectangular lower cavity that held the firing chamber or stoke-hole, on top of which sat a cylindrical or box-shaped upper chamber where the

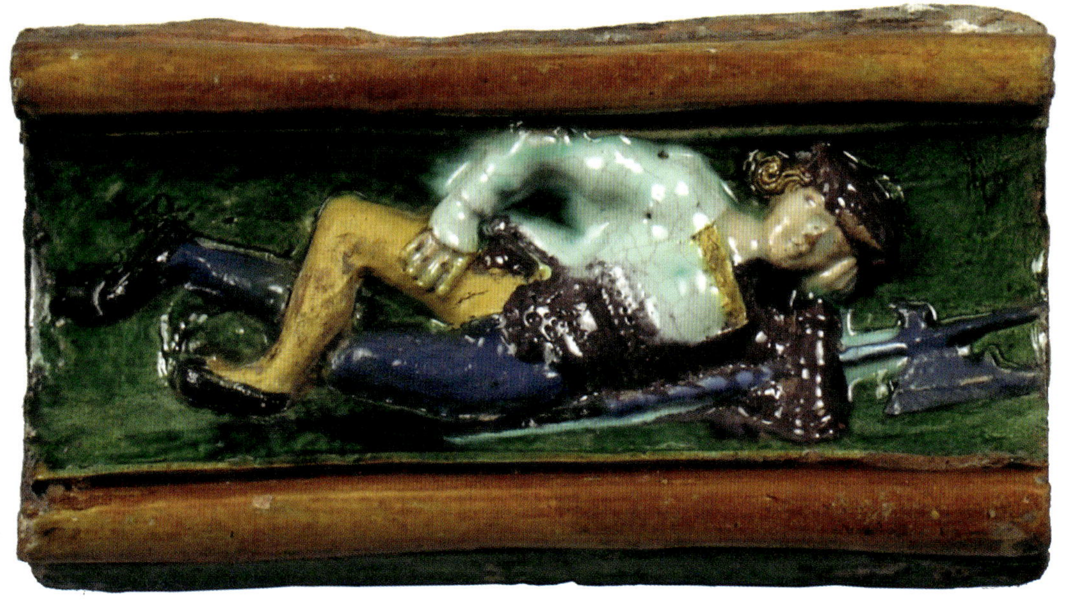

3.4 (cat. 13) Unknown, *Frieze Tile with a Sleeping Guard with a Halberd*, first quarter of the sixteenth century, German (Ochsenfurt). Dark-glazed earthenware, 10.0 x 18.5 cm. Germanisches Nationalmuseum, A948.

© Germanisches Nationalmuseum.

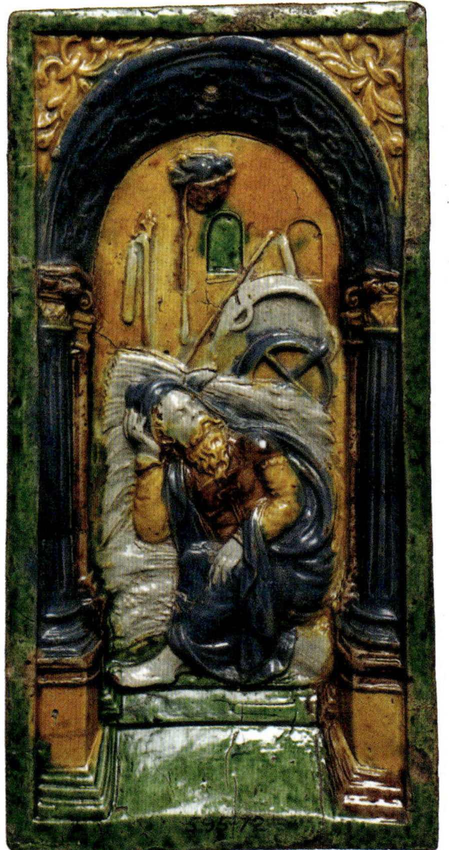

3.5 Unknown, *Stove Tile Depicting Tobit Asleep Under an Arch*, sixteenth century, German (Nuremberg). Glazed earthenware, 29.85 x 15.24 cm. London, Victoria and Albert Museum, 595-1872.

© Victoria and Albert Museum, London.

Twelve Women of the Old Testament, produced by Nuremberg printer and designer of woodcuts Erhard Schön (1491–1542) in c. 1530.[34]

Iconographic shifts in tile design reveal much about the theological divisions that marked the age of reformations. Crucially, they also identify *Kachelöfen* as the centrepieces of household religious practice for both Catholics *and* Protestants, despite differences in style and content. The large-scale proportions of *Kachelöfen* made them an obvious focal point and their interest was heightened by bright figurative scenes that invited and helped to direct religious observances. Decorative as they were, these scenes perhaps also functioned as protective shields against the sensuous heat that emanated from their surfaces. Several surviving *Kachelöfen* tiles from the turn of the sixteenth century, for example, bear direct warnings about the dangers of unseasonable sleep. The colourful frieze tile depicts a sleeping guard whose weapon has slipped into the crook of his slumbering arm (Figure 3.4). This figure may possibly refer to the guards who failed to observe the central Christian mystery of Christ's resurrection because they fell asleep whilst watching his tomb. The guard's repeated pattern surrounds the base of a *Kachelofen* from the Franconian town of Ochsenfurt, just south of Würzburg in modern-day Bavaria, and a short distance from Nuremberg. The tile dates to 1500 and so is almost exactly contemporary with Dürer's engraving.[35] Another vivid sixteenth-century earthenware *Kachelofen* tile manufactured in Nuremberg illustrates a similar cautionary message about the perils that could be met in sleep, especially when that sleep occurred outside of a suitably enclosed place (Figure 3.5). The biblical figure of Tobit is depicted in pipeclay moulding. Tobit, an elderly Jewish man who has lost his fortune, sleeps outside beneath an archway after his daily labours have exhausted him. Whilst he rests, excrement from a sparrow's nest falls upon his eyes and blinds him.[36]

With the obvious exception of kitchen fires, *Kachelöfen* were often the only heat sources in households, and they provided warmth for most of the day once lit. People's physical proximity to them was therefore assured and it was here that families gathered to give and receive spiritual instruction.[37] As Dürer's engraving reveals, however, the visual power of *Kachelöfen* tiles and the religious practices they often invited could be compromised by their thermal properties. The engraving thus invites the viewer to contemplate the full embodied effects of the *Kachelofen* and not just the impact of its bright reflective surfaces upon the eyes, hearts and minds of onlookers. Tile iconography offered a visual stimulus to virtue and to physical and spiritual vigilance, but these encouragements were only effective when onlookers were awake and able to take action to avoid the perceived dangers of slothful sleep.

Albrecht Dürer was aware of the increasingly close relationship between ceramic tile design, woodcuts and engraving thanks to the culture of artisanal collaboration and the variety of trades for which Nuremberg was renowned.[38] Graphic templates for *Kachelofen* tiles circulated in most artist's workshops at this time, and Dürer may have developed designs for this purpose, as he did for stained glass windows around the city. Fellow woodcut designer Erhard Schön certainly created figurative *Kachelofen*-tile designs for discerning customers in Nuremberg, as did Lucas Cranach (1472–1553) the elder and younger (1515–86) and the engraver and printmaker Georg Pencz (c. 1500–50) who worked in Dürer's workshop from 1523.[39] Given this lively exchange of graphic designs for *Kachelöfen*, it is significant that the concave niche-style tiles in Dürer's engraving lack decoration. Small-scale renderings of tile decorations may have lacked visual impact in the engraving or been difficult to achieve. Dürer produced at least two images featuring *Kachelöfen* that predated *The Temptation of the Idler*. A sketch of c. 1493 depicts a man slouching over a *Kachelofen*. He is framed by a coat of arms and the image caption appears to read '*Hicze – oho!*' (Hot – oho!).[40] A woodcut of c. 1492 that was part of a series illustrating a new edition of the Roman play *Eunuchus* includes a *Kachelofen* with rudimentary decorations on its tiles.[41] Neither of these pieces depicts the *Kachelofen* as prominently or in such careful detail as *The Temptation of the Idler*, but they show that tiles could be adorned with decoration. The absence of iconography in the later engraving appears, by contrast, as a deliberate choice to augment the drama of the scene.[42] By removing an important visual layer of defence against the devil's assault, the recumbent man is helpless to resist the heat of the *Kachelofen* and the heady fragrance of the mandrake fruit that lulls him into lustful sleep and into the peril of nocturnal emission.

Conclusion

Albrecht Dürer's *The Temptation of the Idler* (1498) offers unique insights into the intimate effects that Europe's material Renaissance had on everyday life in the imperial city of Nuremberg. By reconstructing the city's rich tradition of *Kachelöfen*-tile manufacture and use, alongside the visual and material qualities of *Kachelöfen* that proliferated in Nuremberg at the turn of the sixteenth century, this chapter has exposed deep-seated concerns about the power of these new consumer goods to stimulate idleness, sexual transgression and sin amongst their users, alongside fears of the devil's capacity to invade people's homes, attack vulnerable bodies and manipulate mundane matter for nefarious purposes. In so doing, it adds a fresh interpretative layer to characterisations of Renaissance *Kachelöfen* as aesthetically pleasing material innovations and as foci for beneficial religious practices. Whilst their highly glazed tiled surfaces depicted important biblical and allegorical scenes that conveyed moral lessons to the viewer, the immersive heat that *Kachelöfen* emitted could work to counter these virtuous endeavours. Albrecht Dürer's *Kachelofen* creates the thermal conditions necessary for the man's descent into sleep, for his lustful dream, and for the act of nocturnal emission that was likely taking place with the devil's encouragement. The engraving is more than just a standard depiction of the seven deadly sins. It raises important questions about the relationship between acquisition and piety in a transformative period that witnessed an outpouring of consumer objects from artisanal workshops across Northern Europe, and especially in Nuremberg. It also serves as an important reminder that late medieval Christian households were vibrant centres of religious contemplation and practice that were supported and challenged by new materials, production techniques and artisanal expertise.[43] Albrecht Dürer's immersion within a dense network of trades was vital to his nuanced perspective on the effects of Nuremberg's manufacturing culture, and to his characterisation of *Kachelöfen* as iconic yet perilous possessions.

Notes

1   Aimar-Wollheim, *At Home in Renaissance Italy*, 12–15; Sarti, *Europe at Home*; Welch, *Shopping in the Renaissance*, 12–14, 19–61.

2   It is uncertain whether Agnes and Albrecht Dürer had a *Kachelofen* within their own home, yet the 'Dürerhaus' on Nuremberg's Zisselgasse, whose interior was recreated by Friedrich Wilhelm Wanderer in 1885, includes several *Kachelöfen* decorated with glazed green tiles. Dürer's interest in *Kachelöfen* as an essential household feature is also suggested by his c. 1506 sketched design of a house that has *Kachelöfen* on three of its five floors. Oakes, 'A New Proposal for Dürer's Drawing', 3–10.

3   For an overview of the scholarship, see Schoch, Mende and Scherbaum *Albrecht Dürer*, I, 65–7, no. 18.

4   Dürer's careful observation of pillows is apparent from an early stage. See his 1493 pen and ink drawings *Self-portrait, Study of a Hand and a Pillow* (recto) and *Six Studies of Pillows* (verso), New York, The Metropolitan Museum of Art, 1975.1.862; Strauss, *Complete Drawings*, 1493/6 and 1493/7.

5   Dürer scholars debate the volume of attributed woodcuts. Panofsky suggests a one-third attribution, whilst more recent scholarship doubles that estimate. Ashcroft, *Albrecht Dürer*, I, 279.

6   Brant, *Das Narrenschiff*, trans. Strauss, *Complete Engravings*, 44.

7   Anon., *Ein allerhailsamste Warnung*.

8   Simons, *The Sex of Men in Premodern Europe*, 194.

9   Strauss, *Complete Drawings*, 1493/4; there is some debate about the date. Dürer's *Women's Bath* was replicated by his pupil, Hans Springinklee, in 1518. Sebald Beham's circular woodcut *The Women's Bath* (1530–50) features a tall, tiled *Kachelofen* although the scene lacks overtly sexualised meanings (H.III.241.1223). The work of Nuremberg-born Beham was heavily influenced by Dürer, and no doubt by the proliferation of *Kachelöfen* in his home city.

10   Sebald Beham, *Three Women in the Bath-House* (1548), London, The British Museum 1853,0709.78; NH Beham 214.

11   Barthel Beham, *Die Spinnstube* (*The Spinning Room*, 1524), Hollstein German II, 245, no. G154. By the mid-seventeenth century, Beham's woodcut adorned Paulus Fürst's broadside *Kurtze Beschreibung der wunderbarlichen Art unnd Eigenschafften* (c.1650), London, The British Museum 1999,0627.39. With thanks to the anonymous reviewer who suggested these comparisons.

12   Schoch, Mende and Scherbaum, *Albrecht Dürer*, I, 65.

13   Wickram, *Rollwagenbüchlin*, 22.

14   Schoch suggests that the fruit is a 'Bratapfel', or roast apple, which was a symbolic attribute of laziness or sloth that could call forth the devil. On the heating of medicaments on *Kachelöfen*, see Anonymous, *The grete herbal*.

15   See 'Love Apples'. On the influence of Hippocratic medicine amongst Nuremberg physicians, see Murphy, *A New Order of Medicine*, 10–14.

16   This remark is attributed to physician and Hebrew theologian Ovadia ben Jacob Sforno. See Fleisher, 'The Fragrance of Biblical Mandrake', 243–51, 249.

17   Compare the depiction of a dissolute household surrounding such an oven in Barthel Beham, *Die Spinnstube*, 1524, woodcut; Hollstein German II, 245, no. G154. Bellows, and depictions of them, were found in Nuremberg's sacred spaces. See, for example, *Geburt Christi aus der Pfarrkirche St. Sebald,* Nuremberg (c. 1439), Germanisches Nationalmuseum.

18   Ashcroft, *Albrecht Dürer*, II, 990.

19 For digital access to the collections, see: www.nuernberger-hausbuecher.de

20 For more detail, see Simons, *The Sex of Men in Premodern Europe*, 133, 254.

21 There is a strong linguistic equivalence between 'scrautum' (scrotum) and 'scrautum pelliceum', a kind of leather used to craft bags and containers. See Adams, *The Latin Sexual Vocabulary*, 74.

22 Proctor, 'Between Medicine and Morals', 119.

23 Maclehose, 'Captivating Thoughts', 98–131, 123.

24 *Ibid.*, 123.

25 Cochlaeus knew the city of Nuremberg well, having been educated there by Heinrich Grieninger before entering the University of Cologne in 1504, and later returning to work there as rector of the Latin School of Saint Lorenz from 1510–15. See Keen, 'Johannes Cochlaeus', 21.

26 Stove Tile Depicting Jason and Creusa and a Statue of Juno, light red tin-glazed earthenware painted in colours, Nuremberg (1546), Victoria & Albert Museum, C.402-1927.

27 Red earthenware stove tile, Nuremberg (c. 1580–1600), Fitzwilliam Museum, Cambridge, C.142-1933.

28 Walcher von Molthein, 'Arbeiten der Nürnberger Hafnerfamilie', 134–5.

29 On the chronology of *Kachelöfen* development in Europe's monasteries and households, see Mossman, *Rulman Merswin.*

30 Cavallo, *Healthy Living in Late Renaissance Italy*, 70–112.

31 On the development and classification of *Kachelofen* tiles, see Rosemarie Franz, *Der Kachelofen*; Heege, *Ofenkeramik und Kachelofen.*

32 These developments fuelled an expansion of the graphic catalogue of many other stoneware objects. See Gaimster, 'Material Culture, Archaeology and Defining Modernity', 78.

33 Nebelsick, '"Finding Luther",' 1155–1207. For figurated *Kachelofen* tiles in late medieval and Renaissance central Europe, see Strauss, *Die Kachelkunst;* Hallenkamp-Lumpe, *Studien zur Ofenkeramik.*

34 Nebelsick, '"Finding Luther"', 1189. The print is divided into two halves depicting six women each; Hollstein German, XLVII, 86, no. 66.

35 The complete *Kachelofen* with a base of sleeping guard tiles was originally from the Würzburg cathedral chapter in Ochsenfurt, see *Kachelofen*, Ochsenfurt oder Würzburg (first quarter of the sixteenth century), Germanisches Nationalmuseum, A503.

36 Earthenware stove tile with relief decoration and coloured glazes, Nuremberg (sixteenth century), Victoria & Albert Museum, 595-1872.

37 On the idealised didactic function attributed to sixteenth-century stove tiles, see Morrall, 'Domestic Decoration and the Bible', 584–6.

38 On artisanal collaboration in Nuremberg, see Wenderhorst, 'Nuremberg, the Imperial City', 11–26; Zika, 'Nuremberg', 30–4.

39 Pencz and both Cranachs are associated with *Kachelofen* tile designs at Turaida Castle, Latvia. Ose, *Stove Tile Ceramics of the Turaida Castle.* Gaimster, *The Archaeology of the Reformation 1480–1580.*

40 *Wappen mit Mann hinterm Offen* (c. 1493–95), Museum Boijmans van Beuningen, Rotterdam, Netherlands; see Strauss, *Complete Drawings.* 1493/22. Ashcroft suggests the caption may read 'Frize – oho!' and could have been intended as a joke against a specific person. Ashcroft, *Albrecht Dürer*, 1, 56.

41 *Pythias and Chremes speaking while seated on a bench* (Eun.IV.5; Basel Öffentliche Kunstsammlung Inv.Z.461) was drawn onto a block by Dürer but not cut or printed. See Strauss, *Complete Drawings*, 1492/36.

42 The same visual strategy was adopted by Sebald Beham. He depicted his *Three Women in the Bath-House* with their backs turned towards an undecorated *Kachelofen*. Beham's outstanding expertise in miniature engraving strongly suggests that it was a deliberate choice to leave the tiles unadorned.

43 Works that call attention to the dynamism of Catholic household devotional practices and to their material contexts (though principally in an Italian context) include: Cooper, 'Devotion', 190–203; Brundin, *The Sacred Home in Renaissance Italy;* Corry, *Madonnas and Miracles.*

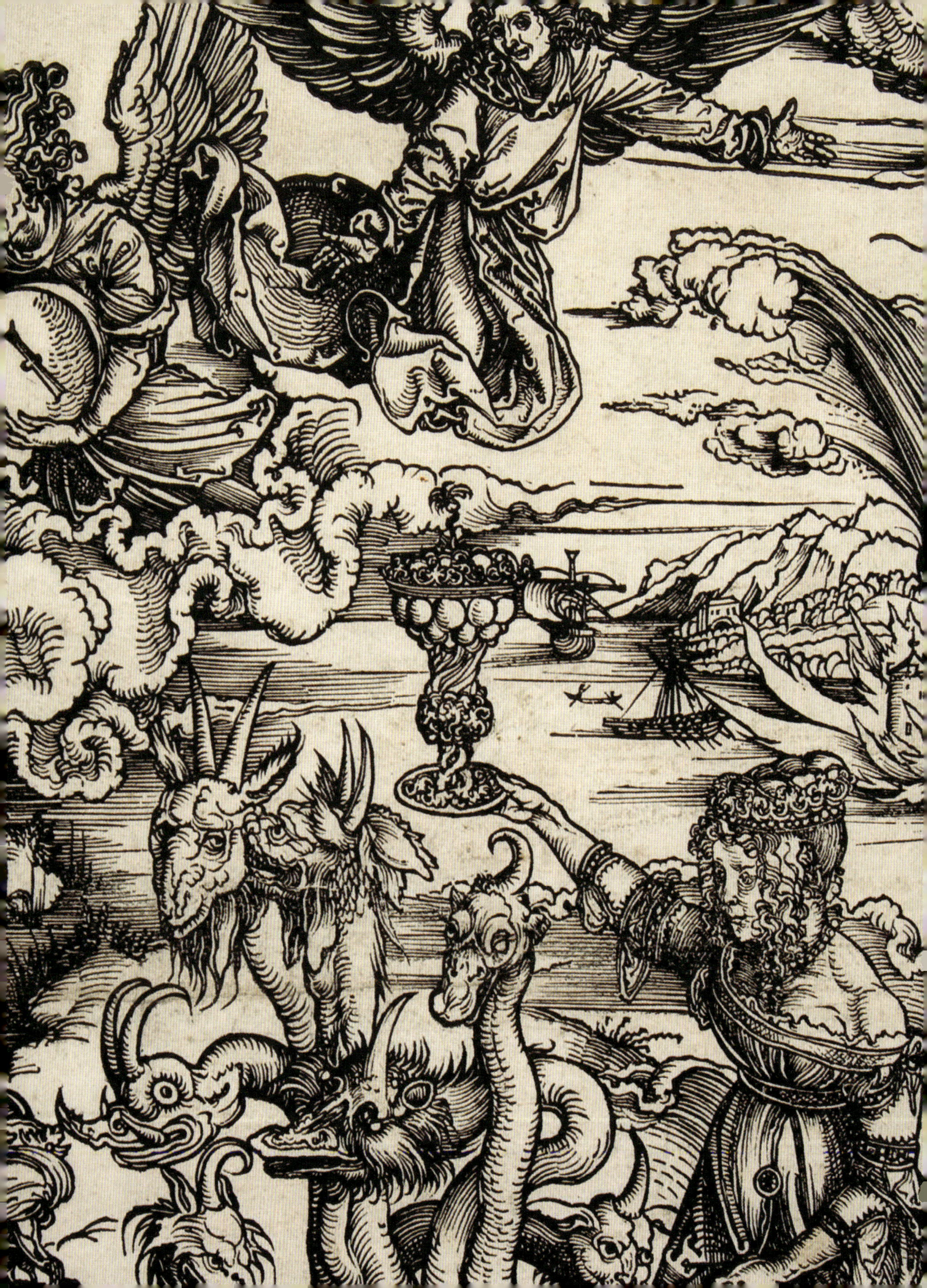

[4] Objects in motion: Albrecht Dürer's *Nemesis*

Jennifer Spinks

Albrecht Dürer's *Nemesis* is a large and ambitious engraving from c. 1501 (Figure 4.1; cat. 34).[1] It depicts a winged goddess soaring above a landscape in a dizzying play of scale and detail that demonstrates the artist's command of technique and his willingness to innovate with composition. The sturdy female figure standing on a globe is reminiscent of Fortune, a figure that Dürer had previously depicted in an engraving of c. 1496 (cat. 36).[2] A preliminary drawing of Nemesis, with its carefully marked-up body sections, demonstrates how Dürer worked on this figure to develop and demonstrate his skills in the construction of human proportion.[3] Fortune, standing on a topsy-turvy ball, embodies the instability of human affairs, and while Dürer's goddess Nemesis also incorporates this idea, she is identifiable as a distinct figure by the objects that she holds: a cup to reward and a bridle to punish.

Dürer presents us here with a bird's-eye view of the town of Klausen in the Valle d'Isarco in the Tyrol.[4] The rich detail in even the tiniest areas of the landscape show how much he appreciated the capacity of engraving to bring his viewer close to every part of the print.[5] The deep topography with a prominent figure in the sky recalls some of the imagery from Dürer's highly successful 1498 *Apocalypse* woodcut cycle.[6] Dürer was likely also influenced by the stunning multi-sheet topographical view of Venice from 1500 printed by the Nuremberg publisher Anton Kolb and created by the Italian artist Jacopo de' Barbari (c. 1460/70–1516), who was soon after based in Nuremberg.[7]

Dürer had travelled through the Tyrol on his first journey to Italy half a decade earlier, and the print draws upon Italian humanist ideas as well as on his memories of travel. In 1902 Karl Giehlow identified Dürer's key source

for this image as the 1482 Latin poem 'Manto' by the Florentine humanist Angelo Poliziano (1454–94), which paid homage to Virgil. In the poem Poliziano invoked Nemesis as an awe-inspiring figure who incorporated dualities, not least those of stillness and motion:

> [A] goddess suspended high upon the vacant air who makes her way girdled by a cloud, but her mantle is of brilliant white, her hair radiant, and her whirling wings produce a shrill sound. She suppresses immoderate hopes and fiercely menaces the proud [...] Stars adorn her brow; in her hands she holds the bridle and the libation bowl [...] she confounds and orders our actions by turns and is borne hither and thither by the force of the whirlwind.[8]

The poem is set against the context of war, and evokes rich landscape imagery, including – in a dynamic phrase that anticipates the steep landscape of *Nemesis* – how 'the forests themselves rush down headlong from the Alpine peaks'.[9] Dürer would have encountered this material through acquaintances in Italy, or, more likely, through humanist friends in Nuremberg like Willibald Pirckheimer (1470–1530), who collected books from the Venetian press of Aldus Manutius and would certainly have owned the 1498 Aldine edition of Poliziano. The imagery of cup and bridle may have also drawn upon a Florentine medal of c. 1480–85 by Niccolò Fiorentino (1430–1514) in memory of Giuliano de' Medici (1453–1478).[10] Another possible source, which also included these elements, is the 'Manual of Roman History' by Julius Pomponius Laetus (1428–98), printed in the early sixteenth century and known in manuscript form in Nuremberg at this time.[11]

The humanist context for this print has generated considerable scholarship, but the material culture that

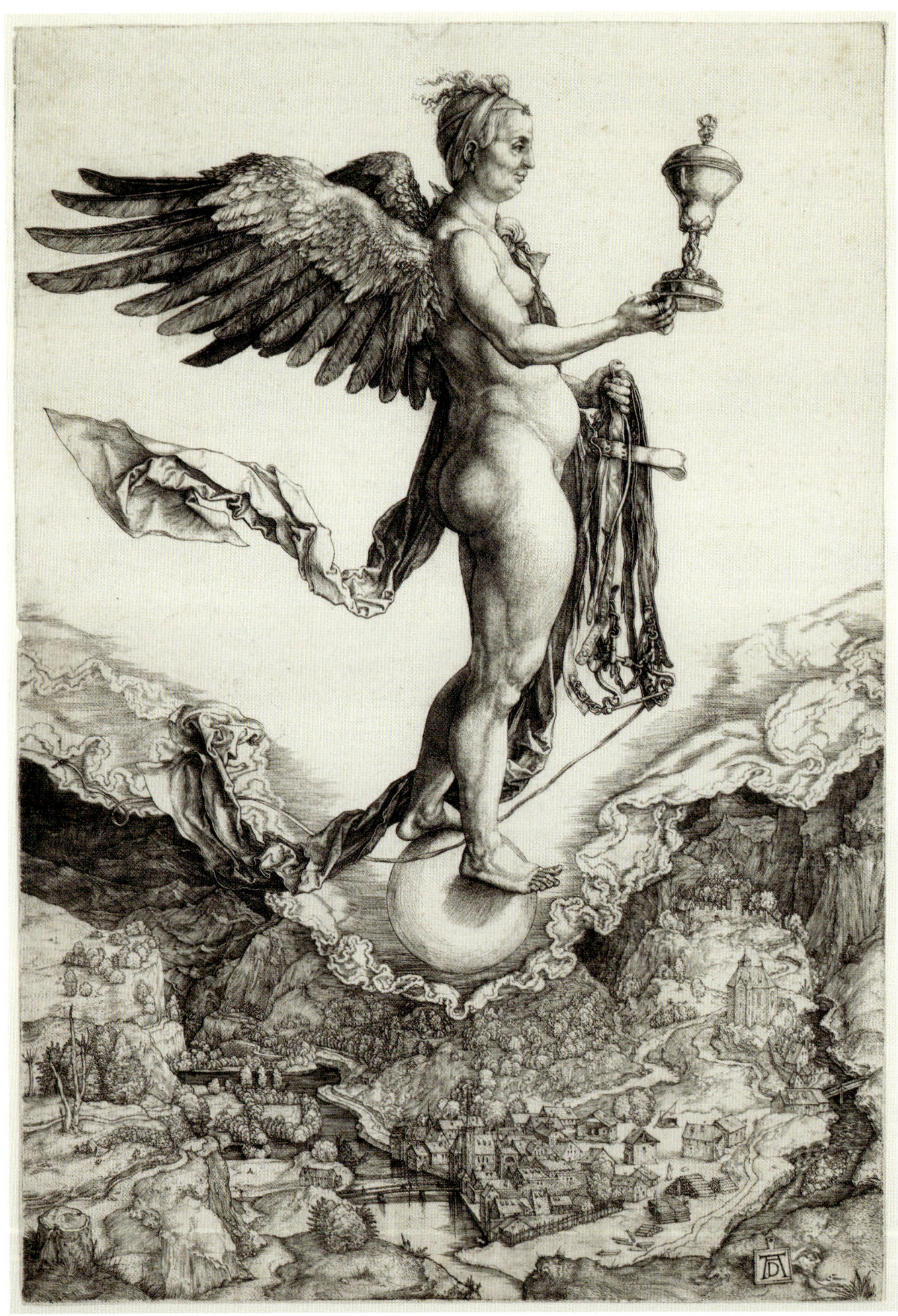

 Albrecht Dürer's material world

is so richly detailed in the engraving also demands attention, as it draws us towards a discussion of the dynamic networks of production and trade in Nuremberg. Dürer was an eager participant in the vibrant 'material Renaissance' that characterised life during a period of growth in consumption, manufacturing, trade and artisanal inventiveness.[12] This participation can be seen in the range of objects that animate the figure of Nemesis. Her carefully detailed wings, for instance, reflect Dürer's well-documented interest in life studies of birds. In Nuremberg, feathers were commodities that were traded and integrated into fashionable clothing.[13] Wings inherently suggest movement, but the stilled image of Nemesis directs our focus instead to the feathers' texture, sheen and pattern.[14] The great swirl of fabric also generates a sense of motion and animates the space around the figure. Dürer flaunts his exceptional skill in detailing the twists and turns of this fabric, which suggests the 'whirlwind' of the poem. Nemesis's earrings and rings are relatively plain, recalling simple Gothic jewellery rather than the more elaborate jewels and enamelling that would become common later in the Renaissance.[15] Their plainness throws into relief the extraordinary vessel which she holds aloft, and which draws the eye of the viewer. The more workaday, but nonetheless complex, shape of the bridle serves as an effective counterpoint to the luxury of the vessel.

The son of a Hungarian goldsmith who benefited from Nuremberg's lack of the closed guild system that dominated most other cities of the time, Dürer apprenticed in goldsmithing before turning to the less prestigious profession of painting.[16] The development of printmaking as an innovative field of artistic activity in the late fifteenth century was partly fostered by an overlap of skills and networks across printmaking and metalworking. The latter was especially concerned with decorative lines and with

line-making, and printmakers like Dürer deployed techniques from metalworking to develop their skills in forms of printmaking using metal plates.[17] The skills that Dürer acquired in his goldsmithing training served him well when he turned to printmaking as an avenue for artistic and commercial success. Over 50 per cent of the city's extensive manufacturing workshops created objects from metal. Indeed, Nuremberg was well-known across Europe as a centre of expertise in skilled metalworking: from the creation of wire and associated small screws and rods – made since the fourteenth century according to the city's secret technique – to the production of the latest fashions in armour, household metalwork and the design and manufacture of highly specialised measuring instruments.[18]

This essay explores how the two most significant objects associated with the figure of Nemesis – the cup and bridle – immerse the viewer in aspects of the crafted, civic, intellectual and religious worlds of Dürer's Nuremberg. However, these connections with Nuremberg do not anchor or pin down the objects, which are dynamic and have their own lives, as recent scholarship on material culture often demonstrates. Objects are not static, but manufactured, acquired, used, shared, altered and passed on.[19] Just as Nemesis herself is a point of rest in the whirlwind of this engraving, so Dürer allows his audience to pause on beautifully crafted objects, to examine them in close detail, and then to envisage them set in motion.[20]

The cup

Dürer evidently intended that the viewer's eye be immediately drawn to the beautifully crafted cup that Nemesis holds out on the tips of her fingers. Her delicate gesture belies the real weight of a metal cup filled with wine: the organic stem mimics a growing plant, and its leaves elegantly support the bowl of the vessel with an apparent lightness that echoes the lightness of Nemesis's grip on the object.[21] The base and lid handle are made with decorative flourishes that are not entirely natural, but bring to mind curling hair, water or clouds, further blending the organic and the artificial. Dürer explored a similar combination

4.1 (cat. 34) Albrecht Dürer, *Nemesis (The Great Fortune)*, c. 1501, engraving, 333 x 231 mm.

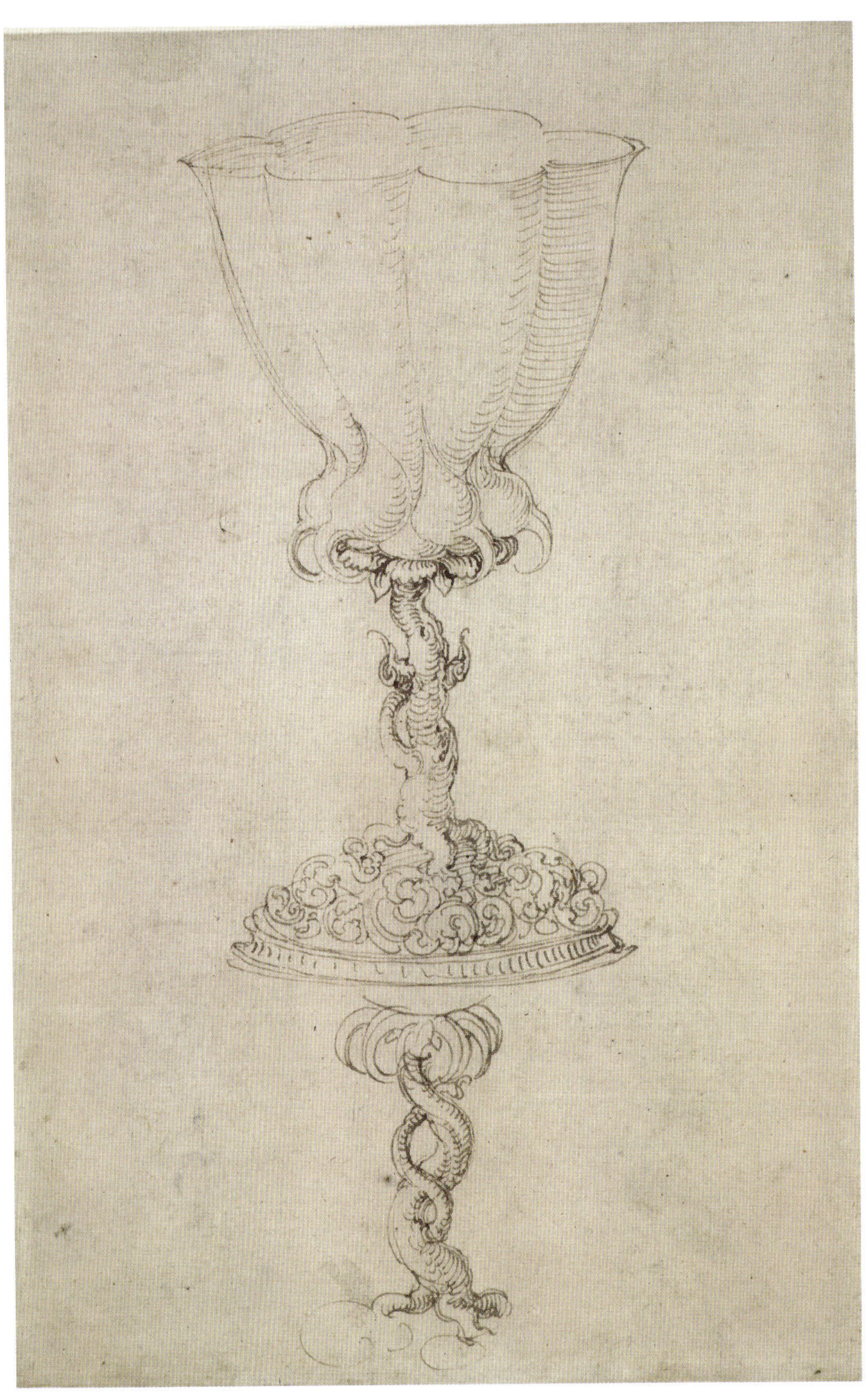

4.2 (cat. 35) Albrecht Dürer, *Design for a Gothic Cup*,
c. 1495–1500, pen and brown ink, 256 x 166 mm.

London, The British Museum, SL,5218.78. Bequeathed by Sir Hans Sloane.
© The Trustees of the British Museum.

of vegetal forms and elaborate metalwork design in his *Design for a Gothic Cup*, which was completed at roughly the same time as his *Nemesis* engraving (Figure 4.2; cat. 35).

This type of vessel, made of glass, or more often metal, and usually lidded, was known as a *Pokal*.[22] Vessels made of metal were works of considerable artistic innovation in late medieval and Renaissance Europe. German cities, Nuremberg included, became well known for their output of these high-status objects, which allowed metalsmiths to show off their skills to maximum effect. They reveal a use of innovative design and technique including the *gebuckelte* or dimpled shape.[23] The cup held by Nemesis, a *Birnpokal* in the shape of a pear, does not seem to be a direct copy of any existing vessel but rather Dürer's creative adaptation of cups like the *Apfelpokal* or 'apple cup' of

1510–15 (Figure 4.3).[24] Its material manufacture in the city, its physical use and its appearance in other forms of visual culture mark it out as a significant object that takes us to the world of Renaissance Nuremberg where *Pokale* were used in celebratory meals in luxurious private homes as well as in civic rituals, as we shall see. The vessel that Nemesis holds is therefore one of the most high-status artistic objects that Dürer could have chosen to depict in a print, and it recalls his beautiful, decorative drawings of vessels that were likely potential designs rather than reproductions of existing objects.[25] They are evidence of Dürer's fertile imagination as well as the desirability and beauty of objects made by master craftworkers.

Through social, civic and especially workshop networks, Dürer would have had access to items like this vessel, and he would likely have even made one himself. It

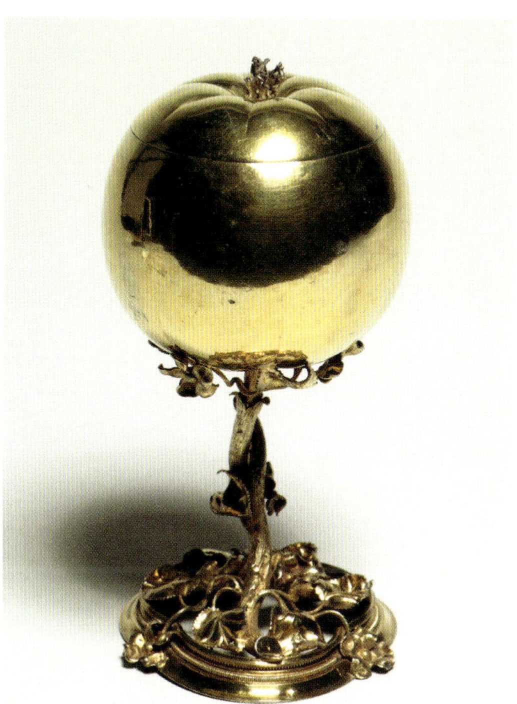

4.3 *Apfelpokal* (apple cup with lid), 1510–15, gilded silver, 21.5 x 11.3 x 11.0 cm.

Nuremberg, Germanisches Nationalmuseum, inv. HG8399, © Germanisches Nationalmuseum, Nuremberg.

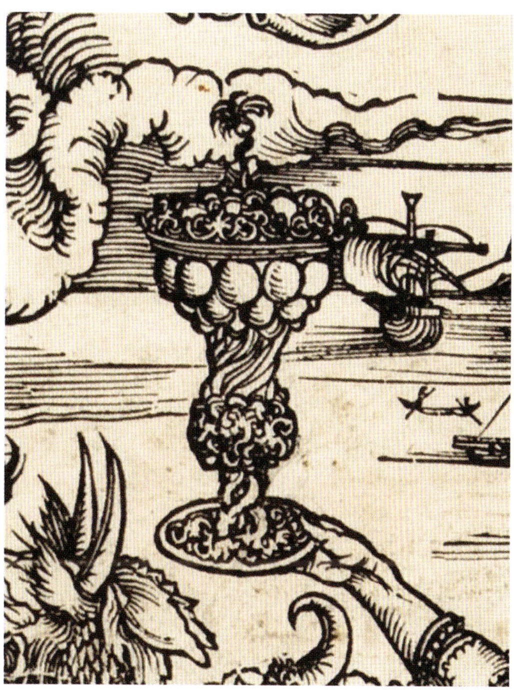

4.4 (Detail of cat. 42) Albrecht Dürer, *The Babylonian Whore* (*Apocalypse*), 1498, woodcut, paper: 387 x 282 mm, plate: 387 x 280 mm.

The Whitworth, The University of Manchester, P.3070. Presented by George Thomas Clough in 1921. © The Whitworth, The University of Manchester. Photo: Michael Pollard.

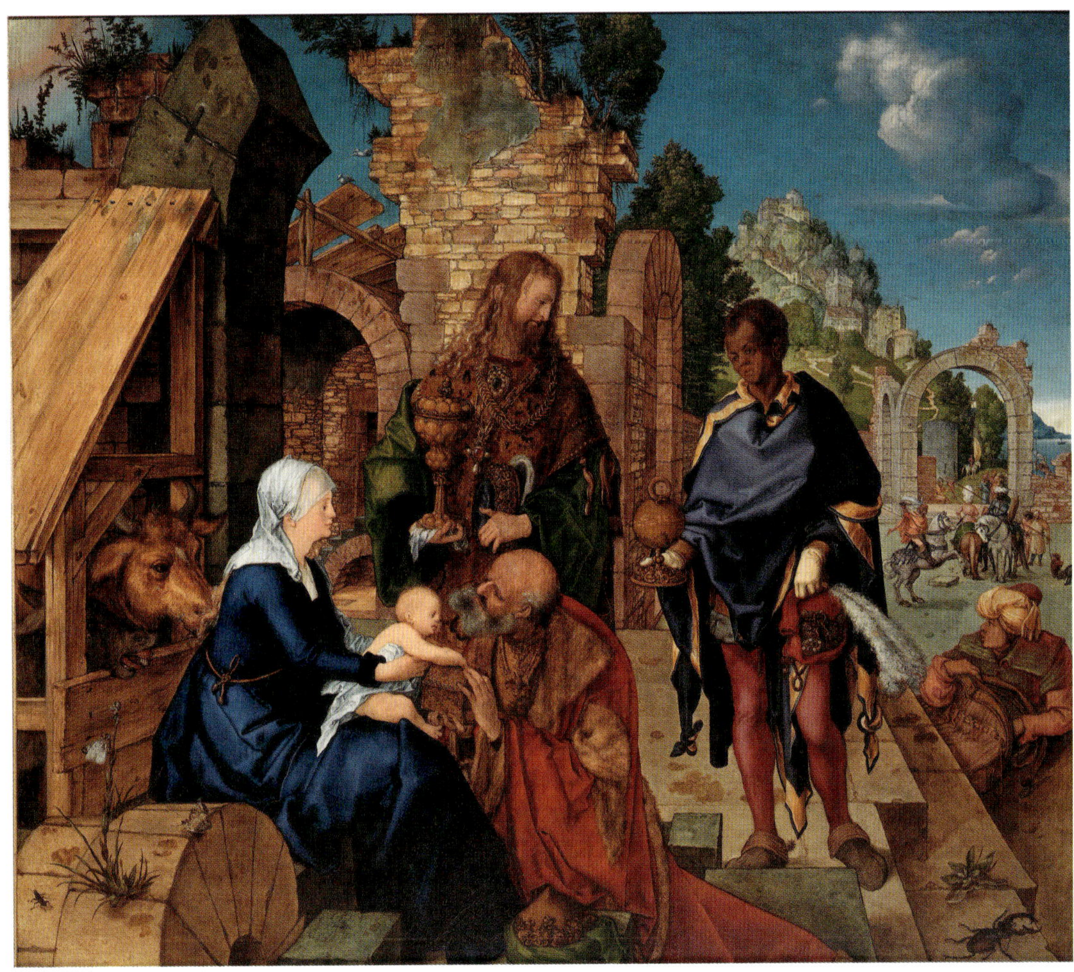

4.5. Albrecht Dürer, *The Adoration of the Magi*, 1504,
oil on wood, 99.0 x 113.5 cm.

Florence, Ministero della Cultura, The Uffizi, inv. 1890 n. 1434.
© Ministero della Cultura.

is likely that Dürer, following in the footsteps of his
father, completed his own goldsmith training before
training as a painter. If so, he may have completed a
'masterpiece' to mark the end of his apprenticeship, and
this work might have been retained in the household
as an important object. In her 1538 will, Agnes Dürer,
the artist's widow, left 'a drinking vessel which was his
masterpiece' to Albrecht's brother Endres (1484–1555).
It is unclear whether the vessel was made by Endres
and was returned to him on her death, or – less likely
but still possible – if the piece was made by Albrecht

and left to Endres in memory of his brother.[26] Either
way, beautifully made vessels were among the most
significant objects in the households of goldsmiths, as
these testified to the metalworker's skill. Between 1489
and 1492 Albrecht Dürer the Elder (1427–1502) was
at work on a commission of drinking vessels for Holy
Roman Emperor Friedrich III (1415–93). The commission
is recorded in the Nuremberg City Council notes of 24
March 1489. On 24 August 1492, the elder Dürer was in
Linz and wrote jubilantly to his wife Barbara (c. 1451–1514)
that Friedrich III had taken 'great delight' in the design

    Albrecht Dürer's material world

drawings. Even better, the emperor had crossed the room to speak to Dürer the Elder – a significant mark of favour – and pressed four gulden into his hands as an extra gratuity on top of the agreed payments.[27] While none of Dürer the Elder's goldsmithing work survives, it is certain that this was a landmark commission for his workshop and a source of family pride. The young Albrecht was on his journeyman travels at this time, and it would surely have been repeated to him as a family story of considerable significance upon his return at Pentecost in 1494.

Pokale and other such vessels formed part of Dürer's physical and imaginative worlds, and we can see his interest in this imagery in several other important works. The gesture of a woman holding a vessel aloft would have been a familiar one to viewers of Dürer's prints. Only a few years earlier, he depicted the whore of Babylon in his famous *Apocalypse* cycle of fifteen woodcuts (cat. 42), which were published as a book in an innovative blending of single-printmaking and book publishing. In this image the female figure also holds aloft a vessel that reflects the heights of German metalwork in its most fashionable and luxurious form (Figure 4.4).[28] The New Testament text of the Book of Revelation describes this as 'a golden goblet … full of abominations and filthiness of her fornication'.[29] Thus, the earlier print demonstrates how luxury could be used for negative purposes; it is no accident that the whore of Babylon and Nemesis are both forbidding figures. The vessel sits at the centre of the *Apocalypse* image, a fulcrum in a chaotic scene that encompasses the whore of Babylon's worshippers, angels, ghostly soldiers and the destruction of the city. Like Nemesis, she is a figure caught in a moment of stillness, having travelled to the centre of this scene on the back of the seven-headed beast whose grotesque heads offset the vessel that outshines her jewellery and rich clothing. Dürer here indicates how, through its richly crafted form and surface, a vessel might carry layers of meaning as well as draw the eye of the viewer in the tactile medium of print. This was an idea that he would develop further in his *Nemesis* print.

Similar elaborate vessels were also familiar from the New Testament iconography of the three Magi or three kings.

Scenes of eastern rulers journeying to worship Christ at his birth were enormously popular in the fifteenth century, and European rulers sometimes identified with the kings during public events and in visual imagery.[30] Dürer depicted the Magi several times in woodcuts because of his special interest in the imagery of the life of the Virgin: he did so first in c. 1503, as part of his 1511 *Life of the Virgin* series (cat. 24), and then again in a separate woodcut from 1511.[31] The three Magi formed the theme of one of his most prestigious painting commissions, *The Adoration of the Magi*, completed in 1504 for the Saxon Elector Friedrich the Wise (1463–1525; Figure 4.5; Friedrich would later be depicted by Dürer, cat. 4). This large oil painting was created for the chapel of the castle church in Wittenberg, the town which would famously become the birthplace of the Lutheran Reformation only a decade later. Dürer's painting builds on fifteenth-century traditions by emphasising the dignified bearing of the Black king and showcasing the gifts held by two of the kings as beautiful examples of a contemporary goldsmith's work. The rich, Venetian-inspired colours of the painting allow the dazzling vessel at the centre of the scene to blend into the colour of the rich curling hair of the king holding it. With his striking features, hair and unusual beard, this king figure echoes Dürer's own appearance in several self-portraits. In such images Dürer drew upon tradition but also innovated by using Italian perspective and colour schemes, and with the placement of a bold self-portrait where he grasps a metalwork object in a nod to his origins and presents himself as a master of all art forms. Having reached their destination, the three kings occupy the centre of Dürer's painting, and the final moment of movement is encapsulated in the delicate gesture of the grey-haired king who reaches to touch fingertips with the Christ child. One of the core ideas underpinning the three Magi is, of course, travel; and the incorporation of symbolic versions of the Magi into public processions in medieval and Renaissance Europe is a testimony to their association with movement. Like Nemesis, the kings have traversed vast distances with their vessels and in coming briefly to rest they orient themselves by the star that has drawn them to Christ.

This range of biblical associations reminds us that lidded vessels could also be used in a variety of religious rituals.

The ciborium or pyxis was used for holding the host (consecrated eucharistic bread available to members of the church during mass), and reliquaries holding holy remains sometimes had similarly elaborate shapes.[32] Saints, like gods, could hold objects (or 'attributes') that identified them in paintings for churches and other sacred settings. In representations of Saint Barbara, for example, the saint often held up a cup, representing the eucharist. Similarly, the vessel held by Nemesis surely reminded viewers of the chalices used for wine during the mass, which was taken only by the priests in pre-Reformation Germany and was therefore imbued with an especially sacred, elevated aura. The vessel in this image thus possessed a rich range of potential religious reference points that were meaningful for Dürer.[33]

Dürer's engagement with the theme of Nemesis and with the work of Poliziano, among other humanist sources, demonstrates his growing fascination with classical mythology, the iconography of antiquity and its renewal in the Italian Renaissance. This was certainly fostered by his travels to Italy, but it was also nourished at home in Nuremberg through friendships and professional circles in the city. These connections gave him access to a range of important civic rituals that brought together members of the Nuremberg community and provide yet another way to interpret the vessel, distinct from its religious meanings. The libation cup held by Nemesis not only suggests wine and travel across distances to offer it to those she favoured, it also indicates how integral drinking and drinking rituals were to early modern German society, and how drinking vessels served as a reminder of the importance of status, ritual and friendship.[34] Indeed, one of Dürer's 1506 letters from Venice to Pirckheimer refers to an elite drinking group.[35]

More publicly, metalwork vessels were part of the processional rituals of civic life in the Nuremberg government, and they would have been familiar in this context to well-connected, upwardly mobile men like Dürer. In the fifteenth century, as the city sought to deepen its close connection with the Holy Roman Empire, a tradition was established that the first visit to Nuremberg by the emperor was accompanied by

processions and events, including the presentation of an elaborate, double-bodied metalwork vessel filled with coins. Habsburg emperors Friedrich III (in 1442) and Maximilian I (1459–1519; in 1489 as king of the Romans and in 1500 as emperor) both took part in this ritual.[36] It was a ceremony that was meant to bolster a connection that was not always as strong as Nurembergers might have wished; Emperor Friedrich, for example, prevaricated on confirming the city's privileges.[37] So significant was the ritual that it was extended in 1521 to seventeen-year-old Archduke Ferdinand (1503–64) who was acting as deputy to Holy Roman Emperor Charles V (1500–58).[38] The crafts of Nuremberg were central to this civic tradition, and detailed descriptions of the 1521 entry indicate that craftsmen and their households used borrowed armour and weaponry in order to dress up as foot soldiers. Making this equipment available from the municipal armoury meant that over '100 crafts' could be represented, and Ferdinand was presented with an ewer and two valuable drinking cups.[39] Dürer would have been familiar with this prestigious civic use of a vessel in motion and conveyed to the holy roman emperor by representatives of a city eager to maintain its prominent status in the Empire.

Vessels could also be presented as markers of prestige and civic gratitude in other contexts. Pirckheimer, Dürer's closest friend, was presented with a golden cup on his return from leading the city's troops in the 1499 Swabian war between Swiss and Habsburg forces.[40] The war had a significant impact on Pirckheimer, who wrote a history of his experiences during the conflict, which concluded with a Swiss victory. He would certainly have discussed the war extensively with his friends and colleagues in Nuremberg who saw the soldiers in their bright red outfits coming and going from the city.[41] It was in the years immediately afterwards that he would likely have introduced Dürer to the ideas in Poliziano's poem – also concerned with war – that inspired the *Nemesis* print.[42] There was likely no one 'original' vessel that Dürer drew upon for the *Nemesis* engraving. Rather, the image reflects a constellation of interwoven associations that would have been meaningful to Dürer and to his audiences. They remind us of the role played by vessels in a Renaissance city and the rich layers of meaning that they embodied, which ranged from the processes of making, to the rituals, processions and other forms of movement that activated the objects once they were created.

The bridle

The exquisite vessel held by Nemesis has rightly attracted scholarly attention, but we should not overlook the bridle that Nemesis holds in her other hand. Its detailed depiction forms part of the still centre of this print where motion is simultaneously suggested and arrested. A tie-line from the bridle trails away between Nemesis's feet, activating the space with a flourish that is echoed in the swirls of fabric. Nemesis holds the bridle in a drooping, aloof gesture that only symbolically represents its normal use of curbing, restraining and directing. Later, highly sexualised images inspired by Dürer's print, by Urs Graf (c. 1485–1527/8) and others, depicted bridle-like chains that fetter naked female bodies.[43] In 1513 Niklaus Manuel Deutsch (1484–1513), for example, created an extraordinary image of a witch flying in the sky, her nakedness emphasised by the chains that are draped over her body.[44] Dürer's Nemesis is certainly voluptuous, but her nakedness here is a

sign of her status as a goddess, and his depiction of the bridle set alongside her naked flesh reinforces her power, not her sexual availability.[45] But the bridle for Dürer is not just an attribute of Nemesis; like the elaborate cup, it conveys important symbolic as well as material links to the world of Nuremberg and reflects the metalworking culture of the city in a more quotidian way. Unlike *Pokale* and other examples of luxury metalwork, original bridles are hard to find in museums today. Modern reconstructions are often displayed alongside the more elaborate armour and decorative saddle fittings that have survived.[46] Dürer's print focuses our attention on this often-overlooked piece of early modern material culture.

The undecorated bridle is certainly a much more workaday item than the luxuriously engraved vessel, but it is not a humble or impoverished object. As a piece of material culture typical in the life of the well-off in a Renaissance city, it suggests solid craftsmanship rather than decorative ingenuity and references the possessions in daily use by the middling sort of residents of Nuremberg rather than luxury items for special occasions. It is the kind of craft that is celebrated in the manuscript *Hausbücher* of the *Zwölfbrüderstiftung*, which from the fourteenth century on depicted craftworkers like the *Zaummacher*, skilfully creating bridles. Indeed, a

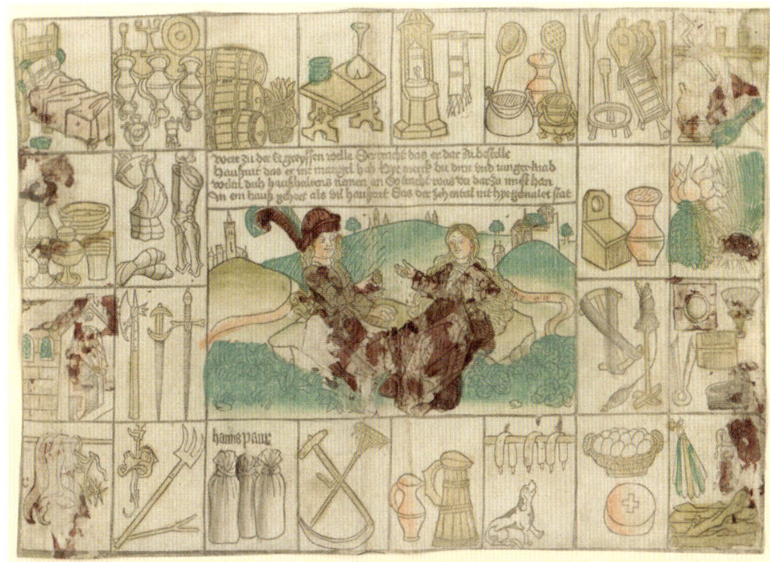

4.6. Hanns Paur, *Leaflet for Betrothed Couples*, c. 1480, woodcut, 253 x 364 mm.

Munich, Staatliche Graphische Sammlung München, inv. 118321 D. © Staatliche Graphische Sammlung München.

c. 1480 Nuremberg betrothal print of items deemed desirable for a well-run household included armour and a bridled horse (Figure 4.6).[47] This simple but fascinating woodcut acts as a kind of visual inventory and demonstrates how the counting and acquiring of crafted objects was deemed worth commemorating in print. Horse riding for Nuremberg residents took one outside the walls of the city and into the surrounding countryside where wealthy people had houses. Dürer would have had his own garden, as his capacity to participate on an equal footing with the more elite residents of the city grew alongside his status and income.[48] Thus objects like bridles could be markers of status, and linked to other possessions and opportunities, even when not ornately decorated or obviously luxurious to the modern eye.

Dürer was fascinated by horses, as many of his early prints and drawings demonstrate, and he regularly depicted bridles.[49] The depiction of horses allowed him to explore courtly and knightly themes, to create dynamic images filled with movement, and to continue his explorations of bodily proportion. Several of these obsessions would culminate in his master print *Knight, Death and the Devil* of 1513 (cat. 75), but a number of his earliest images were also of horses. A few years before the *Nemesis* engraving, Dürer had created the woodcut *Knight on Horseback and Lansquenet* of c. 1496–8 (Figure 4.7).[50] In this print the vigorous horse, its noble rider – in a pose emphasising his fashionable clothing – and the running foot soldier are arrested in a frozen moment, while the bridle controlling the horse's head presents a counterpoint to the beast's surging legs and its larger figure a contrast to the tiny, excitable dog.

The bridle held by Nemesis may also echo, for Dürer, the figure of Erichthonius, who appears as the personification of a constellation in some star maps of the period. Erichthonius was a king of Athens thought to have been the first to harness four horses to a chariot, and his attribute was a bridle loosely slung from his hand.[51] If Dürer also had this in mind, it would have likely been a nod to Nuremberg's importance at this time in creating and manufacturing tools for mapping the heavens. In 1515 Dürer would draw upon two 1503 manuscript maps made in Nuremberg to create star maps of the two hemispheres.[52] Dürer's *Celestial Map – Northern Hemisphere* (cat. 86) included a representation of Erichthonius, showing that this imagery was already circulating in Nuremberg in the first few years of the decade.[53] In 1492/3, Martin Behaim (1459–1506/7) created his *Erdapfel* or gored globe in Nuremberg, a breakthrough in the conceptualisation of mapping and curved space, and an object that would remain on display in Nuremberg's town hall for a decade after its creation.[54] Dürer's possible secondary reference to Erichthonius, alongside his primary focus on Nemesis, echoes an idea that is also central to 'Manto': Nemesis soaring across the curving heavens. In a city that pioneered the creation of globes in the 1490s and created exceptionally detailed and delicate instruments for astronomical measurement, Nemesis's place in the skies resonated. Her still, dangling but impeccably crafted bridle – a staple of Nuremberg's metalwork trade – arrests the viewer's attention, but it also acts as a prompt to consider movement – that of horse riding or the motion of the heavens.

* * * * *

The vessel and bridle draw the viewer into a series of reflections on *Nemesis* but also on the artist's own world. They focus our attention on the kind of metalwork that was so important to the city, printmaking and to the artist personally. These objects also activate the space of the print in unexpected ways. The bridle falls in a slack gesture, and the vessel – which should be heavy and filled with wine – balances almost on the very tips of Nemesis's fingers. Just as Nemesis's sturdy body soars, the objects play with the viewer's perception of space and weight, of stillness and motion. Nemesis flies over a landscape that is deeply realistic but at the same time almost hallucinatory, and the objects – with their symbolic range of meanings and physical tangibility – form part of how the viewer and purchaser becomes drawn into a world that is simultaneously intimate and vast.

4.7. Albrecht Dürer, *The Knight on Horseback and Lansquenet*, c. 1496/98, woodcut, 392 x 283 mm.
New York, The Metropolitan Museum of Art, 1975.653.103.
© The Metropolitan Museum of Art.

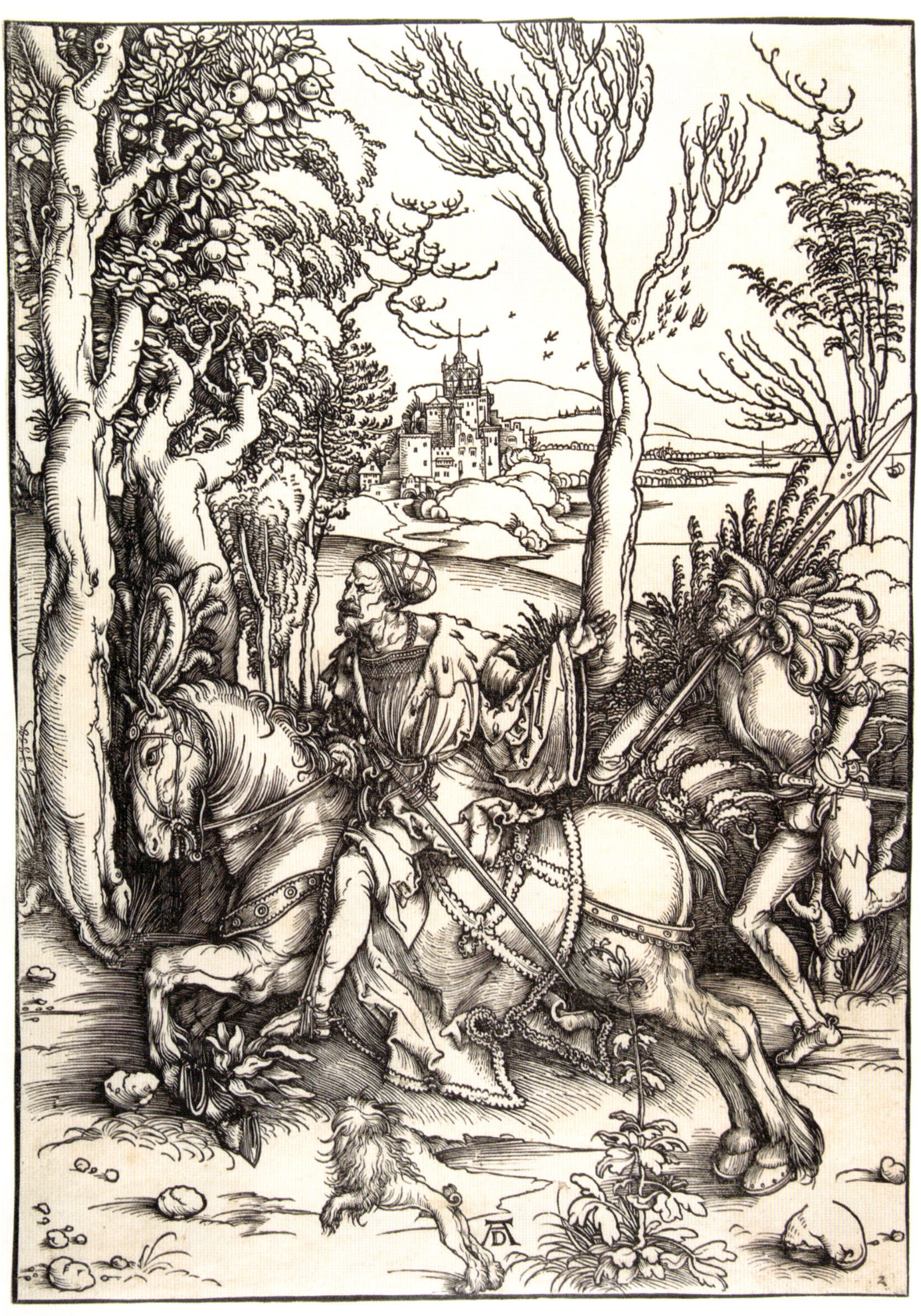

Dürer was not the first artist to lovingly depict objects, but he was one of the first to send them out into the world on a much wider scale through his sales networks for prints – objects, of course, in their own right. Like metalwork cups and bridles, prints could originate in Nuremberg and then travel. The artist's Netherlandish diary of 1520/1 recorded his year-long travels with a focus on expenses, income and trade. It offers a record of diverse objects: from the clothes, paper and other workaday items that Dürer purchased, to exciting *Kunstkammer*-style objects, including shells, skulls and artefacts from India.[55] Dürer also sometimes referred to prints sold or traded either by name or more generically as 'prints'.[56] At a bare minimum, he had six copies of *Nemesis* with him, and almost certainly more. Here we can link *Nemesis* with some of the individuals who were gifted the engraving. In Cologne he gave a copy of *Nemesis* to his cousin Nikolaus's 'man' or valet.[57] In Antwerp he gave city treasurer from 1514–25 Lorenz Sterk 'a complete set of prints, giving the same also to Adrian Herbouts, the public orator of Antwerp'.[58] In the same city he also presented a 'Master Gilles' with a *Saint Eustace* (cat. 104) and a *Nemesis*.[59] He gave the Portuguese factor from 1514 to 1521, João Brandão, a 'small woodcarving of the Christ Child' alongside a prestigious set of prints including 'Adam and Eve, Saint Jerome in his Study, Hercules, Saint Eustace, Melencolia and Nemesis'.[60] Dürer added that he 'gave exactly the same to Signor Rodrigo, the other Portuguese, who has given my wife a little green parakeet'.[61] Rodrigo Fernandez d'Almada (active in Antwerp 1514–40) became a close friend to Dürer, who recorded receiving many objects from him over the course of the year, including 'six Indian nuts'[62] and 'two Calicut cloths, one of silk, and also an embroidered cap, a green jug with myrobalan plums, and a branch from a cedar tree'.[63] Like a Calicut cloth or an embroidered cap, Dürer's *Nemesis* and the objects within it were there to be treasured and to be individually pondered. But they were also there to be understood as dynamic and in motion, and to be, alongside other objects, cumulatively part of the 'material Renaissance' that Dürer helped to craft.

Notes

1 Only Dürer's *Saint Eustace* (cat. 104) engraving is larger; see Koerner, 'Fortune', 259. For an overview of scholarship on *Nemesis,* see especially Schoch, Mende and Scherbaum, *Albrecht Dürer*, I, 95–9, no. 33. I am grateful to Edward H. Wouk, Charles Zika, Matthew Champion and audiences of online papers given in Australia and the UK for suggestions, and to Stefan Hanß for help with microscopic analysis of the print.

2 In addition to his engraving *Little Fortune*, the artist also treated the subject in a drawing, *Fortune in a Niche*, 1498, pen and ink on paper, New York, The Metropolitan Museum of Art, 1975.1.861; Strauss, *Complete Drawings* 1495/7. *Nemesis* has often been referred to as the *Great Fortune*, but the title *Nemesis* dates to Dürer's own reference to the print as 'Nemesin' in his Netherlandish diary of 1521. See the final section of the chapter for these references.

3 Dürer, sketch of the winged figure of Fortune [ie. Nemesis], London, The British Museum, SL,5218.114; Strauss, *Complete Drawings* 1502/25. For further discussions of the body of Nemesis, and Vitruvian proportion, see Kauffman, 'Dürers "Nemesis"', 135 and passim; Koerner, 'Fortune', 263–8, and Panofsky *Life and Art of Albrecht Dürer*, 82–3, which offers a critical commentary on the engraving.

4 Koerner, 'Fortune', 261.

5 Dürer elsewhere expressed frustration with spending time on details in altar paintings that would not easily be seen. In a letter to Jakob Heller on 4 November 1508 he wrote: 'With great care I can scarcely paint one face in half a year. Now the panel has roughly 100 faces, not counting drapery and landscapes and the other things on it. It would be quite unheard of to paint things on an altar so painstakingly. Who would even see them?' Ashcroft, *Albrecht Dürer*, I, 217. Dürer was angling here for a higher payment for the altarpiece commissioned by Heller, but the point remains that printmaking offered a different, up-close experience for the viewer.

6 Kauffmann, 'Dürers "Nemesis"', 142.

7 Damm, Doosry and Scheld, *Der Venedig-Plan von 1500.*

8 'Manto', Poliziano, *Silvæ*, 7.

9 *Ibid.*, 23.

10 Kauffmann, 'Dürer's "Nemesis"', 136–7.

11 See Koerner, 'Fortune', 260, and Panofsky '"Virgo & Victrix"', 23–4. On the humanist literary and iconographical context of Nemesis, see also Kauffman, 'Dürers "Nemesis"' and specifically on medieval connections, see Appuhn-Radtke, 'Fortuna Bifrons'.

12 O'Malley and Welch, eds, *The Material Renaissance*; Rublack, 'Matter in the Material Renaissance'.

13 On feathers, see Hanß, 'Making Featherwork in Early Modern Europe'.

14 For example, the extraordinary roller bird wings (see Stefan Hanß's essay 'The nature of lines' in this catalogue).

15 The headpiece is likely intended to recall Fortune's topknot, which in some traditions could supposedly be seized by those bold enough to confront their own fortunes directly.

16 On the lack of guild systems in Nuremberg, see Kahsnitz and Wixom, eds, *Gothic and Renaissance Art*, 17; on the relative prestige of the two professions, see Smith, *Dürer*, 27.

17 The conceptual, aesthetic and technical links between engraved decorations on metal and the rise of printmaking have been widely explored. See recently Stielau, 'Intent and Independence'; Feulner, 'Tradition and Innovation'.

18 Kahsnitz and Wixom, eds, *Gothic and Renaissance Art*, especially 20–2; Maué, Eser, Hauschke and Stolzenberger, *Quasi Centrum Europæ*; Strieder, 50–6. On armour, see Larry Silver's essay 'Albrecht Dürer's Armour' in this catalogue.

19 See, for example, Spinks, 'The Southern Indian "Devil in Calicut"'; Downes, Holloway and Randles, eds, *Feeling Things*.

20 For a related thematic discussion focused on Dürer's own movement, see Koerner, 'Dürer in motion'.

21 On vegetal forms in northern Renaissance printmaking, see Brisman, 'A Matter of Choice', and on cups see especially 122–4, 146–50.

22 The German term is from the Italian *boccale*, or mug, jug or jar.

23 Kohlhaussen, *Nürnberger Goldschmiedekunst*, 296–350. See also Tebbe, 'Nürnberger Goldschmiedekunst'.

24 *Ibid.*, 164–79 and 296–350.

25 See, for example, in addition to the *Design for a Gothic Cup* noted above, Dürer's drawing of six *Pokale*, in the sketchbook in the Sächsische Staats- und Universitätsbibliothek, Dresden, Mscr. Dresd.R.147.f, fol 193r; Strauss, *Complete Drawings* 1499/6. On Dürer's related table decorations, see Kohlhaussen, *Nürnberger Goldschmiedekunst*, 255–65.

26 Ashcroft, *Albrecht Dürer*, I, 39; see also Feulner, 'Tradition and Innovation', and the following catalogue entries, 26–34.

27 Ashcroft, *Albrecht Dürer*, I, 53.

28 Kohlhaussen, *Nürnberger Goldschmiedekunst*, 261.

29 Revelation 17 and 18.

30 Trexler, *Journey of the Magi*, 76–123.

31 Schoch, Mende and Scherbaum, *Albrecht Dürer*, I, 348–51, no. 225; H. 208.

32 Hahn, *The Reliquary Effect*, 90–151.

33 On liturgical objects in Nuremberg, see Charles Zika's essay 'Objects of devotion' in this catalogue.

34 On drinking rituals and cultures in early modern Germany, see Tlusty, *Bacchus and Civic Order*.

35 See Dürer's letter of 8 September 1506 in Ashcroft, *Albrecht Dürer*, I, 159–62.

36 Bate, 'Portrait and Pageantry', 129–30. Bate writes of Friedrich III: 'The city's official welcome continued on the following day when five councillors presented him with "two gilt cups on top of one another," i.e., a double goblet, containing one thousand gulden' (130).

37 *Ibid.*, 123.

38 *Ibid.*, 132–3.

39 *Ibid.*, 133.

40 Thausing attempted to connect this directly to the *Nemesis* engraving, Thausing, *Albrecht Dürer*, I, 230–9. Schoch observes that attempts to directly link this print to individuals (notably Caritas Pirckheimer) have not been successful. Schoch, Mende and Scherbaum, *Albrecht Dürer*, I, 97.

41 Thausing, *Albrecht Dürer*, 231–2.

42 Giehlow, 'Poliziano and Dürer', 293.

43 On the imagery of women soaring in the sky inspired by the print, which he suggests develops misogynistic iconography not detectable in Dürer's orginal print, see Koerner, 'Fortune', 269–72 and 275–84.

44 On this image, see *ibid.*, 281–4.

45 The vaguely phallic shape of the bridle possibly also lends a masculine air to Nemesis' pose. I leave aside the unconvincing proposal that the bridle hangs in the shape of the cross (Lanckorańska, 'Dürers Kupferstich "Nemesis"', 293).

46 See, for example, the excellent displays in the Germanisches Nationalmuseum, Nuremberg.

47 On this print, see Lange-Krach, *Stiften gehen!*, 230–1.

48 McColl, 'Agony in the Garden', 176.

49 Cuneo, 'The Artist, His Horse, a Print and its Audience'.

50 Schoch, Mende and Scherbaum, *Albrecht Dürer*, II, 49–52, no. 106; H.265.

51 The Auriga constellation today, also known as the Charioteer.

52 Schoch, Mende and Scherbaum, *Albrecht Dürer*, II, 430–5, nos 243 and 244; H.260 and H.259.

53 Gaab, *Die Sterne über Nürnberg*.

54 Bott, *Focus Behaim-Globus*.

55 For a discussion of this, see Koerner, 'Fortune', 273. On Dürer's fascination with objects, see Smith, 'Albrecht Dürer as Collector'.

56 Griggs, 'Dürer's Diary of His Journey'.

57 Ashcroft, *Albrecht Dürer*, I, 566.

58 *Ibid.*, 575.

59 *Ibid.*, 559. Master Gilles was Petrus Aegidius, city clerk of Antwerp, a humanist and close friend of Erasmus. *Ibid.*, 597.

60 *Ibid.*, 559.

61 *Ibid.* Rodrigo Fernandez d'Almada was first secretary to João Brandão and would himself become factor in 1521. *Ibid.*, 597.

62 *Ibid.*, 567.

63 *Ibid.*, 573. Dürer made an ink drawing of Rodrigo and gave him an oil painting of Saint Jerome. *Ibid.*, 576–7.

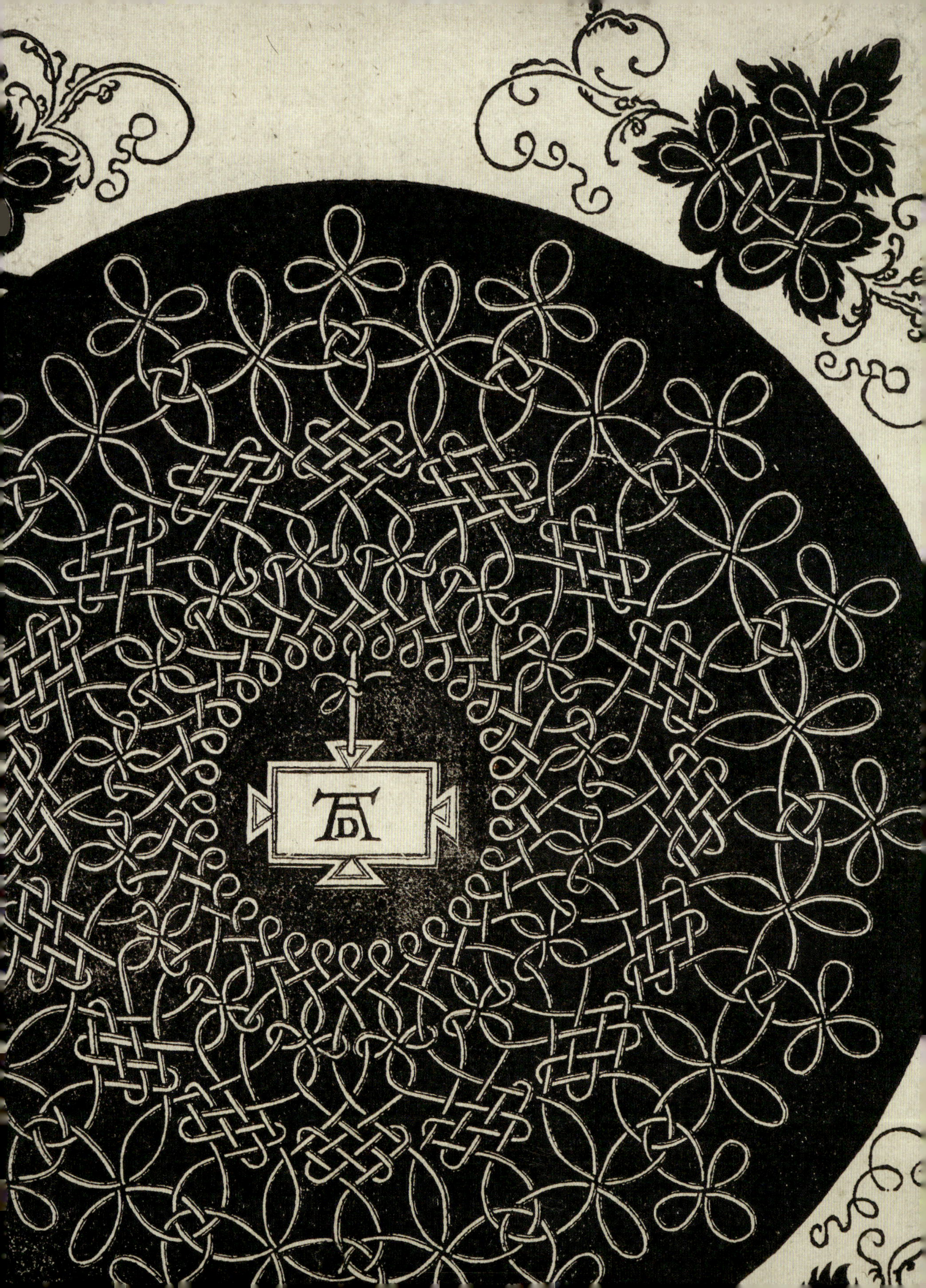

[5] The nature of lines: enviromateriality and ingenuity in Albrecht Dürer's material world

Stefan Hanß

nulla dies sine linea

no day without a line

Pliny the Elder, *Natural History*,
as quoted in the Nuremberg edition of Cardano,
De Sapientia, 45.

Albrecht Dürer's series of six intricately interlaced, symmetrical designs of knots is a visual and intellectual feat (Figure 5.1; cat. 68–70). Art historians have interpreted the woodcuts in reference to earlier engravings by Leonardo da Vinci (1452–1519), which contain a similar motif (Figure 5.2). During his sojourn in Venice (1505–7), Dürer might well have purchased Leonardo's works and copied them upon his return to Nuremberg to feed a growing North Alpine market for rare Italian arts. Indeed, the earliest copies of the *Knots* are printed on 'Venetian paper', which was considered particularly 'subtle' and which Dürer tried to source for his close friend the Nuremberg humanist Willibald Pirckheimer (1470–1530) while in Venice. Dürer's *Knots* thus materialise the artist's interest in the decorative arts, as well as the close artistic and consumerist exchanges between Nuremberg and Venice in the age of the 'material Renaissance'.[1]

However, the comparison with Leonardo often presents Dürer's *Knots* as a product of secondary quality – that is, as a Nuremberg copy *after* the Italian Renaissance polymath. In contrast to such interpretations, this essay outlines the extent to which Dürer's *Knots* reflect his broader conceptual artistic understanding, especially of lines, and how this artistic thinking was anchored in the artist's engagement with nature. Dürer's *Knots*, I argue, take an experimental approach to the links between nature and art, matter and crafts, as well as making and the mind. The *Knots* establish a conversation between 'enviromateriality',

making and ingenuity. 'Enviromateriality' is a recently coined word that evokes the material qualities of natural matter. Understood together, these terms invited the artist's reflections on the essence of life: growth, motion and becoming. Like Dürer's more celebrated prints, the *Knots* positioned the artist as a visual entrepreneur in the new medium, for which Nuremberg was a pioneering hub.[2] By 'knotting' the hands of the artist and the eyes of the beholder, the lines of the *Knots* provide a critical interface of mediation between the workings of natural materials and the artist's working on matter – a point of contact that was used by Dürer to problematise the workings of the image in the Northern Renaissance.[3]

Marketing *The Knots*

In January 1521, Dürer presented 'the six knots (*knodn*)', together with the *Apocalypse*, to the famed Antwerp glass painter and printmaker Dirck Vellert (1480–1547), thus affirming the *Knots*' embeddedness in a wider commercial world of artisanal designs.[4] Across the continent, Nuremberg metal cups had gained fame for intricate designs that pushed the boundaries of established ornamental practices.[5] Such artefacts were familiar to Dürer, himself a trained goldsmith, and they feature in his art, perhaps most prominently in *Nemesis* (cat. 34) and *The Babylonian Whore* from the *Apocalypse* (cat. 42).[6] Glass makers and painters from across Europe, in Venice for instance, copied Nuremberg cup designs to speak to an expanding European market and cater to north alpine tastes.[7] Similarly, contemporary Nuremberg artists contributed to the febrile atmosphere of artisanal change and innovation: Sebald Beham (1500–50), for instance, designed elaborated goblets, and Peter Flötner (1490–1546) held ornamental woodcuts in his possession which, after their posthumous publication, came to shape 'the ornamental grotesque' of Renaissance Germany.[8]

Dürer's *Knots* contributed to the expansion of metalworkers' iconographic repertoire of vegetal decorations. As a goldsmith apprentice, Dürer had trained his hand in the elaborate, symmetrical floral designs of metalwork which he also applied to the *Knots*.[9] By introducing vegetal elements to the arrangement, Dürer made Leonardo's knots accessible to the vibrant craft cultures of entrepreneurial Nuremberg artisans. Goldsmiths like Wenzel Jamnitzer (1508–85), would go on to turn sixteenth-century Nuremberg into a hub of experimental approaches to lifelike goldsmithery, pioneering life-casting techniques of actual plants and animals, for instance, to translate life into making and to allow living matter to represent the matter of life.[10] Dürer's *Knots* hint at the innovative role played by goldsmiths in shaping Renaissance visual tastes, echoing the interlaced elements of gold chains and the symmetrical floral designs of fine goldsmithery as captured by Martin Schongauer (1440/53–91) who was a perennial source of inspiration for Dürer (see Introduction, Figure 1.2). Dürer's skills and training in goldsmithery and drawing were useful when adapting Leonardo da Vinci's work for a transalpine audience, and his *Knots*, therefore, are an example of artisanal intersections across Renaissance craft cultures.

Though he did not use his monogram on the earliest impressions, Dürer must have taken personal pride in the *Knots*. In choosing them as a gift for Vellert – by then deacon of Antwerp's famous Guild of St Luke, the patron saint of artists – he might even have considered them somehow representative of his overall artistic skills. Dürer's investment in the marketisation of his art and his self-fashioning as a leading, innovative artist, especially when travelling in the Low Countries, suggests that it is likely that the gift of the *Knots* was intended to document and advertise his cutting-edge ingenuity – a key yardstick for the contemporary appreciation of material culture.[11] We should therefore consider the *Knots* in light of Dürer's broader artistic thinking and practice, especially regarding lines.

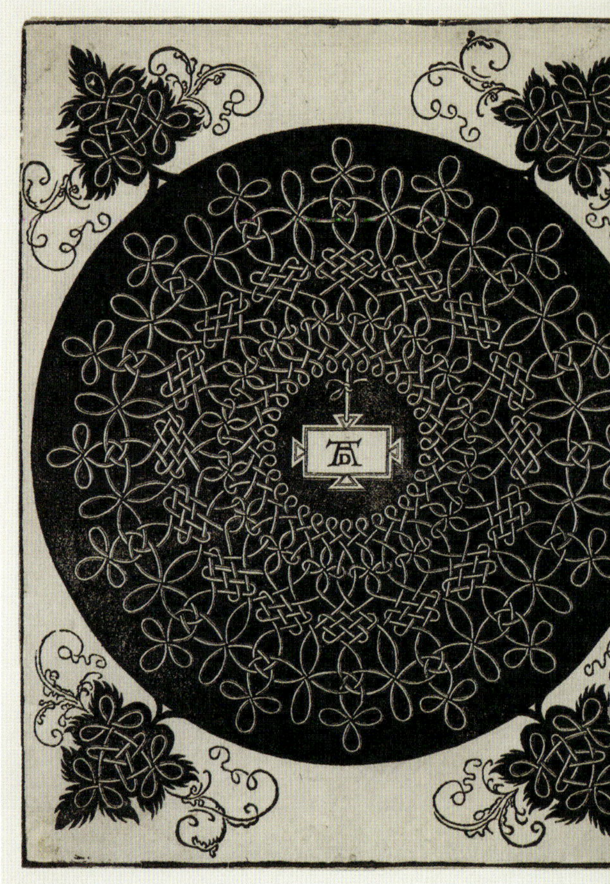

5.1 (cat. 68) Albrecht Dürer, *The Second Knot*, undated, woodcut, 273 x 213 mm.

The Whitworth, The University of Manchester, P.3055.
Gift by George Thomas Clough in 1921 © The Whitworth,
The University of Manchester.

Thinking through lines

Lines are at the centre of Dürer's grammar of visual expression and artistic ingenuity, the treatise *Underweysung der messung* (1525) (cat. 57). According to Dürer, the theory of proportions encapsulates nothing less than 'the truth and benefit of nature or art and beauty'.[12] Translating the proportions of nature into the medium of art, he writes, is key to any artist,

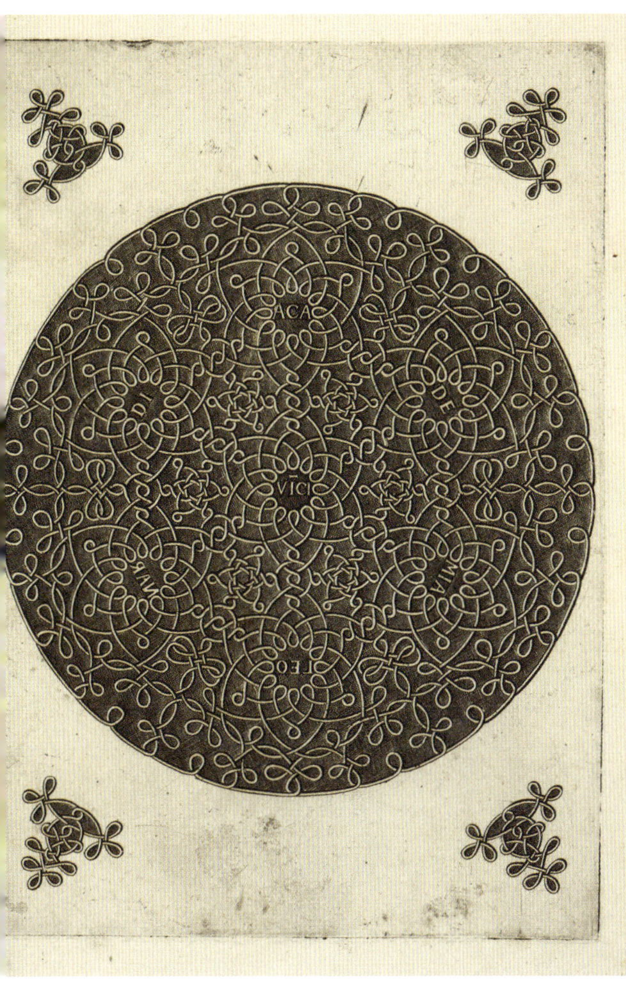

5.2 Leonardo da Vinci, *Knot Design*, c. 1490–1500, engraving, 293 x 207 mm.

'since truthful measuring is what makes the art'.[13] Dürer thus instructs painters using lines to think about the practising of art itself. Grids, for instance, facilitate the translation of life into lifelike visual representation.[14]

When writing about lines, Dürer self-fashions as an author-practitioner spearheading the Renaissance interest in the written codification of knowledge of making.[15] Nuremberg humanists considered

Dürer's treatise a means to help understand, reveal and preserve 'all art and secrecy of nature'.[16] Dürer himself claims to codify knowledge about ingenuity (*schickligkhait*) that had been forgotten since the loss of the art theoretical writings of the fourth-century Greek artist Apelles. Yet Dürer also stresses that ingenuity is most powerfully performed by nature itself, which 'brings to light more sublime and ingenious art' than any artist possibly could.[17] Celebrated by contemporaries as 'the new Apelles', writing about lines put Dürer at the vanguard of Renaissance artistic thinking.[18] In 1528, Erasmus of Rotterdam (c. 1466–1536) praised Dürer for surpassing the works of ancient painters and achieving by the mere use of lines what Apelles was only capable of achieving with 'the blandishment of colours'.[19] After reading the treatise on proportions, Renaissance humanists also equated Dürer with the medieval natural philosopher Albertus Magnus (c. 1200–80).[20] As we shall see, Dürer aligned the theory of lines and ingenuity with the material world of nature.

Since nature itself embodies ingenuity, capturing life was key to Dürer's understanding of artistic practice. He instructed readers to draw 'according to nature' and to portray 'each thing in its natural essence', 'as it is given by nature'.[21] Thus, the artist should not alter appearances by adding to or reducing from them. Dürer states, 'Too much is not worth it', and echoes the Aristotelian golden mean in concluding that 'a true mean is the best'.[22]

He suggests that the artist's own ingenuity can, in fact, be measured by the extent to which he captures the ingenuity of nature. To 'draw naturally', in Dürer's understanding, thus defined the artist's capacity to 'draw (...) things in a skilled manner'. Techne shapes the artist's capacity 'to bring ingenuity (*geschicklikeit*) into each thing'.[23] For the product to be considered art, Dürer advised artists to draw 'according to nature',[24] and suggests that with diligence, they shall capture appearances 'with natural lines' considering 'how nature masterly has made the man'.[25] Since God's making comes to the fore in nature, Dürer advises artists to 'never think of yourself as being capable of making a better similitude of a thing'.[26]

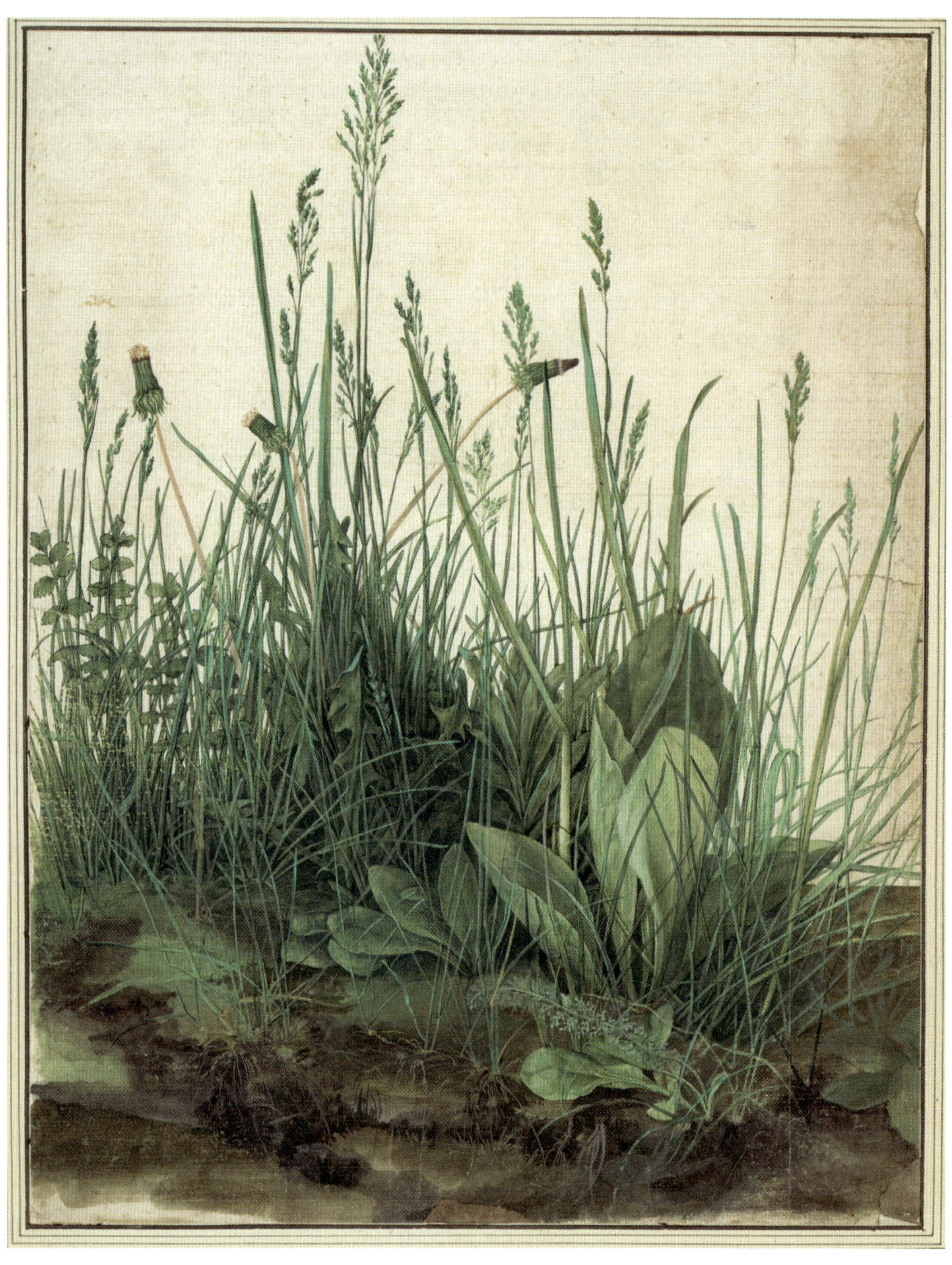

5.3 Albrecht Dürer, *The Great Piece of Turf*, 1503, watercolour, 408 x 315 mm.

Vienna, The Albertina Museum, 3075.
© The Albertina Museum, Vienna.

> 5.4 Albrecht Dürer, *Dead Blue Roller*, c. 1500, watercolour, 274 x 198 mm.

Vienna, The Albertina Museum, 3133.
© The Albertina Museum, Vienna.

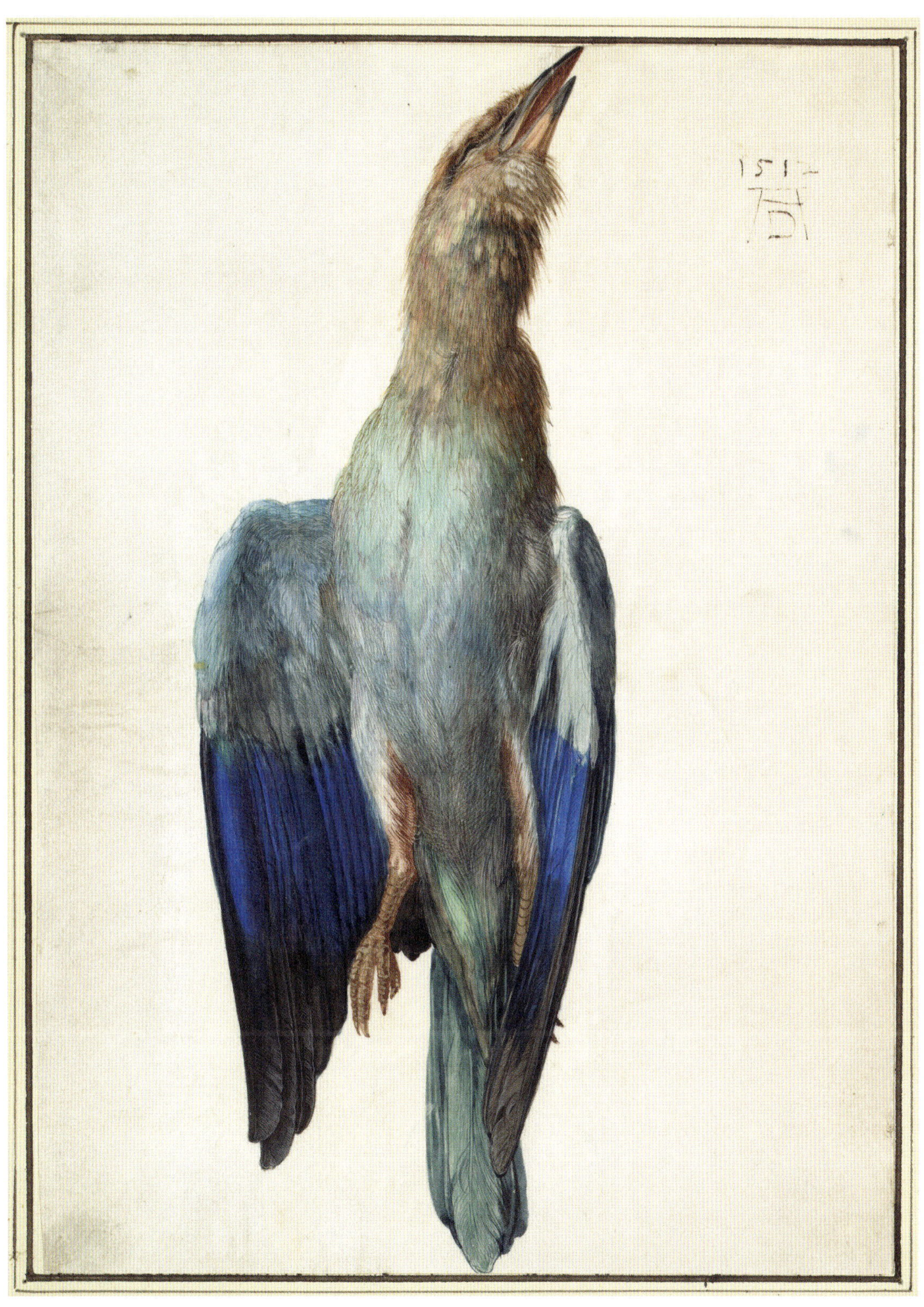

'Natural lines': the matter of lines

The artist's thinking about lines was thus anchored in the natural world. Indeed, natural matter was a source of constant inspiration for Dürer, who was an assiduous observer and collector of naturalia.[27] He collected corals, feathers, coconuts and stones, but also tortoise and snail shells, fish scales and horns – materials that inspired the artist's imagination in translating surfaces into lines, for instance, in *The Sea Monster* (cat. 96).[28] Engagement with enviromateriality trained the mind, eye and hand, by extension shaping the artist's material thinking and doing.

Already as a young goldsmith apprentice, Dürer came to realise that nature was full of lines. When touched with the maker's 'mindful hand' and viewed with magnifying lenses, even the smooth surfaces of metals were characterised by a mesh of lines.[29] *The Great Piece of Turf* (Figure 5.3) exemplifies Dürer's interest.[30] The lifelike rendering of plants, resulting from the perfection with which Dürer captures the proportions of measures, colours and shapes, serves the depiction of growth and motion – key characteristics that define enviromateriality as living matter.

Dürer was also an avid collector of feathers. In Venice, he sifted through the shops of featherworkers to find rare crane feathers for his friend Pirckheimer.[31] When holding a rare roller in his hands, Dürer worked with natural matter to capture the liveliness of enviromateriality (Figure 5.4; cat. 101–2).[32] Using a personal recipe, Dürer would typically saturate existing ultramarine pigments with nut oil to animate the vibrancy of this colour.[33] To achieve lifelikeness meant consciously working with living materials. The artist's minute observation did not miss that it was the lines of the barbs that gave motility and liveliness to the feathers (Figure 5.5). In his drawing, Dürer uses lines to enliven the haptic depth and sensuality of feathers. Similarly, the artist's subtle manual movements translated the materiality of fur, hair and textiles into lines (see Introduction, cat. 2–4). Since they captured the life of natural matter, Dürer considered lines key to communicating lifelikeness.

The artist's ingenuity was manifested in the degree to which artisanal skills aligned observation and making

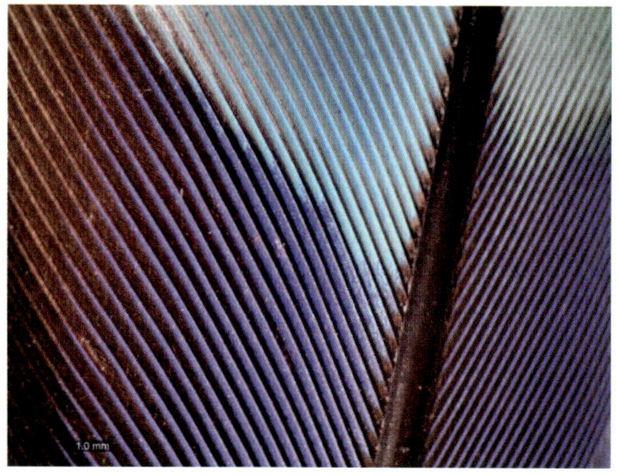

5.5 Feather of an Indian Roller (*Coracias benghalensis*) seen under a Dino-Lite USB Digital Microscope, 35.8 magnification scale.
© Stefan Hanß.

when translating nature into what Dürer calls 'natural lines'.[34] In 1522, Dürer collaborated with the sculptor Veit Stoß (1447–1533) to turn rare reindeer antlers into a striking chandelier for the Nuremberg council. Dürer elongated the antlers' organic, wavy lines and turned them into the central artistic principle of the overall piece. The wooden dragon seems to naturally merge with and organically grow from the antlers to form an artist's comment on the beauty that may emerge when nature and craft are aligned.[35] In *Saint Eustace* (cat. 104), too, Dürer aligned the natural appearance of the stag's antlers with the wavy branchwork of the trees, and the lines of nature more generally.

Since Dürer considered nature a source of perfection, his study of lines and proportions was a way to come to terms with the secrets of natural perfection itself.[36] It is 'the life of nature that reveals the truth of things', Dürer claimed, and 'art is embedded in nature. He who can extract it, has it'.[37] The *Knots* provide a witty commentary on the nature of this extraction and thus on the ingenuity of the artist in light of nature's ingenuity. Since Dürer approached artistic practice to a large extent through lines, the *Knots* can be considered a pun on the artist's engagement with the nature of lines.[38]

Knotting artist and audience: cognition and contemplation

In fact, the *Knots* make prominent reference to nature. In contrast to Leonardo da Vinci, Dürer's work foregrounds vine leaves and perennials to build on a range of visual and material associations. Wine, for instance, necessarily evoked religious motifs. In *The Mass of Saint Gregory* from 1511 (cat. 8), Dürer addressed the miraculous transubstantiation of wine into the blood of Jesus Christ – the Christian *Urmotiv* of material transformation.[39] Tendrils of vines feature prominently in contemporary religious material culture, including on the embroidery of clerical vestments or altar frontals such as the Whitworth's German *Altar frontal with the Tree of Jesse* (cat. 9). There can be no doubt that the glass painter Dirck Vellert, himself a specialist in devotional motifs, was familiar with the woodcut's religious iconographic references.[40]

Dürer associated wine with the mocking of Christ when he represented the subject in one of the woodcuts of his *Small Passion* of c. 1508.[41] In a devotional poem from 1510, Dürer laments that Christ was given vinegar instead of wine when suffering agony at the cross.[42] Years later, when drawing *Christ Carrying the Cross*, Dürer framed the figure with clouds that merge into grapevine-like lines. He elaborates on the tendril motif more explicitly in the corresponding image of Nuremberg city council secretary Lazarus Spengler (1479–1534) with whom the artist shared a close friendship and a common enthusiasm for Reformation ideas (Figure 5.6). The biblical references portray Spengler as a true follower of Christ, willing to carry his cross when defending Christian principles. Evoking the path ahead, the vine tendrils serve as an allegory of the fruits that true faith will bear. The tendrils frame an image of consolation (*Trostbild*), a private devotional artefact that invited the beholder to pause in contemplation.[43]

By associating the *Knots* iconographically with wine, the religious connotations of this motif strongly resonated with specific viewing practices – contemplative forms of engagement commonly associated with devotional art – that Dürer sought to establish for the *Knots*. At a time when 'transcendental

contemplation was initiated by abstract means', these woodcuts were provocative artefacts.[44] Their lines, which guide (or mislead) the eye, stir curiosity and provoke the mind, call for visual engagement and interpretation.[45] To borrow from the artist Paul Klee who once said that 'a line is a dot that went for a walk', the lines in the *Knots* are dots that set the eye in motion and demand the beholder's engagement with the print.[46] The artist's lines also halt the motion of time by asking for a break; they capture a moment in the passing of time, seen for instance in the growth of plants. Dürer's *Knots* both depict and pause the principle of life, growth and becoming, that defines the natural world to which the woodcuts' iconography allude.[47] By highlighting the association between lines and plant matter, Dürer elaborates on the visual and temporal practices associated with the *Knots*. Building on the established religious grammar of the materiality of wine, he calls for a specific mode of visual engagement, encouraging the beholder to view and engage with the *Knots* as a quasi-devotional contemplative exercise.[48]

This interpretation resonates with other works in which the curly lines of grapevines allow Dürer to call for a contemplative visual engagement with art. In *Virgin and Child on a Grassy Bank* (cat. 20), the tendril's meandering lines draw the viewer's eye, calling for a more detailed engagement with the print. In *Saint Jerome in His Study*, the flourishes of the chandelier echo the lines of the antlers, gourd and wine leaves, as much as the saint's immersion in studious contemplation (cat. 73; see also Dagmar Eichberger's 'The material and the immaterial' in this volume). The flourishes of the *Knots* likewise call the observer to engage with the puzzle of the line's origins, and by extension provoke reflections on the originality of art.

Lines of thought: moral philosophy, vision and the nature of art

Connecting the artist's hand with the beholder's eye by calling for contemplative engagement, the *Knots* touch upon the very nature of knowledge. As the further life of the motif demonstrates, Dürer understood the *Knots* as a means of reflective

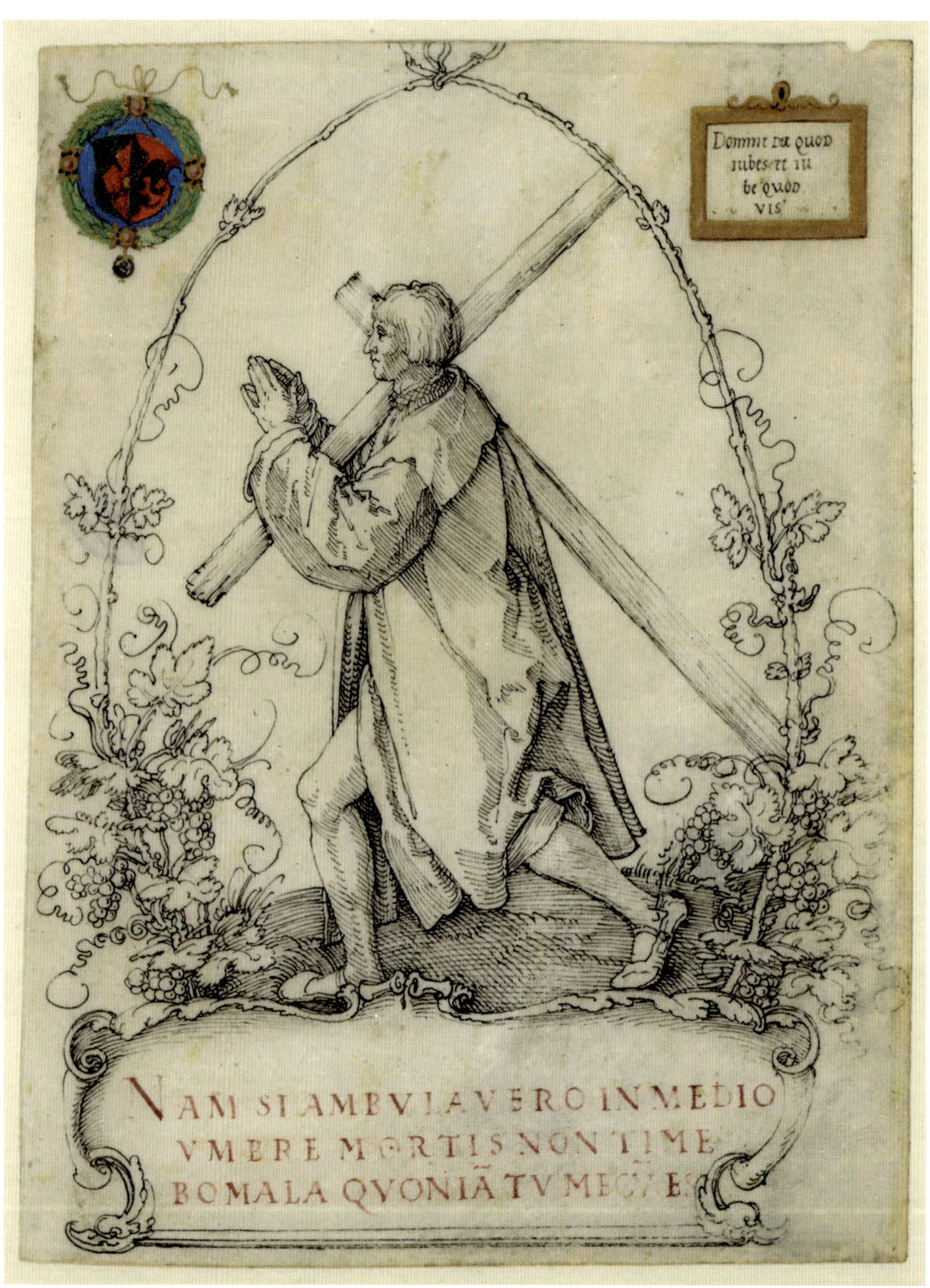

Domine da quod
iubes et iube
quod
vis
NAM SI AMBVLAVERO IN MEDIO
VMBRE MORTIS NON TIME
BO MALA QVONIĀ TV MECV ES

contemplation and epistemic enquiry – a play with the general curiosity of the human mind. 'It is ingrained in us by nature', Dürer writes, 'that we would like to know much.' This urge for knowledge reveals 'the right truth of each thing'.[49] Here, Dürer references the first sentence of Aristotle's *Metaphysics* – 'all men naturally desire knowledge' – and a similar quote in *De imitatione Christi* (Nuremberg, 1492) by Thomas à Kempis (1380–1471).[50] Dürer's intricately knotted lines were intended to spark curiosity for the mind and the eye, perhaps the reason he chose curly perennial lines to accompany his illustrations on the margins of the prayerbook of Emperor Maximilian I (1459–1519).[51]

Much of Dürer's understanding of lines was, in fact, driven by theoretical reflections on the nature of knowledge and shaped by the Renaissance rediscovery of works of ancient authorities like Euclid, in particular his theory of optics and proportions. Dürer collaborated with Pirckheimer in the study of Euclid as early as in 1507, and he singled out Euclid, 'the prince of geometry', as the most prominent reference for his *Perspectiva naturalis*.[52] When editing Plutarch's writings on moral philosophy in 1522–23, the same year that Dürer celebrated the lines of nature in the Nuremberg council's impressive antler chandelier, it was perfectly obvious that Pirckheimer had asked his artist friend Dürer, the celebrated 'new Apelles', to illustrate the title page. Dürer chose a knot design to comment on what would be the reader's very first impression of Plutarch's texts: a parable on the value of the artist's judgement (Figure 5.7). At the very beginning of Pirckheimer's edition, in Plutarch's *On the Control of Anger*, the character Sulla says:

> A good plan, as it seems to me, Fundanus, is that which painters follow: they scrutinise their productions from time to time before they finish them. They do this because, by withdrawing their gaze and by inspecting their work often, they are able to form a fresh judgement, and one which is more likely to seize

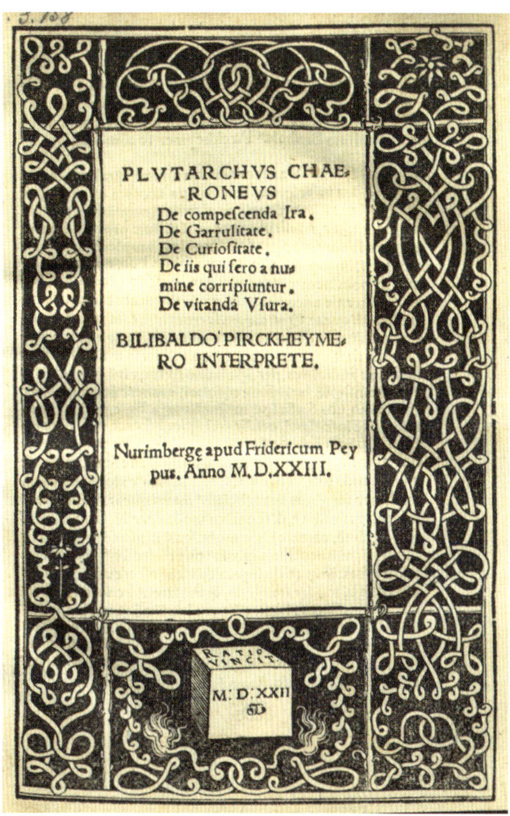

5.7 Albrecht Dürer, *Knot Design*, 1522, title page for Plutarch, *De compescenda Ira*, trans. Willibald Pirckheimer (Nuremberg: Friedrich Peypus, 1523).

upon any slight discrepancy, such as the familiarity of uninterrupted contemplation will conceal.[53]

Dürer's knot design is a spirited comment on this statement. The lines call for exactly this kind of intellectual engagement: a mode of ever-renewed contemplation, tied together by knots whose mêlée of lines guide and confuse the eye, urging viewers to take a step back, to reflect, to discard any sense of self-certainty and to engage over and over again – encouraged by Dürer's provocative statement that 'ratio wins'. By demanding a certain mode of visual thinking, Dürer's knots allegorise the artist's own judgement. The *Knots* thus materialise humanist

5.6 Albrecht Dürer, *Lazarus Spengler Carrying the Cross*, c. 1520–25, pen and black ink on vellum, 137 x 104 mm.

debates on moral philosophy, the status of vision and the nature of art in Renaissance Germany.

However, the vegetal connotations of the *Knots* reach beyond visual associations to touch upon the nature of matter and the matter of art. Since the grapevine was considered animated matter, Dürer's alignment of the *Knots* with viticulture broadened the woodcut's material grammar of motion. The organic form of the knots, especially their vegetable and growing dimension, resonate with Renaissance ideas about how enviromateriality itself engenders motion. German medical and botanical manuals associated grapevine with the cold humoral qualities that had a profound impact on the fluxes of the body. Vine was thus one of the most common ingredients of medical recipes. Pulverised vine bark was thought to have anti-haemorrhagic properties. Referencing ancient authorities like Pliny, Dürer's contemporaries praised vine leaves' power to cure wounds and 'to extinguish (...) all heat of the fever'. The cooling properties of wine brought relief to what Galenic theory considered the body's hottest parts, the eyes and brain in particular, and cured 'ulcers, heat or inflammations' that derived from bodily processes of overheating. Vine leaves were also a remedy against 'strong headaches' and vine resin 'soothens hotly afflictions of the eye'.[54] According to medical understanding, vine leaves also lowered the temperature of the head – a body part considered particularly hot in Renaissance medicine. Further, German authors praised their power to 'strengthen and reinvigorate the brain'.[55] The grapevine, thus, facilitated the kind of contemplative engagement called for in the *Knots*. Referencing established contemporary medical and botanical knowledge about natural materials, Dürer's *Knots* materialise vision, calling for a reconsideration of the very nature of lines and the matter of art.

Dürer was himself highly versatile in reading the humoral qualities of the material world. In his art, he established a powerful conversation between materials and humours as most lucidly evidenced in his iconic *Melencolia I* (cat. 79).[56] Already in *Little Fortune* (cat. 36), Dürer addresses the effects of botanical matter on the human body, namely the use of eryngium (*Mannstreu*) as an aphrodisiac.[57] Dürer

ate quinces to decrease his bodily temperature and to strengthen the mind; he worked mint geranium and fleaworts, depicted in *The Great Piece of Turf* (Figure 5.3), into wound healing ointments; and he also praised the cooling properties of 'good chilly wine'.[58] Dürer would have been familiar with the medical impact of enviromateriality in general and the grapevine in particular. His collaboration with Konrad Celtis (1459–1508) and his own studies of the writings of ancient 'physicians' had heightened his sensitivity for the correlation between the humoral constitution of materials and their physical proportions. The observation of proportions and natural lines, Dürer believed, allowed for inferences to be drawn on the 'nature', and thus the inner humoral complexion of matter.[59] The artist's role was to capture the 'truth' that nature has given to all things, and to make the complexions of enviromateriality visible in art.[60]

Thus, according to Dürer and contemporaries, nature could itself be 'natured' (*genaturt*) since materials were characterised by different forms, complexions and correlations.[61] The physician-philosopher Paracelsus (c. 1493–1541) also called for a materials-specific 'chiromancy' that draws specific attention to natural lines. Reading a material's arrangement of lines of disposition and experiences like wooden growth rings or the linear arrangement of fibres, vessels and cells (similar, for instance, to palm reading) allows, according to Paracelsus, a deeper understanding of the inner character of things.[62] Dürer believed that art could extract natural materials' complexions through lines, and this is an observation that is key to the broader understanding of how the *Knots* comment on the matter of art itself.

The ingenuity of the *Knots*

To produce the woodcut for the *Knots* required a masterfully trained hand and a profound engagement with the living materiality of wood as a grown substance to connect to the lines of nature that structured the surface and inner workings of the material. The linguistic resemblance of the German nouns 'grapevine' (*Weinstock*) and 'woodblock' (*Holzstock*) further strengthened the

Knots' association between matter and vision, nature and making. If the tendrils recalled the parable of the workers in the vineyard (Mathew 20:1–16), the *Knots* also invited beholders to reflect on the artist's effort and skill. Examining the surviving woodblock of *Saint Veronica between Saints Peter and Paul* from *The Small Passion* allows us to see how Dürer worked with the lines of nature to extract the nature of lines itself (cat. 45).[63] There could be hardly a more powerful pun on what Dürer considered the key to artisanship: 'art is embedded in nature. He who can extract it, has it.'[64]

Providing an ingenious comment on the nature of lines, the *Knots* portray the ingenuity of Dürer as the 'master of the line'.[65] Leonardo used engraving to design his knots, a technique which Dürer also mastered to a remarkable degree. Microscopic analysis conducted for this exhibition has shown that Dürer managed to engrave thirteen separate lines within a space covering 2 mm – a striking achievement that bears witness to 'Dürer's eye for detail' and his astounding manual dexterity (compare Figures 1.3, 1.4).[66] Among contemporaries trained in miniature art, such achievements instilled awe and admiration.[67] Giorgio Vasari (1511–74), for instance, praised Leonardo's 'most difficult and beautiful' knots as a testimony to the artist's unrivalled ingenuity. 'There was infused in that brain such grace from God, and a power of expression in such sublime accord with the intellect and memory', Vasari states, that Leonardo 'even went so far as to waste his time in drawing knots of cords, made according to an order, that from one end all the rest might follow till the other, so as to fill a round.'[68] In his artistic response, Dürer showed that he too was capable of similar achievements, and in 'the considerably more difficult woodcut technique'.[69] The much darker background and the vegetal elements of the print directed Renaissance observers to the Nuremberg artisan's departure in technology. Woodcutting required reverse thinking and a different demand of manual control when carving subtly bent lines. As the humanist Joachim Camerarius (1500–74) commented in his Latin translation of Dürer's treatise on proportions (1532):

What shall I say of the steadiness and exactitude of his hand? You might swear that rule, square, or compasses had been employed to draw lines, which he, in fact, drew with the brush, or very often with pencil or pen unaided by artificial means, to the great marvel of those who watched him.[70]

The *Knots* made concrete what contemporaries like Camerarius saw as Dürer's ingenuity, whose 'hand so closely followed the ideas of his mind'.[71] Building on a rich medieval discussion of the intellectual properties of knots uncovered in recent research by Anke Bernau, sixteenth-century humanists debated whether knots, as examples of subtlety and ingenuity, related to the properties of matter or the mind.[72] Dürer's *Knots* thus evoked a whole range of associations with the ingenuity of manual dexterity. Adam Riese (1492–1559), with his best-selling prints on 'calculations on lines' (Nuremberg, 1527), had turned lines into an epistemic tool of complex algebra. The Nuremberg edition of Riese's treatise was published by Friedrich Peypus (1485–1535), an active member of Dürer's humanist network. Peypus had printed the letters of Dürer's friend Christoph Scheurl (1481–1542) to Willibald Pirckheimer's sister, Caritas (1467–1532), the abbess of the Convent of Saint Clara. Peypus's father-in-law, Ulrich Pindar, published works illustrated by Dürer's apprentice Hans Baldung (1484/85–1545). Four years prior to Riese's treatise on the usefulness of lines to conduct advanced calculations, Peypus had published Pirckheimer's edition of Plutarch's writings on moral philosophy which included Dürer's title page of an intricate knot design.[73] Dürer was at the heart of a humanist community that connected the contemplation of lines to refined Renaissance minds and hands.

Dürer also contributed to the development of scientific images using lines for the calculation of time and cosmic constellations. Further, the *Knots* echoed calligraphic flourishes at a time when Nuremberg calligraphers considered the 'extraction' (*ziehen*) of lines an embodied skill.[74] The *Knots* resonated with the ingenious intricacy of lacework and gold embroidery too, both forms of manual cognition based on thinking through complex patterns of lines (cat.. 65).[75] Such associations across craft cultures mattered for Dürer, who understood his theory of lines and proportions to be of use for painters, wood sculptors, stonemasons, goldsmiths, metal casters, silk embroiderers and potters – craftspeople who mastered the complex cognitive-manual achievement of working with natural matter.[76] In nature, such materials were considered alive, yet it required the artist's ingenuity to turn the matter of life into craft. Such ingenuity could be brought to perfection through industry, which again was associated with lines, for instance, in the saying 'no day without a line', a quote by Pliny that the Nuremberg edition of *On Knowledge* by Italian polymath Girolamo Cardano (1501–76) attributes to Dürer's alter-ego Apelles.[77] Shared across the crafts, reflections on making were aligned with an interest in lines.

Recontextualising Dürer's *Knots* with artefacts like embroidery or lacework, natural materials like plants and metals, and contemporary prints like herbals or botanical manuals and philosophical treatises, this essay illustrates how Dürer's engagement with environmental matter impacted his artistic thinking and practice regarding lines. The *Knots* are a contribution to the Northern Renaissance theory of what art is and what art does. In it Dürer comments on humanist debates about whether ingenuity originates in nature or the mind, and he takes a stance on issues of vision and the matter of art itself. The *Knots* thus tie together Renaissance debates on ingenuity in making, and the lines materialise the artist's subtle alignment of hands, minds and materials.

* I owe special thanks to Jennifer Spinks and Edward Wouk for commenting on and improving this essay. I also thank Hannah Spracklan-Holl for providing cross references to English translations in Ashcroft, *Albrecht Dürer* where available. Translations are my own unless otherwise noted.

Notes

1   Rupprich, *Nachlass*, I, 53 (quote). For this text see also Ashcroft, *Albrecht Dürer*, I, 152; Schoch, Mende and Scherbaum, *Albrecht Dürer*, II, 145–57, nos 142–7; H. 274–9. Costello, 'Knot(s)'; Metzger, *Dürer*, 316; Gombrich, *Sense of Order*, 87.

2   Pettegree, *Book in the Renaissance*. Methodologically, I follow here Wouk's call for 'an anthropology of print'. See Wouk, 'Toward an Anthropology of Print'.

3   For this interpretation, Marr, 'Ingenuity'; Marr, *Logodaedalus*; Oosterhoff, *Ingenuity in the Making*; Smith, *Body of the Artisan* are a major source of inspiration.

4   Rupprich, *Nachlass*, I, 164; Ashcroft, *Albrecht Dürer*, I, 573.

5   Mattheus Epfenhauser, double cup, Nuremberg, 1574/75, silver gilt, 52.1 x 15 cm, New York, The Metropolitan Museum of Art, 17.190.607a, b.

6   On *Nemesis*, see Jennifer Spinks' essay 'Objects in motion' in this volume.

7   Standing cup, c. 1530, Venice (Murano), glass, enamelled and gilt, 29.5 cm, New York, The Metropolitan Museum of Art, 1982.60.130.

8   Sebald Beham, *Three Goblet Designs*, 1530, New York, The Metropolitan Museum of Art, 21.11.7; 23.70.12; 23.70.13; Flötner, *Das Kvnstbvch*; Warncke, *Die ornamentale Groteske*.

9   Pilz, 'Der Goldschmied Albrecht Dürer.'

10 Smith, 'Nature and art'; Smith, 'Sixteenth-Century Goldsmith's Workshop.'

11 Marr, *Logodaedalus*; Oosterhoff, *Ingenuity in the Making*.

12 Rupprich, Nachlass, III, 170.

13 *Ibid.*, II, 145–6.

14 See Kemp, *Science of Art*; Dupré, *Perspective as Practice*.

15 Smith, *Lived Experience*.

16 Rupprich, *Nachlass*, I, 99; Ashcroft, *Albrecht Dürer*, II, 706.

17 Rupprich, *Nachlass*, I, 97–8; Ashcroft, *Albrecht Dürer*, II, 704.

18 Sullivan, 'Alter Apelles'.

19 Koerner, *Moment of Self-Portraiture*, 168–9.

20 Rupprich, *Nachlass*, III, 460; Ashcroft, *Albrecht Dürer*, I, 77.

21 Rupprich, *Nachlass*, II, 404–6, 462; III, 216, 277; Ashcroft, *Albrecht Dürer*, I, 432.

22 Rupprich, *Nachlass*, III, 283; Ashcroft, *Albrecht Dürer*, I, 521.

23 Rupprich, *Nachlass*, II, 101, 329; Ashcroft, *Albrecht Dürer*, I, 253; Williams, *Theory and Culture*.

24 Rupprich, *Nachlass*, II, 464.

25 *Ibid.*, III, 174.

26 *Ibid.*, III, 287. For this text, see also Ashcroft, *Albrecht Dürer*, I, 525–6.

27 Koreny, *Tier- und Pflanzenstudien*; Eichberger, 'Naturalia and artefacta,' 18–9; Smith, 'Albrecht Dürer as collector.'

28 Eichberger, 'Naturalia and artefacta', 28.

29 Roberts, *The Mindful hand*; Zuidervaart, '"Most rare workmen"'.

30 Strauss, *Complete Drawings* 1503/29.

31 Rupprich, *Nachlass*, I, 53, 55; Hanß, 'Making Featherwork', See also Ashcroft, *Albrecht Dürer*, I, 152, 159.

32 See, for example, Strauss, *Complete Drawings* 1502/10 and 1502/11.

33 Rupprich, *Nachlass*, I, 216.

34 *Ibid.*, III, 174.

35 Heikamp, 'Dürers Entwürfe für Geweihleuchter'.

36 Rupprich, *Nachlass*, I, 325. For this text, see also Ashcroft, *Albrecht Dürer*, II, 1024.

37 Rupprich, *Nachlass*, III, 286–7, 295. See also Ashcroft, *Albrecht Dürer*, I, 526–7; II, 878.

38 Faietti, *Power of Line*; Ingold, *Life of Lines*.

39 See Charles Zika's essay 'Objects of devotion' in this volume.

40 See the glassworks and prints of Dirck Vellert in the Rijksmuseum, Amsterdam. Cf. Bynum, *Wonderful Blood*; Bynum, *Christian Materiality*.

41 Schoch, Mende and Scherbaum, *Albrecht Dürer*, II, 308–9, no. 200; H. 139.

42 Rupprich, *Nachlass*, I, 136. For this text, see also Ashcroft, *Albrecht Dürer*, I, 303. On Dürer's c. 1509 *The Flagellation* from the *Small Passion* series, see Schoch, Mende and Scherbaum, *Albrecht Dürer*, II, 313–14, no. 203; H. VII, 123.142.

43 Albrecht Dürer, *Christ Carrying the Cross*, c. 1520–25, pen and black ink on vellum, 138 x 104 mm, London, The British Museum, SL,5218.149, see Strauss, *Complete Drawings* 1525/7; Merback, 238–46.

44 Kessler, *Seeing Medieval Art*, the quote is from the back.

45 Not unusual for Dürer's art; see Brisman, 'Image that wants to be read'.

46 Klee, 'Schöpferische Konfession,' 60–6.

47 On Renaissance experimental and experiential approaches to time, see Nagel, *Anachronic Renaissance*; Champion, *Fullness of Time*.

48 Enenkel, *Meditatio*.

49 Rupprich, *Nachlass*, II, 106.

50 Aristotle. *Metaphysics*, I, 3; Kempis, *De imitatione Christi*, aij'.

51 Teja-Bach, *Struktur und Erscheinung*, 177.

52 Rupprich, *Nachlass*, II, 127 (quote), 372–8. For these texts, see also Ashcroft, *Albrecht Dürer*, I, 240–1, 381–2.

53 Plutarch, *De compescenda Ira*, aij'; Plutarch, *Moralia*, 93.

54 Rylff, *Lustgarten der Gesundheit*, 16ʸ. See the many references to the use of wine in Fuchs , *New Kreüterbu[o]ch*. Cf. Rublack, 'Fluxes'.

55 Rylff, *Lustgarten der Gesundheit* ,16ʸ.

56 Rupprich, *Nachlass*, I, 132. See also Ashcroft, *Albrecht Dürer*, I, 292–3; Panofsky, *Dürers Melencolia I*; Merback, *Perfection's therapy*. See also Matthew Champion's essay 'Measure and the material world' in this volume.

57 Schoch, Mende and Scherbaum, *Albrecht Dürer*, I, 36; Brisman, 'Sternkraut'.

58 Rupprich, *Nachlass*, I, 164, 192, 217–8. See also Ashcroft, *Albrecht Dürer*, I, 217–8, 466, 572.

59 Rupprich, *Nachlass*, II, 98, 127; III, 286. See also Ashcroft, *Albrecht Dürer*, I, 381–2, 526.

60 Rupprich, *Nachlass*, III, 286–7. For this text, see also Ashcroft, *Albrecht Dürer*, I, 526–7.

61 Rupprich, *Nachlass*, III, 291, 298; Ashcroft, *Albrecht Dürer*, II, 872–82.

62 Baxandall, *Limewood Sculptors*, 32–3; Meurer, 'Translating the Hand into Print'.

63 The Museum Bautzen holds the woodblock of Dürer's *Fifth Knot*.

64 Rupprich, *Nachlass*, III, 286–7. For this text, see also Ashcroft, *Albrecht Dürer*, I, 526–7.

65 Metzger, *Dürer*, 316.

66 Egmond, *Eye for Detail*, 198.

67 Scribner, 'Ways of Seeing'; Kessler, *Seeing Medieval Art*; Hanß, 'New World Feathers.'

68 Vasari, *Lives*, 230.

69 Metzger, *Dürer*, 316.

70 Koerner, *Moment of Self-Portraiture*, 145.

71 *Ibid.*

72 Bernau, 'Figuring with Knots'; Cardano, *De Svbtilitate*; Scaliger, *De Subtilitate*.

73 Keunecke, 'Friedrich Peypus'; Lassnig, 'Dürer's *Melencolia-I.*'

74 Riese, *Rechnung auff der Linien*; Marr, 'Ingenuity', 62; Murphy, 'Scribal marks'.

75 Wilckens, 'Ein Modelbuch'; Hanß, 'Digital Microscopy'.

76 Rupprich, *Nachlass*, I, 101, 115; II, 144, 150; *Albrecht Dürer*, I, 253; II, 777; II, 697–8; II, 868–9. Only a few decades later, in fact, the goldsmith Jamnitzer released his own study of the proportions and perspective of abstract figures based on Euclid's works, see Smith, 'Sixteenth-Century Goldsmith's Workshop'.

77 Cardano, *De Sapientia*, 45. On industry, see Marr, *Logodaedalus*, 1.

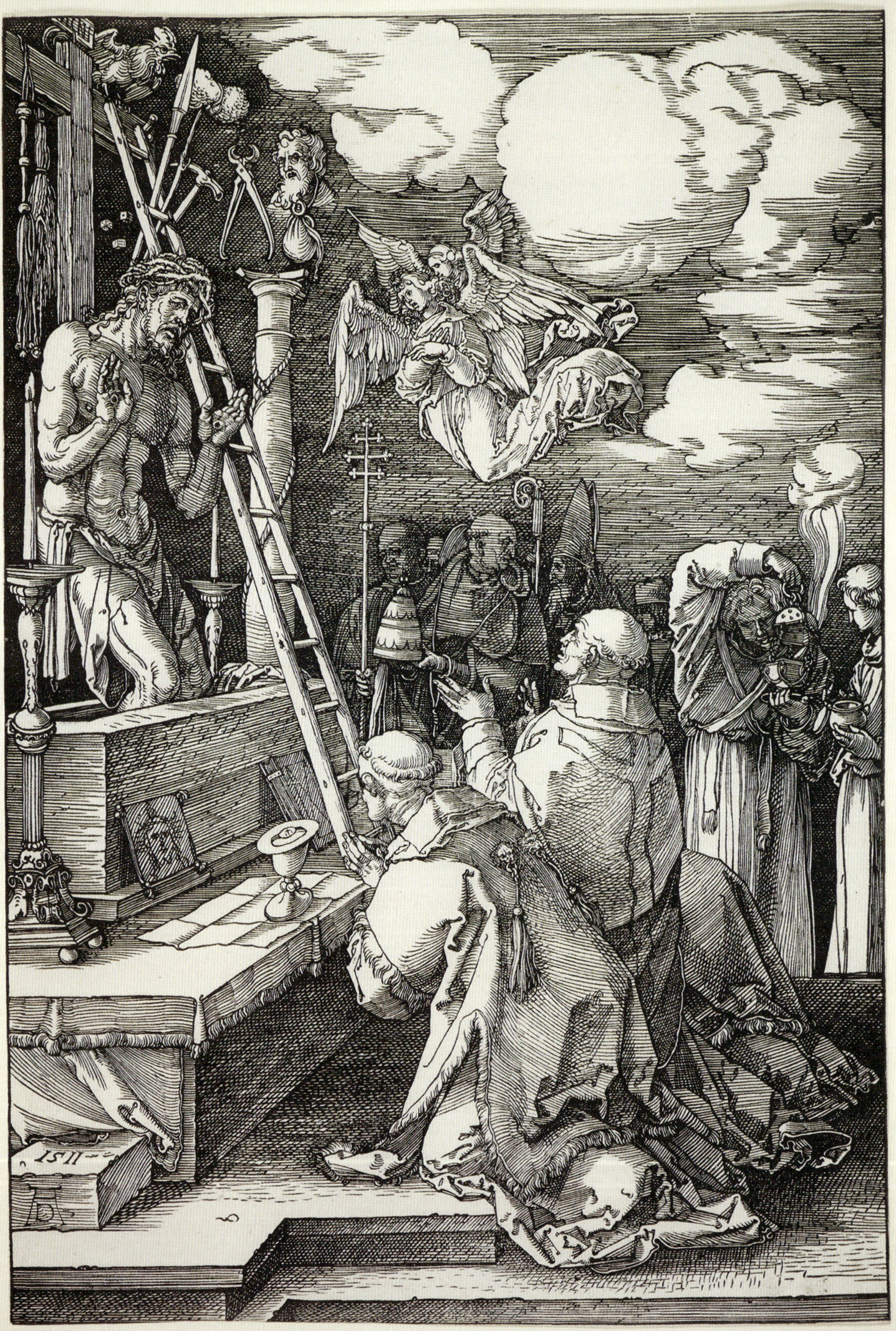

1511

[6] Objects of devotion and instruments of memorialisation: *The Mass of Saint Gregory*

Charles Zika

When Albrecht Dürer completed his woodcut of *The Mass of Saint Gregory* in 1511 (Figure 6.1; cat. 8), the scene he depicted was already a well-established subject among early sixteenth-century artists.[1] The print illustrates the dramatic story of Pope Gregory (d. 604) celebrating mass. Just as he was about to consecrate the bread and wine, he experienced a vision of Christ as the Man of Sorrows, rising from a sarcophagus on the altar and displaying the wounds in his hands. Surrounding Christ were the so-called *arma Christi*, literally 'the weapons of Christ', that is, the objects used to inflict his suffering and death. The print also shows a deacon on Gregory's left and various clerics and assistants – one holding a processional cross, a cardinal holding the pope's tiara, a mitred bishop and his crook, and two attendants filling a thurible with incense from an incense boat. Except for the deacon, they are positioned very much in a shaded background created by Dürer's crosshatching. The backgrounding of the clerical attendants and the absence of any church architecture suggests a transcendent heavenly moment, one in which angels also appear, and serves to direct the viewer to the interaction between Gregory and Christ as they lock eyes and mirror each other's gestures.

The theme of Dürer's woodcut may go back to an eighth-century miracle story about a woman's doubts that the host offered to her by Gregory was actually the body of Christ. The iconography, however, relates more closely to a Byzantine mosaic from about 1300 that was brought from the Sinai to Rome in 1380

and then framed within a honeycomb of relics. The image was then presented to the Carthusian church in Rome, Basilica di Santa Croce in Gerusalemme, which itself was built upon a field of Passion relics. The Carthusians inserted this Man of Sorrows into the Gregory Mass miracle story, identifying it as Gregory's vision, and thereby heightening the sacred power of their newly framed mosaic object. The Carthusians also succeeded in getting various popes to grant extremely large indulgences to prayers said before the mosaic in Rome, and in the later fifteenth century, to prayers said before printed copies of it.[2] Given that the *arma Christi* had become widely popular objects by the mid-fourteenth century and that indulgences could also be earned by saying prayers before them, it is hardly surprising that the Carthusians linked these objects to their version of Gregory's miraculous vision during the celebration of mass. As the devotion spread, references to the icon and church in Rome disappeared, and the *arma Christi* began to feature ever more prominently in illustrations of the Gregory Mass story.

This essay argues that Dürer's woodcut sought to instil new meaning into this late medieval subject, shaped by his city's possession of sacred Passion relics and Dürer's own personal involvement in their communal celebration. The side-view Dürer adopts in representing this miraculous scene in his print provides a depth of vision that allows the Man of Sorrows to become intensely present, stretching out over the altar, a movement accentuated by the positioning of the ladder. The gradations in the hatching provide the scene with a depth hardly seen in Dürer's earlier prints. Dürer's sophisticated technique serves to illuminate the *arma Christi* against the dark background so that these objects seem to float freely, thereby also

6.1 (cat. 8) Albrecht Dürer, *The Mass of Saint Gregory*, 1511, woodcut, 297 x 206 mm.

The Whitworth, The University of Manchester, P.3053. Presented by George Thomas Clough in 1921. © The Whitworth, The University of Manchester. Photo: Michael Pollard.

highlighting their significance for the artist and his city. Some objects – the cross, Christ's crown of thorns, the nail and especially the prominent lance – were strongly linked to Nuremberg's status in the Holy Roman Empire. Relics of these sacred objects, together with the imperial regalia, had been given to the city by Emperor Sigismund (1368–1437) for safe keeping in 1424, and were celebrated in the annual rituals of the *Heiltumsfest* (Feast of the Sacred Relics), also called the Feast of the Holy Lance and Nails. Moreover, Dürer was directly involved in these rituals in 1511 when he completed *The Mass of Saint Gregory* print.

As well as opening up Dürer's connection to the role of these devotional objects in the Nuremberg of his time, this print provides a useful entry into the production and use of liturgical objects in Nuremberg's approximately twenty churches and chapels. *The Mass of Saint Gregory* is the only Dürer work that depicts the celebration of mass – the most important religious ritual of memorialisation and re-enactment that took place on numerous Nuremberg altars daily. Both sets of objects played a significant role in the city's political pre-eminence, cultural appeal and economic wealth from the fourteenth through to the seventeenth century. Liturgical objects, such as chalices, altar candlesticks, altar cloths, paxes and mass-books, were considered sacred by virtue of their contact with the bread (in the form of the round host) and wine believed to be the body and blood of Christ. These items contributed significantly to Nuremberg's metal, cloth and printing industries for which the city was celebrated in the fifteenth and sixteenth centuries, and they were exported through much of central Europe. Devotional objects, such as relics of the bodies of Christ and his saints, or relics of objects with which they had come into contact during their lives, and the different types of containers or reliquaries used to hold them – caskets, shrines, monstrances and reliquary paxes – also drew on the city's craft and intellectual expertise to help shape its reputation as one of Europe's leading centres of artistic production.

The objects seen on the altar in this Dürer print would have all been recognisable to viewers of the time as items manufactured in Nuremberg. Chalices, for instance, were primarily made from silver which was gilded and often embossed – as was the paten or communion plate on which the host is shown resting. The earliest surviving Nuremberg examples date from the mid-fourteenth century, when there were already sixteen goldsmiths working in the city.[3] Dürer's chalice in the Gregory Mass print is similar to the form of those depicted in his other prints, such as the chalice held by the angel putting the seal on the foreheads of God's servants in Dürer's *The Four Angels Holding the Winds* (1498) from the *Apocalypse* series, or the chalices held by angels collecting Christ's blood from his hands, feet and side as he hangs from the cross in the c. 1498 *Crucifixion* from *The Great Passion* series (published in 1511), and in the 1513 *Christ on the Cross with Three Angels*.[4] Dürer's 1523 woodcut, *The Last Supper*, depicts a very similar chalice, even if a slightly more slender version.[5] All these chalices represent a far simpler and chronologically earlier style than those being produced in Nuremberg in the first decade of the sixteenth century. The foot or base is simply round, not at all raised, engraved or decorated as seen in many later fifteenth- or sixteenth-century examples; the stem is quite short, without a collar; the node (slightly varied in the different prints) comprises four small cylindrical or diamond shapes; and the cups are full and funnel-shaped. The flat rounded foot or base of Dürer's chalices seem similar to those of the later fourteenth or fifteenth centuries as do some of the nodes, quite unlike the feet comprising six round petal- or diamond-shaped lobes and hexagonal shafts found c. 1500.[6]

The candlesticks displayed on the altar may also have been part of a strategy that set the scene in an earlier period. Pricket candlesticks with tall shafts resting on elaborate bases and supported by a number of feet, were far more common three or four centuries earlier.[7] More common by 1500 were candlesticks with a circular base and wax pan, which had come to Europe from the Middle East via Venice in the fourteenth century.[8] Taller pricket candlesticks were used on the altar, while candlesticks with sockets for holding the candle were more common in domestic spaces – as Dürer clearly shows in his prints, *The Birth of the Virgin* (cat. 22) and *Saint Jerome in his Study* (cat. 73; see also Dagmar Eichberger's 'The material and the immaterial' in this volume).[9] Dürer includes a less extravagant altar candlestick in his woodcut of *The Penitent David*, a pricket type with a long shaft, but also with a rounded base without feet.[10] In Dürer's *Saint John's Vision of Christ and the Seven Golden Candlesticks* from the *Apocalypse* series (Figure 6.2; cat. 39), reprinted with Latin text in 1511, the highly ornate and varied filigreed forms of these extraordinary objects have more in common with his designs for luxury objects like ornamental goblets and table fountains.[11] Perhaps the altar candlesticks in *The Mass of Saint Gregory* are an attempt to locate Gregory's vision in a more distant past rather than in the present. Alternatively, they may have been at least inspired by candlesticks he had seen in Italy, for a revival of the earlier Gothic style was underway at the turn of the sixteenth century. The workshop of Vicenzo Grandi in Venice, for instance, produced a set of six elaborate bronze pricket candlesticks with a triangular base and feet c. 1520–25.[12]

Other items on the altar in the Gregory Mass print include a corporal, a pax displaying the Holy Face of Christ and what is most likely a mass-book. The corporal, a square linen cloth which was folded out on the altar during the celebration of the mass to protect the vessels that hold the host or wine and to catch any spillage or crumbs, would certainly have been produced in Nuremberg, as would the altar cloth beneath. Textile production and dyeing, just like the production of metal goods, was one of the city's key crafts, for which it was known throughout Europe. Nuremberg also created different liturgical hangings, altar frontals and tapestries in the fifteenth century, with one workshop located in the Dominican convent of Saint Catherine.[13] By 1500 Nuremberg was the most important centre for the production of cloth in South Germany, and a century later the chief location for dyeing throughout the German territories as a whole.[14] The master cloth and linen makers (who in most cases in Nuremberg were also dyers) were strongly represented amongst the middle and also high income master craftsmen in the city,[15] and the City Council was actively involved in supporting their productivity. This support was very clear in the Council's funding and building of the so-called *Sieben Zeilen* (Seven Rows) for fustian weavers, primarily from Augsburg – five rows with fifteen houses in 1488, and a further two rows with six houses in 1524. This spearheaded the city's production not only of fustian, but also of various types of linen and canvas.

Paxes or pax-boards, like the one depicted on the altar in Dürer's print, had become common objects in liturgies of the later fifteenth and early sixteenth century. They were introduced as part of the liturgical ritual of the pax, the kiss of peace, a tradition originating in earlier centuries that took place in the mass after the host had been consecrated and before it was consumed.[16] The ritual was understood as an act of cleansing and preparation – a ritual of peace, unity and reconciliation before the spiritual union with Christ through the taking of the Sacrament. Instead of a physical kiss between the celebrants and congregation, the priest would kiss the pax-board, and then have it offered to other attending clerics and then the lay congregation. In kissing the pax-board it was imagined that each person took up the kisses deposited there, symbolically creating unity among the worshippers.

These pax boards included images of Christ, Mary or the saints – such as scenes of the Crucifixion, the Deposition from the Cross and Entombment, or the Nativity, Annunciation or Visitation of the Virgin. In images of the Gregory Mass, paxes are frequently depicted, and in a very small number prior to the year of Dürer's woodcut, they feature the suffering Holy Face of Christ.[17] Whether Dürer knew of these earlier images with the pax is unknown; but he certainly would have known of the appearance of the Veronica cloth in depictions of the Gregory Mass, given that in Nuremberg alone at least eight images created before 1450 included the Veronica cloth.[18] The Holy Face, the *vera icon* imprinted on Veronica's cloth during Christ's way to Calvary, was frequently included as one of the *arma Christi* in depictions of the Mass of Saint Gregory. In a number of these, it is draped over the side of the sarcophagus – as in the case of the epitaph painting of Heinrich Wolff von Wolffsthal from the Nuremberg Dominican convent of Saint Catherine, created c. 1500 by a Nuremberg artist and donated to the convent church (Figure 6.3).[19] In some other Nuremberg

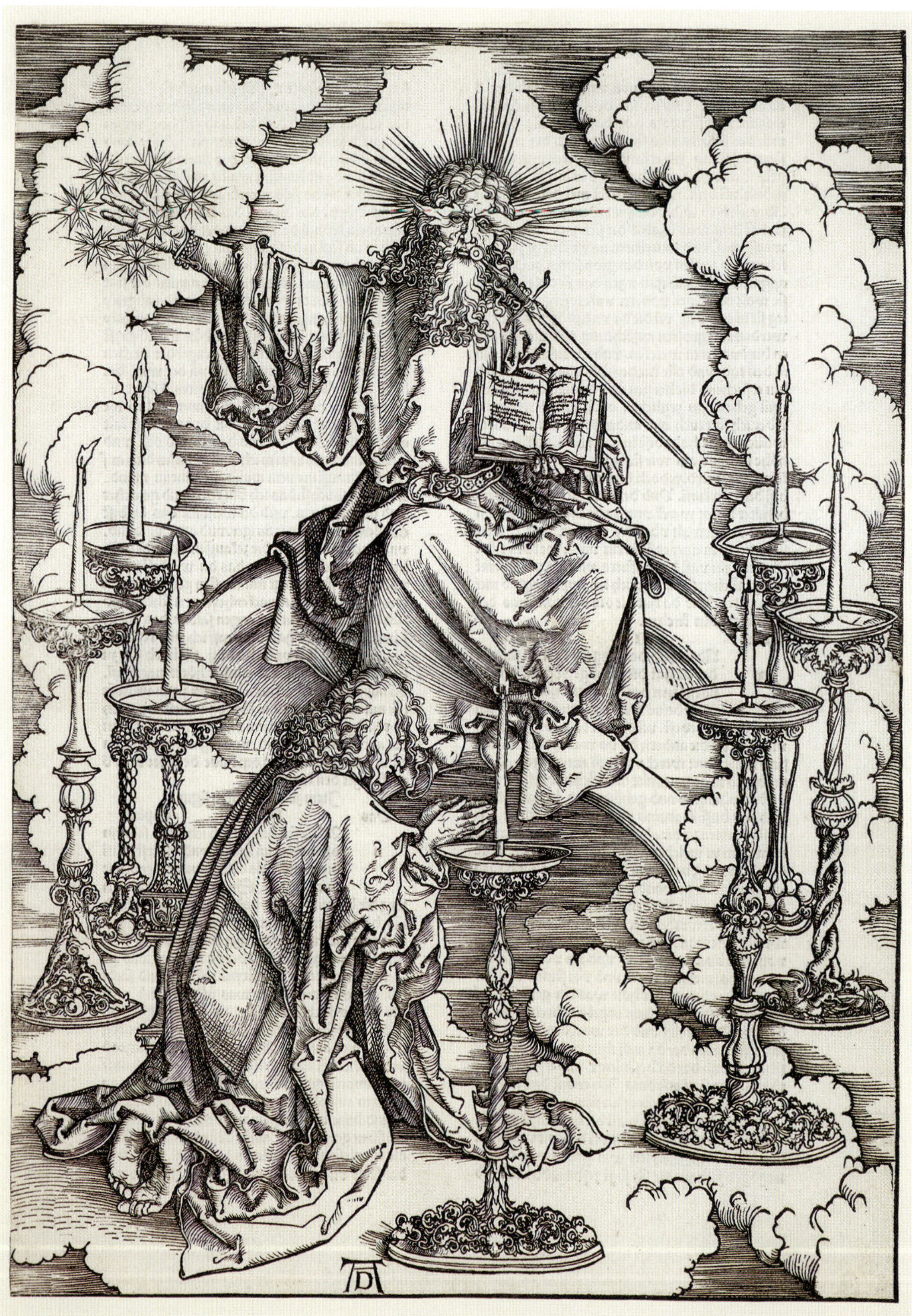

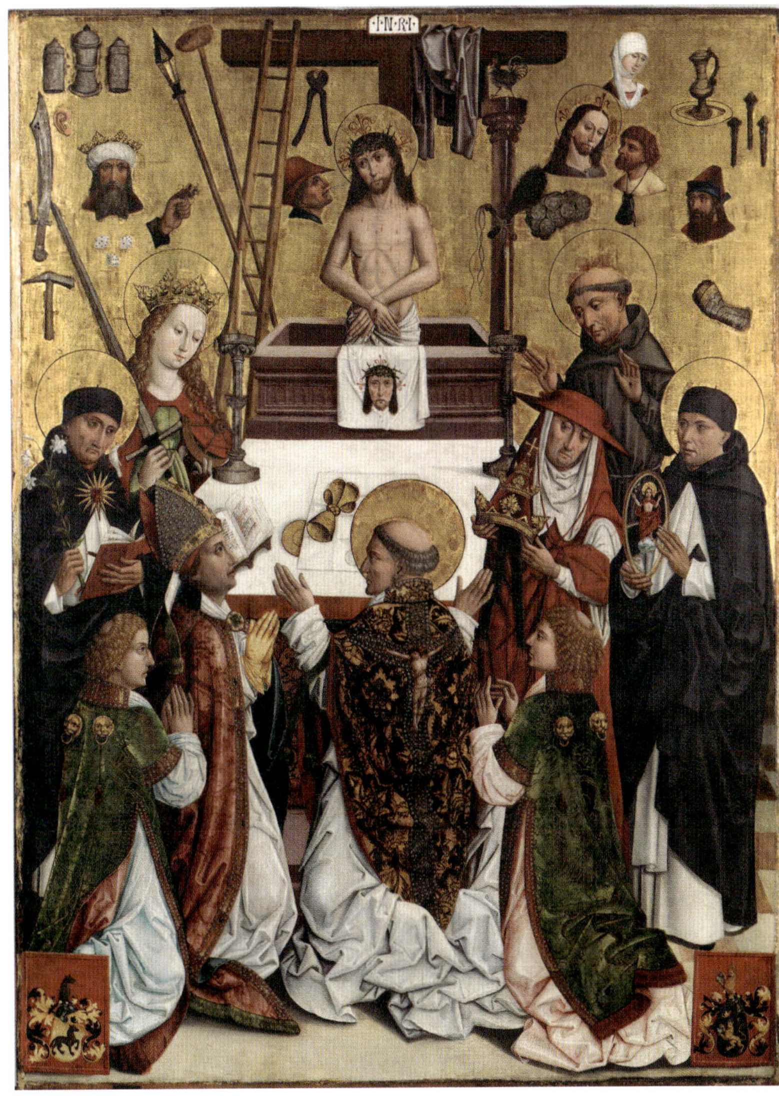

< 6.2 (cat. 39) Albrecht Dürer, *Saint John's Vision of Christ and the Seven Golden Candlesticks*, c. 1498, woodcut, 394 x 286 mm.

The Whitworth, The University of Manchester, P.3059. Presented by George Thomas Clough in 1921. © The Whitworth, The University of Manchester. Photo: Michael Pollard.

6.3 Unknown Nuremberg artist, *The Mass of Saint Gregory from the Dominican Convent Church of Saint Catherine, Nuremberg (Epitaph of Heinrich Wolff von Wolffsthal)*, c. 1500, oil and metal overlay on panel, 187.9 x 138.2 cm.

Nuremberg, Germanisches Nationalmuseum, Gm154. © Germanisches Nationalmuseum, Nuremberg.

images, the Veronica cloth appears as an altar frontal hanging from the edge of the altar.[20]

It seems as though Dürer has intentionally taken the Veronica cloth with Christ's imprinted face, a devotional image and relic often presented as one of the *arma Christi*, and incorporated it into the liturgical object and materiality of the pax-board. This seems a novel move and indicates that Dürer was actively engaged in his subject and not simply re-presenting traditional iconography. As the ladder links the

historical Crucifixion on Calvary to its sacramental re-enactment on the altar, so the pax, a liturgical instrument used to memorialise and make real the power and benefits of that event on the altar, appropriates to itself the power of the historical relic. Many paxes did indeed contain relics. Perhaps Dürer is creating something similar, a liturgical object that accrues power by taking on the power of the Veronica Passion relic. Or perhaps he wishes to present an everyday act of devotion and compassion analogous

to Pope Gregory's miraculous gaze and communion
with the suffering Christ, for the deacon directs his
gaze over the host stamped with the image of the
Crucifixion on to the pax displaying the Holy Face.

So what is the meaning of the other devotional objects
in Dürer's print, the *arma Christi*? There is the cross,
first of all, and hanging from it, a rope scourge and a
birch-rod; and further to the right, a pillar or column
strung with the rope with which Christ was tied to the
column and flogged.[21] The cock seated on the cross
refers to the cock that crowed after Peter denied his
association with Christ three times; the male head
with a bag represents Judas's betrayal of Christ's
location to the Roman authorities in return for a bag
of silver. The nail in the horizontal beam of the cross
and the hammer represent the nailing of Christ to the
cross with three nails; the pliers reference the removal
of those nails when the dead body of Christ was
taken down; the three dice evoke the executioner's
assistants who fought over who would receive Christ's
discarded clothing. There is also the sponge on the
end of a stick, saturated with wine vinegar and offered
to Christ on the cross in order to slake his thirst; the
lance used to pierce Christ's side, in order to confirm
that he had died; and on Christ's head, the crown of
thorns placed there by the Roman soldiers to mock
the claim that he was a king – and only removed after
his dead body was taken down from the cross.

These objects referencing Christ's suffering and death
were common in most of the Gregory Mass images
preceding Dürer.[22] They had been objects of special
veneration since the late twelfth century and became
widely popular through much of Europe from the mid-
fourteenth. A fundamental reason for their popularity
was that the recitation of particular prayers before
them, such as the *Adoro te*, would earn indulgences
from the fires of purgatory – initially for three years, but
as verses were added, so were the number of years.
The inflation was so great that a north Netherlandish
prayer book of c. 1505–15 claimed that one would
receive 200,000 years indulgence if one recited the
nine-verse *Adoro te* on one's knees while looking at
what Pope Gregory saw, viz. the Man of Sorrows and
the *arma Christi*.[23] While Dürer was surely aware of this
popularity, there are no suggestions that indulgences

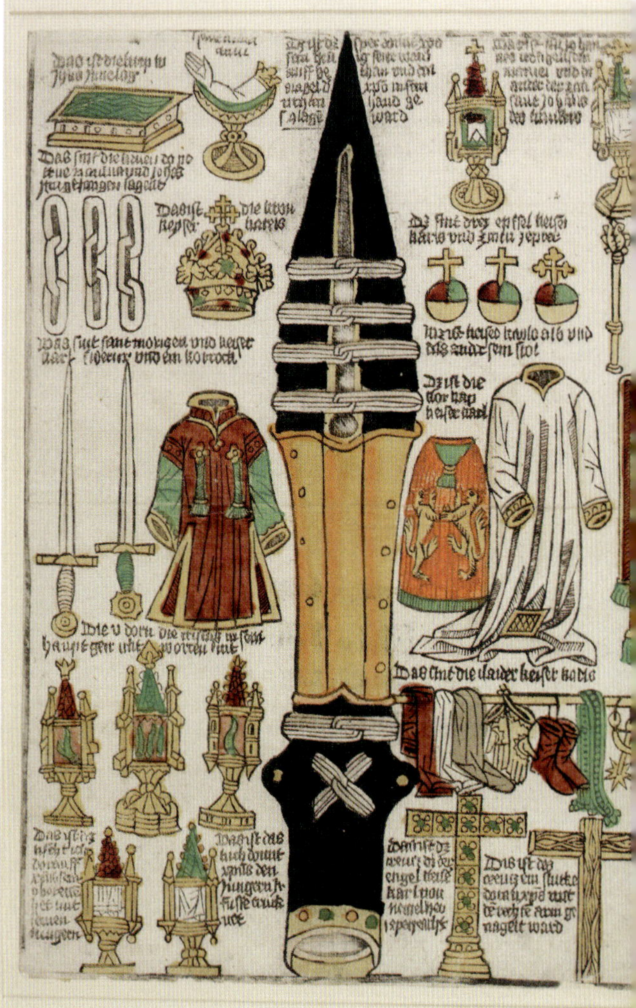

6.4 Unknown artist, *The Relics, Vestments, and Insignia of
the Holy Roman Empire*, c. 1470–80, woodcut with hand-
colouring, 434 x 298 mm.

impacted on the design and content of his print. It was
more the religious and political significance of these
arma Christi for Nuremberg and for himself, I would
suggest, that was critical for its creation.

In 1510 Dürer was commissioned by the Nuremberg
Council to paint twin panels of Emperor Charlemagne
(747–814) and Emperor Sigismund. Several designs
for the commission have survived.[24] An advance

payment was made by the Council in July 1511 and a second payment in late March 1513, when the paintings were likely finished.[25] The panels were used during the city's annual festival, the *Heiltumsfest*. This began in Nuremberg in 1424, when Emperor Sigismund transferred these precious objects from his palace in Visegrád in Hungary (to where they had been transferred just three years earlier from Karlštejn Castle in Bohemia) to the safe-keeping of the city

6.5 Unknown artist, *Heiltumsstuhl (Display Tower of Sacred Relics)*, coloured woodcut, 210 x 155 mm., in *Heiltumsbüchlein* (Nuremberg: Peter Vischer, 1487).

Nuremberg, Staatsarchiv, Rst. N. Handschriften Nr. 399a.
© Nuremberg, Staatsarchiv.

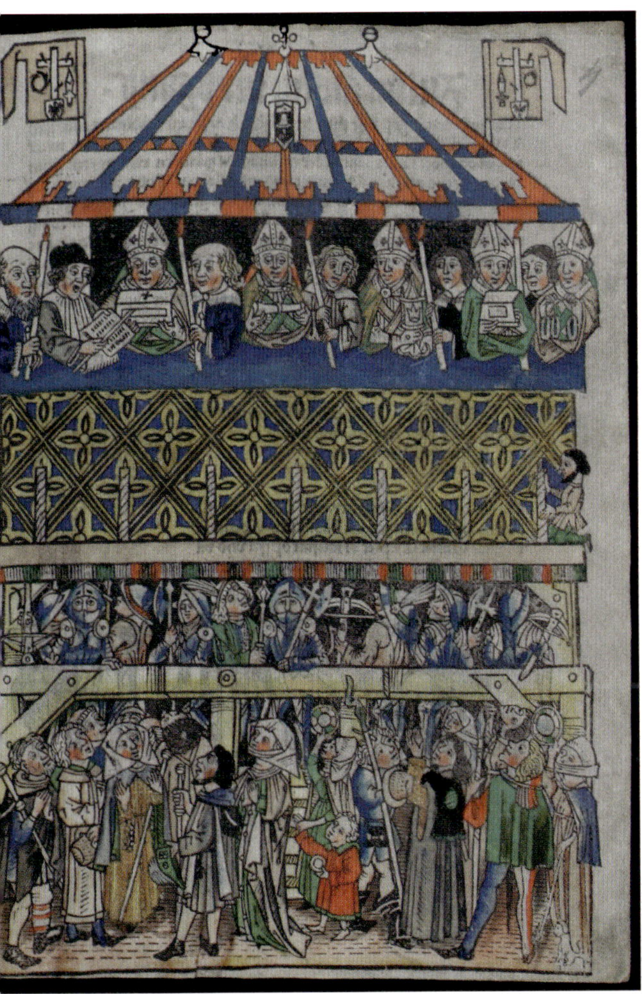

of Nuremberg 'forever and irrevocably', ostensibly because of dangers associated with the Hussite wars.[26] The *Heiltum*, literally 'holy things', came to mean holy or sacred relics by the fifteenth century, and it included both imperial regalia and sacred relics, because the former were considered relics by their association with Charlemagne, who was canonised a saint in 1169.[27] They were celebrated in a number of woodcuts (Figure 6.4),[28] and pride of place was given to the Passion relics: the Holy Lance, the nails, a fragment of the Holy Cross and five thorns from Christ's crown of thorns. The *Heiltum* also included pieces of Christ's apron and the tablecloth used at the Last Supper, a splinter from Christ's crib, the arm bone of Saint Anne and the chains that bound Saints Peter, Paul and John the Evangelist. The imperial regalia included the crown of Otto the Great from the tenth century, the sword of Saint Maurice, an orb and sceptre and various coronation robes and pieces of imperial clothing related to Charlemagne.[29]

The transfer of these relics brought considerable benefits to individual Nuremberg families as well as to the city in general.[30] They were to be kept in the church of the *Heilig-Geist-Spital* (Holy Spirit hospital), the only church in the city under full control of the Council,[31] except for the period of the *Heiltumsfest* and any temporary relocation such as for imperial coronations. This close association with Emperor Sigismund meant that Nuremberg, already specified in the 1356 Golden Bull of Emperor Charles IV (1316–78) as the location for the first imperial diet of a new emperor, became something of a royal centre in the Empire and a lead representative of the so-called Imperial Cities, cities independent of the power of regional princes. It strengthened the city's power in ongoing disputes and economic conflict with the *Burggraf* (castellan), from which it was finally released in 1431. The city also acted as a creditor to Sigismund through the power of twenty-seven of its wealthiest families, while members of those families, such as Peter Volckamer (d. 1437) and Sigmund Stromer (d. 1435/7), were actively engaged in the royal court, often representing the city's and their own family's interests. Sigismund, in turn, supported the city's manufacture, for instance, through his large purchase of armour and armaments in the mid-1430s.

Shortly after the relics arrived in the city in March 1424, and following various decrees and bulls provided by the Bishop of Bamberg, Emperor Sigismund and Pope Martin V (1369–1431), the first *Heiltumsfest* was held two weeks after Good Friday.[32] For the public display of the relics, a three-story display tower (*Heiltumsstuhl*) was built, and each year on the evening before the feast, the relics were also brought from the *Heilig Geist* church and kept in the *Heiltumskammer*. Dürer's twin paintings of Emperor Charlemagne and Emperor Sigismund, commissioned by the city council in 1510, served as hinged partitions and doors to this chamber. When opened, the portraits of the two emperors were revealed; when closed, inscriptions and coats of arms were seen on the reverse.[33]

The *Heiltumsweisung* (sacred relics display) occurred in three segments: first, relics related to the childhood of Christ were shown; second, the imperial regalia; and third, relics related to Christ's Passion – the most important group and highpoint of the ceremony. In a coloured woodcut published in a small pamphlet of 1487 describing the ceremony and related indulgences (Figure 6.5), we see the pilgrims and people below, soldiers protecting entry above, the different ecclesiastical officials and attendants with the reliquaries at level three, and at top left the *Heiltumsschreier*, the sacred relics crier, announcing and identifying each relic. The public would not have been able to see the relics, nor most of them even the caskets in which they were encased, but the main relics were prominently displayed on the flags flying on the *Heiltumsstuhl*. They would have learnt from the crier during the ceremony, if not before, that their presence alone could gain them many indulgences, and if they visited the city's five main churches in honour of Christ's wounds and recited particular prayers they could gain even more. From 1493 people could also access these requirements for gaining indulgences and details of the ceremony in a cheap and uncoloured paper version of the more expensive booklet of 1487, which had been printed on parchment (Figure 6.5).[34] The ritual culminated in the showing of the Holy Lance. After describing how the lance opened a deep holy wound from which poured out 'a bath of blood and water', the crier was

instructed to pause and allow the people to look at the lance – through which each person's sins would be washed away.[35]

The relics were also very much connected to the city's economic power, given that their display was accompanied by a trade fair that ran initially for fourteen days, and from 1431 for twenty-four. The fair was also given imperial status, which meant merchants could participate without cost and received safe passage. In 1463, for instance, 1,974 carts and wagons entered the city. We know that Dürer sold his prints at this festival, most likely those involving Christ's Passion. These privileges were celebrated in various publications, such as in the 1493 *Nuremberg Chronicle* (cat. 1), published by Dürer's godfather, Anton Koberger (1440–1513). The compiler, the Nuremberg physician and humanist, Hartmann Schedel (1440–1514), wrote at the end of his encomium of the city: 'This city is also specially adorned with the invaluable and most holy lance that pierced Christ's side on the cross, as well as with a remarkable piece of the cross and other holy objects revered throughout the world, which are shown annually at Easter time with great solemnity and splendour.'[36] As if to underline this close identification of the city with the sacred relics of Christ's Passion, the iconic woodcut of the city by Michael Wolgemut (1434–1519) in that work inserts three crosses in the approach to the city in the foreground: a central larger cross surmounted by the Holy Lance and a stick with the sponge (and what seems to be a crown of thorns), and two side crosses from which hang clubs, depicted in some scenes of the Crucifixion as the instruments with which the legs of the two thieves were broken.[37] As Jeffrey Chipps Smith has shown, this view of Nuremberg defined the city through to the mid-sixteenth century.[38] The three crosses also survived, at least through to the 1530s, with close copies appearing in the second edition of Nuremberg's new legal code of 1498, and in the manuscript account of significant Nuremberg families, the 'Haller-Buch' of 1533–36.[39]

For most of the year, the sacred relics were kept in a new reliquary shrine commissioned by the City Council that hung above the altar in the choir of

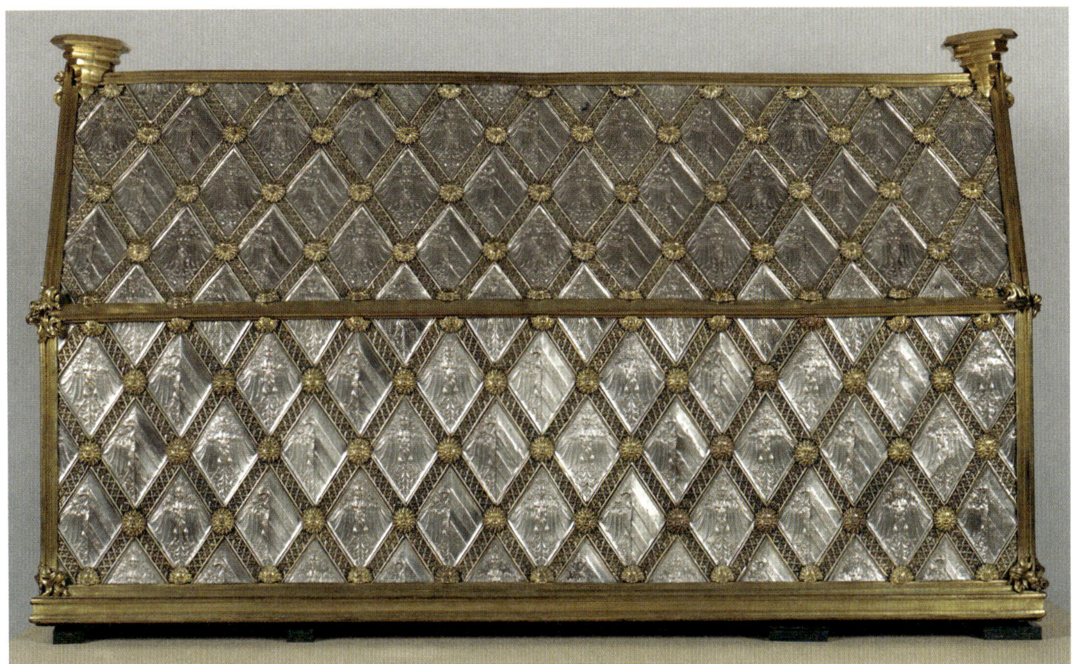

6.6 Peter Ratzko and Hans Scheßlitzer, *Heiltumsschrein (Reliquary Shrine)*, 1438–40, wooden shrine covered with silver plates, 102 x 175 x 505 cm.

Nuremberg, Germanisches Nationalmuseum, KG187. © Germanisches Nationalmuseum, Nuremberg.

the Holy Spirit church (Figure 6.6).[40] The wooden structure was built from oak by a Nuremberg cabinetmaker, Hans Nürnberger, between 1438 and 1440 in a shape similar to the Deocarus shrine (1437) in Saint Lawrence and the Sebaldus shrine (1391–97) in Saint Sebald.[41] It was called a *Sarg* (coffin), and although it did not hold body relics like those of the two saints, this term clearly alluded to Christ's death that the Passion relics had caused. The striking aspect of the shrine is the exquisite metalwork by Peter Ratzko (d. 1453) and Hans Scheßlitzer (d. 1472), and especially the rhomboid silver sheets embossed with the city's greater and lesser coats of arms featuring the *Jungfrauenadler* (Maiden Eagle). The shrine was also hung in such a way that viewers could see the underside painting by an unknown artist, Lucas: two angels holding the two most important relics kept inside, the holy lance and the cross. The shrine was clearly a communal object involving many of the city's craftspeople and artists (including locksmiths

for its complex locking system), emblazoned with Nuremberg's coats of arms and the Nuremberg mark, a reversed 'N' stamped on four of its panels.[42] It signalled the city's legitimate custodianship of these relics, its special relationship with the emperor and its strong links to Christian devotion and faith. But it also demonstrated the city's wealth, its artistic prowess and craft skills.

Dürer was certainly aware of the city's deep investment in its sacred relics when working on *The Mass of Saint Gregory* in 1511. His inscriptions on the front and reverse of his portrait of Emperor Sigismund emphasised the *sunder gnaden*, the special favours or benefits these relics had brought to the city.[43] Dürer himself seems to have been especially attuned to their deep significance at this time. During 1510–11 he was almost entirely focused on religious themes in his prints and paintings. In 1511 he republished the *Apocalypse* book with a new, now illustrated, title-page

and Latin bible texts. He added four new woodcuts
on Christ's Passion (1510) and an illustrated title-page
(1511) to create the 1511 book of the *Great Passion*, with
Latin verses by the Benedictine humanist, Benedict
Chelidonius (c. 1460–1521). Chelidonius's Latin verses
also featured in Dürer's *Small Passion* book of 1511,
which included thirty-two prints and an illustrated
title-page, all completed in that year, and four prints
created in 1509–10. The other major book publication
of 1511 was the *Life of the Virgin*, for which Dürer added
two woodcuts in 1510 and an illustrated title-page
and Chelidonius's verses in 1511 to seventeen earlier
prints.[44] Moreover, all the single prints Dürer published
in 1510–11 had religious themes as their subject, and his
major painted work was *The Adoration of the Trinity*,
commissioned by Matthäus Landauer (d. 1516) for the
All Saints chapel in the Twelve Brethren House.[45] A
major theme running through all this work was Christ's
Passion, evident not only in the Passion series, but also
in the Landauer Altar painting and the 1511 print of *The
Holy Trinity*, in which the angels carry the instruments
of the Passion, the *arma Christi*.[46] The theme is also
very evident in much of Dürer's writing at this time.
His poem, *Seven Times of Prayer*, published as an
illustrated broadsheet in 1510, is an intense meditation
on the stages of Christ's suffering and death.[47]

The subject of *The Mass of Saint Gregory* was clearly
one of immense interest for Dürer when he created
the print in 1511. His artistic and literary activity
from 1509 to 1512 was strongly focused on Christ's
Passion in thinking about how to lead a Christian life.
The City Council's commission for Dürer to make a
significant contribution to the feast that proclaimed
Nuremberg's special benefits and pre-eminent status
may well have encouraged that thinking. The print
included some small but important deviations from
the traditional iconography of the Gregory Mass. It
sought to emphasise visually the way in which the
material manifestation of Christ's Passion in devotional
objects, some of which were held by his city, made
that narrative more immediate and present, thereby
also transforming liturgical rituals, spaces and objects
as frames through which one could share in Pope
Gregory's vision.

Notes

1   Smith, *Nuremberg, A Renaissance city*, 106. Six copies by other
    artists survive, indicating the work's influence (Schoch, Mende and
    Scherbaum, *Albrecht Dürer*, II, 364, no.15). For the subject in the late
    Middle Ages, Gormans and Lentes, eds, *Das Bild der Erscheinung*;
    Meier, *Die Gregorsmesse*; Rudy, *Rubrics, Images and Indulgences*,
    101–36.

2   See especially Rudy, *Rubrics, Images and Indulgences*, 116–30.

3   For chalices, see Kohlhaussen, *Nürnberger Goldschmiedekunst*,
    9–10, 118–37, 180–202; Kahsnitz and Wixom, eds, *Gothic and
    Renaissance Art*, 182, nos. 48, 49.

4   Schoch, Mende and Scherbaum, *Albrecht Dürer*, II, 82–4 (no. 117),
    200–2 (no. 161), 380–2 (no. 236); H.169 (IIa), H.13b, H.182b.

5   *Ibid.*, 486–8 (no. 259); H.182b.

6   For fourteenth-century examples, see Kohlhaussen, *Nürnberger
    Goldschmiedekunst*, nos 212, 214, 215, 223 = figures 214, 217, 218,
    233 in contrast to most later examples, figures 301–27. For those
    approximating Dürer's chalices, figures 325–6.

7   See Mende, *Die mittelalterlichen Bronzen*, 249–55; Germany,
    mid-late twelfth century, cast bronze, London, Victoria and Albert
    Museum, 4437-1857; Mosan Workshop, late twelfth century, gilt
    bronze, Walters Art Gallery, Baltimore, VO.56.

8   For socketed late fifteenth- to sixteenth-century brass and bronze
    candlesticks, see Mende, *Die mittelalterlichen Bronzen*, 264–9, nos
    90–2; London, Victoria and Albert Museum, M.17-1964, M.651-1926,
    M.56-1967; and for the taller version, with a pricket instead of a
    socket, M.2-1954.

9   One of the two socket candlesticks depicted in the *Birth of the
    Virgin* has double arms. For other such examples, see Mende, *Die
    mittelalterlichen Bronzen*, 264–78.

10 Schoch, Mende and Scherbaum, *Albrecht Dürer*, II, 168–70, no. 151;
    H.108.

11 Albrecht Dürer, *Design for a Large Table-Fountain*, 1495–1500,
    pen and brown ink, with watercolour and touched with red chalk,
    London, The British Museum, SL,5218.83; Strauss, *Complete
    Drawings* 1499/1. Dürer, *Design for a Gothic Cup* (cat. 35). For
    this image from the *Apocalypse* cycle, see Schoch, Mende and
    Scherbaum, *Albrecht Dürer*, II, 72–4, no. 113; H.165 (IIa).

12 Workshop of Vicenzo Grandi, *Pair of Altar Candlesticks*, c. 1520–25,
    bronze, Morgan Library and Museum, accession no. AZ035.1-2;
    New York, The Metropolitan Museum of Art, 1973.287.2

13 For four examples of tapestries used as antependiums or dossals,
    see Kahsnitz and Wixom, eds, *Gothic and Renaissance Art*, 198–200,
    nos 55–8 (entry by Leonie von Wilckens). Also Wilckens, *Die
    textilien Künste*, 302–14.

14 Sakuma, *Die Nürnberger Tuchmacher*, 365–6.

15 *Ibid.*, 182–200.

16 See Rudy, 'Kissing Images'; Koslofsky, 'The Kiss of Peace'.

17 See a print by the Monogrammist d (c. 1470) and a painting by the
    Master of the Holy Kinship (c. 1500), in Gormans and Lentes, eds,
    Das Bild der Erscheinung, 92, 147. For the large literature on the
    Holy Face, see Murphy et al., *The European Fortune of the Roman
    Veronica*; Kessler, 'Veronica's Textile'; Rudy, *Rubrics, Images and
    Indulgences*, 60–6.

18 Meier, *Die Gregorsmesse*, 58.

19 Hess et al., *Die Gemälde des Spätmittelalters*, II, 928–41, no. 64: also
    I, 288–98, no. 20; Meier, *Die Gregorsmesse*, figure 21.

20 Hess et al., *Die Gemälde des Spätmittelalters*, I, 156–71, no.9; Lentes, 'Verum Corpus und Vera Imago', figure 9; and figures 4 and 6 (where the Veronica cloth hangs over the sarcophagus and over the altar edge).

21 In *The Flagellation* from Dürer's *Great Passion* series, a knotted rope scourge and a birch of bundled twigs are both used by the executioner's assistants, the latter also shown being bundled by a soldier. Both are also used in the *The Engraved Passion* series, whereas only birches are used in *The Small Passion* series (Schoch, Mende and Scherbaum, *Albrecht Dürer*, I, 137; II, 193, 313.) Both were commonly shown hanging from the cross in later fifteenth-century images (see Parshall and Schoch, *Origins of European Printmaking*, 237, 243, 249).

22 For a fuller list and later accretions, Rudy, *Rubrics, Images and Indulgences*, 55–60, 116, 120–2.

23 *Ibid.*, 107–13, especially 112.

24 Ashcroft, *Albrecht Dürer*, I, 329–33; Kahsnitz and Wixom, eds, *Gothic and Renaissance Art*, 307, figure 130.

25 Ashcroft, *Albrecht Dürer*, I, 336–7, 389–90.

26 For the relics and festival, see Smith, *Nuremberg, A Renaissance City*, 28–30; Schier and Schleif, 'Seeing and Singing'; Schnelbögl, 'Die Reichskleinodien'; Kahsnitz and Wixom, eds, *Gothic and Renaissance Art*, 304–7 (entry by Kurt Löcher); Price, *Albrecht Dürer's Renaissance*, 102–10.

27 Schnelbögl, 'Die Reichskleinodien', 88–90.

28 As well as Figure 6.4, see *Sacred Relics and Imperial Regalia*, c. 1440, woodcut, Germanisches Nationalmuseum, Inv. Nr.HB24755; reproduced with commentary in Parshall and Schoch, *Origins of European Printmaking*, 212–14.

29 For the extract from Emperor Sigismund's decree listing the objects, see Schnelbögl, 'Die Reichskleinodien', 89. Since 1800 they have been in Vienna, except for the period 1938–46. They are now in the *Schatzkammer* (Treasury) of the Kunsthistorisches Museum, Vienna.

30 For the following, Kammel, 'Kaiser Sigismund und die Reichstadt Nürnberg'.

31 In accord with Sigismund's decree that 'no priest should have power over the sacred relics' (Schnelbögl, 'Die Reichskleinodien', 90).

32 This largely followed the establishment of the feast in 1354 by Pope Innocent VI, when the imperial relics were displayed in Prague (Schnelbögl, 'Die Reichskleinodien', 86–7).

33 Ashcroft, *Albrecht Dürer*, I, 333; Kahsnitz and Wixom, eds, *Gothic and Renaissance Art*, 304–7, no. 128.

34 For this and the following on the feast and the fair, Schier and Schleif, 'Seeing and Singing', 408–15; Schnelbögl, 'Die Reichskleinodien', 125–6.

35 Schnelbögl, 'Die Reichskleinodien', 156.

36 Schedel, *Das Buch der Chroniken* [*Weltchronik*], fol. CIr. Also see fol. CXCVr, for an illustration of the Holy Lance (as in Figure 6.4 above, with the nail embedded) and a short account of its discovery and benefits.

37 See Merback, *The Thief, the Cross and the Wheel*, 61, 96, 116–21, 187 ('the men with clubs') and especially figures 32, 37, 40, 41, 73 (clubs hanging from the thieves' crosses).

38 Smith, 'Nuremberg and the Topographies of Expectation', par. 9.

39 Smith, 'Nuremberg and the Topographies of Expectation', par. 8, figure 3; Fleischmann, ed., *Norenberc - Nürnberg 1050 bis 1806*, 30–1.

40 The imperial insignia and clothing were kept in sealed chests and cupboards above the sacristy. See Kahsnitz and Wixom, eds, *Gothic and Renaissance Art*, 179–81, no. 47 (entry by Kahsnitz); Kohlhaussen, *Nürnberger Goldschmiedekunst*, 95–7, no. 169. Also descriptions and twenty-six images, in Germanisches Nationalmuseum Collection Online, Inv. Nr. KG187.

41 In 1508–19, Peter Vischer the Elder and his two sons created the elaborate brass *Sebaldus tomb* for the Sebaldus shrine.

42 Tebbe et al., *Nürnberger Goldschmiedkunst*, I, 499 for this unique mark.

43 See above n. 32.

44 For these 1510–11 publications, see Schoch, Mende and Scherbaum, *Albrecht Dürer*, II, 69, 176–344.

45 Ashcroft, *Albrecht Dürer*, I, 326–7; Strieder et al., *Dürer*, 312–15, nos 413–15.

46 Schoch, Mende and Scherbaum, *Albrecht Dürer*, II, 361–9, no. 231.

47 Ashcroft, *Albrecht Dürer*, I, 300–5; Price, *Albrecht Dürer's Renaissance*, 123–32.

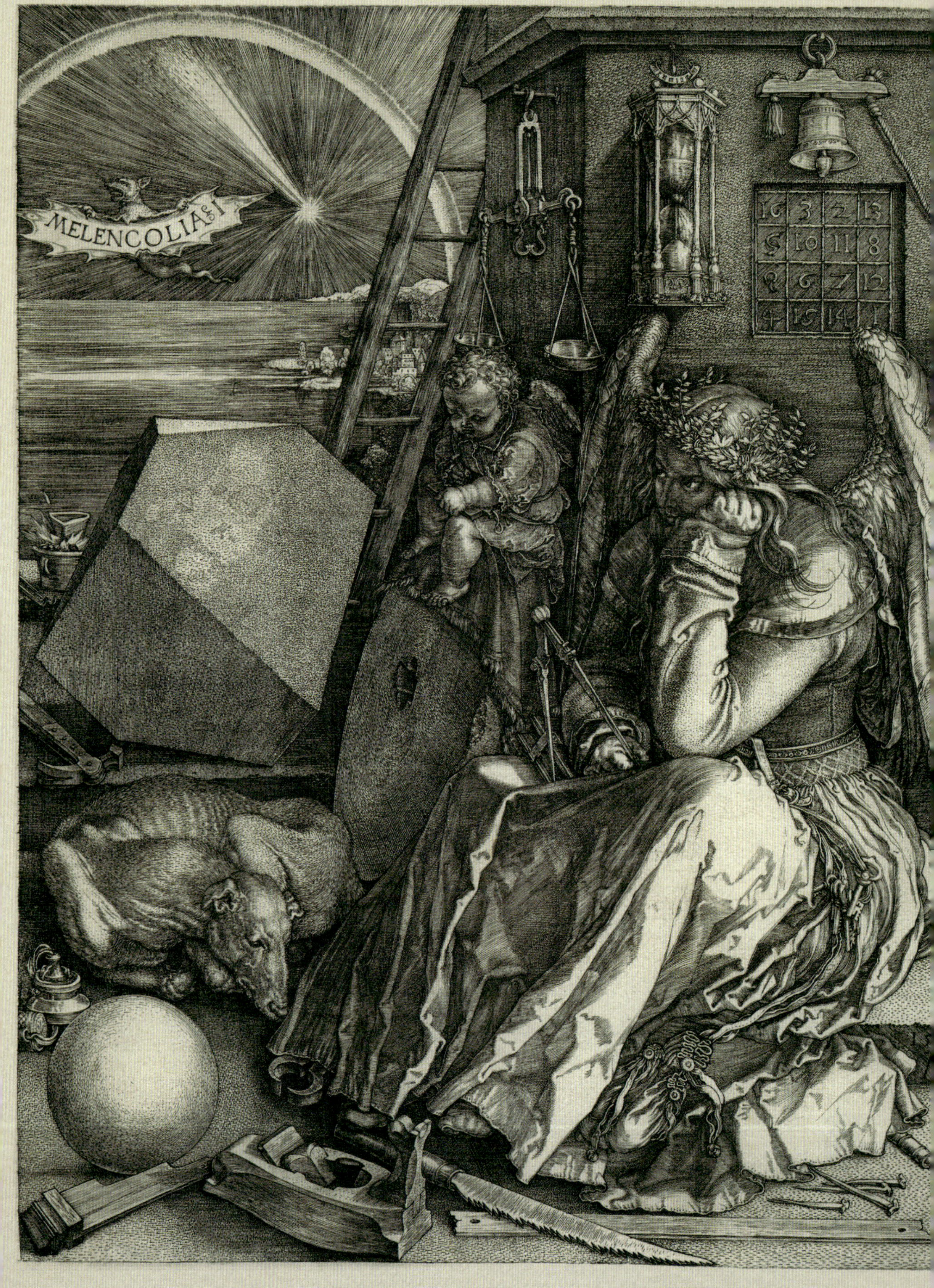

MELENCOLIA §I

[7] Measure and the material world of Albrecht Dürer's *Melencolia I*

Matthew S. Champion

For if the most meaningful works prove to be precisely those whose life is most deeply embedded in their material contents – one thinks of Giehlow's interpretation of Dürer's *Melencolia* – then over the course of their historical duration these material contents present themselves to the researcher all the more clearly the more they have disappeared from the world.[1]

Walter Benjamin, *Strenge Kunstwissenschaft. Zum ersten Bande der* Kunstwissenschaftlichen Forschungen, 1933.

Sixteenth-century Nuremberg was a city where measures mattered.[2] The daily life of its inhabitants was shaped by complex and interweaving systems of time measurement, reaching from the celestial time of the planets to timekeeping devices owned in the home and carried on the person. Accurate and reliable measures of weight undergirded the city's reputation as a centre of exchange, playing a critical role in maintaining Nuremberg's reputation as a hub at the intersection of trade routes across Europe.[3] Nuremberg's famed craftsmanship relied, too, on careful measurement at every level of production: in design, in materials, and in the processes and procedures of manufacture, not least in the production of measurement devices themselves. Careful measures of time, and records of number, length and weight, were also critical to mercantile practices of letter exchange and recordkeeping that formed part of systems of personal and corporate regulation in the period.[4] Measure, too, played important roles

in the materialisation of Nuremberg's religion, not only in the manufacture of religious objects, but also in measurements that could be used to remember sacred journeys and sacred objects and to render them present once more.[5] All these varieties of measurement intersected in the personal and professional world of the renowned Nuremberg artist Albrecht Dürer, and are brought into compelling focus in his famous engraving *Melencolia I* (Figure 7.1, cat. 79).

The engraving shows a seated figure of melancholy, winged, with compass in hand, keys hanging askew from her belt, and purse fallen into the folds of her gown. This personified Melencolia sits surrounded by an array of tools and objects – wood plane, saw, nails, hammer, tongs, crucible, ladder, scales, hourglass, bell and magic square, where each row of numbers adds to the sum thirty-four, and which embeds in its lowest row the date 1514. Amid the assemblage lies an emaciated dog, a sphere and a fantastic polyhedron.[6] Beside the seated figure is a large, chipped millstone on which sits a putto with a slate and an instrument, perhaps the engraver's tool, the burin.[7] In the background, lit by a blazing celestial body, a watery, perhaps flooded, landscape is seen, while a rainbow arches over a bat inscribed with the text *Melencolia I.*

Such a description is a radical oversimplification of the image. Made in 1514, and often located alongside his *Saint Jerome in His Study* (1514, cat. 73), and *The Knight, Death, and the Devil* (1513; cat. 75), as one of Dürer's so-called *Meisterstiche* ('master engravings'), *Melencolia I* has given birth to an astonishing proliferation of interpretations.[8] This proliferation of interpretation uncannily mirrors the proliferation of objects that are placed in the image. Rather than offering a systematic theory of this image, as if that were possible, this chapter offers a series of reflections

7.1 (cat. 79) Albrecht Dürer, *Melencolia (Meisterstiche) I*, 1514, engraving, 240 x 190 mm.

The Whitworth, The University of Manchester, P.3018. Presented by George Thomas Clough in 1921. © The Whitworth, University of Manchester. Photo: Michael Pollard.

on the materialisation of measurement in some of the engraving's objects. The chapter argues that a consideration of contemporary sixteenth-century measurement devices and their significance enlarges our vision of the print. The overwhelming complexity of the measured material world of Dürer's Nuremberg is a trigger for melancholic abstraction and obsessive reflection – the subject of the engraving itself.[9]

Dürer and measurement

Dürer was deeply engaged with measurement. His family background and early training – his father was a Hungarian goldsmith – and later professional life in Nuremberg involved immersion in the city's craft culture. His work shows an intimate concern with how measure affected the representation of the world and structured the imagination. The most obvious witness to this interest is the *Underweysung der messung mit dem zirckel un richt scheyt* ('Instruction in Measurement by Means of the Compass and Ruler') published in 1525 (cat. 57).[10] This treatise shows how understanding, controlling and deploying measure, number and mathematics lay at the heart of Dürer's conception of the artistic process.[11] It also shows the crucial roles played by instruments of measurement – the compass, the ruler – in making across multiple spheres of early modern production. Such instruments were not simply aids to production, they also formed part of Nuremberg's output as an innovative centre in the European marketplace of measurement.

Early drafts of materials relating to Dürer's *Underweysung* survive from the years just before the production of the engraving *Melencolia I*. In these early reflections, Dürer declares that he will start by considering 'measure, number and weight': 'for whoever pays attention to these will also find the root' of the art of representation.[12] Indeed, these three – measure, number and weight – are traditional signs of divine knowledge. The passage quoted is taken directly from the biblical Book of Wisdom 11:21. In the tradition of Jewish and Christian reflection on numbers and measurement on which Dürer here draws, precision of knowledge is something that always lies beyond human grasp. It may be desired, sought and approached, but never absolutely attained.

Dürer's knowledge of the geometry and mathematics associated with measure, and his knowledge of instrument-making, also sat within a history of Nuremberg's emergence as a site of mathematical and astronomical knowledge production in the fifteenth century. A central figure in this story is Johannes Regiomontanus (1436–76).[13] Regiomontanus, perhaps the most important figure in fifteenth-century astronomy, was resident in Nuremberg from 1471–75. His collection of instruments and his library remained in the city in Dürer's lifetime (although some instruments were stolen in 1514), a resource drawn on by the network of artisans and humanists with whom Dürer was closely associated.[14]

Measuring the heavens

Astronomical and astrological time measurement is perhaps the first and most prominent of the measurement systems within which we can place Dürer's *Melencolia I*, with its obvious connections to the planet Saturn. By the early sixteenth century there was a long and venerable tradition of associating the planet Saturn with melancholy and its humour, black bile. The god Saturn was also the god of time, and he was associated, too, with other kinds of measurement, from the minting of accurate currency to the measure of weight.[15] According to the ancient Roman author Varro, scales hung in the ancient temple of Saturn.[16]

Astronomical measurement of the kind attentive to the movement and influence of planets such as Saturn was closely bound up with the production of scientific instruments such as the astrolabe, which allowed users to measure the zodiacal signs. Georg Hartmann (1489–1564) oversaw the production of engraved brass instruments, such as astrolabes (cat. 82), as well as engravings which could be turned into paper instruments.[17] Measurement with such instruments, whether of durable metal or paper, was also profoundly involved with practical questions of meteorological and medical prediction and treatment.[18] Such knowledge was materialised in the form of calendars and almanacs which formed part of Nuremberg's burgeoning early sixteenth-century print

7.2 (cat. 86) Albrecht Dürer, *The Celestial Map – Northern Hemisphere* (*Imagines coeli Septentrionales cum duodecim imaginibus zodiaci*), 1515, woodcut, paper: 455 x 430 mm, block: 430 x 430 mm.

culture. Surviving examples from the late fifteenth century printed in Nuremberg include single sheet almanacs with timetables for bloodletting and works known as *Bauernkalendar* ('Farmer's Calendars'), which co-ordinated the celestial time of the zodiac with ecclesiastical time reckoning.[19] Nuremberg printers also produced editions of best-selling works that related celestial and terrestrial time, including by the sometime Nuremberg resident Leonhard Reynmann.[20]

Among these was a 1515 calendar designed to calculate birth signs, significant for their effects on humoral temperaments.[21]

Writing in around 1508, Dürer emphasised the necessity of attention to this kind of astrological measurement in choosing an apprentice: 'First of all, you should consider in relation to the young person what sign they were born in, with various explanations. Pray God that it is a fortunate hour.'[22] Dürer brings the measure of time here into focus not as a neutral ground, but instead as something to be understood, interpreted and analysed for its effects upon character, profession and ultimately the course of a life itself. This kind of measure could also be deeply personal: Dürer's own genius could be understood as melancholic through humoral and astrological systems that measured the properties of the human body.[23]

An interest in astrological time measurement and the measurement and mapping of celestial space is evident in Dürer's 1515 woodcut of the northern heavens, with its depictions of the signs of the zodiac – the sign Capricorn particularly associated with Saturn (Figure 7.2).[24] In contrast to *Melencolia I*'s idle compass and blank sphere, we might notice the figure of Ptolemy in the woodcut's upper right corner, where the sphere of the heavens is mapped and measured using a compass. Nuremberg was a city famed for the production of celestial and terrestrial globes, objects of masterful measurement of heavenly bodies and of the earth's surface. Nicolas of Cusa had purchased a celestial globe in the city in the 1440s.[25] The famous terrestrial globe made in the early 1490s for the Nuremberg merchant Martin Behaim (1459–1506/7) survives. It is an object which combined the work of artisans across trades, including printers.[26] Dürer's solitary figure, trapped in melancholic reflection and accompanied by a blank globe and idle compass, stands in contrast to the city's productive community of artisans and intellectuals who united to produce these objects.

The sundial

If a saturnine light spreads out over the image from its source in *Melencolia I*'s upper left, another form

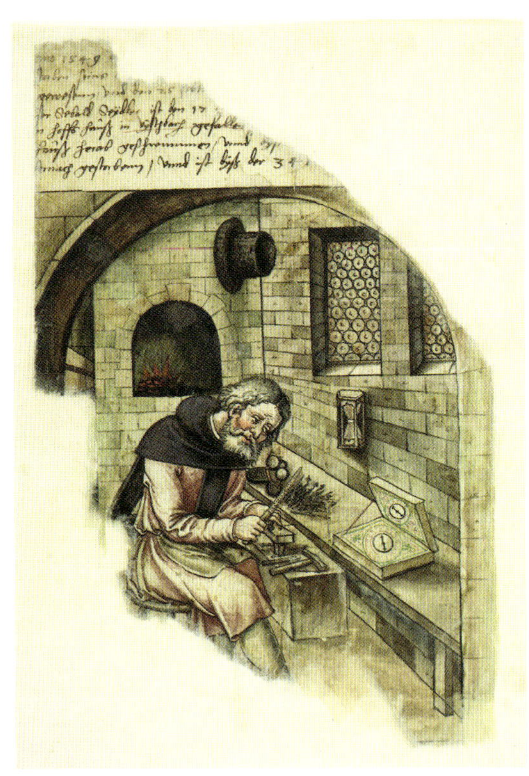

7.3 Sebald Spydler, *Kompassmacher*, c. 1550, 230 x 195 mm.

Hausbuch der Mendelschen Zwölfbrüderstiftung. MS Nuremberg, Stadtbibliothek Nürnberg, Amb. 317b.2° (Mendel II), fol. 1v. © Stadtbibliothek Nürnberg.

of time measurement by the movement of celestial bodies is distinguished by absence. Above the large sandglass which hangs over the seated figure's head is a small sundial. Sundials were part of a plethora of time-keeping devices which enabled cultures of attention to time to proliferate in the fifteenth and early sixteenth centuries.[27] Nuremberg was a centre for the production and manufacture of sundials. Large public sundials adorned buildings, allowing both for co-ordination of time and for the symbolic representation of the city's good order in time. Johannes Stabius (d. 1522), Dürer's collaborator on the celestial projection of 1515 (see Figure 7.2), had designed a large sundial for the Church of Saint Lawrence (*Lorenzkirche*) in 1502.[28] The production of personal ivory, wooden and printed paper sundials began to blossom in the late fifteenth and early sixteenth century, although peak production occurred only later in the sixteenth century (cat. 83, 84).[29]

Manufacture of these objects involved large-scale trade networks across Africa and Europe for the supply of ivory, alongside the close filing of metal, and geometrical and astronomical precision: a focused attention to the deployment of space in the fixing of time.[30] The intense focus required in manufacturing these miniaturised measuring objects can be sensed in a later sixteenth-century image taken from the book of Nuremburg's *Zwölfbruderstiftung*, showing a compass-maker, the trade responsible for the manufacture of sundials (Figure 7.3).[31]

Dürer himself dwelt on the geometry and technique of sundial-making in some detail in his *Underweysung der Messung*. Again, it was the compass, that object that swings idly in the engraving *Melencolia I*, that was used to fix, divide and quantify the correct form of the instrument, tracing out its carefully measured arcs of space and time.[32]

Normally a sundial would be used to measure the hours by shadows, and to synchronise other devices such as a large bell, or sandglass or a weight-driven wall clock of the kind that was becoming normal in the homes of wealthy urban families in the period.[33] In *Melencolia I*, though, the instrument can perform no such task for either sandglass or bell. The sundial now stands useless in the gloomy half-light of the image, offering no fixed point of reference in the state of nocturnal trance. Its lack of measure is remarkably emphasised, as Hartmut Böhme has noted, by the shadow cast by the large hanging sandglass: no such shadow marks the hours on the sundial, rendering time's measure unknown.[34]

The sandglass

The most prominent and obvious measurement instrument in the engraving is the large and elaborately worked sandglass – in German *Sanduhr* ('sand clock') – which hangs above Melencolia's head. The sand clock is an object that appears repeatedly in Dürer's oeuvre. Most often it comes as a sign of

death and the transitory vanity of human life, and it frequently comes topped with a moveable clock dial for recording the passing of the hours.[35] As an example here, we might take the menacing *Death and the Lansquenet* of 1510.[36] The sandglass, or sand clock, becomes an object-in-focus in the three *Meisterstiche* of 1513–14, where its appearance forms part of a well-ordered and regulated humanist study in *Saint Jerome in his Study*, and as a marker of the threat of unseen, yet immanent, death in *The Knight, Death, and the Devil*, (cat. 73 and cat. 75).[37]

The sandglass of *Melencolia I* is without doubt Dürer's most overworked and detailed engagement with the sandglass as a form.[38] It stands in marked contrast to the smaller and simpler sandglasses in images such as Dürer's earlier *Saint Jerome in his Cell* of 1511 (cat. 72; see Figure 8.7).[39] The 1511 Jerome sand clock conforms to surviving representations and examples of early sandglasses with provenances associated with Nuremberg crafts (Figure 7.3).[40] These objects seem to point toward a well-ordered relationship to time: to productive, focused and carefully timed work. These smaller objects measure shorter lengths of time. As opposed to obsessive stasis, they require turning at regular intervals to maintain their measured precision.

The sand clock of *Melencolia I* is an entirely different order of object. Its size implies a longer duration, most likely a full hour. Its decoration is elaborate and fantastic. Are there any surviving objects that might help us further reflect on its form? As a point of comparison, we might consider a surviving sandglass made in 1506 and now in the collections of the Germanisches Nationalmuseum in Nuremberg (Figure 7.4).[41] This sandglass is an intimate devotional object, with beautiful intricate silverwork casing of Gothic tracery. Reminiscent of a small reliquary, at each end of the object is a devotional image – the sacred heart of Jesus emblazoned with the holy name of Jesus in the centre of a cross, and on the reverse a clock dial with a hand pointing almost to the apocalyptic hour of midnight.[42]

This object suggests a devout attention to time, the kind of measured piety associated with the clock that had burgeoned across Europe in the wake of the famous fourteenth-century *Horologium divine*

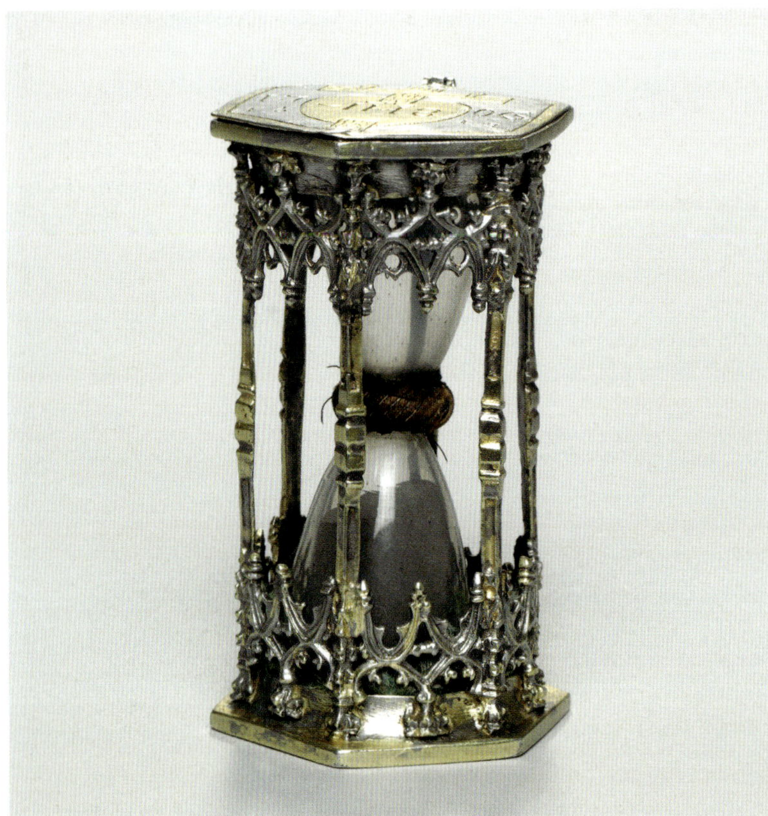

7.4 *Sanduhr (Sand clock)*, Nuremberg (?), 1506, silver and gilded-silver, glass, wax and silk thread, lead sand (?), 87 x 50 mm.

Nuremberg, Germanisches Nationalmuseum, inv. no. WI 1955. © Germanisches Nationalmuseum, Nuremberg.

> 7.5 Anonymous Master, *Tucheraltar*, c. 1445–50, oil and tempera on wood. Frauenkirche, Nuremberg, originally for the Church of Augustinian house of Saint Vitus (Augustinerklosterkirche Sankt Veit).

© Theo Noll / www.nuernberg. museum.

sapiencie (The Clock of Divine Wisdom) by Henry de Suso (c. 1295–1366).[43] It found expression in a later anonymous work, the *Horologium devotionis* by a brother Bertholdus, that was printed three times in Nuremberg prior to 1500, first in Latin and then later in the German edition known as the *Zeitglöcklein des Lebens und Leidens Christi* (The Little Clock – literally: little time bell – of the Life and Suffering of Christ). The combination of time measurement and devotion would find startling expression a little later in the century in crucifix sundials made by Georg Hartmann, where time was measured by the cross, and attention to time called attention to God's action in the world (cat. 83).[44] Texts and objects such as these were designed to make the knowledge and contemplation of time a trigger for mystical and contemplative ascent into a quasi-eternal knowledge of the order of salvation. Taking time's measure might mean getting its measure, in the sense of a

mastery of time that moves beyond the weariness of temporal existence.[45]

It is in this light that we can also compare the sand clock of *Melencolia I* with perhaps its closest Nuremberg parallel, a sandglass depicted on the mid fifteenth-century Tucher Altarpiece (*Tucheraltar*) painted for the city's Augustinian house around 1445–50 (Figure 7.5).[46] On one of the altarpiece's outer panels, Saint Augustine's eyes rise above the clutter of worldly knowledge on his shelves to a vision of the Trinity. A trio of objects suggest how Augustine's vision moves beyond temporal, worldly sensory perception: spectacles and a small convex mirror, associated with physical vision and incapacity to see clearly, and an arched sandglass that suggests how the vision has moved beyond the realm of time.[47]

In comparison to the *Tucheraltar* and the miniature 1506 sandglass, then, and seen alongside the piety

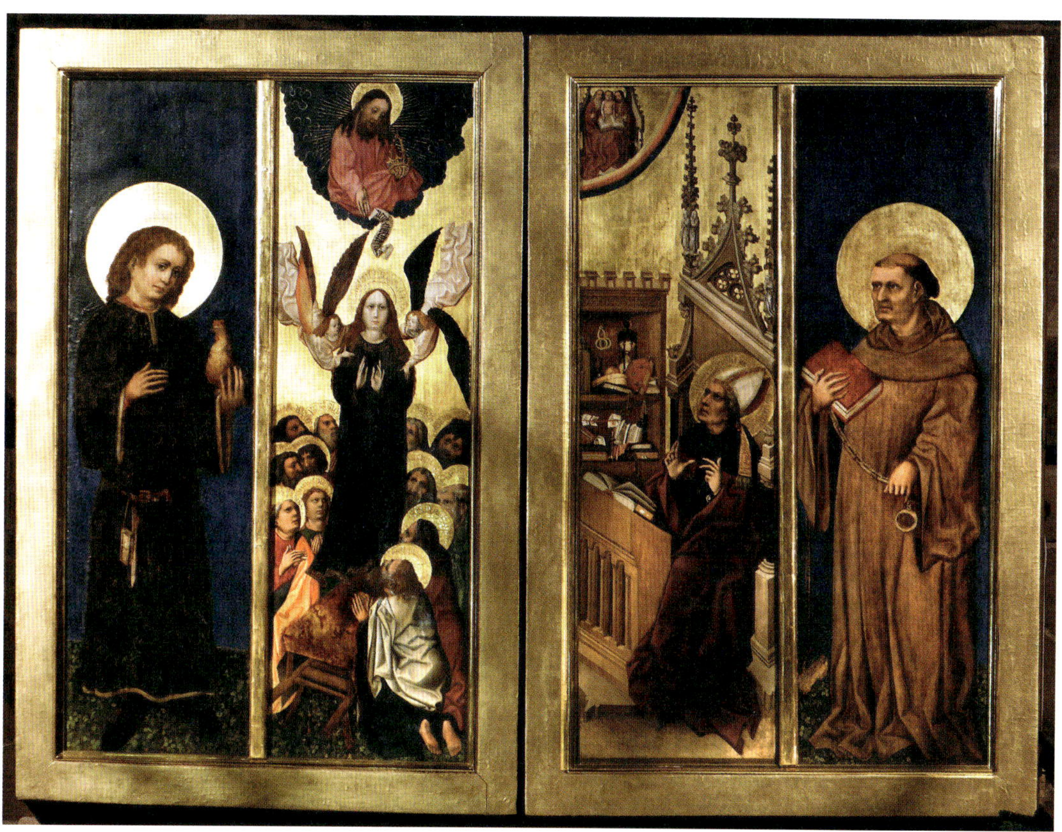

attached to the measure of the hours in the period, the sandglass of *Melencolia I* can be seen to take on a different set of qualities. It suggests time frozen as a never-ending, and ultimately overwhelming, stream.[48] Measure pitches over into a sense of being lost in time. There is no vision of eternity here. Time's weight hangs heavy over the seated figure.

Viewed this way, we might place *Melencolia I* in the wider context of a proliferation of time measurement in the period – including the manufacture of domestic wall clocks, watches and table clocks (cat. 85), an emerging Nuremberg industry which would flourish in the sixteenth century.[49] With its celestial bodies, sundial and sand clock, *Melencolia I* is further evidence of the plurality of times in sixteenth-century Europe, a plurality repeatedly emphasised in recent scholarship on the history of temporalities.[50] Both earlier and later images of contemplation and scholarship stressed

the power of the diversity and complexity of time measurement to overwhelm, potentially trapping the intellect in a web of worldly time.[51] In Dürer's engraving, too, times multiply, adding to the sense of the weight on the seated figure's shoulders.

The measure of time's weight might draw us to consider further another kind of material measure present in the sandglass: the sand itself. Surviving recipes show how sandglass sand required careful attention to materials, their weight and measure, to flow with ease.[52] Lead was often used for this task. Indeed, this seems to be the material present in the 1506 sandglass.[53] This dry element was associated with the influence of the melancholic planet Saturn. We are brought back to a knowledge of materials, their properties and significance, and the measure of celestial time.

The bell

Two other weighty objects hang behind the seated melancholic: the bell and the scales. The bell draws us again into the realm of time measurement and well-measured civic life. From the summit of Nuremberg's two most imposing churches, the Church of Saint Sebald (the *Sebalduskirche*), near to Dürer's house, and the Church of Saint Lawrence (the *Lorenzkirche*) across the River Pegnitz, bells rang out the hours.[54] And not only from these two most imposing of the city's ecclesiastical monuments. A further two towers were crucial to the city's time measurement: the *Weißerturm* and the *Laufer Schlagturm*.[55] Beyond these four towers, other bells sounded in the heart of the city from a plethora of towers and institutions. Among these was the Church of Our Lady (the *Frauenkirche*), built on the site of the old synagogue, which was destroyed in the fourteenth century. The *Frauenkirche* was the site of a major new monument to the city's imperial status: from 1506–9, a new automatic clock, known as the *Männleinlaufer*, included bells which chimed the hours over the city's marketplace while automated figures of the imperial electors moved in front of a figure of the Holy Roman Emperor. As Heidi Eberhardt Bate and others have pointed out, good measurement was about good government.[56]

These elevated sites which proclaimed the measured life of the city recall the elevated setting of *Melencolia I*. Is this a scene placed on city walls or a tower, the common location for bells or trumpeters who marked the changing hours of urban time? If we follow this possibility for a moment (and it is just a possibility) we might see the conjunction of sand clock and bell as evoking the long night-watches of the *Turmwächter* (tower watchmen), those who watched the sandglasses in towers to make sure the ringing of the hour bells was measured correctly.[57] But there is no correct measure here, despite the proliferation of time measurement devices. Each of these devices requires active attention and physical engagement: someone to turn the sandglass, someone to ring the bell. Instead, *Melencolia I*'s bellpull extends beyond the image into nowhere. This is a silent reverie unbroken by the well-ordered march of time's measure; time is not passing; the sandglass of the *Turmwächter* will not run out; the bell will not sound. The night of melancholy is a time without measure.

In another sense, though, the bell is a further sign of the most ultimate measure of human life – death. Like the sandglass, where time ultimately runs out, the bell's silence is also the threat of a sound, the death-knell at the end of a fruitless life spent in unproductive, melancholic abstraction.

The scales

The proximity of an ending is also evoked in the last measurement device analysed in this chapter: the scales. Like the other measurement instruments analysed here, scales could be encountered in a variety of settings in fifteenth- and sixteenth-century Nuremberg. The most prominent and public of these scales was the *Stadtwaage* (city weighing station), the site of Nuremberg's public enforcement of standards of weight. A surviving 1497 relief by the famed Nuremberg sculptor Adam Kraft (c. 1455/60–1509) shows the large scales in use, an emblem of the city's prosperity.[58] Scales also appeared in the workshops of the various crafts and played a critical role in the trade of materials reaching from basic goods to precious stones.[59] Here they could become objects of prestige and display. Perhaps the most famous of all surviving scales from the period was made in 1497 for the Nuremberg minter Hans Harsdorfer (d. 1511) (Figure 7.6).[60]

A sense of the importance of scales in the symbolic and practical life of the city can be gained from Dürer's 1521 woodcut frontispiece for the *Reformacion der Stat Nüremberg* (*Reformation of the City of Nuremberg*, 1522).[61] Here the coats of arms of the Empire and Nuremberg are presented, watched over by two winged figures, one of whom carries scales and sword, an emblem of *sancta iusticia* (holy justice). Indeed, scales appear a number of times across Dürer's oeuvre. Their most usual association is with just judgement. In his *Sol justiciae* (Sun of Righteousness) c. 1499, the seated judge turns to look at a pair of carefully balanced

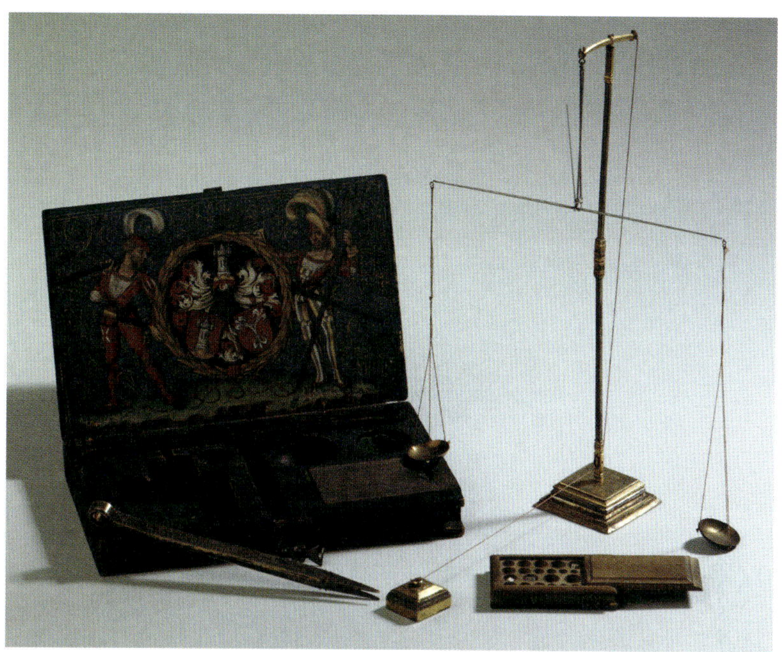

scales.[62] But scales also evoke the coming of the Last Judgement, of course in the figure of the divine judge, and in Dürer's famous *Apocalypse* series of 1497–98, where one of the four horsemen carries scales which fly behind him in a sign of measure out of kilter (cat. 40).[63]

Like the compass, sundial, sandglass and bell, the scales of Nuremberg required close attention and bodily engagement. Each relied on the power of careful observation and the manipulation of human hands to render them active and useful. This point applies both to their practical use and the practice of their representation: in the Harsdorfer scales, for example, a square weight at the base of the stand was moved to alter the height of the cross beam as required; and equally in Dürer's drawing of scales related to *Melencolia I* we can capture something of the intimate embodied engagement of the artist with the object.[64] Measure in this world depended on the close sensory attention and engagement of the viewer and toucher of the object.[65] In contrast to this active world of exchange, measure and embodied knowledge, *Melencolia I*'s scales hang empty, measuring nothing.

Or do they? When we observe the engraving now, these objects do in fact become active partners in a task of engaged interpretation and imagination. In the words of Shira Brisman, this is an image that wants to be read.[66] *Melencolia I*'s scales, as with the other objects analysed in this essay, can be held in the mind's eye, evoking just measure and the prosperous good order of the city, celestial time, divine oversight and judgement, and even the time of death, judgement and apocalypse: they are objects for work, literally and semantically. Even as *Melencolia I*'s instruments seem idle, the networks of objects and images summoned up by their presence stretches out across time to make the image again present to us, to produce a reflection on the role of measurement and its materialisation in the creation of melancholic reflection itself.

Notes

1   Benjamin, *Gesammelte Schriften* III, 367. Translation from Wood, ed., *The Vienna School Reader*, 444. The reference is to Giehlow, 'Dürers Stich, "Melencolia I"'. Translations in this essay are my own, unless noted otherwise.

2   For a study of the general culture of measure in the period, see Bate, 'The Measures of Men'. Nuremberg's measured world mirrored wider cultures and practices of measure across Europe's urban centres in the period, while also developing its own distinctive features.

3   See, for example, Maué, Eser, Hauschke and Stolzenberger, *Quasi Centrum Europae*.

4   See, for example, Westermann, 'Das "Journal" der Nürnberger Handelsgesellschaft Hans Walther'.

5   For Dürer and engagement with measure and holy, imperial objects in Nuremberg, see Wood, *Forgery, Replica, Fiction*, 151–4. Also Kiening, 'Mediating the Passion'.

6   On the polyhedron, see recently Bubenik, 'The Shape of Things to Come'.

7   On the burin, see Klibanksy, Panowsky and Saxl, *Saturn and Melancholy*, 343–4. Also Koerner, *Moment of Self-Portraiture, 27.*

8   As has been observed more than once, the scholarship on *Melencolia I* is enough to induce melancholy. For three important gateways into the wider scholarship: Klibanksy, Panowsky and Saxl, *Saturn and Melancholy*; Böhme, *Albrecht Dürer, Melencolia I*; and Merback, *Perfection's Therapy*. See also the literature cited in Schoch, Mende and Scherbaum, *Albrecht Dürer*, I, 179–85, no. 71. On *Saint Jerome in His Study* see also Dagmar Eichberger's 'The material and the immaterial' in this volume.

9   In developing this case, this chapter follows numerous interpreters on the image. See, for example, Böhme, *Albrecht Dürer, Melencolia I*, or Koerner's pithy articulation in *The Moment of Self-Portraiture*, 23.

10   Albrecht Dürer, *Underweysung der messung mit dem zirckel un richt scheyt* (Nuremberg: Hieronymus Andreae, 1525). For an English translation, see Strauss, ed., *The Painter's Manual*. On the *Underweysung*, see Andrews, 'Albrecht Dürer's Personal *Underweysung*'.

11   See further Schröder, *Dürer, Kunst und Geometrie*.

12   Ashcroft, *Albrecht Dürer*, I, 340 (73.1); Rupprich, ed., *Dürer: Schriftlicher Nachlass*, II, 104.

13   Zinner, *Regiomontanus*, 103–49 on his time in Nuremberg.

14   On the afterlife of Regiomontanus's library and instruments, see Zinner, *Regiomontanus*, 157–60. See also Andrews, 'Albrecht Dürer's Personal *Underweysung*', 410–11; Petz, 'Urkundliche Nachrichten'.

15   See Klibanksy, Panowsky and Saxl, *Saturn and Melancholy*, 135.

16   Varro, *De lingua latina*, V.183. See also Klibanksy, Panowsky and Saxl, *Saturn and Melancholy*, 333.

17   Schmidt, 'Making Time and Space'.

18   On the longer history of medicine in Nuremberg, see Murphy, *New Order of Medicine*.

19   See, for example, the *Bauernkalendar* printed in Nuremberg by Georg Glockendon the Elder in 1493 (Nuremberg, Germanisches Nationalmuseum, Graphische Sammlung, inv. HB 14913). For a brief discussion, see also Kress, *Divine Diagrams*, 215, 517. For one such almanac printed in Nuremberg by Peter Wagner in c. 1486, see San Marino, CA, Huntingdon Library, 89402, available at https://hdl.huntington.org/digital/collection/p16003coll14/id/277 [accessed 19 February 2023].

20   On this production, see Johnston, 'Printing the Weather'.

21   See Smith, *Nuremberg*, 164.

22   Ashcroft, *Albrecht Dürer*, I, 246 (51.3.2); Rüpprich, ed., *Dürer: Schriftlicher Nachlass*, II, 92.

23   On Dürer as melancholic, see the discussion and further literature in Merback, *Pefection's Therapy*, 190, 306. n. 30.

24   On this point, see Zika, 'Dürer's Witch, Riding Women and Moral Order', 126; and Schoch, Mende and Scherbaum, *Albrecht Dürer*, II, 430–5, no. 243; H. 260.

25   For Cusa's globe, see Hauschke, 'Globen und Wissenschaftliche Instrumente', 365, 386.

26   Nuremberg, Germanisches Nationalmuseum, inv. no. WI 1826. See Bott, ed., *Focus Behaim-Globus*.

27   On this question, see Hanß, 'Fetish of Accuracy'.

28   Dürer, *The Painter's Manual*, 21, citing Johann Gabriel Doppelmayer, *Historische Nachricht von der Nürnbergischen Mathematicis und Künstlern* (Nuremberg: Peter Conrad Monath, 1730), 32, 46. See also the publications of Johann Schöner, who published on cylindrical portable sundials in 1515.

29   On the early history, see Gouk, *Ivory Sundials of Nuremberg*, 28–9. For a sample of early objects, see the *Klappsonnenuhren* in Nuremberg, Germanisches Nationalmuseum, inv. no. W 128 (wood, 1511); inv. no. HB 13104 (paper, 1501/1515); inv. no. WI 355 (ivory, late fifteenth century); inv. no W 17 (metal, and attributed to Regiomontanus, 1464/7); London, The British Museum, 1877,0521.23 (cat. 84). On Dürer and the printing of instruments, see Marr, 'Ingenuity in Nuremberg'; Schmidt, *Interactive and Sculptural Printmaking*, chapter 8. Sundials could also be made in more simple ways, for example by holding a straw in one's hand. See Johnston, 'Printing the Weather', 428–31.

30   See Gouk, *Ivory Sundials of Nuremberg*, 32–5.

31   For Nuremberg's known compass makers, see Gouk, *Ivory Sundials of Nuremberg*, 64.

32   Dürer, *The Painter's Manual*, 246–57. For further reflections on the compass and its role in constructing *Melencolia I*'s polyhedron and rainbow, see Sohm, 'Dürer's "Melencolia I"', 17–21.

33   I have not, as yet, found any clear examples of sandglasses topped with sundials prior to Dürer's *Melencolia I*. Later images, however, combine *Melencolia I*'s sundial–hourglass pair with Dürer's *Nemesis* (c. 1501, cat. 34) to make a hand-held sundial–sandglass pair. See Maué, Eser, Hauschke and Stolzenberger, *Quasi Centrum Europae*, 414–15. For a possible exception, see Nikolaus Manuel Deutsch's pen and ink drawing of a witch with skull and sandglass, c. 1513, in the Kupferstichkabinett of the Kunstmuseum in Basel, which may be topped by a sundial, although a clock dial or mirror are also possibilities. On this image, see Zika, *Appearance of Witchcraft*, 111–12.

34   Böhme, *Albrecht Dürer, Melencolia I*, 27.

35 Clock dials on hourglasses are also featured in a number of Northern panel paintings. See, for example, the sandglass in the panel of Saint John from Gabriel Mäleßkircher's 1478 Tegernsee altarpiece (now Museo Nacional Thyssen-Bornemisza, Madrid, inv. no. 235 (1928.17)) and in the Annunciation from Sebastian Taig's *Karmelitenretable* of 1518 in the Stadtmuseum Nördlingen.

36 Schoch, Mende and Scherbaum, *Albrecht Dürer*, II, 149; H. 239. Further examples include Albrecht Dürer, *A Couple and Death*, engraving, c. 1498, see ibid., I, 68–70; H.195; Albrecht Dürer, *Death and a Noble*, *The Prayer Book of Maximilian I*, fol. 12r, see Strauss, *Complete Drawings*, 1515/7. For images less securely attributed to Dürer: *Death and the Lady* c. 1510–12, Rotterdam Museum Boijmans van Beuningen, see ibid., 1510/28; *Merry Company and Death*, Dresden Kupferstichkabinett c. 1500, see ibid., XW.215.

37 The presence of sandglasses across these three images is often observed, but rarely analysed. See, for example, Stumpel, 'Dürer and Death', 81.

38 On sandglasses more generally, see Dohrn-van Rossum, *History of the Hour*, 117–18, 380. I am currently writing a longer study of the sandglass and its history.

39 Schoch, Mende and Scherbaum, *Albrecht Dürer*, II, 360–2, no. 360, H. 228. See also Dagmar Eichberger's 'The material and the immaterial' in this volume.

40 See, for example, two sandglasses in the Germanisches Nationalmuseum, Nuremberg: inv. no. Z1314 (sixteenth/seventeenth century? Nuremberg?) and inv. no. Z573 (fifteenth/sixteenth century?, Nuremberg?). On these objects, see Hasselmeyer, 'Sanduhren aus Nürnberg'; Schindler, Keller, and Schürer, eds, *Zünftig!*, 168–9, 180; Thomas Schindler, 'Tempus Fugit'.

41 Nuremberg, Germanisches Nationalmuseum, inv. no. WI 1955. For brief descriptions of the object, see Eser, *Die älteste Taschenuhr*, 184–5. I have been unable to time this object as yet. It is smaller than the other glasses in the GNM that run for around 15 minutes. For another short-running *Sanduhr*, see the glass attached to the leg of Matthäus Schwarz in his *Trachtenbuch* (Herzog Anton Ulrich Museum, Braunschweig) and which is described as running for eight minutes. See Rublack and Hayward, eds, *The First Book of Fashion*, 281–2.

42 On this iconography, see Champion, 'Pointing to a Deeper Now'.

43 On the dissemination of this important work, see Künzle, *Heinrich Seuses Horologium Sapientiae*.

44 See also GNM WI 133; Maué, Eser, Hauschke and Stolzenberger, *Quasi Centrum Europae*, 367–71.

45 For further discussion, see Champion, *The Fullness of Time*; Champion, 'To See Above the Moment is Delightful'.

46 On the altar, see Strieder, *Tafelmalerei in Nürnberg*, 37–40.

47 On early mirror production, see Büchert, 'Die mechanische Herstellung von Glasspiegeln', 51–2.

48 Compare Barikin, 'After the End', 111.

49 See Eser, *Die älteste Taschenuhr*.

50 See, for example, Hanß, 'Fetish of Accuracy'. Also Champion, *The Fullness of Time*.

51 For images that chronologically bracket *Melencolia I* in this regard, see MS Brussels, KBR IV 111, fol. 13v (mid-fifteenth-century French translation of the *Horologium* of Henry Suso, with Suso seated in contemplation, surrounded by a plethora of time keeping devices) and Francesco Petrarch, *Von der Artzney bayder Glueck* (Ausgburg: Heinrich Steiner, 1532), book 2, chapter 15 (woodcut by the Petrarch Master, showing a seated figure wrapped in contemplation with a sandglass, domestic clock and large clock dial). I am currently preparing a study of this image and its dissemination. On Suso and melancholy, see recently Thompson, 'The Solar History of Acedia'.

52 See, for example, Pope, 'Powder for Hourglasses'; Coole, Drover, Sabine and Tyler, 'Sand-Glass "Sand"'.

53 For other surviving sixteenth-century glasses probably filled with lead, see Basel, Historisches Museum, inv. no. 1877.35.1.–2 and Basel, Historisches Museum, inv. no. 1982.1139.

54 On the ringing of the hours at the church of Saint Sebald, see Mummenhoff, 'Die Anbringung des Viertelschlagwerks'.

55 See the view of Nuremberg on the frontispiece of Konrad Celtis's *Norimberga* of 1502. See also the discussion in Eser, *Die älteste Taschenuhr der Welt?*, 17, 175.

56 Bate, 'The Measures of Men'. See also Rooney, *About Time*, 53–64.

57 For a seventeenth-century device from the Thomaskirche in Leipzig used for this purpose, see Basel, Historisches Museum, inv. no. 1880.190.

58 Adam Kraft, *Stadtwaage*, 1497 (Nuremberg, Germanisches Nationalmuseum, inv. no. Pl.O.2849). See also Bate, 'The Measures of Men', 155. For further literature, see https://objektkatalog.gnm.de/wisski/navigate/55560/view [accessed 24 March 2022].

59 On the gem trade, see Siebenhüner, *Die Spur der Juwelen*.

60 See Kahsnitz and Wixom, eds, *Gothic and Renaissance Art*, 218–19.

61 Schoch, Mende and Scherbaum, *Albrecht Dürer*, III, 165–7, no. 273; H. 285. See Smith, *Nuremberg, A Renaissance City*, 114; Bartrum, *Dürer and his Legacy* 213–14, no. 161.

62 See Schoch, Mende and Scherbaum, *Albrecht Dürer*, I, 79–80. See also the drawing of Justice in Strauss, *Complete Drawings* 1495/56.

63 See further Leahy, Spinks and Zika, *The Four Horsemen*. Also Sohm, 'Dürer's "Melencolia I"', 22

64 See Strauss, *Complete Drawings* 1495/56.

65 See, more generally, Smith, *The Body of the Artisan*.

66 Brisman, 'The Image that Wants to be Read'. See also Brisman, *Albrecht Dürer*, 122.

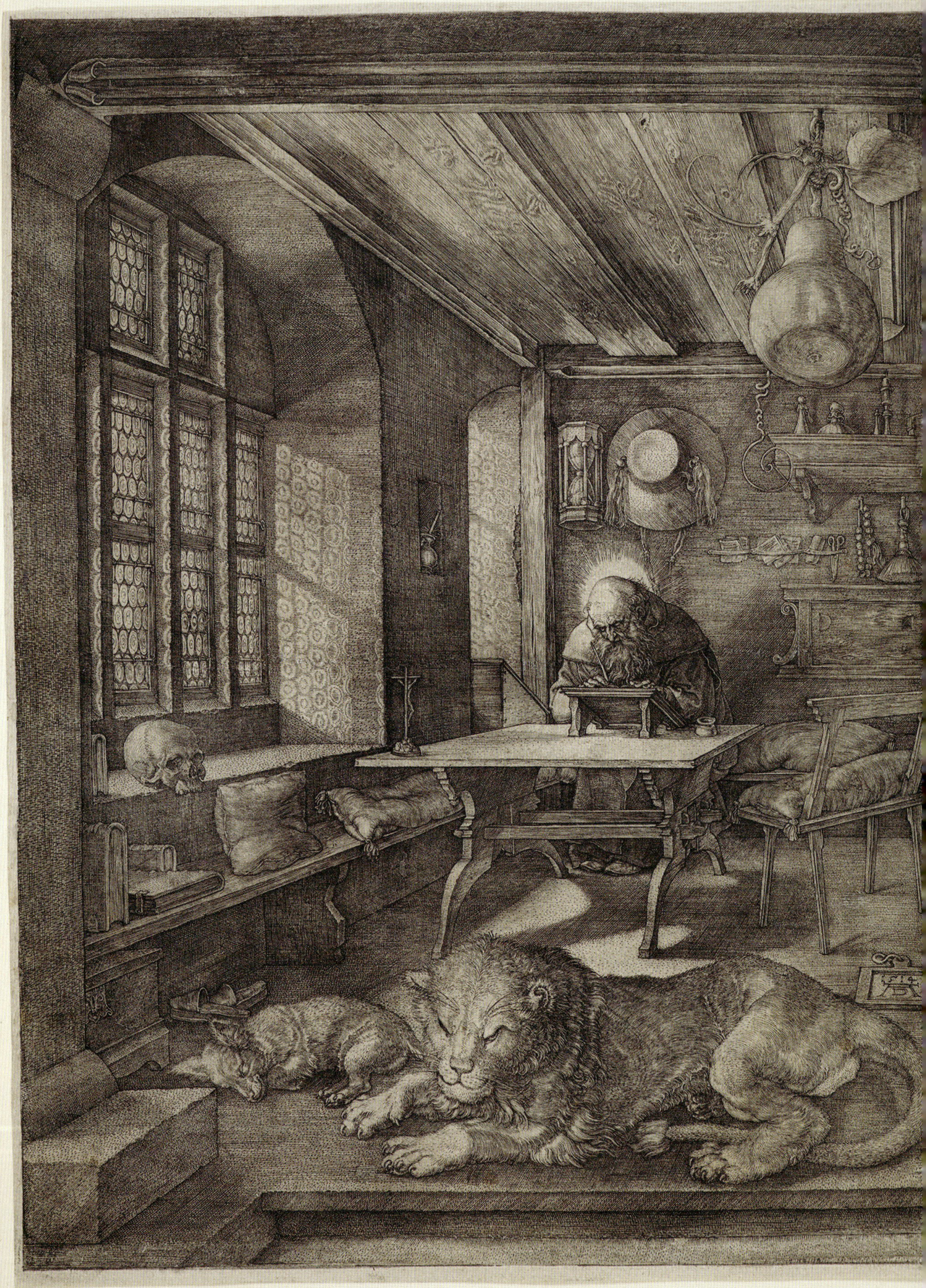

[8] The material and the immaterial: *Saint Jerome in his Study*

Dagmar Eichberger

Saint Jerome (354–430) was one of the most popular saints of late medieval and Renaissance Europe. In Italy, Germany, Spain and the Netherlands he was depicted on the walls of frescoed churches, on panel paintings, in illuminated manuscripts and in prints.[1] Jerome was venerated as a model of spirituality and erudition by members of the Catholic and, after the Reformation of 1517, of the Protestant church (Figure 8.1). He is best known for his translation of the bible from Greek, Hebrew and Aramaic sources into Latin. The so-called *Vulgate* remained the standard Latin bible translation well into the nineteenth century.[2]

In 1295, Jerome was given the epithet 'Doctor of the Church' and according to the *Golden Legend* written by Jacobus de Voragine (1228–98), he was ordained as cardinal. In 1483, the Latin *Vulgate* was translated into English and published by William Caxton (c. 1415/24–c. 1491/92).[3] Many popular texts embellished the biography of Jerome by adding entertaining anecdotes such as story of the lion Jerome tamed by removing a thorn from its paw, or the episode in which he accidentally put on a woman's dress and got into trouble.[4] His popularity increased even further when Erasmus of Rotterdam (c. 1466–1536) composed a biography of the saint.[5] Soon after, Martin Luther (1483–1546) wrote annotations to several texts by Saint Jerome.[6] In the second decade of the sixteenth century, the theologian Johannes von Staupitz (1460–1524) was largely responsible for the rise of a cult of Saint Jerome among Nuremberg humanists.[7] At that time the Nuremberg city scribe Lazarus Spengler (1479–1534)

translated the Latin text 'De morte Hieronymi', that was attributed to Eusebius of Cremona into German.[8] Dürer, who was part of Staupitz's circle, designed the woodcut *Saint Jerome Writing in a Cave* (1512), reproduced on the verso of Spengler's title page in 1514.[9]

It is well known that Jerome had a complex personality, being both sensitive and fiery, sometimes even belligerent and pugnacious. In a recent biography by the theologian Alfons Fürst, the church father is described as 'a choleric with features of a misanthrope, a militant propagandist for the ascetic ideal, a versatile and productive author, a diligent translator and an original scientist'.[10] Many of these qualities featured in depictions of the saint in late medieval and Renaissance Europe. There are two types of images, and these relate to different phases of the saint's life. Jerome could either be portrayed as a scantily clad hermit, performing acts of penitence in the wilderness,[11] or as a scholar in his study sometimes wearing his cardinal's cloak. Less frequently, the saint was shown in the process of removing the thorn from the lion's paw.[12] Occasionally, the different iconographic strands were blended, as in Albrecht Dürer's above-mentioned 1512 woodcut depicting Jerome as an author in a cave.[13]

During his life, Dürer produced at least ten images of Saint Jerome: two oil paintings,[14] three woodcuts,[15] three drawings,[16] one dry point[17] and two engravings, including *Saint Jerome Penitent in the Wilderness* of 1496 (cat. 71; compare Figure 2.3), and *Saint Jerome in his Study* (Figure 8.1; cat. 73), the subject of this essay.[18] In the beginning, Dürer produced images of the penitent Jerome; later, he was seemingly more interested in the saint's intellectual activities. The engraving examined here, dating from 1514, belongs to the latter category, and for that reason this study concentrates on the image of the scholar in his

8.1 (cat. 73) Albrecht Dürer, *Saint Jerome in his Study (Meisterstiche)*, 1514, engraving, 243 x 186 mm.

The Whitworth, The University of Manchester, P.3015. Presented by George Thomas Clough in 1921. © The Whitworth, University of Manchester. Photo: Michael Pollard.

study. The haptic qualities of the room as well as the abundance of material objects placed on the table, benches and wooden shelves in the large-format print captivates the viewer. Books, letters, writing utensils, candlesticks and household items as well as liturgical objects fill the space and create a homely atmosphere.

Albrecht Dürer, *Saint Jerome in his Study*, 1514

Dürer's *Saint Jerome in his Study* belongs, along with *Nemesis* (cat. 34), *Saint Eustace* (cat. 104), *Knight, Death and Devil* (cat. 75) and *Melencolia I* (cat. 79), to his so-called large engravings.[19] These prints can be considered autonomous works of art comparable to small panel paintings.[20] In a journal made of his trip to the Netherlands, Dürer noted down all the prints he sold or gave away as gifts. In it, he makes a clear distinction between three different sizes of paper: whole-sheet, half-sheet and quarter-sheet prints.[21] As Robert Griggs has argued convincingly, Dürer took with him more than one type of Saint Jerome. The different expressions used in his diary therefore leave room for interpretation: 'Jerome in his cabinet' (four references), 'Jerome' (one reference), 'Jerome sitting' (three references), 'engraved Jerome' (five references), 'a Jerome sitting, engraved in copper' (one reference). Unless we assume that Dürer took the early engraving of *Saint Jerome Penitent in the Wilderness* with him, we can deduce that he gave away his 1514 print at least ten times. As Griggs points out, Saint Jerome prints by far outnumber all other images. In comparison to fourteen prints of Saint Jerome, he gave away only seven prints of *Melencolia I* and five engravings of *Saint Eustace*.[22] Thus it can be assumed that the subject of Saint Jerome was as popular in the Netherlands as it was in Germany.[23]

What made Dürer's engraving of *Saint Jerome in his Study* so special? Even the Italian theoretician Giorgio Vasari (1511–74) – who is known to have been critical of German art generally – described it as an unsurpassed 'marvel' (*meraviglia*).[24] Albrecht Dürer was famously described by Conrad Celtis (1459–1508) and his contemporaries as a 'second' or a 'modern Apelles'.[25] Erasmus of Rotterdam emphasised Dürer's ability to express every detail of the visible world in a monochrome medium, that is in black-and-white. Paraphrasing Erasmus, Erwin Panofsky later called Albrecht Dürer 'the Apelles of the black line'.[26]

When looking at the print itself, the qualities that impressed these authors are clear. Dürer convincingly captures the effects of daylight as it falls through bullseye panes of glass and leaves a geometric pattern on the thick stone walls. A clear distinction is made between this soft natural light and the rays of bright light that emanate from the head of the saint. The fur of both dog and lion are reproduced in a highly illusionistic manner. We can identify the various surfaces that define the differing materials: soft cushions, textile slippers, wooden furniture, leather-bound books and a gourd hanging from the beam that frames the scene. Jerome's cardinal's hat hangs on the wall, and a skull is placed on the windowsill.

Equally impressive is the spatial definition of the large room in which Jerome sits. It is not a confined cabinet as is known from other representations of Jerome in his study, but a proper living room as might have existed in Dürer's own time.[27] The heavy beams, the wooden panelling, the deep window recess, the benches and chests are typical of a comfortable patrician home of the period.[28] By choosing an oblique angle, Dürer makes the room appear deep. Jerome is not sitting in the central axis but has been moved slightly to the right. The drastic foreshortening is achieved by using the method of central perspective. The saint sits at the back of the room and takes up only a small proportion of the entire space. He is separated from the viewer by a large wooden table and by two animals that are lying at the step leading into the room. While the dog is sleeping, the lion – one of Jerome's foremost attributes – is half awake, his eyes almost closed. The unusual layout prompted Matthias Mende to describe the room as almost claustrophobic.[29]

What are the many objects that have been portrayed in this image and what do they stand for? The symbols most frequently associated with Jerome are the skull, the crucifix and the hour-glass, all of which allude to his meditations. His spirituality and devotion are further underlined by the rosary beads attached to the wall. Equally prominent is his attire as a cardinal:

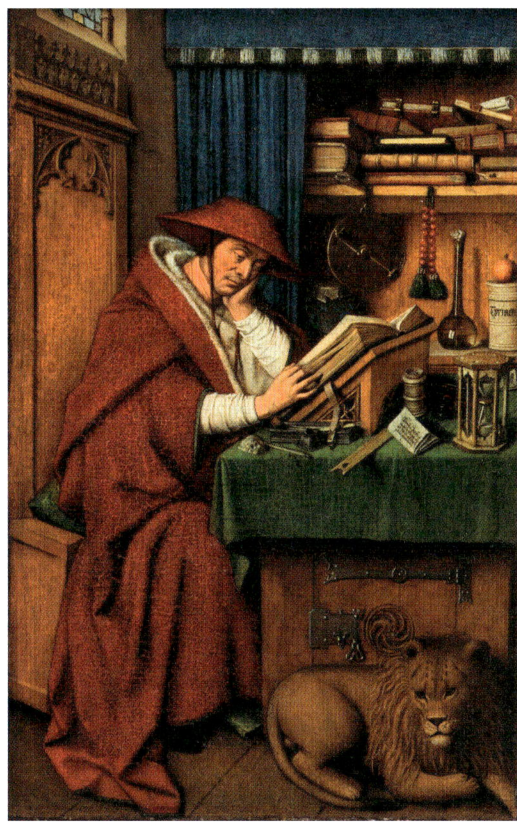

8.2 Jan van Eyck and workshop, *Saint Jerome in his Study*, c. 1435, oil on linen paper on oak panel, 206 x 133 mm.
Detroit Institute of Arts, City of Detroit Purchase, 25.4.
© Detroit Institute of Arts.

a voluminous red overcoat and a broad-brimmed hat with tasselled strings. A rather unusual element is the aspergill in an ewer deposited in a niche on the wall between the two windows, possibly referring to Jerome's role as priest. The leather-bound books placed on the bench underneath the window refer to the intellectual life of the saint. Certain attributes pertain to Jerome's role as prolific author: the writing desk, the inkwell, the candlestick on the upper shelf, the letter and the pair of scissors attached to the wall. The broom hung from a nail must be another tool of the trade, as it appears in many of Dürer's prints of the subject.[30] Most of the material objects depicted here correspond to the living space of an educated citizen of Nuremberg who would study or complete paperwork in his home.

The most unusual object in Jerome's study is the oversized pumpkin or gourd hanging in the front right corner of the room. According to Ulrich Kuder, this attribute is to be understood as a reference to a dispute between Augustine and Jerome about the correct identification of the botanical plant – pumpkin or castor bean – under which the Old Testament prophet Jonah had sought shade.[31] Jerome decided in favour of the bottle gourd which is depicted prominently in Dürer's print. Quite obviously, this object does not belong to the daily sphere of material objects that populate most of Dürer's images of Saint Jerome but refers instead to the intellectual life of the saint.

Earlier images of *Saint Jerome in his Study*

The materiality as well as the symbolism of Albrecht Dürer's print has its roots in earlier depictions of this well-known saint. There is a plethora of late-medieval images depicting Saint Jerome in his study.[32] The most relevant for Dürer's engraving, as well as the earliest and most famous, is a small panel attributed to Jan van Eyck (c. 1390–1441) and his workshop (Figure 8.2).[33] It is slightly smaller in size than Dürer's print and dates from approximately 1442. Like Dürer's version, Jerome's *studiolo* here is filled with numerous objects: a lectern, books, writing utensils, a folded letter, a sand spreader, a ruler, a rosary and an hourglass. In contrast to Dürer's print, however, Jerome is not portrayed in the act of writing but is instead reading a book on the writing desk in front of him. An additional element is the astrolabe hanging from one of the shelves. An ancient instrument that was used by astronomers to measure the altitude of the stars, its inclusion in the work emphasises his role as a scholar. On the lower shelf the following objects are visible: a transparent glass carafe, a jar covered with a stopper made from cloth and an apothecary's vessel with the Latin inscription 'Tyriaca'. *Therica* was a highly prized antidote for snakebite that was produced in Venice during the Renaissance period.[34] Based on Arthur Pease's investigations of Jerome's interest in medicinal treatments and healing, such details demonstrate how differentiated the image of Saint Jerome was in the mid-fifteenth century.[35] In Dürer's engraving, two glass vessels with stops are placed on the upper shelf. Their meaning is not as clear but may allude to similar concepts. There is no indication that Dürer had seen the painting by van Eyck, but it is conceivable that information about such an important work of art was accessible to him indirectly. His father, Albrecht Dürer the Elder (1427–1502), spent several years in the Netherlands, and we can assume that he was familiar with Jan van Eyck's oeuvre.[36]

In several instances, images of Saint Jerome have been interpreted as 'historiated' portraits, that is, images in which a real person is represented in the guise of a historical, biblical or mythological figure. In the case of van Eyck, it has been suggested, for instance, that the figure of Saint Jerome is a disguised portrait of Cardinal Niccolò Albergati (1375–1443), the famous theologian who travelled to Arras in 1435 to participate in a peace congress during the Hundred Years' War.[37]

Another famous representation of this studious saint was produced by the Sicilian artist Antonello da Messina (1430–79), probably during his time in Venice (Figure 8.3).[38] While Antonello's work is a small painting, it is filled with details and its structure is more complex than the van Eyck painting. The wooden cubicle in which Jerome undertakes his studies is situated in a medieval church that is filled with light and offers views into the countryside beyond. Dora Thornton has examined how built-in wooden cabinets like these may have looked in the early modern period.[39] A church, however, is not a typical environment for a domestic study, thus it is probable that Antonello da Messina used this device to draw attention to the spirituality of the saint. An additional layer of space was added to this unusual construction by placing the cubicle and the church behind an open stone arch which serves as a frame for the picture. As in Dürer's engraving, the scholar is removed from the foreground and is deeply embedded in his scholarly environment. The perspectival floor and the additional step at the lower ledge add to the growing distance between the viewer and the protagonist. By presenting the scene in this way, the space is turned into a stage. In addition to the

more common attributes – books, writing utensils, a crucifix, a lion, glazed stoneware, etc. – we can detect more unusual details, such as the saint's slippers at the bottom of the wooden stair. Among the various animals – the lion, the cat, the birds – a partridge and a peacock stand out due to their position and size. Based on the *Physiologus*, an anonymous early Christian text which contains didactic descriptions of animals, birds and fantastic creatures, as well as on the writings of Isidor of Seville (d. 636) and Konrad von Megenburg (1309–74), the partridge was seen as a bad and disloyal bird, while the peacock had more positive

8.3 Antonello da Messina, *Saint Jerome in his Study*, c. 1475, oil on limewood, 45.7 x 36.2 cm.

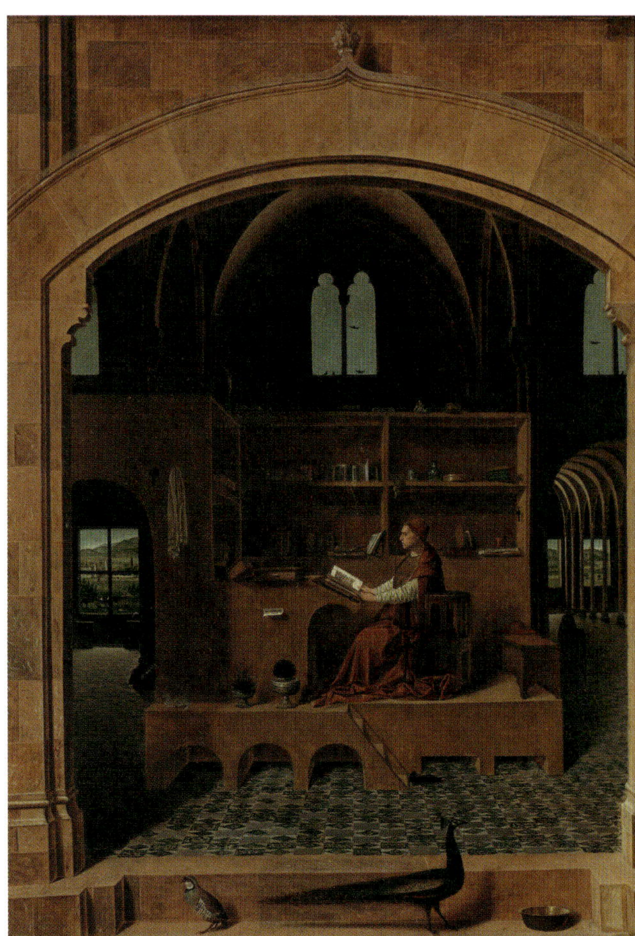

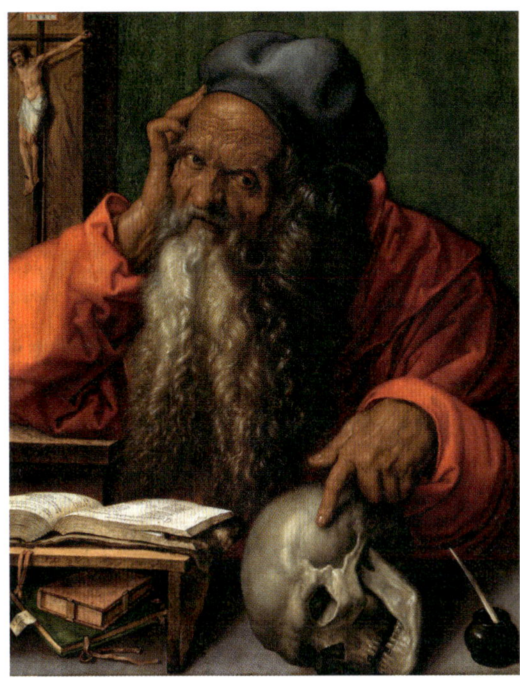

8.4 Albrecht Dürer, *Saint Jerome in Meditation*, 1521,
oil on oak, 59.5 x 48.5 cm.

Lisbon, Museu Nacional de Arte Antiga, Direção-Geral do Património
Cultural. © Arquivo e Documentação Fotográfic.

associations.[40] Their inclusion acts as a reminder that animals as well as manufactured objects bring images of the saint to life in a tactile, material way.

In Dürer's engraving of *Saint Jerome in his Study*, the bearded old man at the desk was not intended to be a portrait of a living individual. Instead, Jerome here represents the prototype of the wise church father who lives the solitary life of a scholar. Dürer's panel painting of *Saint Jerome in Meditation* takes up this idea in which old age is associated with wisdom (Figure 8.4). Dürer painted this half-length portrait during his trip to the Netherlands.[41] While he stayed in Antwerp, he portrayed the face of a ninety-three-year-old man with the intention of producing an idealised image of saint.[42] In contrast to his earlier print, he moved away from the idea of the scholar's study and focused essentially on four key elements: the skull, the cross, the books and an inkwell with quill. Jerome's intense gaze and the index finger pointing to the skull

forces the viewer to remember death. It is an intensely captivating image of *Memento Mori*.

Later artists, such as Lucas Cranach the Elder (1472–1553), reinterpreted Dürer's iconic image by turning it into a historiated portrait. The most famous examples of these are two paintings by Lucas Cranach the Elder from 1525 and 1526 that show Cardinal Albrecht of Brandenburg (1490–1545) as Saint Jerome in his study.[43] Dürer's original layout was reproduced in mirror image, explained by Cranach's use of a print made after Dürer.[44] Looking at the clean-shaven face of the thirty-five-year-old cardinal with his red beret, there can be no doubt that this is a portrait of a contemporary dignitary in the guise of Jerome. Albrecht has no halo but instead surrounds himself with all the trappings of the erudite saint: the crucifix, the books, the desk, the writing utensils, the hourglass and the lion. Albrecht of Brandenburg was more interested in displaying his precious gold and silver vessels than projecting the image of a man interested in medicine or astronomy. In contrast to van Eyck and Dürer, Cranach turns the late-medieval chamber into a menagerie, adding further animals to the dog and the lion. In the 1525 Darmstadt painting we can detect two partridges and a pair of pheasants with eight chicks. In the 1526 painting, now at the Ringling Museum in Sarasota, Florida, the artist added further animals: a squirrel, a deer, a beaver, a rabbit and a grey parrot. These wild creatures are entirely out of place in a scholar's study, and the meaning of the animals remains oblique. Andreas Tacke proposed that by placing a parrot on the table and by hanging a painting of the *Virgin and Child* on the wall, Cranach underlined Albrecht's loyalty to the teachings of the Catholic church and emphasised his opposition to Martin Luther.[45] If that reading is correct, Albrecht Dürer's humanist image can be interpreted as a political statement that responded to the religious strife of the Reformation period. A few decades later, the anonymous artist W. S. produced another historiated portrait that was closely modelled on Dürer's 1514 print. The small engraving is a posthumous homage to Martin Luther in which he is portrayed as Saint Jerome.[46] The Latin inscription at the bottom of the print shows Luther's late motto 'Pestis eram vivus, moriens tua mors ero, Papa' (Living I was your plague, dying, I will be your death, Pope).

A parallel case: *The Vision of Saint Augustine*

At the time when the image of Saint Jerome as scholar was popularised in art, Saint Augustine (354–430) was also being portrayed as an intellectual in his study. The motifs used for characterising both saints and their environment are similar, but not identical.[47] Looking at representations of Augustine further illuminates our understanding of aspects of the Jerome imagery – in particular, the issue of materiality.

The most famous representation of the *Vision of Saint Augustine* is a large painting on canvas by Vittore Carpaccio (1465–1525/26), painted in 1502. The preparatory study for Carpaccio's *Vision of Saint Augustine* has survived and allows us to trace the artist's creative process (Figure 8.5).[48] Carpaccio had been commissioned to decorate the newly acquired Saint Catherine hospital in Venice, now occupied by the brotherhood of the Dalmatians. He executed nine paintings for this building, which was named the Scuola di San Giorgio degli Schiavoni.[49] The series contains scenes from the lives of the brotherhood's four patron saints: Saints George, Jerome, Augustine and Tryphon. At first sight one might ask, what exactly is the theme depicted in this image? Carpaccio illustrates an episode which is known from a thirteenth-century letter by Pseudo-Augustine addressed to Cyril of Jerusalem. The letter mentions a vision in which Saint Jerome appeared to Saint Augustine while in his study.

This happened at the very hour of his death in distant Bethlehem and the vision was accompanied by supernatural light.[50] The mystic appearance of Saint Jerome is revealed to the viewer only indirectly. Saint Augustine looks to the window and perceives the light emanating from Jerome. The white spitz (dog) in the painting, sitting in the middle of the room, stares towards the window; he is probably also aware of the heavenly vision.

The subtle quality of Carpaccio's interpretation becomes obvious when comparing the image with one of the scenes in a painting by the Flemish Master of Saint Augustine (Figure 8.6).[51] In the architectural niche in the upper left of this representation, dating from 1490, we see that the saint, seated in his study, has stopped his work on a manuscript and looks at a supernatural apparition of Saint Jerome as cardinal, bathed in a bright aureole of light. One might go so far as to say that the central theme of Carpaccio's painting is pushed into the background by the minute portrayal of a study chamber filled with all sorts of material objects.[52] There is an unprecedented wealth of books on shelves, on the table and on a rotating lectern situated in an adjoining cabinet at the left side of the painting. Close to Augustine's desk a manuscript with musical notes is visible, as is a folded document with a large red seal and an hourglass. Further, various astronomical devices are scattered across the room, including an armillary sphere, and are meant to characterise Saint Augustine

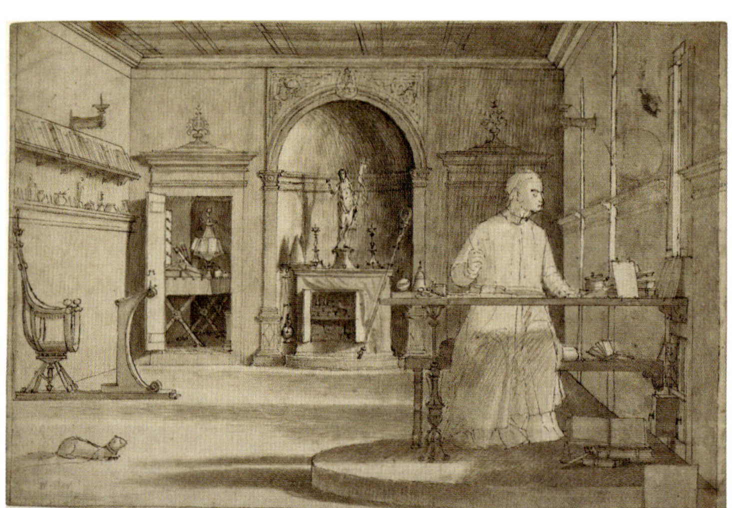

8.5 Vittore Carpaccio, preparatory sketch for the *Vision of Saint Augustine*, 1502, pen, ink and wash, 278 x 426 mm.

 Albrecht Dürer's material world

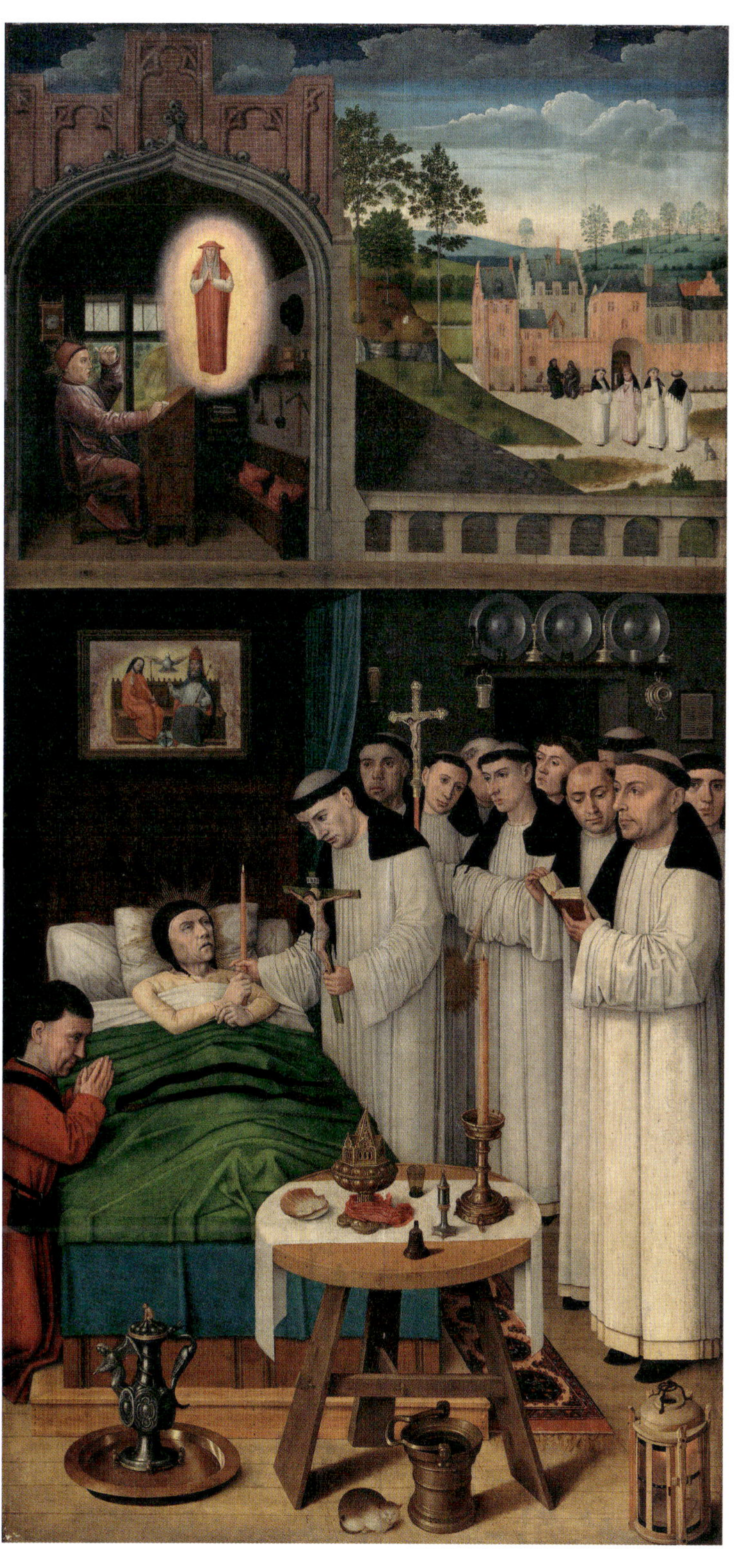

8.6 Master of Saint Augustine, *Scenes from the Life of Saint Augustine*, 1490s, oil on oak panel, 136.1 x 66.4 cm.

Dublin, National Gallery of Ireland, NGI.823. © National Gallery of Ireland.

as an erudite man and a versatile thinker. New, however, is the inclusion of small statuettes, possibly antique objects, placed on a ledge at the left side of the room. Another innovation within the standard typology of the scholar's study is the inclusion of an altar with liturgical instruments which has been placed in the central apse. The bronze statue of a risen Christ, the mitre and the crosier refer to Augustine's role as a representative of the Catholic church and emphasise the saint's spirituality.[53] What Dürer's engraving and Carpaccio's painting have in common is that Jerome's literary activity is characterised by his environment and he becomes part of the space in which he resides. The light penetrating through the window plays an essential role in both works and underlines the spirituality of both Augustine and Jerome.

Variations on the theme of Saint Jerome in Dürer

Albrecht Dürer was fascinated by Saint Jerome. For most of his life, he worked on different versions of the subject, emphasising different elements of the saint's biography. During his journeys to northern Italy, he visited Venice at least twice. It is likely that he was familiar with the versions created by Antonello da Messina (1475) and Vittore Carpaccio (c. 1502). In 1511 – only three years before he published his famous 1514 engraving – Dürer worked on a slightly smaller woodcut, *Saint Jerome in his Cell*, that encapsulated many aspects of the later print (Figure 8.7; cat. 72).[54] Saint Jerome sits inside a small wooden closet that has been fitted into a larger room with a tunnel vault. In the final woodcut, the room is obscured by a curtain that has been drawn aside. Jerome is portrayed here as an elderly man dressed in his cardinal's garb. He leans over a writing desk and reads a book of considerable dimensions. A small crucifix has been attached to the front of the desk close to the open manuscript, and six more books have been placed on the shelf to his left. In the foreground we observe a chest with a cushion on which rests yet another leather-covered manuscript with clasps. Fixed to the front of his desk are a pair of scissors, a quill and a folded piece of paper; an inkwell sits at the corner of his desk. At the back of this narrow cubicle, we find more implements: a broom, a second pair of scissors and a rosary. The large hourglass is

surmounted by an object that is reminiscent of a mechanical clock. The box-like cabinet is furnished with a second shelf which is placed above the saint's head. It is filled with still more objects: five bottles with stops, a candlestick and a jug with an aspergill comparable to the one depicted in his 1514 print. The holy water sprinkler differs from the everyday items in Jerome's study in that it is a liturgical object.

A preparatory sketch for this woodcut has survived in the Ambrosiana Library in Milan.[55] The pen drawing is of interest insofar as it reveals more about the room in which the saint sits. First conceived as a rectangular space, it was later turned into a barrel-vaulted room. It opens into a second room of smaller dimensions. At some point Dürer must have decided that it was preferable to concentrate exclusively on the saint and block out the surrounding architecture with a curtain. The drawing suggests that there was a window to Jerome's left, another element that does not reappear in the final woodcut. The Milan drawing can be understood as a preliminary stage for the master engraving of 1514. Even though the wooden furniture and the layout of the room have been greatly altered, the main group with Jerome at his desk and the lion in the foreground is very similar in design. It seems as if Dürer worked on the theme of *Saint Jerome in his Study* after his return from Italy, perhaps drawing on Antonella da Messina's earlier concept of a room within a room. By 1514, however, this idea was abandoned in favour of a living room filled with the kind of everyday objects that were widely used in Nuremberg.

Dürer took up the challenge of illustrating Jerome's life again in the years that followed. In his 1512 dry point print, he returned to the subject of the saint living in the wilderness where once again he is accompanied by the lion.[56] In contrast to his earlier engraving, Dürer does not show the saint beating himself with a stone, but instead emphasises his devotion. Jerome has turned his eyes away from the open manuscript and is leaning towards the crucifix that stands on the left side of the table. With his hands folded in prayer, he looks up to the sky as if seeking to commune with God. Despite dwelling in the desert, Jerome is carrying the garb of the cardinal with him. The hat with the tasselled strings is placed next to the pollard willow. In

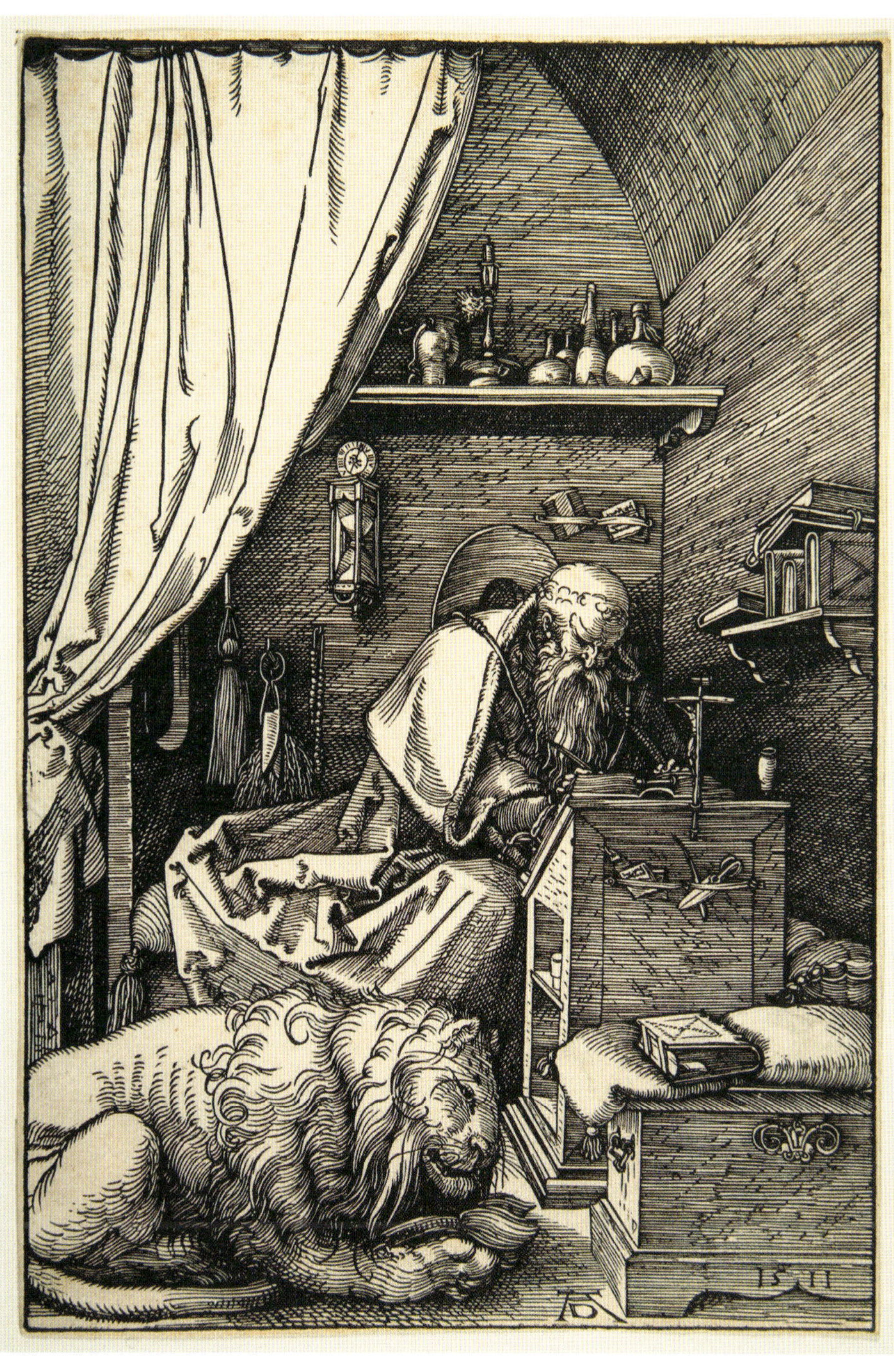

8.7 (cat. 72) Albrecht Dürer, *Saint Jerome in his Cell*, 1511, woodcut, 232 x 159 mm, trimmed.

The Whitworth, The University of Manchester, P.3049. Presented by George Thomas Clough in 1921. © The Whitworth, The University of Manchester. Photo: Michael Pollard.

this print it seems that Dürer did not want to give up the idea of the scholar and therefore equips Jerome with a simple desk and an inkwell.[57]

After 1521, Dürer produced a medium-size drawing in brown ink that dealt for one last time with the subject of Saint Jerome.[58] Since the room contains elements that can be found in earlier versions, the drawing is often referred to as *Saint Jerome in his Study*. Jerome sits on a wooden bench behind a writing desk, both placed in a confined space. The cabinet has a wooden ceiling and a window to the left. The shelf sitting under the ceiling contains two books, a candlestick and two bottles, elements that are reminiscent of the 1512 woodcut. The notion of a purely domestic environment is here reinforced by the vessels that are placed upside down on a wooden rack: a beaker and an ewer with a metal lid. Compared to the other images discussed, this is a relatively sparse image. Dürer has stripped the saint of all his worldly trappings; no reference is made here to his status as cardinal. The upper body of the saint is almost naked, recalling the early images of penitence, and the saint has propped up his face with his left hand while looking intensely at the skull in front of him and his right arm rests on his knee. The crucifix on the table complements the meditative atmosphere and refers to the idea of death and salvation. On top of his small table, Jerome has placed a sheet of paper and an inkwell, as if he is about to note down his thoughts. As was the case with the image of *Saint Jerome by the Pollard Willow*, this drawing is again a hybrid version that combines different facets from the saint's life.

This discussion of the various versions has shown how Albrecht Dürer constantly searched for the best possible representation of Saint Jerome in order to do justice to his various roles as hermit, author, scholar and man of the church. Dürer was inspired by those who experimented with the topic before, both in Italy and in Northern Europe, and they motivated him to find new solutions. With its successful combination of material and immaterial elements, the 1514 engraving of *Saint Jerome in his Study* excels in this innovation: the figure of a wise and spiritual intellectual is paired with a world full of material objects that reflect Jerome's life and also connects the viewer to everyday aspects of Nuremberg.

Notes

1 Rice, *Saint Jerome in the Renaissance*; Ridderbos, *Saint and Symbol*, 15–40; Russo, *Saint Jérôme en Italie*; Aikema, *De Heilige Hieronymus*; Meighörner and Thum, *Hieronymus in der Wilderniss*.

2 https://en.wikipedia.org/wiki/Vulgate

3 De Voragine, *The golden legende*, fol. CCCIXr–CCCXIr: 'Here followeth the life of Jeromme'.

4 De Voragine, *The golden legende*, fol. CCCXr.

5 EXIMII DOCTORIS HIERONYMI STRIDONENSIS VITA EX IPSIUS POTISSIMUM LITTERARIS CONTEXTAPER DEYDERIUM ERASMUM ROTERODANUM, 9 vols., (Basel: Johannes Froben, 1516); see also Erasmus, *La vie de saint Jérôme*.

6 Luther, *Annotierungen*.

7 Matthias Mende, 'Hieronymus im Gehäus', in Schoch, Mende and Scherbaum, *Albrecht Dürer*, I, 176–7, no. 70.

8 'Beschreibung des heyligen Bischoffs Eusebij: der ain junger un[d] diszipel des heyligen Sancti Hieronymi gewest ist…'; published by Lazarus Spengler, Nuremberg: Hieronymus Höltzel, 1514.

9 Albrecht Dürer, *Saint Jerome Writing in a Cave*, woodcut, 1512. See Schoch, Mende and Scherbaum, II, 369–71, no. 232, H.229.

10 Fürst, *Hieronymus, Askese und Wissenschaft*; see also the biographies by Cain, *Jerome of Stridon* and Rebenich, *Jerome*.

11 Currie, Serck and Toussaint, *Saint Jérôme dans un paysage*, 30–4; Ridderbos, *Saint and Symbol*, 63–88; Tricot, *Van Patinier tot Ribera*.

12 Rogier van der Weyden and workshop, *Saint Jerome and the Lion*, c. 1450, oil on wood, Detroit, Institute of Art.

13 Belting, 'St Jerome in Venice', 6–11.

14 *The Penitent Jerome*, c. 1495/94, oil on wood, 23 x 17 cm, London, National Gallery; *Jerome in Meditation*, oil on wood, 60 x 48 cm, Lisbon, Museu Nacional de Arte Antiga, see Figure 8.3, p. 91.

15 *Saint Jerome in his Cell*, 1511; see Schoch, Mende and Scherbaum, *Albrecht Dürer*, II, 360–2, no. 360, H.228; *Saint Jerome Writing in a Cave*, 1512; see Schoch, Mende and Scherbaum, *Albrecht Dürer*, II, 369–71, no. 232, H.229; and *Saint Jerome in his Study Pulling the Thorn from the Lion's Paw*, title page from *Epistolare beati Hieronymi*, 1492, publ. by Nikolaus Kesler, Cambridge University Library (Peterborough D.11.1). The authenticity of this woodcut has recently been questioned by Ramona Brown and Anja Grebe, see Brown and Grebe, 'Albrecht Dürer von nörmergk'.

16 *Saint Jerome in his Study*, 1511, Venice, Ambrosiana; 1512, see Strauss, *Complete Drawings* 1511/15; preparatory sketch for the Lisbon panel painting of Saint Jerome, 1521, Vienna, Albertina, see Strauss, *Complete Drawings* 1521/3; *Saint Jerome in his Study*, after 1521, Berlin, Kupferstichkabinett, see Strauss, *Complete Drawings* 1521/5.

17 *Saint Jerome by the Pollard Willow, Studying*, 1512, Los Angeles, J. Paul Getty Museum. See Schoch, Mende and Scherbaum, *Albrecht Dürer*, I, 158–60, no. 65, H.58.

18 See Schoch, Mende and Scherbaum, *Albrecht Dürer*, I, 38–40, no. 6, H.57.

19 On *Nemesis* see Jennifer Spinks' essay 'Objects in motion', and on *Melencolia I* see Matthew Champion's essay 'Measure and the material world,' both in this catalogue. For *Saint Eustace*, see Schoch, Mende and Scherbaum, *Albrecht Dürer*, I, 92–5, no. 32; H.60, and for *Knight, Death and the Devil*, see *ibid.*, I, 169–73, no. 69; H.74

20 Schoch, Mende and Scherbaum, *Albrecht Dürer*, I, 174–8, no. 70.

21 Griggs, 'Dürer's Diary of His Journey', 404.

22 *Ibid.*, 406.

23 Mende, 'Hieronymus im Gehäus', 174–8; Richter, 'Hieronymus im Gehäus'.

24 Vasari, *Le vite*, 408–9; Mende, 'Hieronymus im Gehäus', 178; Kuder, *Dürers ,Hieronymus im Gehäus*; Hecht, 'Theologische Aspekte'.

25 Sullivan, 'Alter Apelles', 1164–6; Müller, *Apelles am Fürstenhof*.

26 Panofsky, 'Notes on Erasmus' Eulogy on Dürer'.

27 See the so-called chamber of Martin Luther in the Veste Coburg; https://de.wikipedia.org/wiki/Martin_Luther#/media/Datei:Lutherzimmer_Veste_Coburg_by_Vincent_Eisfeld.jpg

28 See the Albrecht-Dürer-Haus in Nuremberg, https://museen.nuernberg.de/duererhaus.

29 Mende, 'Hieronymus im Gehäus', 174.

30 For instance, *Saint Jerome in his Cell*, 1511, see Schoch, Mende and Scherbaum, *Albrecht Dürer*, II, 360–2, H.228 , no. 229.

31 Kuder, 'Dürers Hieronymus im Gehäus', 229–40.

32 Ridderbos, *Saint and Symbol*.

33 Jan van Eyck and workshop, *Saint Jerome in his Study*, c. 1442, oil on linen paper on wood, 20.6 x 13.3 cm (unframed), Detroit Institute of Art; Hall, 'More about the Detroit Van Eyck'.

34 Watson, *Theriac and Mithridatium*.

35 Pease, 'Medical allusions'; see also: Garzelli, 'Sulla fortuna del "Gerolamo" mediceo'.

36 Rupprich, 'Dürer, Albrecht der Ältere'.

37 Weiss, 'Jan van Eyck's "Albergati" Portrait'; Hall, 'Cardinal Albergati'; Hall, 'More About the Detroit Van Eyck'.

38 Barbera, *San Girolamo nello studio*; Aikema, *De Heilige Hieronymus*.

39 Thornton, *The Scholar in his Study*.

40 According to Saint Augustine, the peacock is a bird of heaven and a symbol of immortality, see Ridderbos, *Saint and Symbols*, 51–5. According to Konrad von Megenburg, the partridge is also an unchaste animal for various reasons. It was believed that male partridges practised homosexuality.

41 Van den Brink, *Dürer war hier*.

42 Albrecht Dürer, *93-Year Old Man*, 1521, preparatory sketch, brush drawing on grey-violet primed paper, 415 x 182 mm, Vienna, Albertina; Strauss, *Complete Drawings* 1521/3.

43 Lucas Cranach the Elder, *Albrecht of Brandenburg as Saint Jerome in his Study*, 1525, oil on wood, 115 x 77 cm, Darmstadt, Hessisches Landesmuseum; and Lucas Cranach the Elder, *Albrecht of Brandenburg as Saint Jerome in his study*, 1526, oil on wood, 115 x 79 cm, Sarasota, FL, Ringling Museum. See Tacke, 'Albrecht als Heiliger Hieronymus'.

44 *Ibid.*, 118; Hieronymous Hopfer, *Saint Jerome in his study*, engraving, 22,6 x 15,5, Vienna, Albertina, page of a print album.

45 *Ibid.*, 127–8.

46 Monogrammist W. S. (Wolfgang Stuber?), *Martin Luther as Saint Jerome in his Study*, engraving, circa 1570–80, Kupferstichkabinett, Staatliche Museen zu Berlin, inv. no. 43-10; H.57.I.

47 Fortini Brown, 'Carpaccio's Augustine in his study'; Gill, 'Reformations', 72–5.

48 Vittore Carpaccio, preparatory sketch for the *Vision of Saint Augustine*, drawing, pen and brown ink with grey washes, 278 x 426 mm, 1502, London, The British Museum, 1934,1208.1.

49 Vittorio Carpaccio, *The Vision of Saint Augustine*, oil on linen, 141 x 210 cm, Venice; see: Stoichiță, *Carpaccios Gemäldezyklus*.

50 Gill, 'Reformations', 59, n.2; Gill points to the fact that there is a certain discrepancy between the daily life of the scholar – reading, studying and writing – and the reality of eternal life after death.

51 Master of Saint Augustine, *Saint Augustine having a vision of Saint Jerome*, right wing of a triptych depicting *Scenes from the Life of Saint Augustine*, 1490s, illustrated at Figure 8.6.

52 Nagel and Wood, *Anachronic Renaissance*, 35–44.

53 The art historian Meredith Gill provides an insightful interpretation of Saint Augustine in the light of his writings, see Gill, 'Reformations', 75–9.

54 See n.15, above.

55 Albrecht Dürer, *Saint Jerome in his Study*, pen drawing, 190 x 151 mm; Venice, Bibliotheca Ambrosiana, see Strauss, *Complete Drawings* 1511/15.

56 Albrecht Dürer, *Saint Jerome by the Pollard Willow*, dry point, 210 x 183 mm; Schoch, Mende and Scherbaum, *Albrecht Dürer*, I, 158–60, no. 65; H.58.

57 Belting, 'Saint Jerome in Venice'.

58 Albrecht Dürer, *Saint Jerome in his Study*, drawing, brown ink, 203 x 126 mm, Berlin, Kupferstichkabinett, no. KdZ 4443; see Strauss, *Complete Drawings* 1521/5.

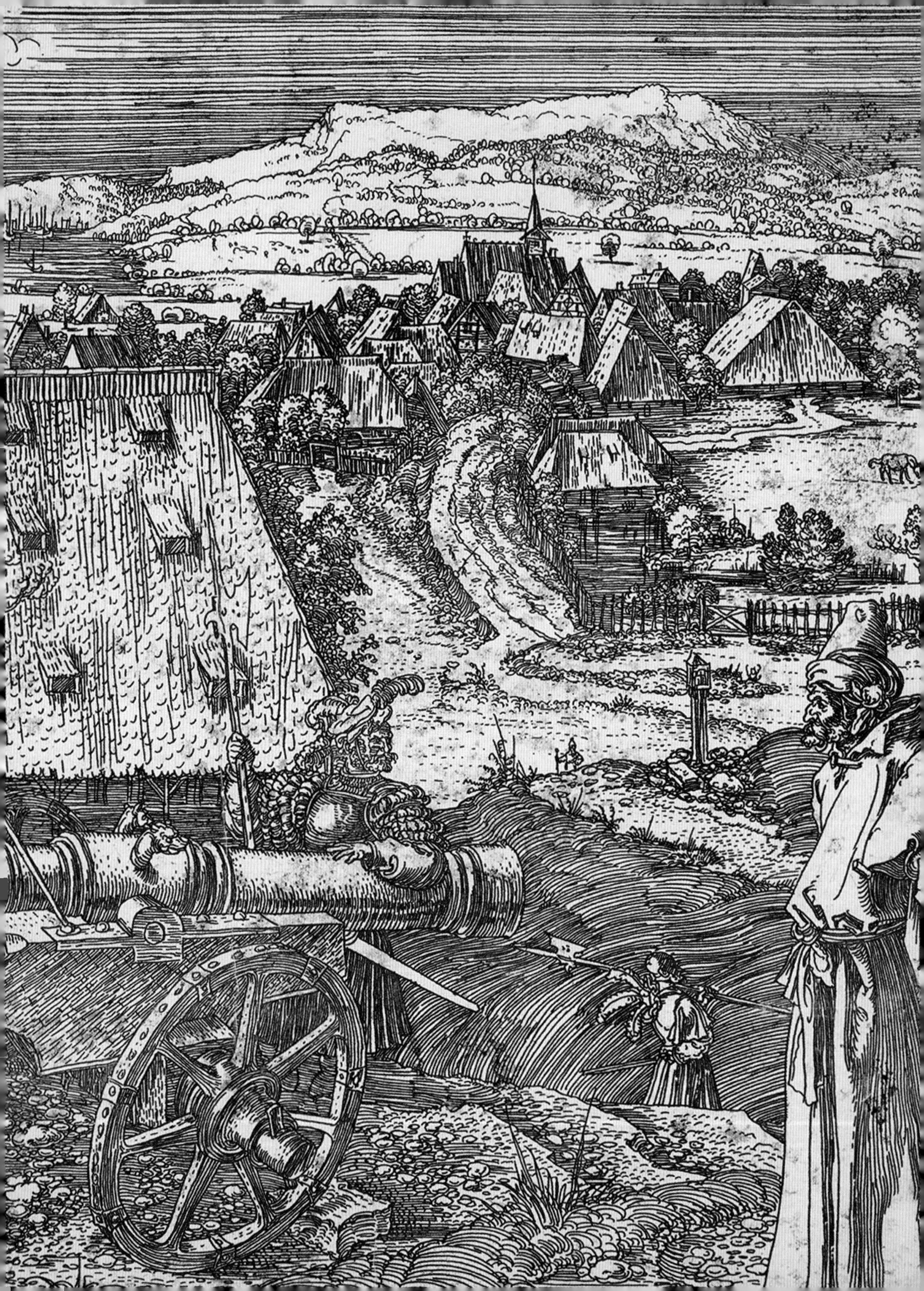

[9] Albrecht Dürer's *Landscape with a Cannon* of 1518: the matter of etching

Edward H. Wouk

Albrecht Dürer's *Landscape with a Cannon* (Figure 9.1; cat. 52) is the final and most ambitious of the six etchings on iron that the artist produced between 1515 and 1518.[1] The oblong print pictures an expansive landscape, which has been identified as an accurate view of the Lindelberg mountain seen from Eschenau, a village close to Nuremberg. Dürer had drawn the site a few years earlier in a delicate metalpoint study, and that drawing may have served as the basis for the background here.[2] The setting appears at first familiar: a cow grazes on a field in the distance and low houses, typical of the region, straddle a winding road in the middle ground. Yet the scene challenges any sense of familiarity. First, there is the matter of the cannon – a garrison gun of medium calibre with the arms of Nuremberg on its breech. The cannon is not only strangely positioned on this leafy hillock; it is also anachronistic. This model of cannon, dating to the last decades of the fifteenth century, had been retired by the city of Nuremberg by 1512, when such earlier firearms were taken out of active use and placed on display in the municipal armoury as museum pieces.[3] Equally inexplicable are the figures in exotic dress in the right foreground, who appear out of place in the German countryside. Likely based on a drawing Dürer made after the *Procession in Piazza San Marco*, a painting by Gentile Bellini (c. 1429–1507) he saw during his travels to Venice which I discuss below, these foreign dignitaries seem to have arrived unexpectedly from another world. Their unusual costumes contrast with the flamboyant uniforms of the *Landsknechts*, or mercenary soldiers, who guard the weapon and patrol the land. Like the viewers of this etching, these foreign statesmen ponder the impressive piece of field artillery that stops them in their tracks. To some, the quizzical gazes of these visitors, directed at the cannon and the landscape

beyond, have suggested an impenetrable cultural divide in the foreground of this strange print.

In this essay, I examine why Dürer brought the seemingly incongruous motifs of landscape, cannon and foreign figures into conversation in a single image, and why he chose to do so in the highly novel medium of etching on iron. Cannons at the time were cast in bronze or iron, with supporting elements like the lafette, the chassis for moving the firearm, generally forged from iron.[4] They belong to a world of firearms that were richly decorated with cast and etched motifs, which transformed these implements of warfare into objects of striking artistry and visual appeal. In its making, then, Dürer's iron etching shared in the materiality and culture of specialist craft knowledge of the cannon it portrays. The resulting print, in turn, represents a juncture of modern military and print technologies staged on a dense, politically fraught terrain.[5] Dürer's *Landscape with a Cannon* reveals the artist's intense interest in the pictorial possibilities that etching might afford, and it represents his most ambitious project to test the limits of a still young printmaking technique.

This essay is divided into three parts. In the first, I consider the relationship between Dürer's *Landscape with a Cannon* and the firearm it represents. The secretive chemical process of etching, using corrosive acid to bite into a metal surface to produce an image or pattern, began as a technique for decorating armour.[6] It emerged tentatively as a graphic artform in the work of Dürer's contemporaries, including Daniel Hopfer (1470–1536) in Augsburg.[7] Dürer's experiments in etching are generally thought to postdate the earliest forays of the Hopfers, but *Landscape with a Cannon* reveals the extent to which he expanded the visual and affective potentials of this new technique

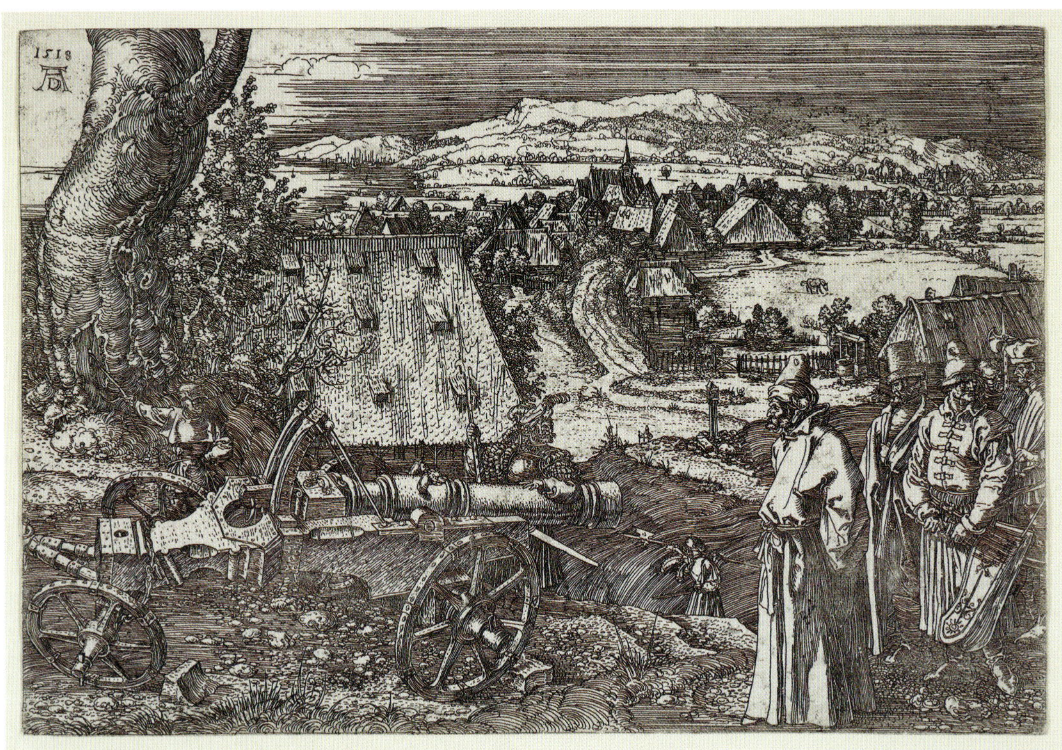

9.1 (cat. 52) Albrecht Dürer, *Landscape with a Cannon*,
1518, etching on iron, 220 x 325 mm.

The Whitworth, The University of Manchester , P.3022. Presented by George Thomas
Clough in 1921. © The Whitworth, University of Manchester. Photo: Michael Pollard.

to explore what etching alone could achieve: lines of uniform thickness that undulate and squiggle with a freedom not afforded by the techniques of engraving and woodcut in which he already excelled.[8]

In the second part of this essay, I address how Dürer used etching to portray the figures in exotic dress and their perplexing arrival into this Germanic landscape. My analysis will question the traditional identification of these figures as Turkish, proposing instead that they represent a more ambiguous gathering of inquisitive foreign dignitaries. In the third and final part of this essay, I consider what the origins of some of these figures in a painting by Gentile Bellini might reveal about Dürer's experimental approach to composition in *Landscape with a Cannon*. My argument juxtaposes Dürer's rivalry with armour on the one hand with his interest in Italian painting on the other in order to

demonstrate how, in *Landscape with a Cannon*, he treated etching as a joint technical and artistic wonder. This interpretation of *Landscape with a Cannon* adds a new dimension to Dürer's self-identification with the materiality and techniques of metalwork, his family's traditional trade.[9] Although we do not know why Dürer ceased to make etchings, this astounding final experiment demonstrates how, in the space of a few brief years, he successfully elevated the technique from a decorative mode associated with adorning armour to an independent pictorial art.

Dürer the etcher

By the time Dürer completed *Landscape with a Cannon*, in 1518, he had established etching as a site of creative experimentation within his graphic oeuvre.[10]

Already in *Desperate Man* (cat. 49), often considered to be Dürer's first etching, the artist began to explore the possibilities of combining experimental technique and a highly unusual, even inscrutable subject matter. This print's strange portrayal of contorted bodies in a cramped space has been described as both dream-like and accidental. Recent interpretations have suggested that the print represents subjects as diverse as an erotic bath, an antique Saturnalian celebration or an unsolved artistic problem.[11] While the iconography of his *Man of Sorrows* of 1515 may be more conventional, it too reveals Dürer's continuing exploration of the medium's distinctive graphic potentials.[12] This small print attests to an unprecedented investigation of the pen-like spontaneity afforded by the etching needle, which gave rise to what many have described as an attempt at replicating the properties of drawing in print.[13] The tentative lines of *Man of Sorrows* and the obvious corrections, perhaps deliberately left visible, provide important insight into the artist's creative process and his seemingly spontaneous approach to the medium.[14] In contrast to the sparsity of line in *Man of Sorrows*, in *Christ on the Mount of Olives* (*The Agony in the Garden*) of 1515 (cat. 50) and *Abduction on a Unicorn* of 1516, Dürer introduced a novel treatment of tone to his etching practice by playing with the density of lines of uniform thickness.[15] Exercising a greater degree of control over the medium, the artist gave startling radiance to Christ's head in *Christ on the Mount of Olives* by creating stark contrasts between areas of brilliant light, produced by blank expanses of paper, and dark fields heavily worked with etched lines. These disparate passages produce the effect of an ethereal light around the praying figure. The plate of this etching was later coated in gold. Ceasing to be useful for printing, it became a resplendent art object in its own right, inviting admiration of Dürer's virtuosic experiment in etching on the part of its owner, Emperor Rudolph II (1552–1612), who was an important collector of the artist's work.[16]

Dürer's *Sudarium Displayed by an Angel*, also of 1516 (cat. 48), has been widely discussed in terms of the artist's exploration of the resonances between materiality and meaning in etching.[17] The print represents an angel holding aloft the veil with which Veronica wiped the sweat from Christ's face on his way to Calvary, creating a miraculous impression that might be described as the first Christian printed image. Dürer had already treated the subject in a woodcut of 1510 (cat. 46) and an engraving of 1513 (cat. 47), in which the face of Christ bears striking resemblance to the artist's own self-portraits.[18] But his etched depiction stands apart for its self-awareness as a printed image.[19] In *Sudarium Displayed by an Angel*, the archetypal imprint of the holy face appears not at the centre of the image and displayed to the viewer, as in Dürer's other depictions of the motif, but rather flutters upside-down on a foreshortened cloth at the top of the print. The holy face is legible to the angel basking in the radiance of this miraculous image-within-the-image, but we, as viewers of the print, must work to read its inverted form, which is rendered in a sparse outline obscured by the transecting network of lines forming the cloth. By these means, Dürer suggests an analogy between the origins of the miraculous image and the etching itself. Like the linear rendering of Veronica's sweat-stained veil it depicts, Dürer's etching emerged from an act of pressing a receptive medium, in this case paper, against a form-giving surface – an iron plate marked with lines drawn by Dürer's hand and etched by acid, which created a lasting impression.

Yet for all his prior experimentation with etching, Dürer's *Landscape with a Cannon* stands apart in terms of size and ambition. It features a panoramic view that is rare in the artist's printed oeuvre. Turning the page to landscape format and exploiting the pictorial values of the linear technique of etching, Dürer interspersed areas of light and dense hatching, so that the terrain appears to undulate as it recedes toward the distant horizon. The tree at left offers an exquisite display of the artist's agility with the etching needle. Its gnarled bark and branches curve and twist. Animated and almost anthropomorphic, this knotted trunk and branch flaunt the fluidity of the etched lines from which they are made. These range from short flicks of the needle to longer, sweeping curves that bend and flow with energy and purpose around the rings of growth which extend upward and beyond the field of vision. Rising from an outcropping between the cannon and the house, the tree delimits the left

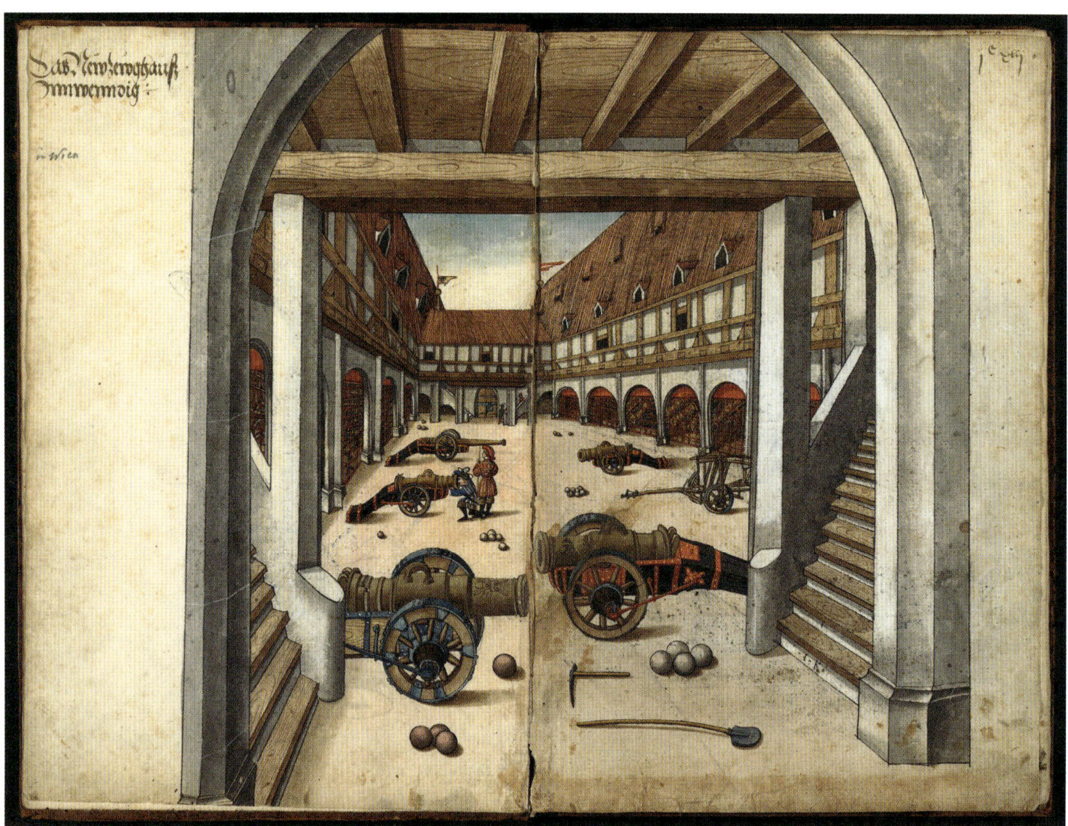

9.2. Jörg Kölderer, *Inventory of Maximilian I's Armaments in Tyrol* from *The inventory of Maximilian I's Armaments in Tyrol*, between 1504 and 1508, pen and ink and watercolour, 430 x 290 mm.

© Yale Center for British Art, Paul Mellon Collection.

edge of the composition. It simultaneously frames a view of the distant harbour and of the landscape spreading out to the right. As a successful *repoussoir*, it also helps establish scale and perspective within the print, providing a relative measure for assessing distances between the foreground, middle ground and background and offering a vertical balance to the horizontally placed cannon that has given this image its title. In no other print did Dürer devote so much space to technological innovation, from the abundant dimensions of the iron plate that produced the image, to the substantial size of the cannon it portrays. In the foreground, the metallic properties of the iron etching intersect with those of the bronze cannon, which

takes shape through the curves, hatchings and dots that Dürer deployed to conjure this impressive firearm.

The political cannon

Dürer was an artist keenly interested in armaments and other implements of war.[20] We find detailed depictions of cannons in several images by Dürer or in projects he oversaw. These include some of the woodcuts on the massive *Triumphal Arch of Maximilian*, a collaborative effort among artists guided by the historian Johannes Stabius (1460–1522), which was completed around 1517, just one year before *Landscape with a Cannon*, to honour Dürer's most important patron, the Holy

Roman Emperor Maximilian I (1459–1519). The Holtorp collection in The John Rylands Research Institute and Library owns an impression of *Maximilian Successful in Battle Against France in 1492–1493* (cat. 53), attributed to Dürer's assistant Wolf Traut , which comes from the historical scenes above the Gate of Honour, near the centre of the *Triumphal Arch*.[21] This woodcut, one of many battle scenes appearing on the *Triumphal Arch*, portrays no fewer than ten cannons of different sizes and constructions which have brought the opposing city to ruin. Six large cannons or bombards, with either round or polygonal barrels, are arranged in a line in the foreground of the image, while another four cannons of varying magnitudes at right all show signs of having been recently fired from behind wooden blinds, with

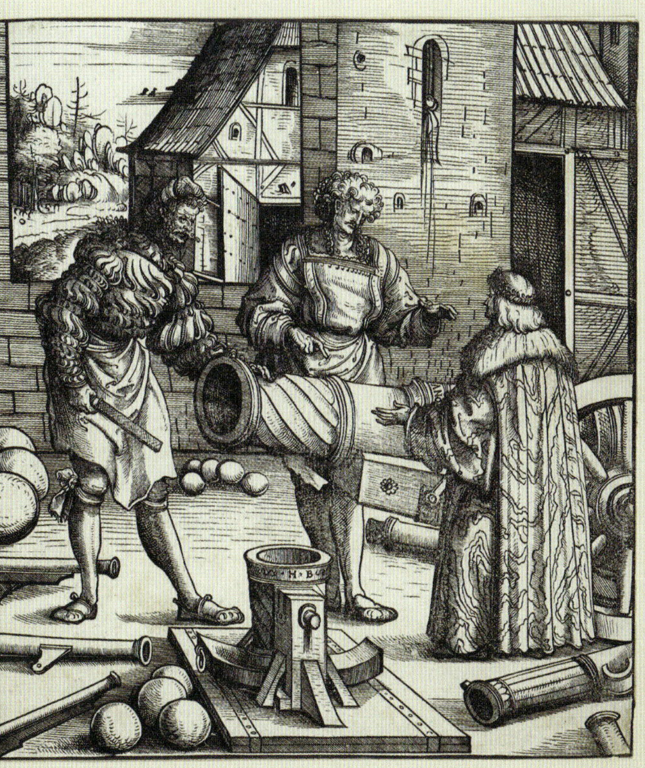

9.3 Hans Burgkmair, *The Young Weisskunig at the Gunnery* from *Der Weisskunig*, 1514–16, woodcut on paper, 220 x 200 mm.

implements for cleaning and preparing the guns scattered messily at their bases. In the foreground, imperial forces proudly celebrate the capture of the enemy flag, embracing one another and revelling in the triumph they achieved with this novel military technology. Another woodcut on the arch shows the young Maximilian standing alone in the middle of a crowded field strewn with an abundance of field artillery of varying shapes and sizes. This detailed woodcut has been attributed to Dürer's contemporary Albrecht Altdorfer (1480–1538), the German artist whose nine landscape etchings of 1518–22 come closest to *Landscape with a Cannon* in their expansive pastoral vistas. The text accompanying this scene explains the emperor's lavish spending on firearms.[22]

Dürer was undoubtedly aware of Maximilian's passion for firearms and the huge sums he was prepared to spend on them. Maximilian's stock was carefully inventoried, with individual cannons being assigned names.[23] A watercolour from the *Inventory of Maximilian I's Armaments in Tyrol* (Figure 9.2), one of several manuscript inventories of his armaments, shows how such cannons were stored around the courtyard of the new arsenal. Maximilian embraced the potentials of novel arms technologies and promoted casting cannons and handguns at the nearby foundries he had established at Mühlau.[24] This watercolour has direct bearing on Dürer's *Landscape with a Cannon*, because it demonstrates a culture in which the display of such artillery was as important as the firing power of the object itself. We see figures admiring and maintaining the cannons, which have been pulled out of their special berths for inspection, while their potential use is only hinted at by the other implements scattered on the ground. Cannons were important instruments of war, but they also offered incredible soft power as symbols of Maximilian's wealth, the technical superiority of the founders in his realm and the sheer abundance of the weaponry at his disposal.[25]

Not surprisingly, we find cannons in a number of the images appearing in two important book projects that celebrated the emperor's lineage and achievements through a mix of allegory and history:

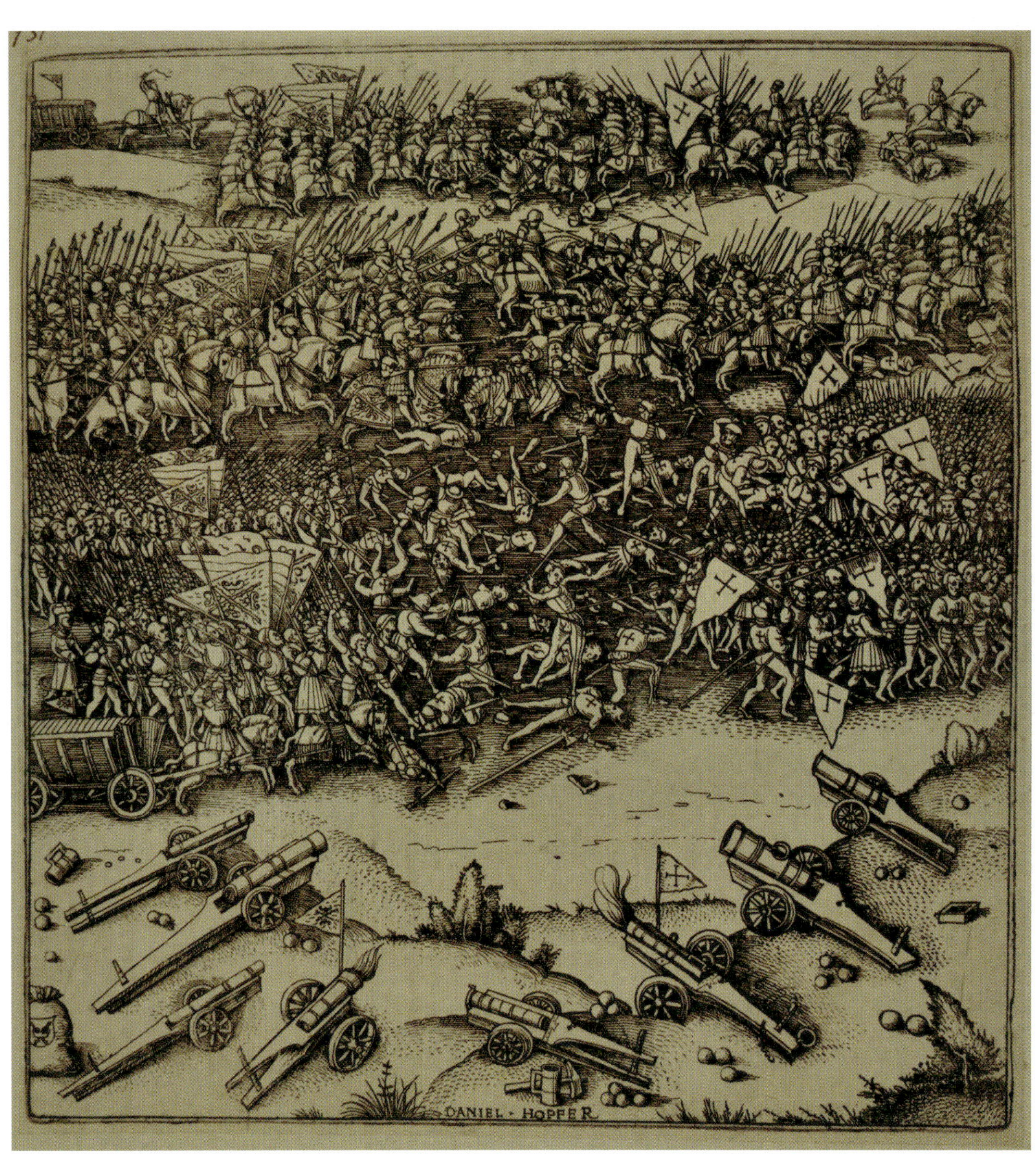

9.4 Daniel Hopfer, *The Battle of Thérouanne*, c. 1493, etching, 230 x 231 mm.

© Bologna, Gabinetto delle Stampe, Pinacoteca Nazionale.

the *Weisskunig*, which remained unpublished at the time of Maximilian's death, and the *Theuerdank*, a celebratory text recalling the conventions of late medieval courtly romance, published in Augsburg by the imperial printer Hans Schönsperger (c. 1455–1521).[26] In addition to advancing Maximilian's image as a confident commander of field artillery, these projects developed a powerful affinity between esteemed arms manufacturers and printmakers in ways that are immediately relevant to Dürer's *Landscape with a Cannon*. For example, one of the woodcuts in the *Weisskunig*, cut by Hans Burgkmair (1473–1531), shows the young king visiting a cannon foundry (Figure 9.3), where he discusses a major piece of artillery with its creators.[27] The arms maker, dressed in an elaborate garment with slashed sleeves and a work apron tied at his waist, holds a file in his right hand while his left hand rests on the smooth, polished neck of the cannon. His gesture recalls that of the *Landsknecht* guarding the cannon in Dürer's print, who holds a wooden lance in one hand while placing his other hand on the cool metallic surface before him as he engages visually with his interlocutor. By stressing the tactile properties of the gun, these images engage with a culture deeply attuned to the material properties of metalwork.

Although working in woodcut and not etching, Burgkmair suggested an affinity between his art and the esteemed craft of firearms manufacture when he signed his initials prominently on an adjustable mortar, held vertically in a vise and not yet attached to its shaft.[28] With this gesture, Burgkmair – responsible for 118 prints in this ambitious cycle – advanced a connection between his work and that of the prestigious firearms makers, whose mastery of a recent and potent technology captures the interest of the king. Burgkmair also experimented in the technique of etching on iron, producing a single example, his *Venus, Mercury and Cupid*, of c. 1520 (cat. 51). To date, discussions of Burgkmair's etching have focused on its iconography, its technique and whether the print constitutes a success or failure.[29] Yet the experiment itself attests to a wider interest among printmakers to work with materials that had hitherto remained in the purview of specialist armourers. In the case of Burgkmair's *Venus, Mercury and Cupid*, metallurgical

analysis carried out on the surviving plate, now in the British Museum, has demonstrated that the matrix was produced from carburised wrought iron sheets, which were forged together into a pile and then hammered in a process that had been used for centuries to produce sword blades.[30] Although Burgkmair's one foray into the medium probably postdates Dürer's six etchings, it nonetheless helps to situate Dürer's experiments within a wider context of conceptual and material *paragone*, or rivalry, between printmaking and the forging of armour, and between the singular decoration of armour with etched lines and the use of the same processes to produce graphic images.

Dürer was not the first artist to introduce the cannon as a motif in an etching. Hopfer's earliest etching – possibly the very first graphic etching ever, the *Battle of Thérouanne* (Figure 9.4), depicting an imperial victory over the French on 7 August 1479 – includes a prominent display of eight cannons in the foreground. Their intricate forms are far more legible than the profusion of nearly identical bodies crowding the battlefield. Here, Hopfer, the armour decorator, appears to forge an explicit link between the arms trade in which he was active, and the pictorial capabilities of this newfound graphic art derived from the practice of gun manufacture and decoration.[31] He also advanced a significant association between the medium of the printed etching and the depiction of a newsworthy event. The imperial achievement in the battle, won by means of technological as well as military prowess, parallels his own technical achievement in bringing etching to bear in a new graphic form that visualises this event. The self-reflexive nature of his approach to etching the *Battle of Thérouanne* is underscored in the placement of his signature beneath the barrels of gunpower and hammer at the foreground of the print. No soldiers are visible here, and it is not even clear who fired the still smoking cannon. But Hopfer, as arms decorator turned printmaker, asserts his agency as the artist who pictures this noteworthy battle in which technology, rather than human force, delivered the victory.

The spindly cannons splayed across the foreground of this etching are of a decidedly older variety than the firearm Dürer portrayed in *Landscape with a Cannon*. It may be the case that the cannon in *Landscape with a Cannon* had already been retired from use in Nuremberg, but it featured an important innovation in field-artillery of the early sixteenth century that set it apart from earlier models: a trunnion or pivot, visible at the centre of the lafette.[32] This pivot enabled the device to be tipped for firing, then returned to the horizontal position, without being dug into the ground as in older models. The dragons' heads on the cannon call attention to the location of this pivot. Dürer represented precisely such a cannon in his *Etliche underricht zu befestigung der Stett, Schloß und Flecken* (*Several Lessons on the Fortification of City, Castle, and Places* or *Treatise on Fortification*), published in Nuremberg in 1527, just one year before his death. Placed at the end of that treatise, the woodcut depicting such a cannon (cat. 54), extends across the book's opening. It portrays both the large piece of artillery, a cannonball emerging from its bore, as well as the supporting 'Lafette mit Richthörnern', seen from the side and above. This cannon, presented here as a technical marvel, is nearly identical to the firearm in *Landscape with a Cannon*. The guns in both images feature the same dragons' heads and similar coat of arms, although the sighting device that features so prominently on the cannon in the 1518 etching has been augmented in the later woodcut with a crank and gears for raising and lowering the device.

Like the isolated print in Dürer's treatise, the cannon in *Landscape with a Cannon* is the protagonist of the page. Yet, there are no cannonballs, no barrels of ammunition, no brushes or shovels. The cannon is in its horizontal position used for travel, not the diagonal necessary to prepare and fire the gun, but there are also no horses to pull the cannon. These omissions lead us to question whether the cannon has perhaps been left behind, possibly as a relic of battles already fought. Blocks have been placed under its wheels to prevent movement, but the cannon appears oddly unstable,

9.5. Gentile Bellini, *Procession in Piazza San Marco*, 1496, oil on canvas 367 x 745 cm.

Venice, Gallerie dell'Accademia, painted for the Scuola grande di San Giovanni Evangelista. © Gallerie dell'Accademia.

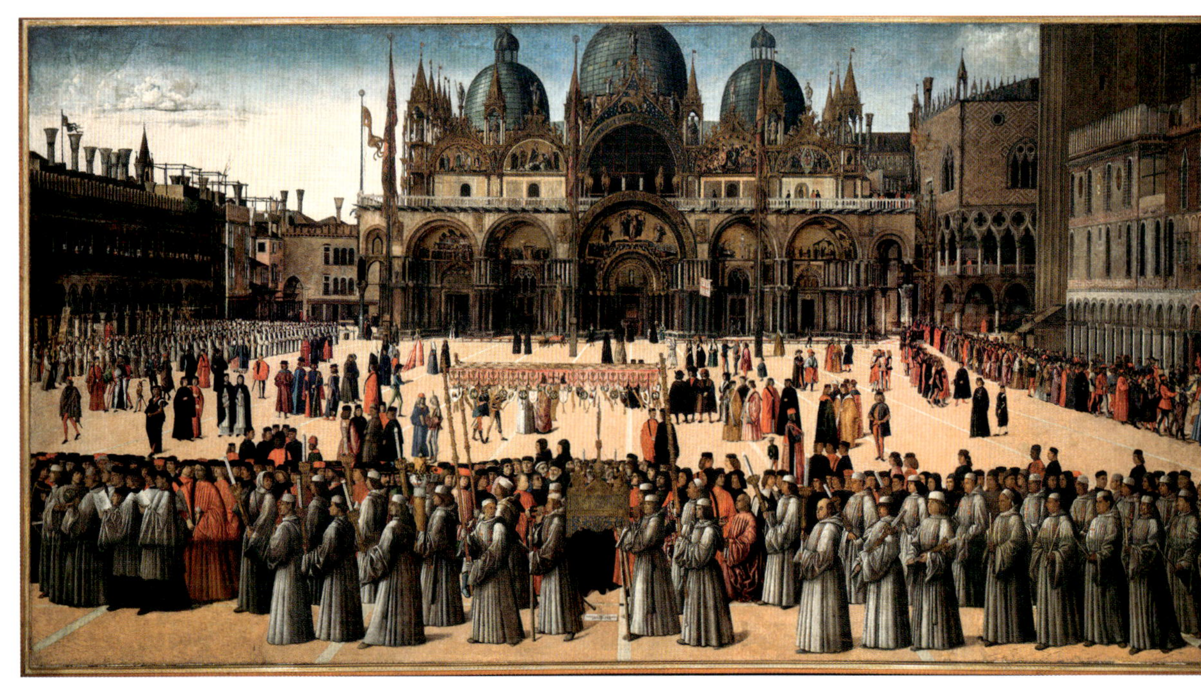

as though a few more degrees of torsion to its axels
might cause this piece of field artillery to tip over and
roll off the page. Rainer Schoch, in his discussion of this
print, argues that the image may allude to the suffering
of war, identifying the twisted wheels of the lafette
as a symbol of hardship.[33] Yet such a reading, while
grounded in contemporary proverbial culture, overlooks
the absolute splendour of the object of attention
dominating the foreground of the print as well as the
apparent prosperity of the well-maintained village in the
distance which bears no traces of armed conflict.

Rather than an implement of active warfare, the cannon
in *Landscape with a Cannon* sits inert at the edge of
a hill. Its presentation here recalls an arms race that
was, as we have seen, as much about the display of
expenditure on beautiful firearms as about their actual
use. At the same time, the idleness of this cannon is also
a reminder of how rapidly even such an impressive gun
might become obsolete. If such cannons had indeed
been decommissioned in Nuremberg and moved to an
armoury for museum-like display, then the presentation
of the unused implement here may underscore its
status as an object of historic significance, rather than
violent use. Exhibited parallel to the picture plane to
be examined from multiple angles, this cannon invites
admiration and wonder, which it visibly elicits from the
foreign visitors in this scene and, implicitly, from the
beholders of the print.

Boundaries drawn

As an object of visual as well as tactile attention,
Dürer's cannon functions as a nodal point for the
cross-cultural interactions among the figures who
straddle the firearm: the *Landsknecht* and his two
compatriots in the middle ground, and the 'foreigners'
who enter stage-left, perplexed and seemingly unsure
of where to fix their gazes as a further *Landsknecht*
follows them closely, possibly as a escort. Larry Silver
has interpreted Dürer's *Landscape with a Cannon* in
relation to an emerging sense of Germanic patriotism,
which developed through the recovery of ancient
sources describing the region and its inhabitants on
the one hand and, on the other, a celebration of the
local terrain.[34] For Silver, the figure of the 'circumspect

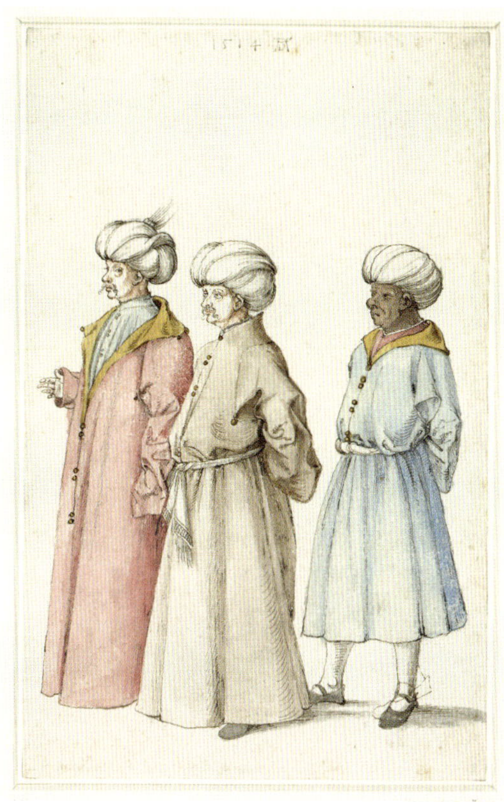

9.6 Albrecht Dürer after Gentile Bellini, *Three Turks
Wearing Long Coats and Turbans*, 1495–1500, pen and
brown ink with watercolour, 306 x 197 mm.

Turk' in the foreground, confronting both the soldier
and the barrel of the gun, 'symbolizes the rival force in
Europe', namely the Ottoman Turks, whose advances
into Habsburg territories were seen to pose an
existential threat to the preservation of the Christian
imperium. The year on the print, 1518, notably
coincides with one of Maximilian's calls for a crusade
against the Turks at the behest of Pope Leo X (1475–
1531). In this context, Silver characterises the print as an
image of the 'protection of the German homeland' as
well as a call to perpetual vigilance against the threat of
Islamic intruders. Ottoman forces were advancing up
the Danube and would lay siege to Vienna in 1529.[35]

While the historical premise of this interpretation
is compelling, the identification of the figures as

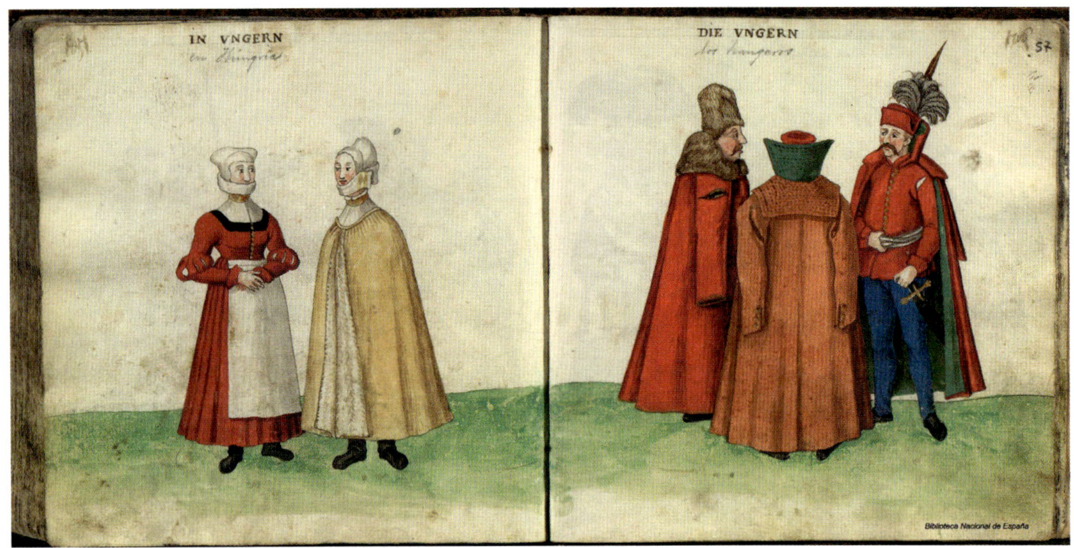

9.7 After Christoph von Sternsee, *Die Vngern* in *Códice de trajes*,
c. 1500–99, fo. 57r, pen, ink and watercolour, 210 x 200 mm.

Madrid, Biblioteca Nacional de España, Res 285. © Biblioteca National de España.

representatives of a threatening Ottoman presence is problematic. The foreign dignitaries appear anything but menacing. Their gestures and expressions suggest interest and even puzzlement. Weighed down in heavy clothes and paused in their journey, they hardly constitute an invading force. Even the figure at right who clutches at the hilt of his sword seems perplexed and perhaps distracted, but not aggressive. What is more, the dress of the figures is notably hybrid, combining elements that are Turkish with others that are eastern European. As discussed above, Dürer's source for the lead figure of this group has long been identified as one member of a trio of Ottoman dignitaries appearing in the far upper right of Gentile Bellini's *Procession in Piazza San Marco*, completed in 1496 (Figure 9.5).[36] Dürer may have examined this work, or preparatory drawings for it, during his trip to Venice, recording the poses of the three figures in a surviving drawing (Figure 9.6).[37] In that pen and wash study, later inscribed with the artist's monogram and the date 1514, Dürer carefully transcribed the features and dress of the two leading figures, changing only their facial hair into twirling moustaches. But he altered the appearance of the third figure considerably, transforming him into a Black servant.

Traces on the sheet reveal that, at first, Dürer drew the figure's left foot raised, as in Bellini's finished painting, but later planted it on the ground. He also coloured the figure's trousers white, rather than red, and changed the colour of his skin.

The significance of these modifications remains unclear, and it is also uncertain why Dürer only returned to this drawing as a compositional source more than a decade after making it. However, it is noteworthy that when Dürer repurposed the middle figure from this group to be the leader of the foreign entourage in his etching, he not only modified the man's facial features and posture but also chose to remove his large spherical turban, the most widely recognisable feature of Ottoman Janissary dress in European print culture at the time.[38] Instead, Dürer dressed his entire cluster of foreigners in high fur hats and berets, which relate more closely to contemporary costumes worn by Hungarians.[39] Similar hats appear on the three figures identified as 'citizens and common people' of Hungary in Christoph von Sternsee's costume album of c. 1548 (Figure 9.7).[40] In a like manner, the robes worn by Dürer's dignitaries combine elements studied from Bellini's Ottoman notables with features of contemporary eastern

European dress. The cloak of the man with the scimitar, for instance, bears close comparison to the *mente* or *pelisse*. Dürer himself may have owned an example of this type of overcoat of Hungarian origin that was worn in eastern Europe and in the Ottoman Empire. A nobleman identified as *Pollachi*, or Polish, wears a similar coat in the *Trachtenbuch* (fol. 59:24r), or costume album, attributed to the French antiquarian Jean-Jacques Boissard (1528–1602) and dated c. 1550–60.[41] Similar dress can be seen on figures identified as *Hungarian* and *Hungarian Nobleman* in Cesare Vecellio's (c. 1521–c. 1601) *Degli habiti antichi e moderni di diverse parti del mondo* of 1590.[42] The remaining foreigners in Dürer's print wear a form of dolman, or fitted, robe-like jacket left open at the front, which had its origins in Turkey but was also worn by Hungarians by the sixteenth century, as seen closed at the front in another drawing from the Boissard *Trachtenbuch* (fol. 70:30r).

It could be that the hybrid dress on these figures was understood as foreign, exotic and eastern in a general sense. The woodcut *Of Foreign Fools* appearing in Sebastian Brant's *Narrenschiff* exhibits a similar variety of costumes and poses, including a figure with a scimitar. Dürer was certainly familiar with this print and its accompanying text, which warns against the foolery of 'Turks, pagans, Saracens in brief / All those who have no true belief, / The heretics to boot (a plague!), / Who have their fool's abode in Prague'.[43] But the figures in *Landscape with a Cannon* seem anything but fools. If they are Hungarians – originating from the same territory as Dürer's family – then this image could be understood to depict an encounter with visitors from a kingdom that was perceived as a Christian bastion against Ottoman military advances at the time, and a significant player in the arms race.[44] Hungarians were slow to enter the so-called gunpowder revolution, but they developed an advanced weapons industry and became important suppliers of artillery to other parts of Europe as well as the Ottoman Empire.[45]

The relations between Hungarian and Ottoman artillery manufacture have been traced to a Hungarian arms producer by the name of Orban. Having failed to sell his knowledge to the Byzantine emperor, Orban purportedly turned to the Ottoman sultan and immediately found employment producing massive

cannons that played an important role in toppling Constantinople.[46] Soon Mehmet II (1431–81) attracted other important cannon founders from Europe, including Jörg of Nuremberg, who apparently was captured from an earlier post in Bosnia and brought into the service of the sultan.[47] Whether or not these accounts are based on fact, they demonstrate how the manufacture of artillery constituted a form of rarefied, specialist knowledge for which courts and cities competed across political boundaries. The acquisition of cannons and cannon manufacture capabilities was one facet in an ongoing cross-cultural rivalry that manifested itself in displays of wealth and of technical as well as artistic virtuosity.[48]

While the visitors in Dürer's print may have registered as Turkish for some contemporary viewers, as they did for later art historians, the careful modification of the figures' dress invites a less polemical reading of the encounter taking place. The possible Hungarian origin of these four elders further complicates any straightforward, stereotyped view on the relationship between the German soldiers and their foreign 'guests'. Entering a strange landscape by unknown means, these foreigners encounter a cannon – an object of great interest in their culture, as in Dürer's. One figure advances to inspect the firearm and possibly to engage its guardian in discussion about the weaponry he touches but does not use.

Setting the stage

If the desire to represent credible foreigners prompted Dürer to return to his earlier studies after Bellini, the challenge of horizontality may have also invited reflection on the Italian artist's approach to the treatment of action and narrative in an expansive setting. Dürer's figural source, Bellini's *Procession in Piazza San Marco*, painted for the Scuola di San Giovanni, unfolds with rich detail a scene of more than fifty years earlier when the procession of the True Cross on the Feast of Saint Mark turned from a civic pageant into a miraculous event in which an injured boy was healed.[49] Scholars have examined connections between Bellini's copious description of setting and the colourful language of a local chronicle tradition in which embellishment could serve as a marker of authenticity.[50] To that end, the carefully observed Ottoman figures in Bellini's large and densely populated painting testify to the cosmopolitan character of contemporary Venice which developed, in part, from a longstanding if at times fraught exchange between that city and the Ottoman world.[51] But as credible witnesses to the scene, these foreigners also play a vital narrative role. Having come to Venice to engage in diplomacy and possibly to trade, they become unexpected witnesses to a mirale. In Bellini's painting, they help to authenticate that miracle and, in so doing, lend credibility to the artist's detailed visualisation of that pivotal historical moment.[52]

As in Bellini's painting, Dürer's men in foreign dress observe and verify the authenticity of the noteworthy yet beguiling sight before them. Their precise place of origin is far from certain, but as unexpected outsiders entering the Germanic landscape near Nuremberg, they represent a group of long-distance travellers who both bring and seek knowledge from afar.[53] Their position in the image, as curious witnesses on the margins, recalls a foreign convention of pictorial narrative description characterised by close observation, inter-cultural dialogue, and historical authenticity that is fostered through the spectacle of abundant and varied pictorial detail.

But while Bellini set his foreign observers toward the back of his image, Dürer brought his forward, posing them close to the position of the print's beholder to serve as models for our gaze. Like Dürer's dignitaries, we find ourselves confronted by an unfamiliar terrain dominated by a strange object: a cannon with no immediate purpose. Neither in use nor abandoned, it stands still, momentarily, to be admired in Dürer's print, which figures this firearm in relation to its own materiality, on the one hand, and in relation to foreign pictorial conventions on the other. In his final etching, Dürer thus portrayed a dual rivalry with two leading artistic media of his time – the Germanic casting and ornamentation of firearms and the rich pictoriality of Italian oil painting. His etching naturalises these forces into a landscape that offers perspectives on its own position at the intersection between a history of technology and a history of art.

Notes

1   Etching, 215 x 320 mm, recorded in at least three states and one roughly contemporary copy by Hieronymus Hopfer (Bartsch 8:518, no. 45). See Meder, *Dürer-Katalog*, no. 96; Schoch, Mende and Scherbaum, *Albrecht Dürer*, I, 210–12, no. 85; H.96; see also Bindewald, 'An Undiscovered State,' 6–7; Veil, *Künstler, Kriege, Kanonen*.

2   The drawing (Strauss, *Complete Drawings*, 1517/18) was formerly at the Museum Boijmans van Beunigen in Rotterdam but is now in Moscow, Puskhin Museum, inv. D.I.121.. There have been attempts to associate the drawing with an actual visit, either in 1517 when Dürer travelled to Bamberg to see the Bishop Georg von Limburg, or when the artist travelled to Kirchenback to visit the famous mathematician, geometer and astronomer Johann Schöner. See Mitius, 'Die Landschaft auf Dürers Eisenradierung', 141–9; Dreßler, 'Nürnbergisch-fränkische Landschaften', 267, no. 16b. It has recently been argued that the drawing was made from the window of the home of Dürer's friend Jakob Muffel. See Jenkins, Orenstein and Spira, eds, *The Renaissance of Etching*, 54, no. 19 (entry by Christof Metzger).

3   Bechtold, 'Zu Dürers Radierung', 112–13.

4   Andrade, *The Gunpowder Age*, 103–14, 201–3.

5   Geddes, *Watermarks*, 134. Toward the end of the sixteenth century, gunpowder and intaglio printmaking both featured in the *Nova Reperta* cycle of new inventions believed to have been unknown in antiquity, designed by Jan van der Straet (Giovanni Stradano) in Florence and published by Philips Galle in Antwerp. See New Hollstein Stradanus, 325 (for *Pulvis pyrius*) and New Hollstein Stradanus, 341 (for *Sculptura aes*).

6   See the account in Landau and Parshall, *The Renaissance Print*, 323–36.

7   Metzger, *Daniel Hopfer*; Spira, 'Between Paper and Sword'.

8   West, 'Albrecht Dürer, Hans Burgkmair', 382, describes Dürer's etched lines as nervous.

9   See Feulner, 'Tradition and Innovation', 23–5, with earlier literature. See also Heuer, 'Evaporating Dürer'.

10 Most recently, Meurer, 'Translating the Hand into Print', esp. 422–7, with earlier literature.

11 Parshall, 'Graphic Knowledge'; Jenkins, Orenstein and Spira, eds, *The Renaissance of Etching*, 46–9, no. 15 (entry by Christof Metzger). Bartrum, *Dürer and his Legacy*, 198, no. 142, discusses the history of the print's title.

12 Schoch, Mende and Scherbaum, *Albrecht Dürer*, I, 197–8, no. 78; H. 22.

13 Jenkins, Orenstein and Spira, eds, *The Renaissance of Etching*, 46, no. 13 (entry by Christof Metzger); see also Dackerman, 'Dürer's etchings', 37–51.

14 Meurer, 'Translating the Hand into Print', 423.

15 For the *Abduction on a Unicorn*, also called the *Rape of Proserpina*, see Schoch, Mende, and Scherbaum, *Albrecht Dürer*, I, 206–8, no. 83; H. 67.

16 Jenkins, Orenstein and Spira, eds, *The Renaissance of Etching*, 49–50, no. 16 (entry by Christof Metzger). The plate, formerly in the collection of Joseph Heller, is in the Staatsbibliothek Bamberg, inv. Kupferplatte 25.

17 Kessler, 'Face and Firmament'; Jenkins, Orenstein and Spira, eds, *The Renaissance of Etching*, 51, no. 17 (entry by Christof Metzger).

18 Bartrum, *Albrecht Dürer and his Legacy*, 82, no. 4.

19 Koerner, *Moment of Self-Portraiture*, esp. 96–8; Meurer, 'Translating the Hand into Print', 444–6.

20 Willers, 'Bemerkungen'; Muller, *Waffen und Rüstungen*; Norman, 'Armour and Weapons', 36–9.

21 Schauerte, *Die Ehrenpforte*, 270–1, no. C 2.12; Alberti, ed., *Le finzioni del potere*, 136, no. 12.[52]. The Holtorp impression comes from a separate edition of the historical panels only, issued c. 1520 by Hieronymus Andreä with Latin text in prose by Benedictus Chelidonius.

22 Silver, *Marketing Maximilian*, 160. On Altdorfer's landscapes, see Wood, *Albrecht Altdorfer*. For a comparison between Altdorfer's and Dürer's approach to etching, see Dackerman, 'Dürer's etchings', 46–50.

23 The manuscript was compiled by Bartholome Freyssleben, Maximilian's chief master of armaments or *Oberst Hauszeugmeister*, and illustrated by Jörg Kölderer. On Maximilian's field artillery inventories, see Boeheim, 'Die Zeugbücher I'; Boeheim, 'Die Zeugbücher II'. See also Hale, *Artists and Warfare in the Renaissance*, 100–3, compare figure 155. On the novel instruments developed to measure of cannons, see Smith, *Lived Experience*, 109–10, fig. 4.9.

24 Terjanian, *The Last Knight*, 266–7, no. 153 (entry by Pierre Terjanian).

25 Silver, *Marketing Maximilian*, 155–6.

26 On these two books, see *ibid.*, 169–214, with earlier literature.

27 B. VII, 224, no. 80.51; Hollstein German V, 117, no. 451. A proof impression of this woodcut is in London, The British Museum, 1912,0513.62.

28 Boudet, *The Ancient Art of Warfare*, 440. figure 462.

29 West, 'Albrecht Dürer, Hans Burgkmair', 379–95.

30 Williams, 'The Metallographic Examination', 92–4.

31 Metzger, 'The Iron Age', 27, notes that this print bears similarities to Israhel van Meckenem's *Judith with the Head of Holofernes*, B.VI.203.1.

32 See Guérout, 'Sixteenth-Century French Naval Guns', esp. 124.

33 Schoch, Mende and Scherbaum, *Albrecht Dürer*, I, 212, no. 11.

34 Silver, 'Germanic Patriotism', 38–68, 216–20.

35 *Ibid.* Silver connects this print to much earlier print, *Five Soldiers and a Turk on Horseback*, generally dated around 1495, in which a turbaned figure rides behind four foppishly dressed soldiers with a fifth seen from behind; see Schoch, Mende and Scherbaum, *Albrecht Dürer*, I, 34–5, no. 4; H.81. The artist engraved his so-called *Turkish Family*, also showing figures in turbans, about one year later; Schoch, Mende and Scherbaum, *Albrecht Dürer*, I, 53–4, no. 14; H. 80.

36 Bechtold, 'Zu Dürers Radierung', 117.

37 The drawing is associated with Dürer's first trip to Italy in Strauss, *Complete Drawings*, 1495/12; Bartrum, *Dürer and his Legacy*, 108–9, no. 38; Aikema and Brown, eds, *Renaissance Venice and the North*, 266–7, no. 38 (entry by Isolde Lübbeke). See, however, Luber, *Albrecht Dürer and the Venetian Renaissance*, 57-58, who rejects the drawing as evidence for Dürer's first Venetian journey and suggests that it derives from a pattern book.

38 Smith, *Images of Islam*, 14–15; Miller, *The Turks and Islam in Reformation Germany*, 77-121.

39 As noted in Cole and Viljoen, *The Early Modern Painter-Etcher*, 86, no. 1 (entry by Larry Silver).

40 See Bond, 'Mapping Culture in the Habsburg Empire', 530-79. Two versions of this manuscript exist: one in Florence, Museo Stibert, and the other in Madrid, Bibliteca National de España, Res 285. See Mezquita Mesa, 'El Códice', 16–41.

41 On the history of this album, see Thimann, 'Erinnerung an das Fremde'. On Dürer's 'Hungarian' coat, see Ashcroft, *Albrecht Dürer*, I, 163.

42 Venice: Damian Zenaro, 1590.

43 Basel, 1506, fol. CXXXr. As cited and translated in Smith, *Images of Islam*, 32–3.

44 Pollak, *Cities at War in Early Modern Europe*, 6.

45 Agoston, *Guns for the Sultan*, 191.

46 Agoston, 'Ottoman Artillery and European Military Technology', 27–8.

47 *Ibid.*, 28–9.

48 See Necipoglu, 'Süleyman the Magnificent and the Representation of Power'.

49 See the summary of events in Rodini, 'Describing Narrative', esp. 26–9.

50 Fortini Brown, *Narrative Painting*, 87–98; Rodini, 'Describing Narrative'.

51 The Fall of Constantinople in 1453 set off a chain of Venetian defeats that resulted in the losses of Negroponte (1470), Tana (1474) and Scutari (1479) in the Aegean. Venice signed a peace treaty with Sultan Mehmed II in 1470 but anxiety over the Ottoman threat continued. See Mack, *Bazaar to Piazza*, 23. See also Kim, 'Gentile in Red'.

52 Carboni, 'Moments of Vision: Venice and the Islamic World, 828-1797', 26.

53 The classic study remains Helms, *Ulysses' Sail*.

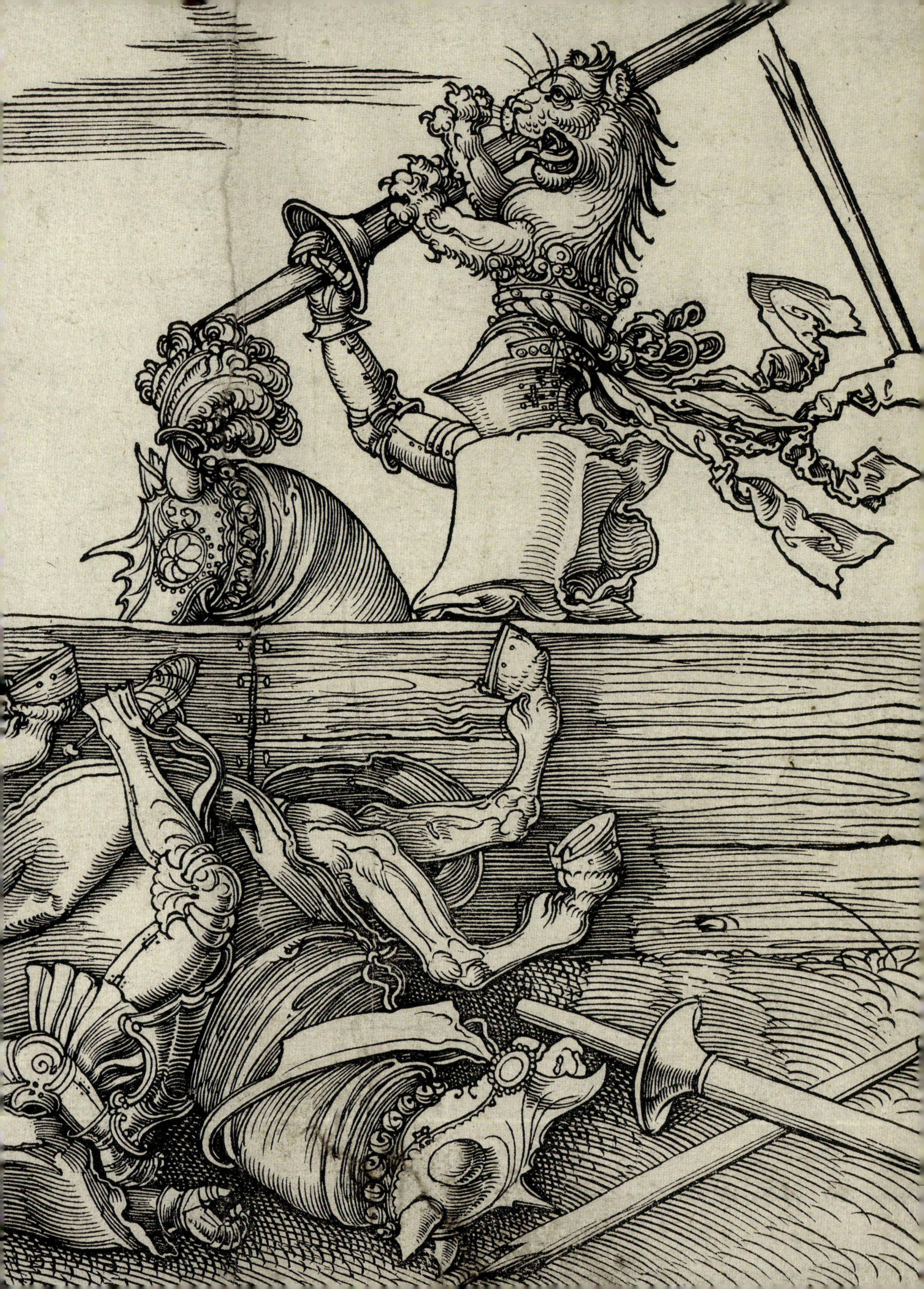

[10] Albrecht Dürer's armour

Larry Silver

Although, of course, Dürer did not make armour, the most expensive of all objects in his day, he often represented it, and made several designs for novel forms of armour for his imperial patron, Maximilian I (1459–1519).[1] As the son of a goldsmith who trained him in metalwork, Dürer was no stranger to thinking about work on and in metallic substances or to applying decorations to them.[2] One major form of armour which Dürer designed, specifically for Emperor Maximilian, was several over life-sized bronze figures for the emperor's tomb (today housed in the Innsbruck Hofkirche).[3]

Armour and Maximilian's tomb project

Original designs by Dürer formed the starting point for three (or more) of the claimed ancestor figures of the emperor on the tomb monument. These were to be fashioned in three dimensions and eventually cast in bronze, sometimes with a middle stage in wood. In one case, for the bronze figure of Maximilian's distinguished ancestor *Count Albrecht IV*, executed after a wooden carving by Landshut-based sculptor Hans Leinberger (c. 1475/80–1537), an original drawing design survives (Berlin, Kupferstichkabinett, though it has recently been attributed instead to an Augsburg artist and Dürer contemporary Hans Burgkmair, 1473–1531).[4] The figure of Albrecht IV (1447–1508) holds a mace and bears a lion on both his shield and his helmet crest. A more certain Dürer drawing design for Maximilian's Tomb is labelled 'Ottoprecht fürscht' (Prince Ottobert) in the artist's own hand and dated 1515.[5] It formed a preliminary sketch for another older, venerable Habsburg ancestor who wears even more fantastic (i.e. ancient) armour that includes a dragon on both shield and crest, and whose imaginary weapon resembles a combination of mace and spear.[6]

Two other bronze ancestors, executed in 1513 by the Renaissance-oriented Nuremberg workshop of Peter Vischer (1487–1528), suggest other, lost designs by Dürer whose drawings surely also fashioned these imposing figures of ancient, legendary heroes claimed as ancestors by Maximilian – *Theodoric the Ostrogoth* and *King Arthur* (!).[7] Both figures lean on their armorial shields in comfortable *contrapposto* poses. While *Theodoric*'s archaic armour displays the same pinched waist design as *Albrecht IV* along with a simple flip-up helmet *bever*, *Arthur* by contrast wears the more rounded design of contemporary Renaissance armour in Germany (particularly Augsburg). Such armour has even come to be described as 'Maximilianic' because of its close association with the current emperor as a design innovator in this exclusive craft.

As the paragon of knightly stature and virtue, *Arthur* closely resembles the principal knightly saint, *Saint George*, as represented in an earlier Dürer engraving of c. 1502 (Figure 10.1).[8] That figure also stands in a relaxed pose and wears contemporary armour while holding his signature red cross banner.[9] At his feet sit both his slain dragon and his feather-crested helmet with visor upraised. The armour already shows the rounded breastplate of Maximilian's devising as well as the lance used for horse combat resting at its right side. The rounded foot covering (*sabaton*) looks natural in contrast to the long, pointed tapered feet (*poulaine*) of previous armour. The plates (*tassets*) above the thigh and knee pieces (*poleyns*) cover an underlying chain mail layer for ease of movement and replace earlier heavily decorated solid pieces.

Maximilian's devotion to his family ancestors was also fully spelled out in woodcuts that illustrated his armoured Habsburg ancestors for his planned *Genealogy of Maximilian I* (1510). These were designed

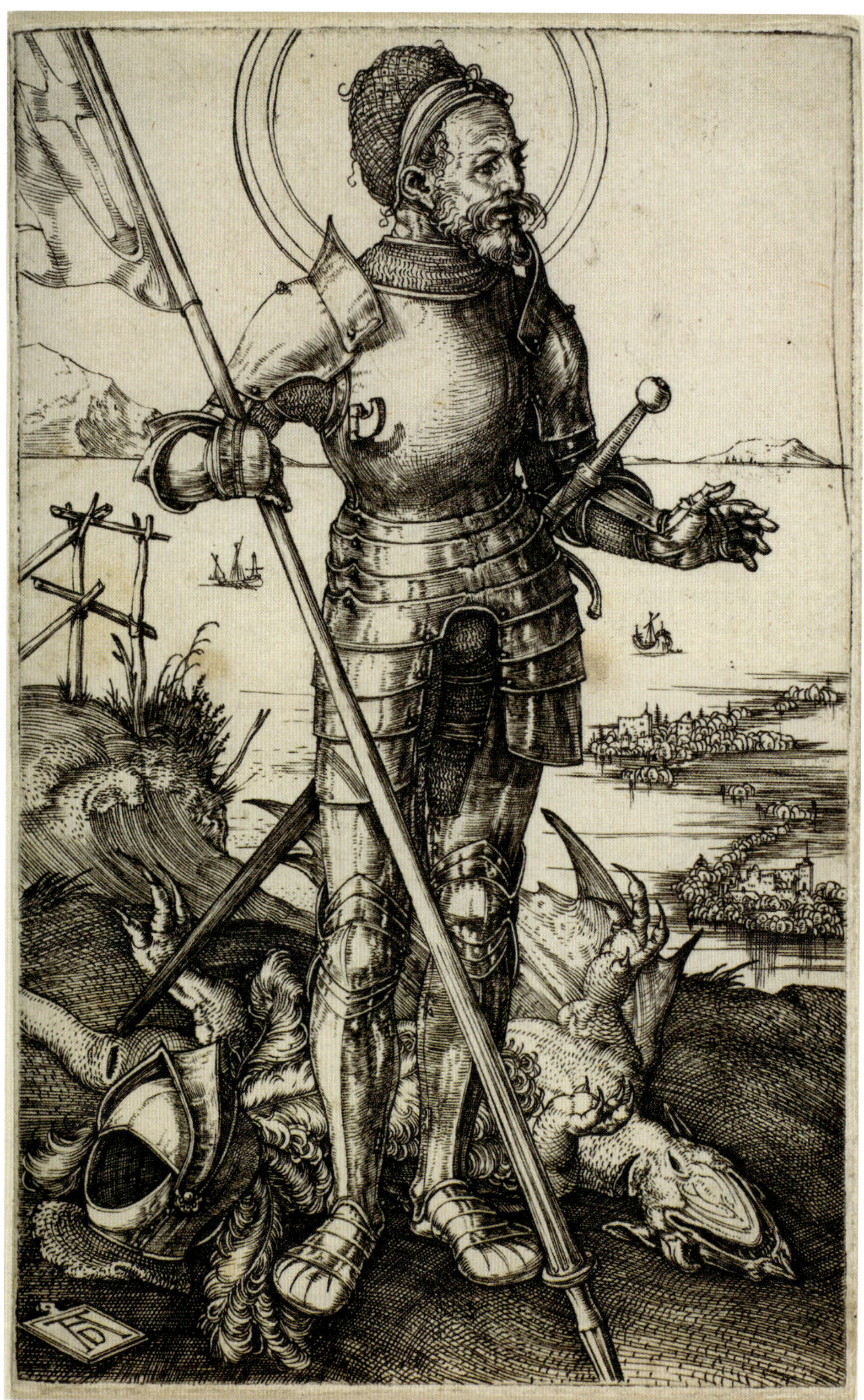

in full by Hans Burgkmair.[10] In Maximilian's lightly
allegorised prose account of his reign's achievements,
the *Weisskunig*, Burgkmair vividly expressed the
emperor's passion for armour production in another
woodcut (Figure 10.2). In a workshop setting, the
emperor is shown personally supervising the creation
of these rounded forms of armour, but the image also
features construction of tournament armour, another
favourite pastime of Maximilian.[11] Despite being active
projects during the second decade of the sixteenth
century, both illustrated projects – the *Genealogy* and
the *Weisskunig* – like so many of Maximilian's efforts
to record his achievements for posterity, were never
finished.[12]

Armour and horseback combat

Besides his cluster of Tomb ancestor figures in
armour, Maximilian avidly pursued various forms of
tournaments and jousts on horseback, a fascination
which, according to the *Weisskunig*, was already
evident in his youth. Another Hans Burgkmair
woodcut shows him as a boy with playmates,
competing across a table with toy knights who joust
on horseback with lances.[13] Maximilian even recorded
his own real-life tournament contests in yet another
planned book of sixty-four tournaments, the *Freydal* (c.
1512–15; also never completed).[14] Preliminary coloured
renderings of those jousts were drawn up for the
Freydal (surviving as a cluster in Vienna and elsewhere),
and Dürer was commissioned to produce woodcuts.
The few that he completed represent each kind of
tournament combat.

Combat on horseback in the joust consisted of two
major kinds of encounters.[15] The first of these was
Rennen, or racing, where lighter lances and armour
tilted with the object of either dismounting the
opposite rider or splintering his shield. Maximilian
devised a new half-helmet for *Rennen* with swept-

10.1 Albrecht Dürer, *Saint George Standing*,
c. 1502, engraving, 113 x 72 mm.

New York, The Metropolitan Museum of Art, Fletcher Fund,
1919, 19.73.61 © The Metropolitan Museum of Art.

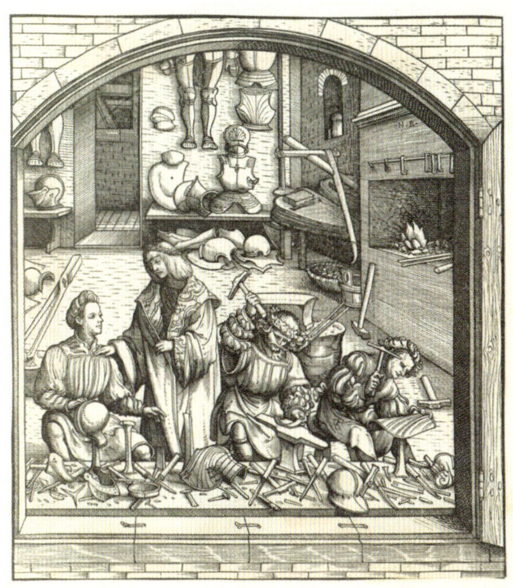

10.2 Hans Burgkmair, *The skill and new invention in armour
mastery* from *Der Weisskunig*, c. 1510–16,
woodcut, 221 x 194 mm.

Vienna, The Albertina Museum, inv. no. HO2006/347
© The Albertina Museum, Vienna.

10.3 Albrecht Dürer, *The Italian Joust*, c. 1516,
woodcut, 224 x 241 mm.

London, The British Museum, Y,8.158
© The Trustees of the British Museum.

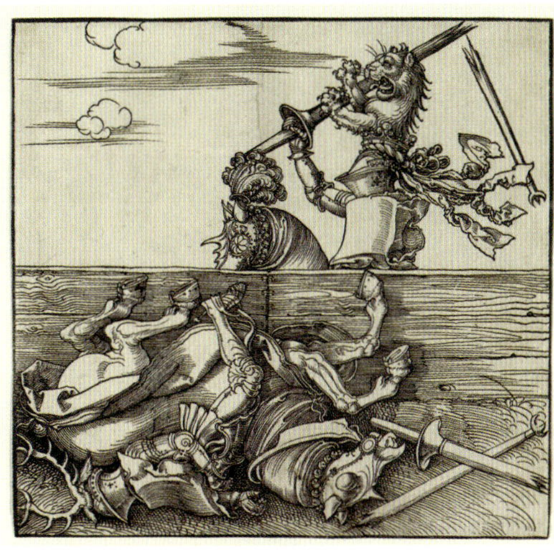

back streamlining, and he standardised the armour for it to include a new feature: exploding shields as targets. These *Rennen* helmets and armour are the ones shown being assembled from component parts in Burgkmair's woodcut. By contrast, *Stechen*, or piercing, involved much heavier armour comparable to that of the battlefield. It featured an especially thick helmet with narrow eye slit and no visor which was tightly attached to the armour and was immobile rather than detachable. *Stechen* lances were massive and often capped so that they could not penetrate the narrow opening of the helmet. Thus the object of *Stechen* was to dismount one's opponent whilst tilting across a barrier. These armoured combatants had to be lifted onto their sturdy warhorses just to compete.

Dürer pictured both types of tournament combats, and his jousting woodcuts for *Freydal* (c. 1517–18) reveal the contrasts between them.[16] His *Rennen* woodcut shows the distinctive helmet forms and expanded chin guards as well as two fly-away shields. The arms of both jousters are exposed to reveal decorative sleeves. By contrast, the *Stechen* woodcut (Figure 10.3) shows the combat across a wooden barrier with splintered lances. As a result of the shock of impact, one horse and rider have fallen over and their bodies lie across the foreground. The added caps on both lances are clearly visible, and these extra-thick helmets are topped by elaborate crests – antlers for the fallen knight and a lion for the upright victor. Dürer's woodcuts conform closely to the coloured preliminary *Freydal* drawings, which are preserved in a volume in Vienna.[17] One can see even more variants on the basic armour equipment for both *Rennen* and *Stechen* in the parade of tournament knights within the sequence of woodcuts – many of them also by Hans Burgkmair – devised for Maximilian's *Triumphal Procession* (also left incomplete at his death in 1519).[18]

Armour studies and designs

Demonstrating his ongoing close observation of contemporary armour, Dürer also incorporated the *Stechen* helmet with its colourful crests into a number of his engravings and woodcuts as a conventional form that supports the display of heraldic coats of

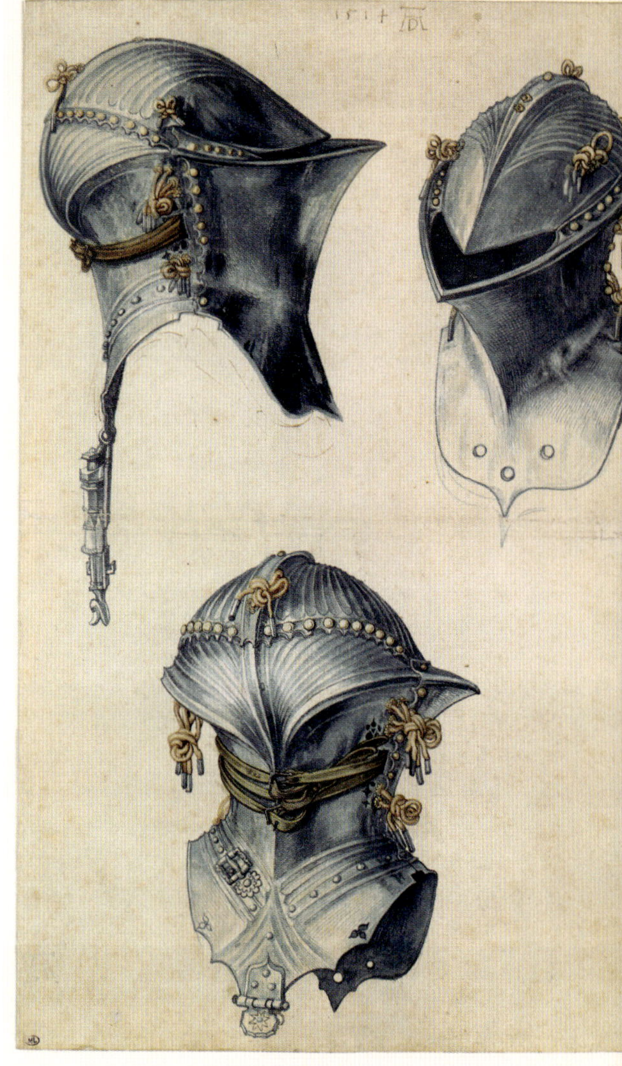

10.4 Albrecht Dürer, *Three Views of a Tournament Helmet*, c. 1498, watercolour 421 x 267 mm.

Paris, Musée du Louvre, Département des arts graphiques, inv.R.F. 5640 © RMN-Grand Palais (musée du Louvre) / Adrien Didierjean.

10.5 Workshop of Albrecht Dürer (possibly Wolf Traut, 1486–1520), *Youthful Maximilian* from *Triumphal Arch of Emperor Maximilian*, c. 1515–17 (detail), woodcut, over 457 x 622 mm.

New York, The Metropolitan Museum of Art, Harris Brisbane Dick Fund, 1928, 28.82.8-41 © The Metropolitan Museum of Art.

arms. Produced around the same time as his *Saint George*, Dürer engraved a *Coat of Arms with Cock* (c. 1502) atop a massive *Stechen* helmet, whose bolt holes are clearly visible.[19] A similar helmet in profile is adorned with a pair of large, lifelike wings in the 1503 Dürer engraving, *Coat of Arms with Skull*.[20] His careful study of *Stechen* helmets derives throughout from a careful watercolour study of a single piece from three viewpoints (c. 1503) (Figure 10.4).[21] It not only shows three bolt holes for attaching the helmet but also the narrow eye opening as well as the tapered neck area that minimised the danger from lances. Rows of streamline grooves also ornament this closely observed object, which is decorated with a favourite Maximilian pattern of armorial pleating.

In 1498 Dürer first depicted a profile mounted man in armour. This image has often been associated with his famous later engraving, *Knight, Death and the Devil* (1513) (cat. 75), in part because both lances display fox pelts.[22] This early watercolour shows Dürer's meticulous interest in contemporary armour; what has seldom been noted is that this cladding is not combat

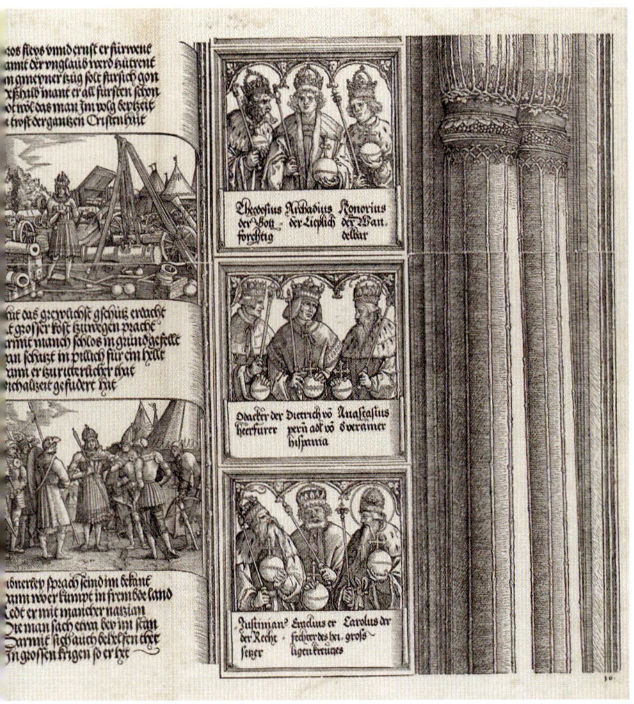

armour but rather the distinctive half-helmet (*sallet*) of a *Rennen* jouster (compare cat. 76). Closer inspection of the 1513 engraving also shows the distinctive *Rennen* helmet, as well as ornamental pleating that was appropriate to festive occasions rather than the battlefield. Both the watercolour drawing and the 1513 engraving underscore the crucial importance of the horse in the conduct of knights in jousting and in warfare. After all, the English term 'chivalry' comes from the French *cheval* ('horse'), and in his diary of his travels to the Low Countries in 1520–21, Dürer expressly called this same engraving *der Ritter*, or 'the knight'.[23]

Unsurprisingly, Maximilian was often portrayed at full length in profile as an armoured knight on horseback. Complemented by a *Saint George*, this imagery appeared shortly after his official coronation in Trent in 1508 in a Hans Burgkmair woodcut.[24] At the same time, a 1509 profile equestrian portrait of Maximilian by Ulrich Ursentaler (1482–1562) was produced as a presentation coin to celebrate the coronation. Here the armour more closely resembles the rounded breastplate and open visor of *King Arthur* and was based on the Augsburg creations by Lorenz Helmschmied (c. 1450/55–1515), the principal court armourer.[25] Maximilian also planned for an equestrian statue to be placed in Augsburg. It was to be based on a profile drawing in armour by Burgkmair (c. 1508–9) and was to be carved by the local sculptor Gregor Erhart (c. 1465–1540/41); it, too, was never executed.[26]

By the middle of the decade, Dürer was working closely for the emperor, principally as designer for the nearly 200 woodcuts of his massive *Arch of Honour* ensemble.[27] One of the first images (as realised by an artist in the workshop, possibly Wolf Traut, 1486–1520) shows Maximilian surrounded by the elements of his military and tournament interests (Figure 10.5). These items chiefly consist of metal objects, including: artillery; cannon and mortar, as seen in *Landscape with a Cannon* of 1518 (cat. 52; see Edward Wouk's 'Landscape with a Cannon' in this volume); metal battlefield weapons; a halberd and a pike. Prominent on the ground before him sits a cluster of various helmets from armour groupings, ranging from an open visor to a closed *Stechen* guard beside it, and on the opposite side a *Rennen* helmet beside a closed visor of battlefield armour. The youthful future emperor, holding both orb and battle sword, stands in the image centre and is fully clad in the very armour that he advanced. Like the armour used for *King Arthur*, it also includes an open visor (here crowned by a plethora of feathers), a rounded breastplate with grooved ornament, layered plates along the legs and square-toed footwear.

While working for Maximilian, Dürer also produced drawings in c. 1517 for pieces of individual luxury decorated armour. The most elaborate of these was a design for a helmet visor that was intended for etched decorations that included a variety of motifs: a dragon in front, a peasant with a bagpipe, an angry heron and a row of vases (perhaps an allusion to a knightly order), as well as vegetal ornament of flower and vines.[28] These decorations would have been imposed onto the steel surface of the armour through an acid used for etching, a technique (*Eisenradierung*) pioneered in Augsburg by Daniel Hopfer (1470–1536) and later used for his own independent single-sheet prints.[29]

An unusual but related drawing by Dürer of a design for a saddle, continued the ornamental inventiveness of his own armour designs while transposing it to a different material: ivory.[30] The unusual configuration of the drawing confirms that it was another courtly design, specifically for the pommel of a particular luxury M-shaped saddle. This traditional late medieval form is known chiefly from Hungary, one of the Habsburg territorial possessions of Maximilian (and of the future Austro-Hungarian Empire) acquired by marriage in 1515. Dürer's decorations include a two-headed heron at the centre, accompanied by a peasant with a bagpipe and a spiky unicorn–serpent monster. Because ivory can be carved with sharp tools like the burin used on a copperplate for engravings, Dürer's complex designs did not have to be compromised from the paper page to the proposed final product. In terms of iconography, the artist has included a pair of dangerous women: the peasant is being tempted by a naked woman with a mirror, and on the opposite side a harpy chimera with wings, a long reptilian tail and a lion's body crouches. Such

images – warnings about the power of women over even the strongest of men – also adorned the armour of knights to challenge their resistance to lust and to reassert their warlike valour.

Unlike Hopfer, Dürer did not directly engage with etching on metal for armour decoration, and his own experiments with the print medium of etching, usually on iron rather than the steel compound of armour, was brief and largely unsuccessful. If we examine carefully the most successful of his etchings, his 1518 *Cannon*, we fail to see the remarkably dense, fine lines of the artist's own extraordinary recent engravings, most notably his *Knight, Death, and the Devil* with its own display of refined, contemporary armour worn by the protagonist. Instead, Dürer's etchings more closely resemble his woodcuts, where the brittle resistance of carving woodblocks necessarily limited both the fineness and the density of lines (though Dürer managed to expand the capacity of woodcuts to imitate the successful naturalistic representation of engravings).[31]

Dürer's imagery for knights, originally more a matter of observing and incorporating the major innovations in contemporary German armour, intensified in the new century as he drew closer to the imperial court. There he produced woodcuts for the planned *Freydal* publication in order to record the emperor's love of tournament jousts, but he also generated decorative designs for new armour pieces (and even for one Hungarian saddle with engraved ivory panels), and additionally designed whole suits of armour, both archaic and contemporary, for several of the bronze standing figures of Maximilian's putative ancestors for the emperor's ambitious tomb project. Thus, across his career, albeit chiefly on paper, Dürer engaged deeply with the representation of armour. He remained aware of its materiality but also, especially in his proposed decorations for new pieces, pushed both the limits and the conventions of that art form.

Notes

1 On Maximilian and armour, see Terjanian, 'The Currency of Power', 17–37; Haag, *Kaiser Maximilian I*; Terjanian, 'Princely Armor'; Silver, *Marketing Maximilian*, 147–59.

2 Smith, 'Dürer and Sculpture'.

3 The basic study remains Oberhammer, *Die Bronzestandbilder*, also Egg, *Die Hofkirche in Innsbruck*; Scheicher, 'Kaiser Maximilian plant sein Grabmal'; Seipel, *Werke für die Ewigkeit*; Terjanian, *The Last Knight*, 298–9, nos. 168–9. For the proposed locations of the Tomb, see Schauerte, 'Annäherung an ein Phantom'.

4 Ink on paper with colour tints, c. 1515. Berlin, Kupferstichkabinett no. KdZ 4260 (W. 677 in the Winkler catalogue); Michel, *Emperor Maximilian I and the Age of Dürer*, 360–1, no. 119. A copy of this drawing survives in Liverpool, Walker Art Gallery. The Berlin drawing has been reattributed from Dürer to Hans Burgkmair by Fredia Anzelewsky, although it might also be a second version of a lost preliminary design. Anzelewsky, 'Entwürfe Hans Burgkmairs', 59–62.

5 Also in Berlin, Kupferstichkabinett; inv. no. 26812.

6 Wood, 'Maximilian I as Archeologist', 1160–5, figure 10, with references, n. 127. Because the drawing has colour notes, it probably served as a sketch for the more finished and coloured Tomb figures, laid out in advanced plans on a parchment scroll by Maximilian's court secretary Jörg Kölderer, on whom, see Scheichl, 'Who Was (or Were) Jörg Kölderer', 80–9, 170–1, no. 21.

7 Views in the round at www.nuremberg.museum/projects/show/198-king-theoderich-innsbruck and https://www.nuremberg.museum/projects/show/197-king-arthur-innsbruck. See also Terjanian, *The Last Knight,* 299, no. 169.

8 Schoch, Mende and Scherbaum, *Albrecht Dürer*, I, 100–1, no. 34a; H.55.

9 For German armour history, see Gamber, 'Der Turnierharnisch'; Nickel, 'Arms and Armor'; Terjanian, 'Princely armor'; Terjanian, *The Last Knight*.

10 B.VII.223, no, 79; Hollstein German V, 110, nos 325–415.

11 B.VII.224. no. 80/50; Hollstein German V, 116–19, nos 431–551; Terjanian, *The Last Knight*, 220–3, nos 114–15.

12 For Maximilian and Burgkmair, see Silver, 'The "*Papierkaiser*"', 91–9; for the *Genealogy* and *Weisskunig*, *ibid*., 168–9, 288–9, nos 20, 74.

13 B. VII, 224, no. 80/17; Hollstein German V, 116, no. 439.

14 Michel, *Emperor Maximilian I and the age of Dürer*, 282–4, no. 72; Krause, 'Die ritterspiel'; Krause, *Freydal*. In a recorded dictation from the period 1505/08 Maximilian uses the name *Freithart*, or open heart, for the allegorical hero (himself) of his self-described 'comedi'.

15 Pfaffenbichler, 'Maximilian I. und das höfische Turnier', 129–65.

16 Schoch, Mende and Scherbaum, *Albrecht Dürer*, III, 154–7, nos 271.1-2. A third Dürer woodcut for the *Freydal* showed armoured combat with weapons on foot.

17 Vienna, Kunsthistorisches Museum, Kunstkammer, inv. Nr. 5073; specifically compare Krause, 'Die ritterspiel', figures II. 50.4, 50.9.

18 Appuhn, 1979; Michel, *Emperor Maximilian I and the Age of Dürer*, 268–71, no. 68.

19 Schoch, Mende and Scherbaum, *Albrecht Dürer*, I, 101–3, no. 35; H.97.

20 *Ibid.*, I, 105–7, no. 37; H. 98. See also his late woodcut (1523) with his own coat of arms, an open door (*Tür*) on a shield below a profile *Stechen* helmet, crested with a 'moor's' head; *ibid.*, II, 484–5, no. 258; H. 288.

21 Paris, Louvre; see Strauss, *Complete Drawings* 1495/49.

22 Vienna, Albertina; see Strauss, *Complete Drawings* 1498/48; Robison, *Albrecht Dürer: Master Drawings*, 90–2, no. 19; Michel, *Emperor Maximilian I and the age of Dürer*, 334–5, no. 101. The work is inscribed in Dürer's hand, 'This was the armour at that time in Germany'.

23 Ashcroft, *Albrecht Dürer*, I, 567. ('At Antwerp, 22 November–3 December 1520'), 'Note: Cashed 2 crowns for expenses. For two *Adam and Eves*, one *Sea Monster*, one *Jerome*, one *Knight....*'

24 Hollstein German V, 74, no. 253. See Silver, 'Shining Armor', 8–29; Michel, *Emperor Maximilian I and the Age of Dürer*, 348–53, no. 113.

25 Terjanian, *The Last Knight*, 33, 101–4, 181–3, 206, 236–41, nos 26, 28, 88, 128–32; Lange-Krach, *Maximilian I. (1459–1519)*, 268–73, nos 55–7; Teget-Welz, *Ingeniosus Magister*, 61–7; for Erhart's role in sculpture for Maximilian's Tomb, *ibid.*, 261–71, no. B-01 (Elisabeth von Görz-Tirol).

26 Vienna, Albertina, inv. 22447; see Lange-Krach, *Maximilian I*, 296–7, no. 72; Michel, *Emperor Maximilian I and the age of Dürer*, 348–53, no. 111.

27 Schoch, Mende and Scherbaum, *Albrecht Dürer*, II, 393–412, no. 238; H. 251; Schauerte, *Die Ehrenpforte*; Michel, *Emperor Maximilian I and the age of Dürer*, 373–6, no. 124.

28 Vienna, Albertina, c. 1515–17; see Strauss, *Complete Drawings* 1517/3. Terjanian, *The Last Knight,* 176–8, nos 83–5; Michel, *Emperor Maximilian I and the age of Dürer*, 340–1, nos 104–5. These pen ornaments closely resemble Dürer's marginal pen decorations for the *Prayerbook of Emperor Maximilian*; Strauss, *The Book of Hours of the Emperor Maximilian the First*; Lange-Krach, *Das Gebetbuch Kaiser Maximilians I*.

29 Metzger, *Daniel Hopfer*, esp. Spira, 'Daniel Hopfer und die geätzte Dekoration von Rüstungen', 68–85; Terjanian, 'Princely Armor'.

30 Morgan Library and Museum, c. 1517, no. I, 256; see Strauss, *Complete Drawings*, 1517/5. See references to this related group of drawings in note 26, and also Robison, *Albrecht Dürer: Master Drawings*, 80–2, no. xxiv. For the unusual structure of Hungarian saddles and a catalogue of extant works, see Radway, *In the Name of Saint George*. The author is grateful to Dr Radway for sharing her research.

31 Silver and Cole, 'Fluid Boundaries', 5–35, esp. 6–7; Dackerman, 'Dürer's Etchings: Printed Drawings?', 37–51. Also, Talbot, 'Printmaking', 59–60.

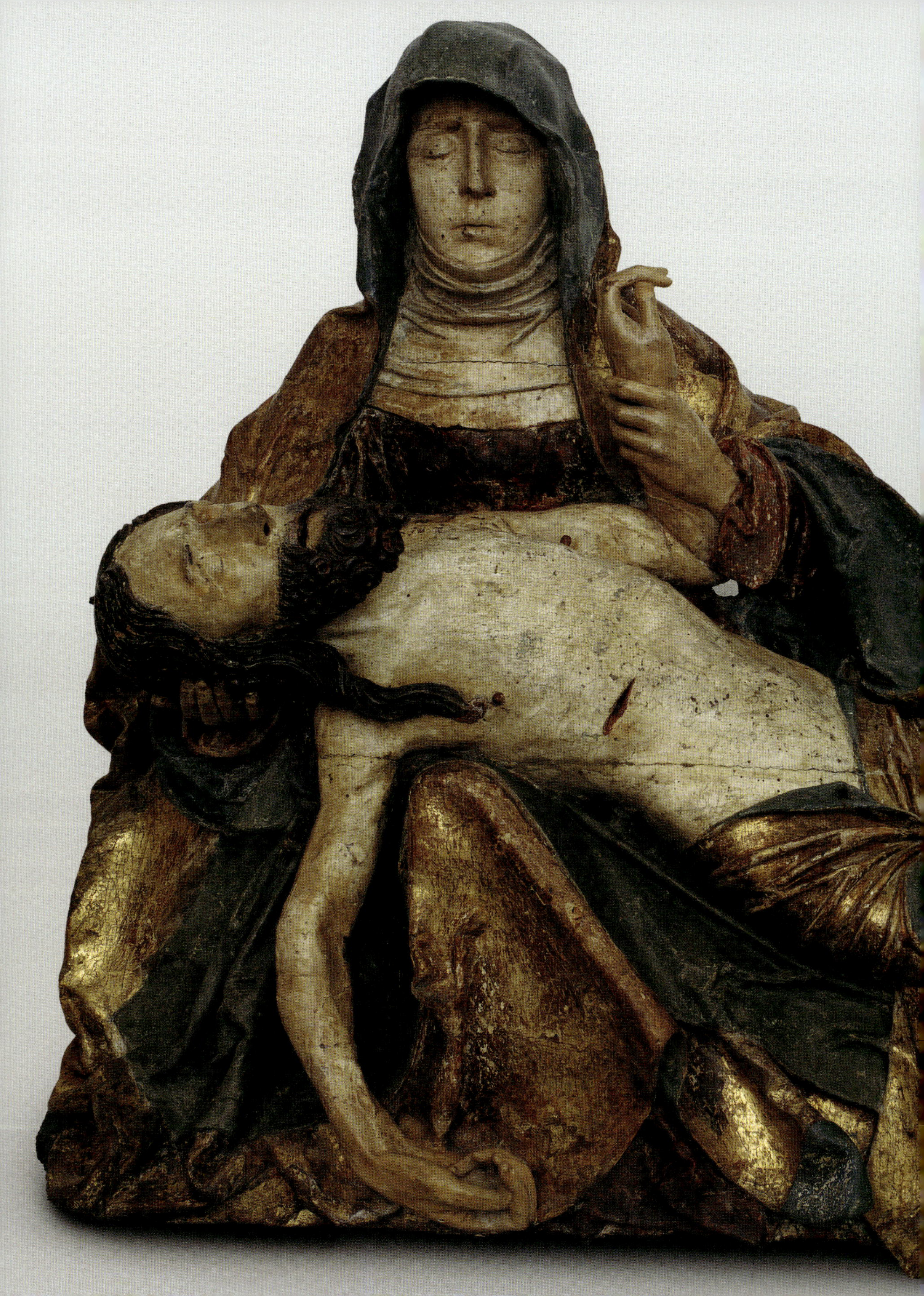

[11] The Whitworth's sculpted *Pietà* from Renaissance Germany

Holly Fletcher

At vespers our Lord was taken from
The Cross and laid before His mother.
His strength and might now lay hidden
In God's bosom on that same day[1]

Albrecht Dürer wrote these lines as part of his 1510 devotional verse on 'The Seven Daily Times of Prayer'. He based the verse on the *Hours of the Cross*, a form of structured devotion focusing on the sequence of Christ's Passion which began appearing from the fourteenth century in Books of Hours, a popular type of prayerbook intended for lay worship. The moment described by Dürer in this section of the text is the same as that depicted in the sculpted wooden *Pietà* in the Whitworth's collection (cat. 7). The pietà, a devotional form which emerged in the German-speaking lands at the end of the thirteenth century, presents the lifeless body of Christ across his mother's knee following his descent from the cross. As Dürer's lines indicate, the bereft Virgin's contemplation of Christ's body was believed to have taken place at the canonical hour of vespers in the early evening, hence the German term for the pietà, *Vesperbild*.[2] In Italian 'pietà' means 'compassion', and this title reflects the suffering the onlooker was meant to experience when viewing such images of grief.

The figure of Christ presented in the Whitworth's *Pietà* aligns with Dürer's meditation on the weakness of his earthly body. Christ's emaciated form lies uncomfortably across Mary's lap in a sloping diagonal. His right arm curves around to the base of the sculpture, and his little finger curls in to meet the wound on his right hand, which is coloured with red pigment, marking where he was nailed to the cross. The entire sculpture has been painted in multiple colours, in a technique called polychromy. The contrast between Christ's pale body and the blue interior of Mary's gown on which he lies focuses the viewer's gaze upon his lifeless form.[3] The gilding that outlines the Virgin's gown surrounds both figures, encircling mother and son. Dürer appealed to the 'heartfelt grief' of Mary for her son's suffering, and in the *Pietà* her sorrow is depicted through her downward gaze and solemn expression.[4] She gently cups Christ's head in her right hand, while her other hand grips his left wrist, alerting the viewer to the wound, which she grazes with her index finger.[5]

Origins

The Whitworth's *Pietà*, acquired in 1972, dates to the beginning of the sixteenth century.[6] The style and treatment of the figures suggest it was created sometime around 1510, most likely in southern Germany.[7] We find Christ's body in a similar position, draped over his mother's knee with his legs outstretched, in a sculpture from 1510–20 in the Bavarian National Museum in Munich (Figure 11.2) showing the *Lamentation*. Such larger gatherings of figures mourning Christ's death, which typically include Saint John the Baptist and Mary Magdalene, formed the basis for the iconography of the pietà. While the figures appear stiffer in this example, the modelling of Christ's body, with his faintly visible ribs, veins and muscles, closely resembles the Whitworth's *Pietà*. The provenance of the Munich sculpture is unknown, but it is believed to have been produced in middle Franconia, the region where Dürer's home city of Nuremberg is located.[8] It is possible that the artist who carved the Whitworth's *Pietà* may also have been based in Franconia, though this is less certain. But the *Pietà*'s sculptor would almost certainly have been familiar with Dürer's work, since by the beginning of the sixteenth century Dürer had already achieved considerable

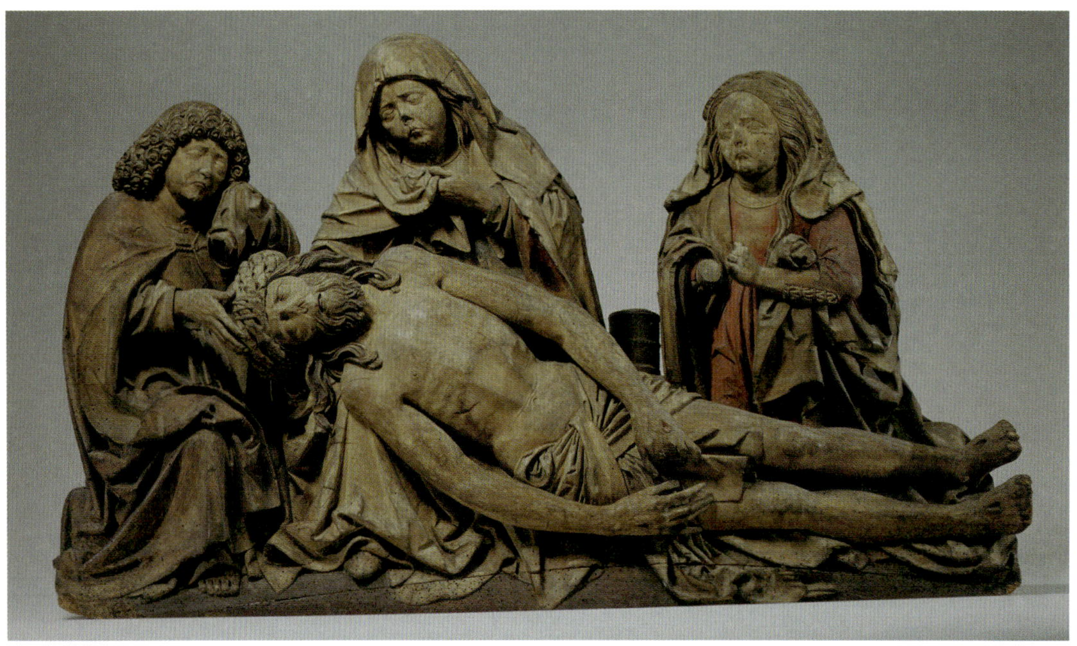

11.2. *Lamentation* (probably from a predella), c. 1510/20, German (Middle Franconia?) wood and polychrome, 61 x 103 x 21.5 cm.

Bavarian National Museum, inv. no. MA 1301. © Bavarian National Museum

fame throughout Germany and beyond, chiefly through the circulation of his prints. The *Pietà* was thus created against the same cultural backdrop as Dürer's oeuvre, and Dürer himself produced an image of *The Lamentation of Christ* for his *Great Passion* woodcut series between c. 1497 and 1500 (cat. 28). Dürer's woodcut *Lamentation of Christ* shares some notable similarities with the Whitworth's *Pietà*. For instance, Christ's body lies horizontally at the bottom of the print while the Virgin, similarly dressed in a wimple to cover her head, holds Christ's hand, drawing attention to the wounds of his Passion. Moreover, this image displays an interest in the affective properties of drapery (see 'The workshop' in this volume) which is likewise evident in the *Pietà* where the heavy, carved folds of the Virgin's gown serve to create a sense of stillness and solemnity, reflecting the personal devotion and prayer which images of the pietà invited.

There is physical evidence that the Whitworth's *Pietà* once formed part of an altarpiece, particularly the carved-out reverse of the sculpture, which suggests that it was intended to be viewed from the front. The *Pietà* may have been incorporated into a predella, the section at the base of an altarpiece, and indeed several contemporary examples of predellas featuring the *Lamentation* do exist.[9] Thus, we might imagine this sculpture as part of a larger visual ensemble that included painted narrative panels and rich embroideries, recalling the Whitworth's earlier German altar frontal depicting the Tree of Jesse against a rich red background (cat. 9), as well as implements of the mass made from a range of materials including brass, silver and gold, which Dürer closely observed in his 1511 *The Mass of Saint Gregory* (cat. 8; see Charles Zika's 'Objects of devotion' in this volume). The *Lamentation* made a particularly fitting subject for a predella because of its theological connection to the transubstantiation, or conversion of the bread and wine into the body and blood of Christ in the Eucharist, which would be performed in front of the predella on the altar. During this ritual, the *Pietà* would have reminded the congregation of the body of Christ which they were to consume. In some examples of other sculpted pietàs from medieval Germany, the host may have even been kept inside the wound on Christ's side, further strengthening this connection with the Eucharist.[10]

The Whitworth's *Pietà* was most likely sculpted from limewood, which was the main type of wood used by sculptors in southern Germany during this period.[11] The use of limewood for the *Pietà* is indicated by the uniform grain structure of the wood when viewed under a microscope. Limewood's even structure

11.3. Monogrammist S, *The Seven Sorrows of Mary*, 1516–45, engraving, 149 x 105 mm.

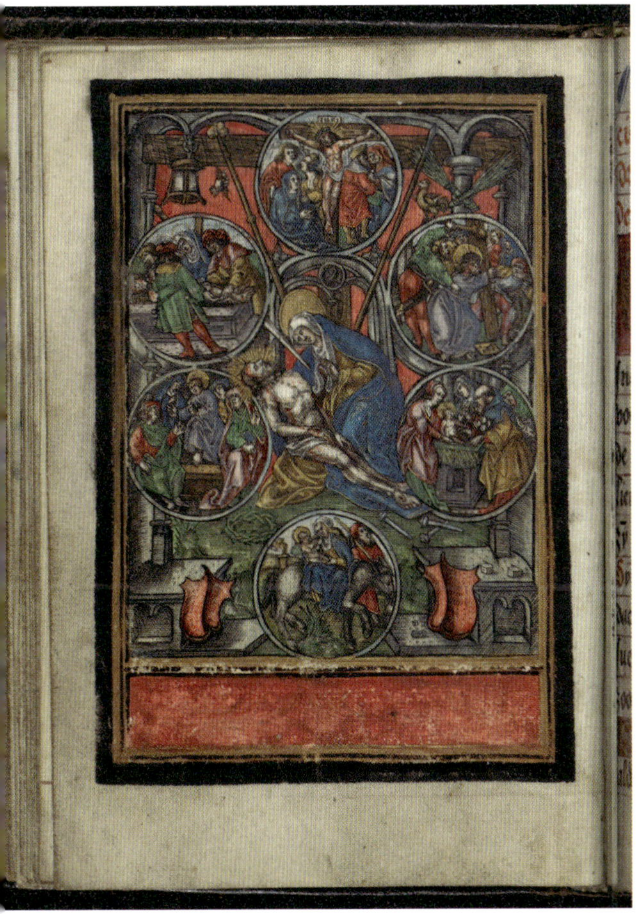

makes it particularly favourable for sculpting, as it possesses greater softness and elasticity than the more heavily cell-structured oak, for example.[12] While it is a relatively stable species of wood, limewood nevertheless undergoes continuous shifting, shrinking and swelling in response to the humidity of its environment. Sculptors would typically hollow-out their limewood before carving, removing its heartwood to minimise the likelihood of the outer sapwood splitting, and thus stabilising their creations. This may also be why the reverse of the Whitworth's *Pietà* has been carved away. At the time it was made, limewood was a relatively expensive and sought-after material. Despite being grown locally in southern Germany, including in two large forests surrounding the city of Nuremberg, the sale of limewood was highly regulated. The value of limewood was also tied to its spiritual and religious significance. In the early modern German language, the word *Linde* could mean both lime tree and holy grove. Lime groves could act as sites of pilgrimage, while holy lime trees might be hung with votive tablets to ward off sickness.[13] Just as the subject of the pietà encouraged devotion, its material also required respect and reverence from both the viewer and the sculptor.

The pietà in devotion

The pietà emerged as an artistic subject in the context of a growing devotional movement in northern Europe which found its clearest expression in German mysticism.[14] Medieval German mystics emphasised a deeply personal and emotional devotion to God, encouraging the development of images which enabled their viewers to visualise and meditate upon the suffering of Christ.[15] Saint Mechthild of Hackeborn (1241–89) recorded a vision she beheld while contemplating an image of the pietà, in which the Virgin asked her to reflect deeply on the redemptive power of Christ's wounds and even to approach and kiss those specific parts of the sculpture.[16] Such pietistic devotion also left its mark in Renaissance Nuremberg. In 1492, the Nuremberg printer Anton Koberger (1445–1513), Dürer's godfather, published the well-known *De imitatione Christi* (The Imitation of Christ) by Thomas à Kempis (1380–1471). Kempis's text emphasised contemplative devotion, and he instructed his readers, for example, to 'rest … in the passion of Christ and dwell willingly in His sacred wounds'.[17] Images of subjects such as the pietà were intended to assist with such contemplation.

One important development emerging from this popular piety was the cult of the Seven Sorrows of the Virgin. The confraternity of the Seven Sorrows was founded in the 1490s in three Netherlandish churches, with the politically motivated intention of inspiring widespread, cultic devotion in regions under Burgundian-Habsburg rule. It spread rapidly throughout the Low Countries and beyond, including in Germany, gaining a substantial number of followers. The veneration of the Seven Sorrows involved meditating upon the Virgin's suffering and her compassion for Christ. This was accomplished through simple spiritual exercises performed by members of the confraternity each week, thus combining private devotion with collective religious experience.[18] Throughout the fifteenth and sixteenth centuries, numerous artworks were created which paid homage to this popular cult. The works typically present the sorrowful Virgin or *Mater dolorosa* and often include small scenes of her various torments. Dürer himself painted a polyptych on this theme for Friedrich the Wise, Elector of Saxony (1463–1525), around 1495–8.[19] The image of the pietà was frequently depicted at the centre of such works, as in *The Seven Sorrows of Mary* by Monogrammist S from the first half of the sixteenth century (Figure 11.3), and sculptures of the pietà were occasionally believed to perform miracles in association with devotion to the Seven Sorrows.[20] It is possible that the Whitworth's *Pietà* may have been created for veneration in a chapel associated with the confraternity of the Seven Sorrows and may even have been believed to be miraculous. Whether or not this was the case, the prominence of the cult within German devotional culture at the time of the *Pietà*'s production would have informed both its creation and reception.

While the pietà's depiction of Mary's grief may have held particular significance for female viewers, her suffering was commonly understood to represent the grief of humankind for Christ's sacrifice and was not gender specific.[21] In images of the *Mater dolorosa*, the Virgin acted as a model for all viewers to participate in

Christ's Passion.[22] In a prayer from 1510, recorded with the verse cited at the outset of this essay and possibly intended for a devotional broadsheet, Dürer entreated the Virgin: 'through the bitter pain you bore with great lamentation when your dead son lay before you, come to my help in my distress'.[23] Dürer's verse thus indicates how both men and women might appeal to Mary's suffering in their devotion. More important than her gender in images of the pietà was Mary's humanity. In the late fifteenth century, emphasis was placed on the tender relationship between Christ and his human mother. Dürer produced several depictions of the Madonna and Child which gave prominence to the very human relationship between mother and son; the pietà acts as a solemn counterpoint to this motif. In his 1514 engraving, *Virgin and Child by the Wall* (cat. 29), the Virgin is shown without a halo, gazing at her baby with palpable tenderness. The Whitworth *Pietà* similarly evokes the humanity of Mary who appears, above all, as a grieving parent.

During the turmoil of the Reformation and Counter Reformation in the sixteenth century the significance of Mary in German devotional culture came under pressure. Reformers rejected the veneration of Catholic saints and Martin Luther (1483–1546) declared the invocation of Mary idolatrous. Although a note written by Dürer in 1523 suggests that he agreed with Luther's teaching on the subject, it also reflects contemporary ambivalence about devotion to the Virgin. Condemning the unruly masses of worshippers at the pilgrimage site of the miraculous Beautiful Madonna in Regensburg, Dürer wrote: 'This superstition has arisen at Regensburg in defiance of Holy Scripture … God help us not to dishonour his worthy Mother in this manner, but rather to honour her'.[24] For Dürer, while images of Mary should not be the subject of idolatrous adoration, the mother of God nevertheless demanded honour and respect. Indeed, many devotional images of Mary remained in reformed cities and churches throughout the Reformation, including in Lutheran Nuremberg.[25] That the Whitworth's *Pietà* has survived in good condition suggests that it continued to be a respected object that encouraged reflection on the passion of Christ and the sorrow of the Virgin.

Notes

1   Ashcroft, *Albrecht Dürer*, I, 303.

2   Jeep, *Medieval Germany*, 391

3   Although its polychromy is mostly the result of later overpainting, conservation work conducted in preparation for this exhibition uncovered traces of original paint layers on Mary's face and in Christ's side wound.

4   Ashcroft, *Albrecht Dürer*, I, 302.

5   The *Pietà* was carved from three pieces of wood which were cut radially and pinned together. Although there are no visible artist marks there is evidence of adze tool markings on the reverse of the piece. The sculpture sustained some damage in transit to the museum in 1972, with some gilding rubbing off and serious grazing to the protruding fold of the Virgin's robe. The figure of Christ is also missing his left toes and left ring finger. This damage notwithstanding, the *Pietà* is in relatively good condition and received conservation treatment at the Whitworth in 2021 when it was thoroughly cleaned, some staining was removed, loose fragments were reattached and the existing paint layers were consolidated. There are some horizontal cracks to the front of the piece due to previous conservation interventions as well as the natural movement of the wood.

6   Curatorial files record that the *Pietà* was sold to the Whitworth by Thomas Howard-Sneyd, a dealer in antiquities, following an assessment of its authenticity by George Zarnecki of the Courtauld Institute in London. Little else is known about the sculpture's provenance.

7   I am grateful to Matthias Weniger for his assistance with dating the *Pietà*.

8   Bavarian National Museum Inv. Nr. MA 1301.

9   See for example the predella on the side altar of the Alte Heilig-Geist-Kirche in Pullach im Isartal. I am grateful to Matthias Weniger for his suggestion that the *Pietà* formed part of a predella.

10 Schiller, *Iconography*, II, 180. See also Bynum, *Wonderful Blood*, 131.

11 See Baxandall, *Limewood Sculptors*.

12 Marincola and Kargère, *Medieval Polychrome Wood Sculpture*, 25. I am grateful to Sarah Potter, conservator at the Whitworth, for her analysis of the grain structure of the wood in the *Pietà*.

13 Baxandall, *Limewood Sculptors*, 27–36.

14 Passarge, *Das deutsche Vesperbild*, 5–7. On German mysticism, see Andersen, Lähnemann and Simon, *Companion to Mysticism*.

15 On the role of images in contemplative devotion, see Hamburger, *The Visual and the Visionary*, especially 111–48.

16 Vavra, 'Bildmotiv und Frauenmystik', 211.

17 Kempis and Benham, *The Imitation of Christ*, 86.

18 Speakman Sutch and van Bruaene, 'The Seven Sorrows', 261–6.

19 The central painting of the Virgin from this composition is currently in the Alte Pinakothek in Munich, inv. 709, while the surrounding panels are at the Gemäldegalerie Alte Meister in Dresden, inv. 1875–1881. For Dürer's later portrait of Friedrich the Wise, see cat. 4.

20 Eichberger, 'Visualizing the Seven Sorrows', 121–9. See also Schuler, 'The Seven Sorrows'.

21 Heal, *Cult of the Virgin Mary*, 270.

22 Schuler, 'The Seven Sorrows', 7.

23 Ashcroft, *Albrecht Dürer*, I, 313. This verse was part of an anthology of poetry and verse prayers which Dürer compiled between 1509–10. Several of his verse prayers formed the basis for religious broadsheets produced in collaboration with other artists such as Hans Baldung. See Ashcroft, *Albrecht Dürer*, I, 294–5.

24 Ashcroft, *Albrecht Dürer*, II, 689.

25 Heal, *Cult of the Virgin Mary*, 264–5.

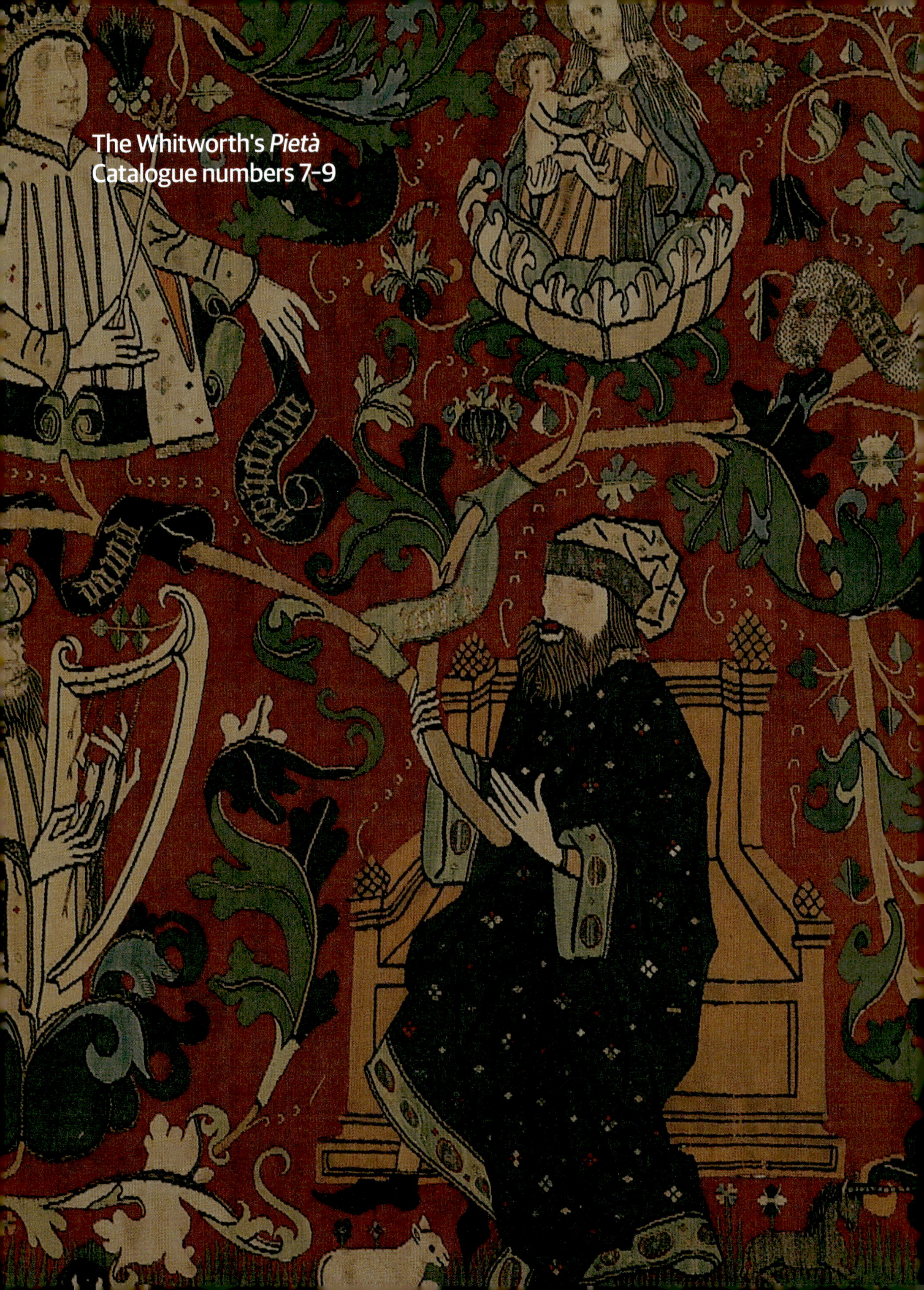
The Whitworth's *Pietà*
Catalogue numbers 7–9

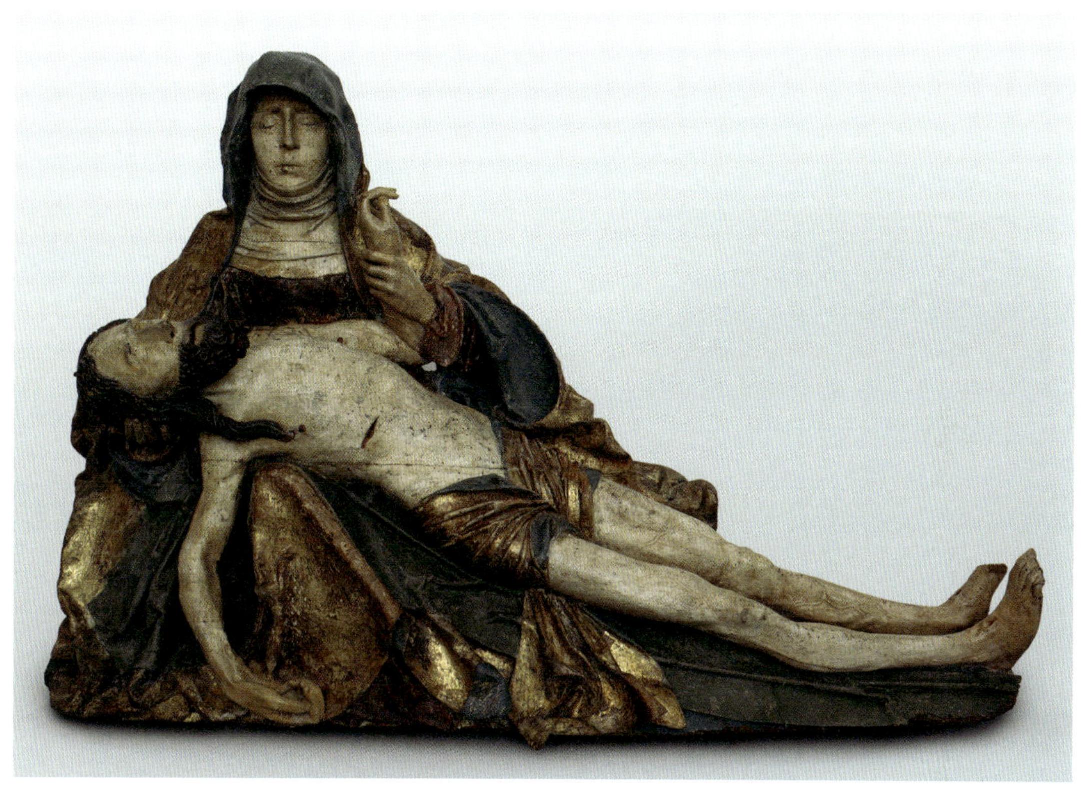

^7

Unknown, *Pietà*, c. 1490–1510, German.

Polychromed and gilded wood carving,
74.5 x 115.0 x 34.5 cm

The Whitworth, The University of Manchester, S.1972.1. Purchased
from Objects Ltd in 1972 with support from the Arts Council England
/ V&A Purchase Grant Fund. © The Whitworth, The University of
Manchester. Photo: Michael Pollard.

8

Albrecht Dürer
The Mass of Saint Gregory, 1511.

Woodcut, 297 x 206 mm, trimmed
Schoch, Mende and Scherbaum, *Albrecht Dürer*, II, 363–5, no. 230;
B.VII.142.123; H.226

The Whitworth, The University of Manchester, P.3053. Presented by
George Thomas Clough in 1921.
© The Whitworth, The University of Manchester. Photo: Michael Pollard.

For illustration, see fig. 6.1, p. 62.

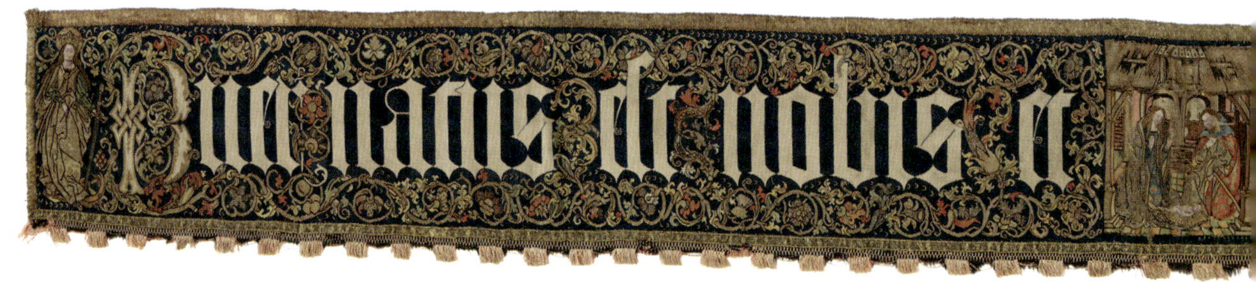

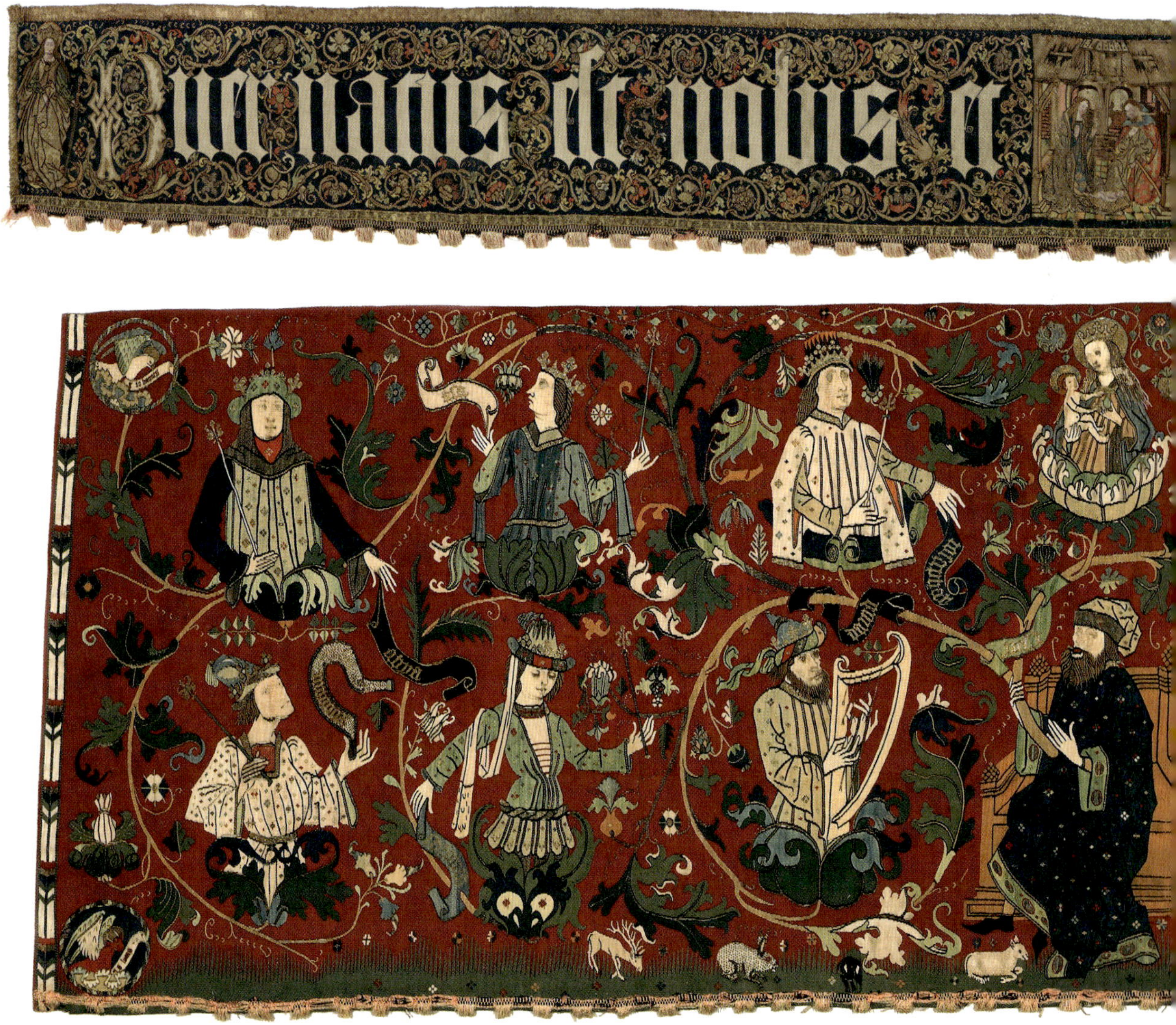

9

Unknown

Altar frontal with the Tree of Jesse, Virgin and Child, and Emblems of the Four Evangelists, c. 1470–9, German (Cologne region) and *Altar Superfrontal Depicting the Birth of Christ and Saints Catherine and Barbara, inscribed* Puer natus est nobis et Filius datus est nobis (Unto us a Boy is Born, unto us a Son is Given), c. 1470-99, German.

Altar frontal: tapestry with linen, wool, silk, gold, silver and metal yarns, ink on faces, 89.0 x 204.7 cm, Superfrontal: tapestry with linen, wool, silk, gold, silver and metal yarns, paint on faces, 16.3 x 199.5 cm. *The Whitworth Art Gallery: The First Hundred Years*, 18–19

The Whitworth, The University of Manchester, T.8247.3 (altar frontal) and T.8247.4 (superfrontal). Purchased from Sir John Charles Robinson in 1891.

© The Whitworth, The University of Manchester.
Altar frontal photo: Michael Pollard; superfrontal photo: The Whitworth.

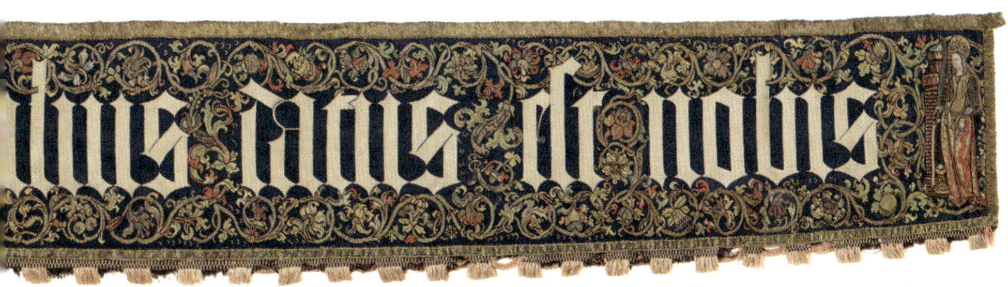

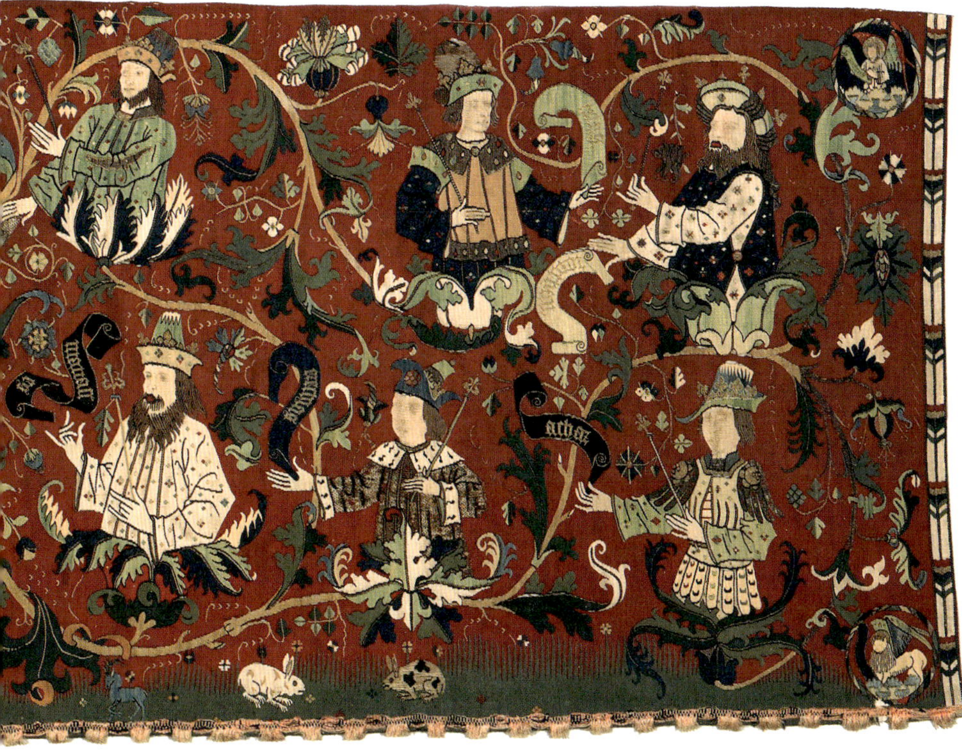

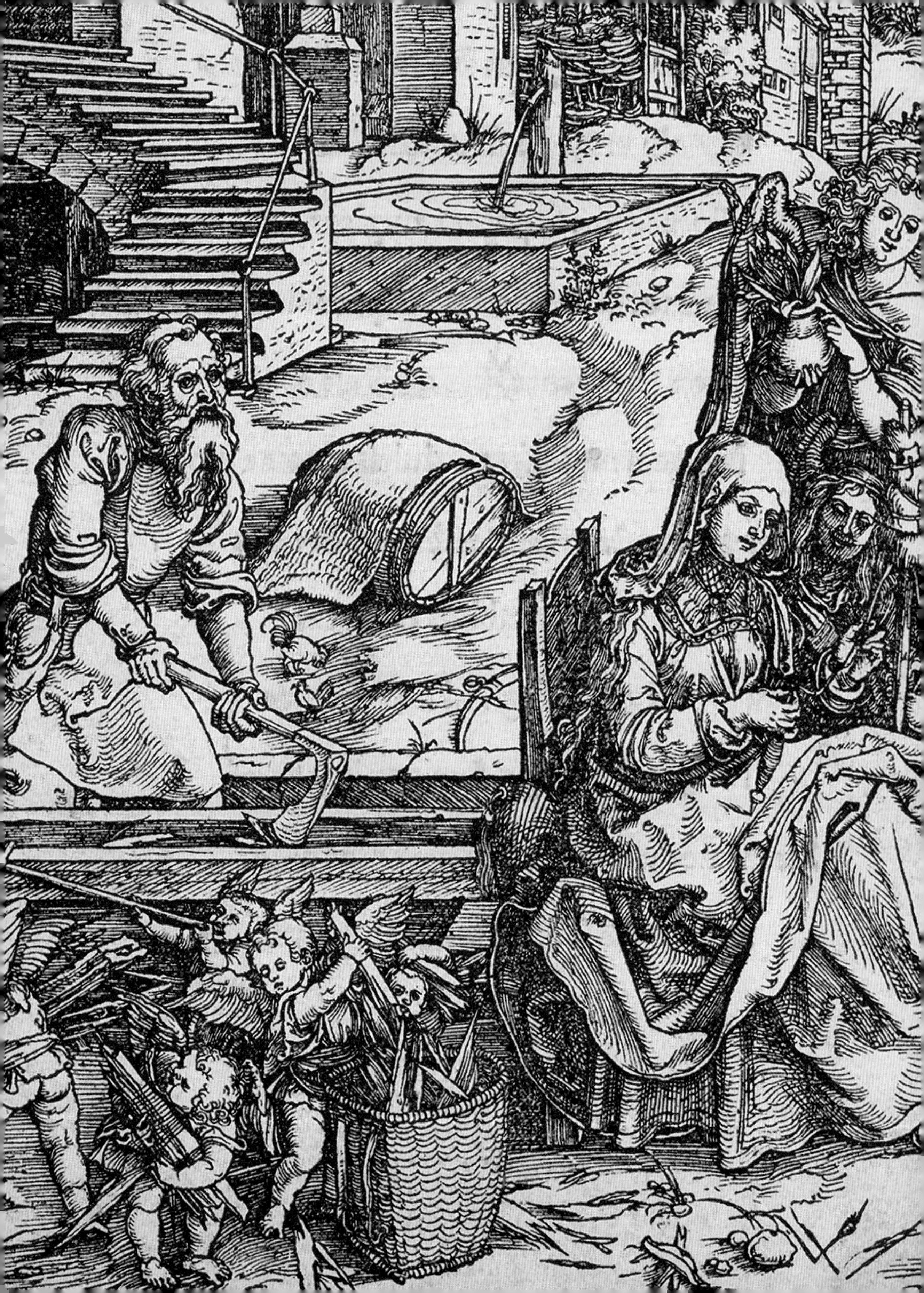

[12] The home

Sasha Handley and Charles Zika

Dürer's neighbourhood

Pre-modern European cities were tightly knit communities in which homes were located in very close proximity. Neighbouring households, often including artisan workshops, formed the basis of the city's social, economic, political and religious networks. This was the case for Albrecht Dürer's city of Nuremberg.[1] At the age of four in 1475, Dürer, his Hungarian-born father, Albrecht the Elder (1427–1502), and his mother Barbara Holper (1452–1514), the daughter of the prominent goldsmith Hieronymous Holper, moved from their small house near the Hauptmarkt (central marketplace) to a prime street location below the castle, Unter der Veste (the current Burgstrasse).

This street linked the Hauptmarkt, Rathaus (city hall), the main church of Saint Sebald and the castle – an axis of commercial, civic, imperial and religious power.[2] Three doors from Albrecht the Elder's residence and goldsmithing workshop was the house containing the largest of Nuremberg's painting and print workshops, that of Michael Wolgemut (1434–1519), to whom young Albrecht would be apprenticed. It was Wolgemut who, with his collaborator stepson Wilhelm Pleydenwurff (c. 1460–94), illustrated the *Nuremberg Chronicle* (cat. 1). The author of that work, the wealthy landowner and humanist, Hartman Schedel (1440–1514), lived a little further down the street, as did the man who commissioned it, Sebald Schreyer (1446–1520), a merchant and churchwarden of Saint Sebald. Anton Koberger (1445–1513), Dürer's godfather, printer of the *Nuremberg Chronicle* and soon to be owner of a large international printing and publishing house, lived only a few streets away, and even closer lived the work's German translator, Georg Alt (c. 1450–1510). The houses of many of the city's leading patrician families

(the Haller, Tetzel, Stromer, Kress and Behaim, to name a few), were on the same street as the Dürers, and so too was the prominent lawyer and later close friend of Albrecht Dürer, Christof Scheurl (1481–1542). The neighbourhood was also home to artisans – such as the carpenter Jobst Wegelin and the coppersmith, Dürer's father-in-law, Hans Frey (1450–1523) – many of whom supplemented their artisanal labour with additional work or financial investment in mining, metallurgy, trade or finance.[3]

Homes, therefore, were not refuges from the social and cultural energy of the city. They were certainly places of familial nurturing, socialising and memorialising, but they were also places of material production, wealth acquisition, social learning and cultural exchange, of bridging boundaries, cultivating patrons, learning new skills and constructing identities. Many of these activities occurred in the *Stube*, a living and work room, and one of the four rooms (with the hallway, working kitchen and small bedroom) that were standard for houses in Nuremberg by the fourteenth century.[4] The *Stube* and kitchen always had a common wall to connect the cooking fire to the tiled stove (*Kachelofen*) that warmed the *Stube*. The tiles found on domestic *Kachelöfen* (cat. 12–14) were often richly decorated with architectural motifs, vernacular subjects and even the arms of Nuremberg, where many were manufactured and where their colourful forms animated domestic interiors while also radiating the stove's heat (see Sasha Handley's 'Perilous possessions' in this volume). Some houses had one or two stories above the ground floor, which would then include a second *Stube*, accessed through stairs in the hallway, and a small room for children and/or for apprentices. Dürer's biography demonstrates the impact of this varied and dynamic entrepreneurial

Nuremberg environment on his artistic interests and choices, which were periodically refreshed by his physical and literary travels and those of his neighbours.[5]

Dürer's homes

In 1509 Albrecht and Agnes Dürer purchased their first house as a married couple. Located on Zisselgasse in the shadow of Nuremberg castle, the half-timbered house was a substantial investment at 275 Rhenish gulden,[6] which they paid to Bernhard Walther (c. 1430–1504), a merchant and astronomer, and former pupil of Regiomontanus (1436–76; see Matthew Champion's 'Measure and the material world' in this volume). No complete inventory of the couple's house survives, but Albrecht compiled a list of his possessions in 1524 where he described his dwelling as 'a fairly well stocked household' that benefited from 'good clothing, pewter kitchen and tableware, good tools, bedding, chests and containers'.[7] In 1520, during their trip to the Netherlands, the couple's possessions were swelled by Agnes's purchase of a washtub, washing-up bowl, a set of bellows to stoke a fire, a pair of women's slippers, two jugs and a cage for a parakeet.[8]

Though modest in comparison with the homes of patrician families like the Tuchers, there is little doubt that the Dürers lived comfortably on Zisselgasse. Here they were surrounded by everyday objects such as linen bedsheets, pillows and tablecloths that could be homespun or purchased from the bustling stalls of the city's Hauptmarkt, and by innovative and high-quality commissioned wares such as *Kachelöfen* that were synonymous with Nuremberg's potters and commanded an international reputation and market. Whether ornate or everyday, the domestic wares of the Dürers' home and of those of their friends and neighbours took centre stage in the artist's work where they were observed in intricate detail and inspired his depiction of highly realistic, personalised and intimate scenes. The artist's prints were, in turn, purchased by the citizens of Nuremberg where they became a focus for household religious practices, education and pleasure. These works reflect the artist's experience of home not as a mundane dwelling

but as a place for communication with the divine, and a dramatic stage for crucial lifecycle events such as childbirth and death.

Adorning the home

Nuremberg's reputation for excellent metalwork, a craft in which Dürer was initially apprenticed and highly skilled, led to the creation of beautiful tableware such as the 'white silver goblets without feet' that Agnes Dürer inherited after her father's death. The experience of being surrounded by such striking objects at home and around the city provided creative inspiration for Dürer's depiction of the extravagant lidded goblet that featured prominently in his *Nemesis (The Great Fortune)* of c. 1501 (cat. 34; see Jennifer Spinks's 'Objects in motion' in this volume) and the goblet at the heart of *The Adoration of the Magi* of 1511.[9] The stems, bodies and finials of these goblets are observed in exquisite detail and Dürer produced several designs for similarly elaborate drinking vessels during his lifetime (see 'The workshop' in this volume).

These vessels, and the ornate table centrepieces of silver and gold that Dürer designed were undoubtedly objects of wonder and pleasure, as well as marks of luxury consumption. But Dürer's prints and surviving household objects from Renaissance Nuremberg also reveal a sense of disquiet about the potential harm that the unmitigated consumption of expensive manufactured goods could bring. The high-status *Kachelofen* in Dürer's *Temptation of the Idler* of 1498 (cat. 10; see Sasha Handley's 'Perilous possessions' in this volume) features in a scene of devilish lustfulness within a *Stube*. A man sleeps on a bench next to the *Kachelofen* whilst a demonic creature prepares to blow air into his ear with a pair of bellows, and a Venus-like figure, with Amor playing on stilts at her feet, gestures toward the source of heat. The bellows, associated with temptation in a roughly contemporary woodcut in the *Ship of Fools* (cat. 11) by Sebastian Brant (1457–1521) suggests a preoccupation with sin, while the handles of a set of four silver-gilt *Apostle Spoons* (cat. 30) manufactured in Nuremberg, are inscribed with biblical figures and moralistic inscriptions such as 'Woe unto those whose god is their belly'. Such texts serve to remind the spoons' handlers of the damaging bodily and spiritual effects of extravagant feasting. In a similar manner, the depiction of the temptation of Adam and Eve in an early-sixteenth-century brass bowl (cat. 32) made this cautionary story of human sinfulness an everyday presence for its users. Likewise, the theme of sin and repentance found in Dürer's 1496 engraving of the *The Prodigal Son* (cat. 27), set before a dense group of buildings particular to the region, provided a model for scenes on several sixteenth-century maiolica plates.[10]

More workaday and plain household objects, such as ceramic jugs, serving dishes, curtains, candlesticks, knives and leather pouches, flood the busy female-centred domestic scene in *The Birth of the Virgin* of c. 1503 (cat. 22). It is one of six prints exhibited here from the *Life of the Virgin*, a series of twenty woodcuts begun around 1500 and published in the form of a book with a Latin text in 1511 (a seventh print from the cycle, *The Visitation* (cat. 55) appears in 'The workshop' in this volume). In this cycle, Dürer staged key events from the Virgin's life – her birth (cat. 22), her death (cat. 26), the holy family in Egypt (cat. 25) – in domestic settings and surrounded by domestic objects. *The Annunciation* (cat. 23), however, takes place in a large, vaulted chamber, Venetian in style, with Mary seated at a prayer stool and shown to have been reading biblical prophecies. The scene is also replete with theological references: above in a roundel is the biblical figure of Judith who holds aloft the head of her enemy Holofernes, while below under the stairs is a badger, chained like the devil in Revelations 20:1–3, both alluding to Mary's conception of Jesus as a victory over sin.[11]

The ordinary objects filling many of the domestic scenes of the Virgin's life were commonplace in Nuremberg homes, as were items such as the brass bell (cat. 33) marked with the Crucifixion depicting Saint John and the Virgin standing by the cross, and tapered jugs resembling a *Bartmannkrug*, or glazed stoneware jug. A later example of one such jug from the town of Frechen, stamped with a bearded man (*Bartmann*) and the arms of Julich-Kleve-Berg, is exhibited here (cat. 31).[12] Together, the bell and jug

reveal how household objects were invested with meaning through use as well as through the sacred and secular images they bore. The household objects in Dürer's works celebrated the ingenuity of Nuremberg's tradespeople within Europe's 'material Renaissance' (see the Introduction) while also warning of the dangers that this new world of material innovation and consumption brought with it.[13]

Objects and emotions

One of Albrecht Dürer's skills as an artist was his ability to make emotions visible, to represent affect through the medium of print. From Dürer's *Gedenkbuch* – the record book in which he penned family events from 1502 – we know of his emotional response to the death of his parents.[14] It has been suggested that it was perhaps the deep and abiding sadness at the death of his mother in 1514 that influenced his engraving of that year, *Virgin and Child by the Wall* (cat. 29). Or perhaps it was the heaviness of melancholy that Dürer had depicted so masterfully in the same year in his *Melencolia I* (cat. 79; see Matthew Champion's 'Measure and the material world' in this volume). The Virgin in his *Virgin and Child by the Wall* is not shown with a halo or radiant aureole but is a woman of Dürer's world. The shimmering folds of her voluminous cloak and shawl contrast with her darkened face and doleful eyes, a bunch of keys and an attractive bag hang from her belt, her arms clutch the Christ child so tightly that he recoils, and her anxiety becomes palpable. She is also located in Nuremberg, the buildings behind her clearly depicting its castle, towers and imperial stables as seen from the city's *Tiergärtnertor* (Menagerie Gate). This cityscape was visible (in reverse) from the third-floor balcony of the Dürer house, where Barbara Dürer had lived with her son Albrecht and his wife Agnes from 1509.

Quite different facial expressions, bodily gestures and clothing are also used by Dürer to depict a grieving mother and son in his 1498–9 woodcut, *The Lamentation of Christ* (cat. 28), as the body of Jesus is about to be laid in the grave. This print was re-published as part of Dürer's so-called *Great Passion* cycle of twelve woodcuts, which was issued in book form with Latin texts in 1511 together with the *Apocalypse*, the *Life of the Virgin*, and the *Small Passion*, indicating a strong focus on devotional themes in that year (see Charles Zika's 'Objects of devotion' in this volume).[15] Dürer uses the Virgin's cloak again to create a sense of intimacy through encirclement, drawing together mother and son in a bond that is also expressed in her holding of Christ's limp right hand – similar to the grieving embrace found in many examples of the pietà (see Holly Fletcher's 'The Whitworth's sculpted *Pietà*' in this volume).[16] Dürer also demonstrates his skilled use of clothing materials and their folds to convey joyful emotions in *The Embrace of Joachim and Anne at the Golden Gate*, a 1504 print also reproduced in the later *Life of the Virgin* (cat. 21). Anne's joy and relief in learning that finally at her advanced age she was to give birth to a daughter, Mary (who would become a powerful queen in heaven and on earth and in turn give birth to a king)[17] is expressed through Anne's forward rush into the arms of Joachim, a physical and also emotional movement amplified by Joachim's awkward grasp and slight push-back of the front folds of Anne's garment as he attempts to encircle her waist with his arms. Such scenes, copied many times over by various artists, soon became intimate devotional images designed to arouse personal religious piety and compassion in the home.[18]

Dürer's *Small Passion*, his most extensive and possibly best-known cycle of woodcuts, is represented here by four prints, including *Christ Parting from His Mother* (cat. 16).[19] In these works, Dürer displays his capacity to focus on the strong and intimate human emotions that link mother and son. Christ is shown blessing his mother Mary as he leaves to carry out his redemptive role, which will lead to his Passion and ultimate death on the cross. His mother seems to be aware of the terrible suffering he is to endure as she sinks to her knees, her hands clasped tightly before her in a gesture of grief and pleading, while Martha places a comforting hand on her shoulder. Indeed, the very next print in the series is *The Last Supper* (cat. 18), in which the Passion of Christ is clearly intimated by the money bag held by the Apostle in the foreground, directly opposite Christ and in his line of sight. This is Judas, holding a bag with

the thirty pieces of silver he received for his willingness to inform the authorities of Christ's location. The bag is a portent of this imminent betrayal.

But the first public event in the *Small Passion* cycle after *Christ's Entry into Jerusalem* (cat. 15) – a quiet welcome as he enters on a donkey, but far from an impassioned response by onlookers – illustrates Dürer's ability to visualise quite different emotions. *Christ Driving the Moneylenders from the Temple* (cat. 17) depicts a furious Christ using a flail to throw the terrified moneylenders out of the Temple, having first overturned their tables and benches, thereby causing their money bags to spill out on the floor. The fury of this Christ figure inspired a range of artistic responses and may well have informed the depiction by Lucas Cranach the Elder (1472–1553) of the subject in the *Passional Christi und Anti-christi*, a Lutheran polemic against the Catholic Church published in 1521 (cat. 19).[20] Characterised by a simpler and more direct treatment of subject, the *Small Passion* prints gave rise to numerous copies and interpretations. Some prints in the cycle were also taken up as sources for objects in more luxurious materials, including Italian maiolica, whereby Dürer's devotional designs were also transmitted internationally as meaningful motifs on objects for domestic use.[21]

1   Hess and Eser, *Early Dürer*, 14–15.

2   Gulden, 'Nuremberg's Elites', 286–8; Gulden, 'Dürer's Neighborhood'.

3   Gulden, 'An Ideal Neighborhood', 31–2.

4   Bedal, 'Wohnen wie zu Dürers Zeiten'.

5   Gulden, 'An Ideal Neighborhood', 35; Eser and Grebe, *Heilige und Hasen*, 11–43.

6   The 'golden [coin]', minted by the Prince Electors of the Rhineland and by Nuremberg, differed from the Netherlandish guilder (Ashcroft, *Albrecht Dürer*, I, 20, 259).

7   *Ibid.*, 191.

8   *Ibid.*, 561.

9   Not included in this exhibition. See Schoch, Mende and Scherbaum, *Albrecht Dürer*, II, 348–9, no. 225; H. 208.

10 *Ibid.*, I, 48. The village has been identified as Himpfelshof, west of Nuremberg.

11 Strauss, *Complete Engravings*, 259. Dürer also represented an enchained devil in *The Angel with the Key of the Bottomless Pit*, the fifteenth and final woodcut in his *Apocalypse* cycle; see Schoch, Mende and Scherbaum, *Albrecht Dürer*, II, 104–5, no. 126; H. 178.

12 On the large-scale export of these jugs to England, see Holmes, 'The So-Called "Bellarmine" Mask'.

13 O'Malley and Welch, *The Material Renaissance*; Rublack, 'Matter in the Material Renaissance'.

14 Hutchinson, *Albrecht Dürer*, 74–7; Ashcroft, *Albrecht Dürer*, I, 95–100, 395–8; Eser, 'Dürer's Self-Portraits', 261–3, 268–9, no. 5.

15 For the history of these cycles, see Bartrum, *Dürer and his Legacy*, 173–4, no. 118.

16 Some art historians, however, identify the standing woman as Mary. See Schoch, Mende and Scherbaum, *Albrecht Dürer*, II, 202–4, no. 162.

17 See Chelidonius's accompanying Latin text and German translation, in Wiener, Scherbaum and Drescher, *Dürers Marienleben*, 112, 117.

18 For later copies of these three discussed prints, see Schoch, Mende and Scherbaum, *Albrecht Dürer*, I, 188; II, 204; II, 234. More generally, see Vogt, *Das druckgraphische Bild*, 31–74.

19 The four prints from the *Small Passion* exhibited here come from the Holtorp Collection in The John Rylands Research Institute and Library and were mounted in this unusual format of four to a card by its compiler, Hiero von Holtorp. See Wouk, *Imprinting the Imagination*. Dürer's *Saint Veronica between Saints Peter and Paul*, represented in both the original woodblock (cat. 45) and an impression (cat. 46) is in the 'The workshop' section of this catalogue.

20 These responses include, most notably, Rembrandt's 1635 etching of the scene. See New Hollstein Rembrandt, 139.

21 Bartrum, *Dürer and his Legacy*, 251–6, nos 207–13; Gabbarelli, *Sharing Images*, 110–23.

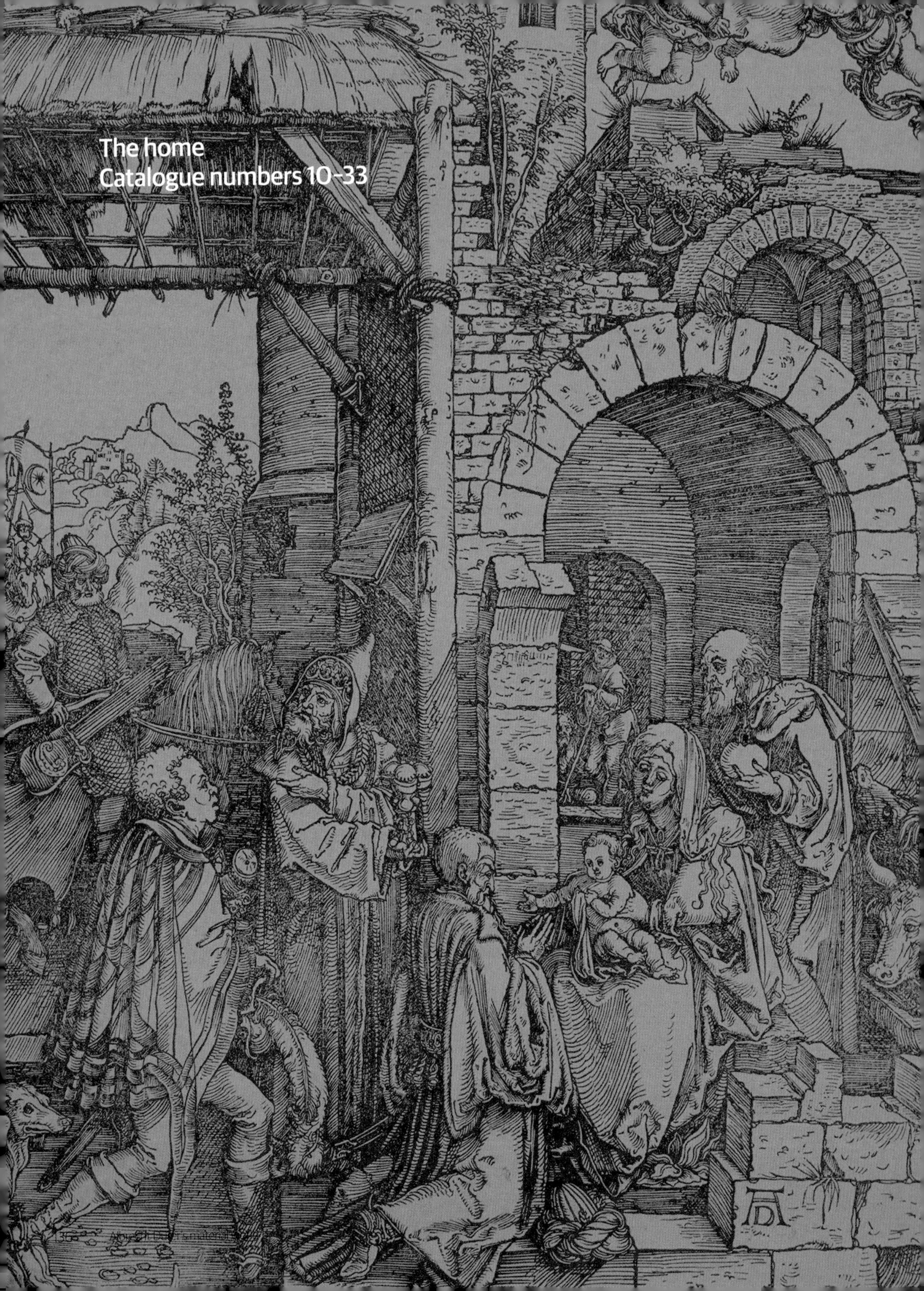

10

Albrecht Dürer
The Temptation of the Idler (*The Dream of the Doctor*),
1498.

Engraving, 185 x 117 mm

Schoch, Mende and Scherbaum, *Albrecht Dürer*, I, 65–7, no. 18;
B.VII.91.76; H.70
Ashmolean Museum, University of Oxford, WA1863.2291.
© Ashmolean Museum, University of Oxford.

For illustration, see fig. 3.1, p. 24.

11

Albrecht Dürer
Devil with Bellows in Sebastian Brant, *The Ship of Fools*
(*Das Narrenschiff*), Basel: Johann Bergmann de Olpe,
1497; and Paris: Johann Philippi de Cruzenach, 1498.

Woodcut 116 x 94 mm

Schoch, Mende and Scherbaum, *Albrecht Dürer*, III, 92–3, no. 266.10
The John Rylands Research Institute and Library, The University of
Manchester, Spencer 9793 (Basel, 1497), to be replaced during the
course of the exhibition with Spencer 17644 (Paris, 1498).
© The University of Manchester.

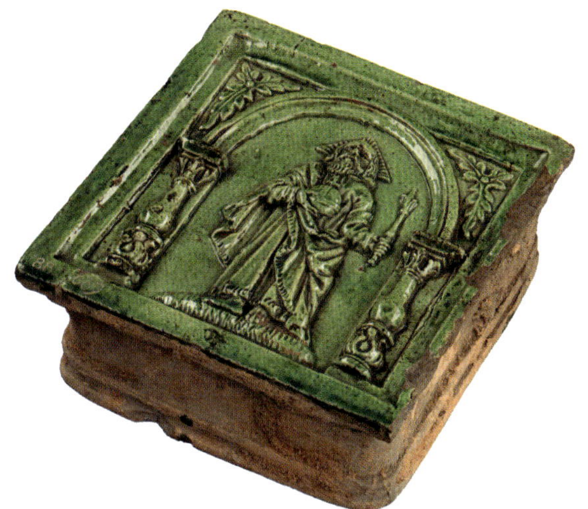

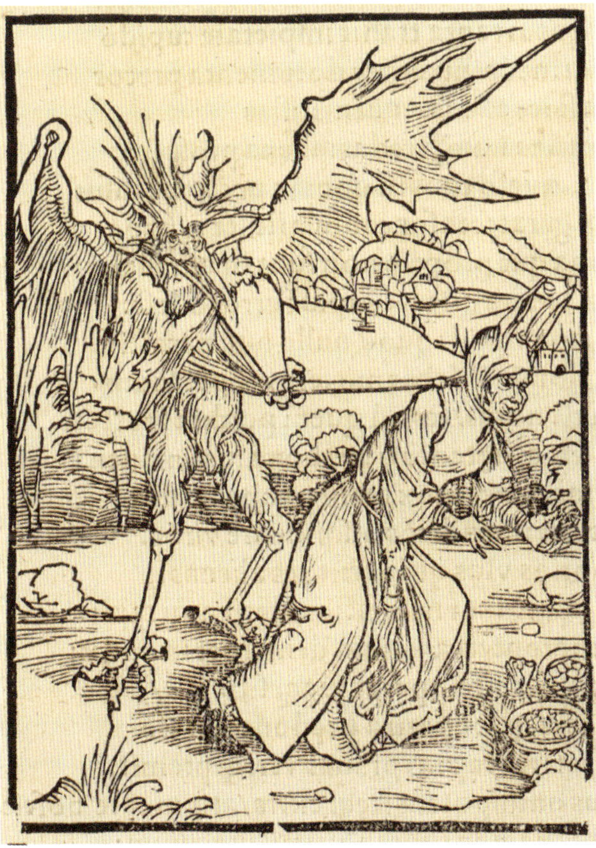

12
Unknown
*Stove Tile with Christ in an
Arched Panel with Baluster
Columns*, late sixteenth
century, German.

Green-glazed earthenware,
17.5 x 17.3 x 6.4 cm

National Museums Scotland,
A.1888.689.
© Trustees of the National
Museums Scotland.

13
Unknown
Frieze Tile with a Sleeping Guard with a Halberd, first quarter of the sixteenth century, German (Ochsenfurt).

Dark-glazed earthenware, 10.0 x 18.5 cm

Nuremberg, Germanisches Nationalmuseum, A948.
© Germanisches Nationalmuseum, Nuremberg.

For illustration, see fig. 3.4, p. 30.

v 14
Unknown
Stove Tile Depicting a Genius Holding the Nuremberg Coat of Arms, first half of the sixteenth century, German.

Green-glazed earthenware, 21.0 x 21.0 cm

Germanisches Nationalmuseum, A605.
© Germanisches Nationalmuseum.

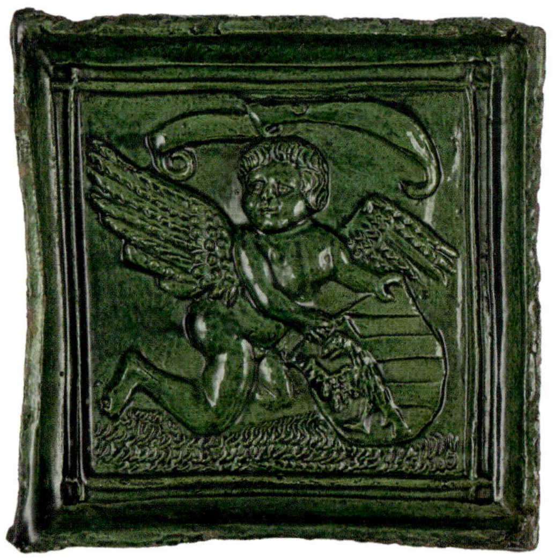

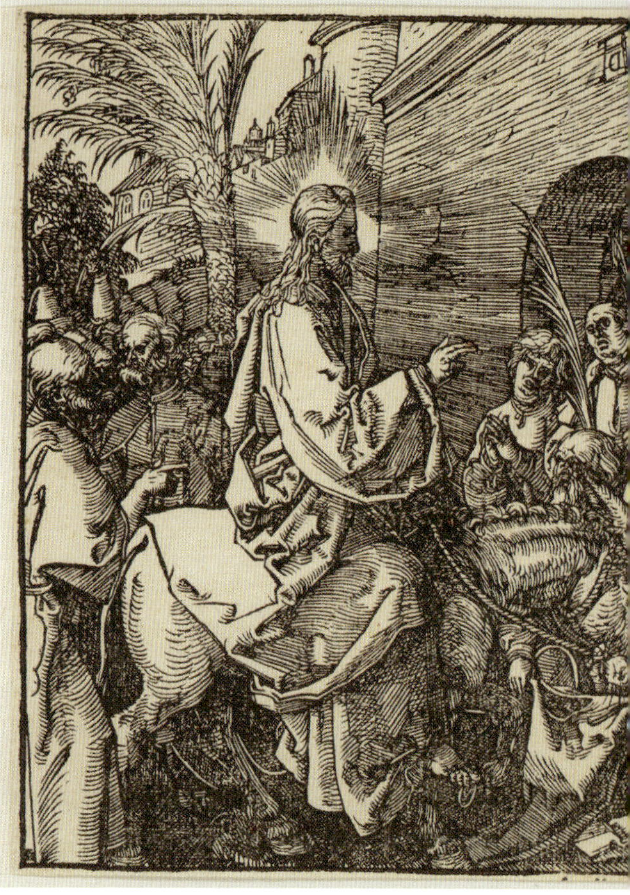

^15
Albrecht Dürer
Christ's Entry into Jerusalem
(*The Small Passion*), c. 1508–9.

Woodcut, 127 x 98 mm
Schoch, Mende and Scherbaum, *Albrecht Dürer*, II, 294–5, no. 191; B.VII.119.22; H.130

The John Rylands Research Institute and Library, The University of Manchester, Holtorp Collection, 5/1/25/3. © The University of Manchester.

> 16
Albrecht Dürer
Christ Parting from His Mother
(*The Small Passion*), c. 1508–9.

Woodcut, 126 x 97 mm
Schoch, Mende and Scherbaum, *Albrecht Dürer*, II, 297–8, no. 193; B.VII.119.21; H.132

The John Rylands Research Institute and Library, The University of Manchester, Holtorp Collection, 5/1/25/3. © The University of Manchester.

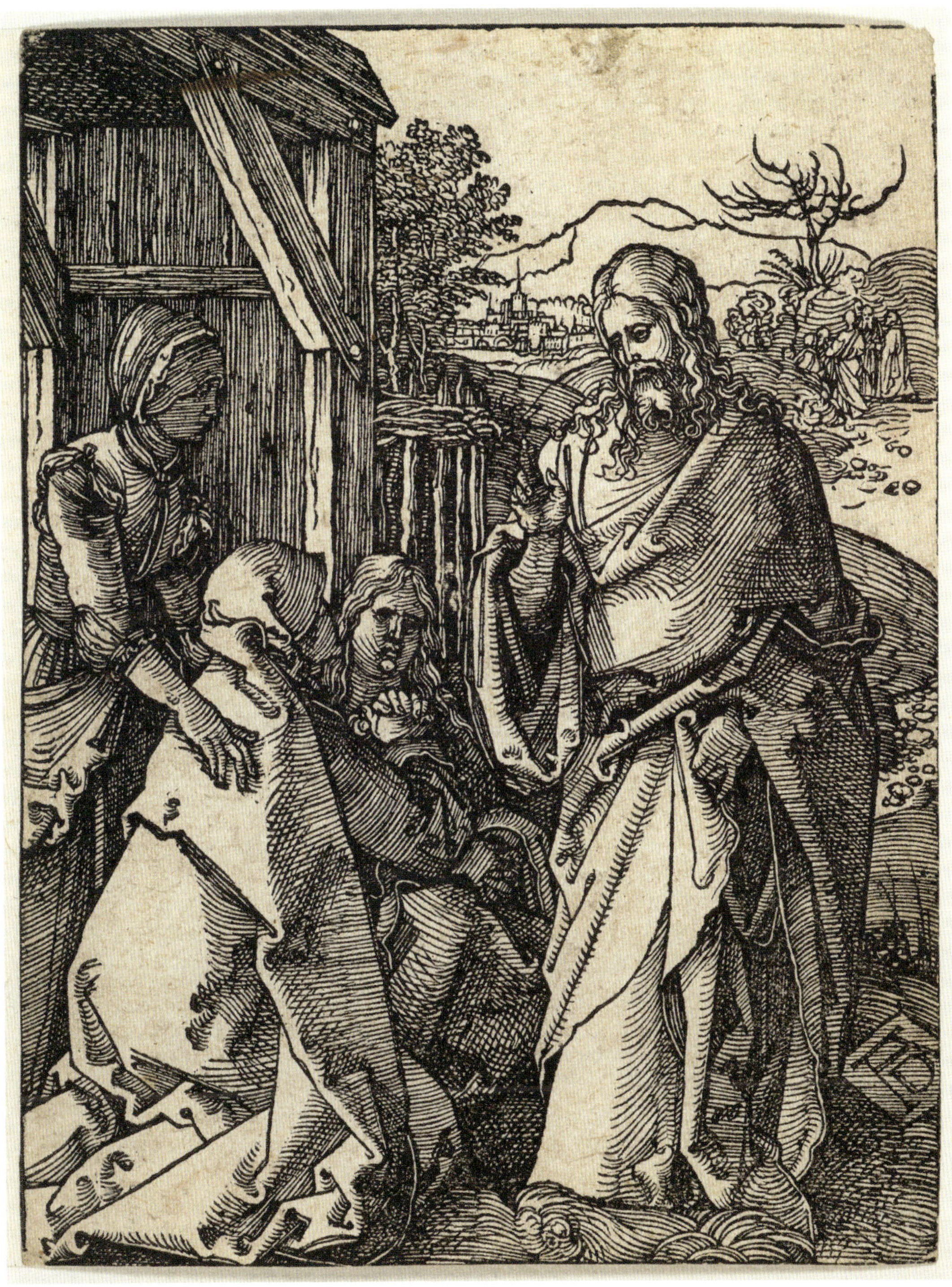

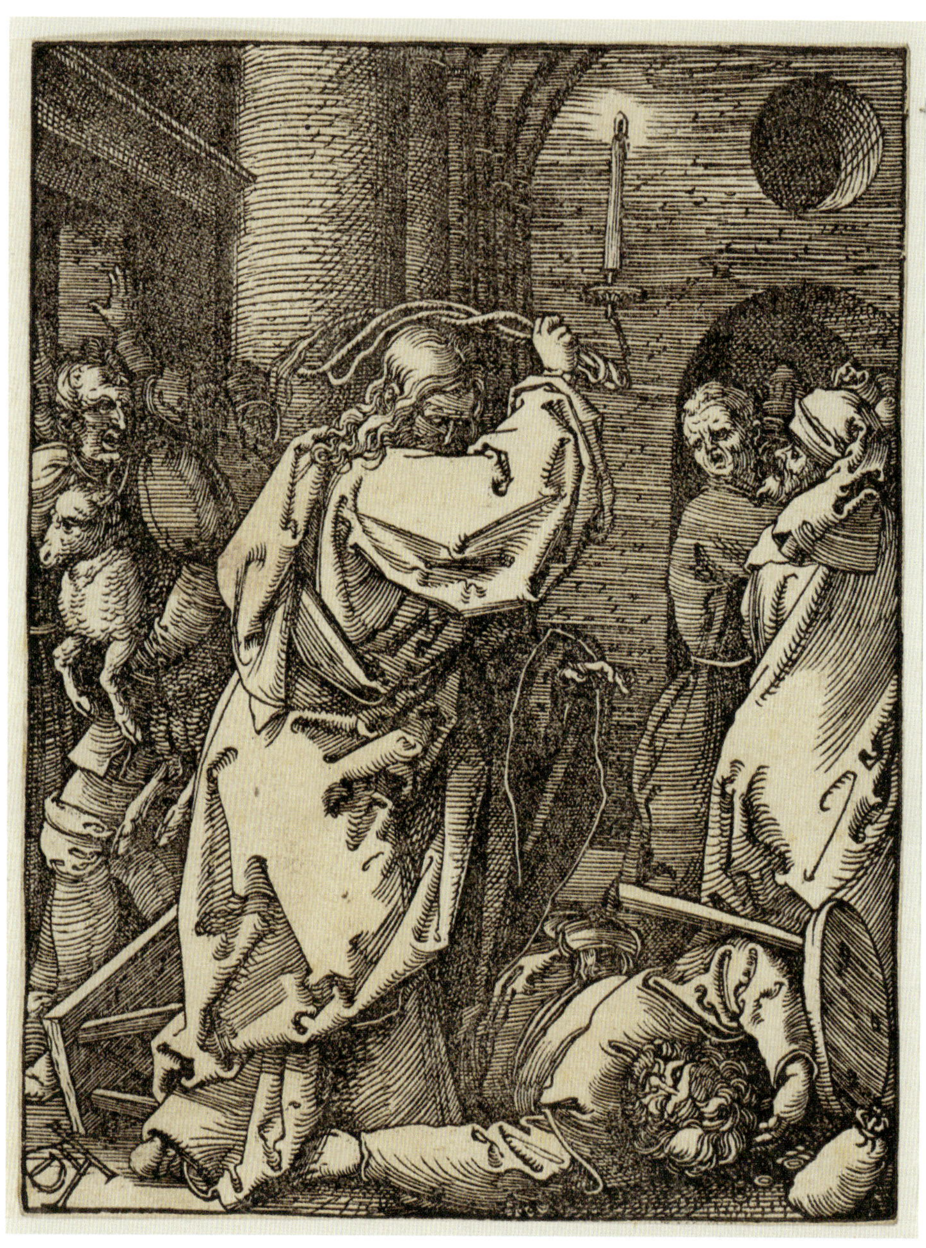

17
Albrecht Dürer
Christ Driving the Moneylenders from the Temple
(*The Small Passion*), c. 1508–10.

Woodcut, 126 x 97 mm
Schoch, Mende and Scherbaum, *Albrecht Dürer*, II, 296–7, no. 192;
B.VII.119.23; H.131

The John Rylands Research Institute and Library, The University of
Manchester, Holtorp Collection, 5/1/25/3. © The University of Manchester.

18
Albrecht Dürer
The Last Supper (*The Small Passion*), c. 1508–9.

Woodcut, 126 x 98 mm, trimmed
Schoch, Mende and Scherbaum, *Albrecht Dürer*, II, 299–300,
no. 194; B.VII.119.24; H.133

The John Rylands Research Institute and Library, The University
of Manchester, Holtorp Collection, 5/1/25/3.
© The University of Manchester.

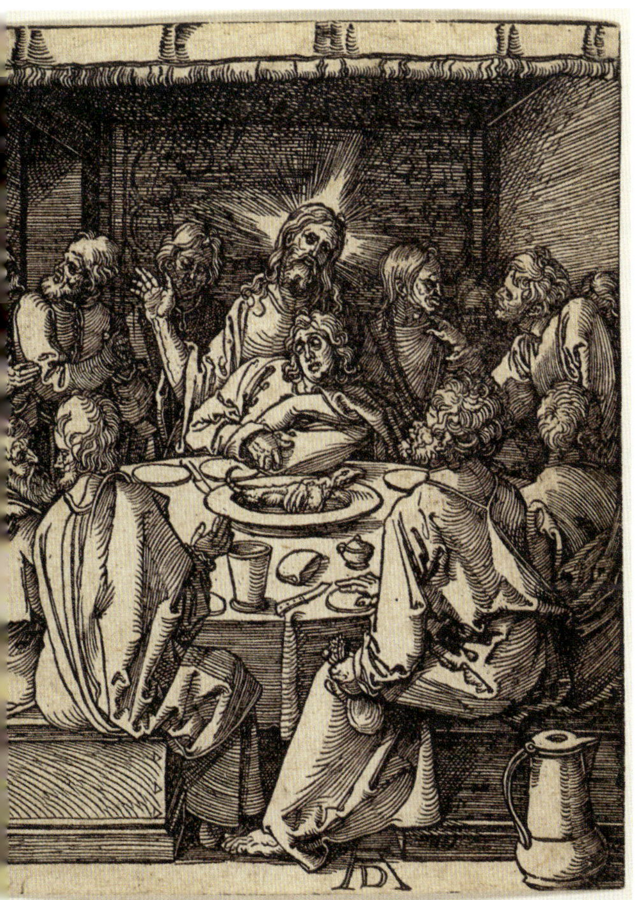

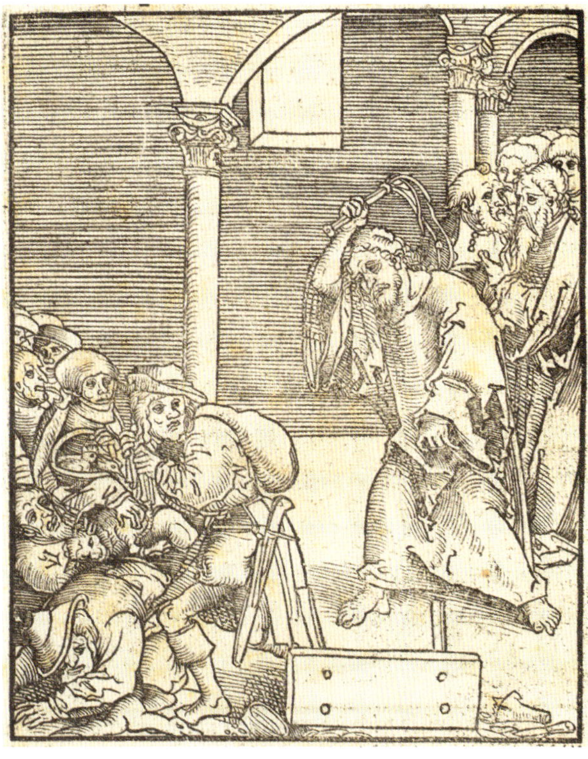

19

Lucas Cranach
*Christ Driving the Moneylenders from
the Temple* in Martin Luther, Philip
Melanchthon and Johann Schwertfeger,
Passional Christi und Anti-christi.
Wittenberg: Johann Rhau-Grunenberg,
1521.

Woodcut, 195 x 145 mm

The John Rylands Research Institute and Library,
The University of Manchester, R232900.
© The University of Manchester.

20

Albrecht Dürer
Virgin and Child on a Grassy Bank, 1503.

Engraving, 114 x 71 mm, trimmed
Schoch, Mende and Scherbaum, *Albrecht Dürer,* I, 103–4, no. 36;
B.VII.54.34; H.31

The Whitworth, The University of Manchester, P.5106. Presented by
the executors of Dr E. J. Sidebotham in 1929.
© The Whitworth, The University of Manchester. Photo: Michael Pollard.

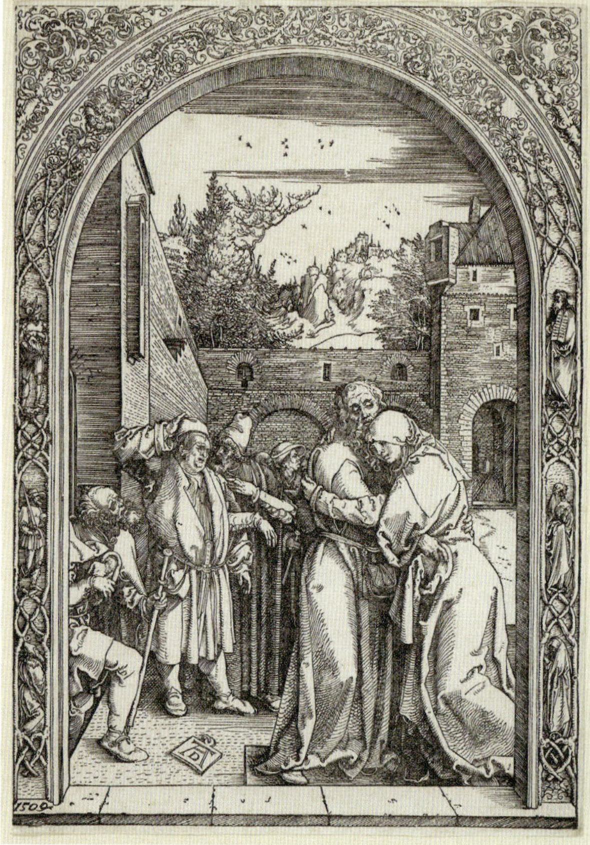

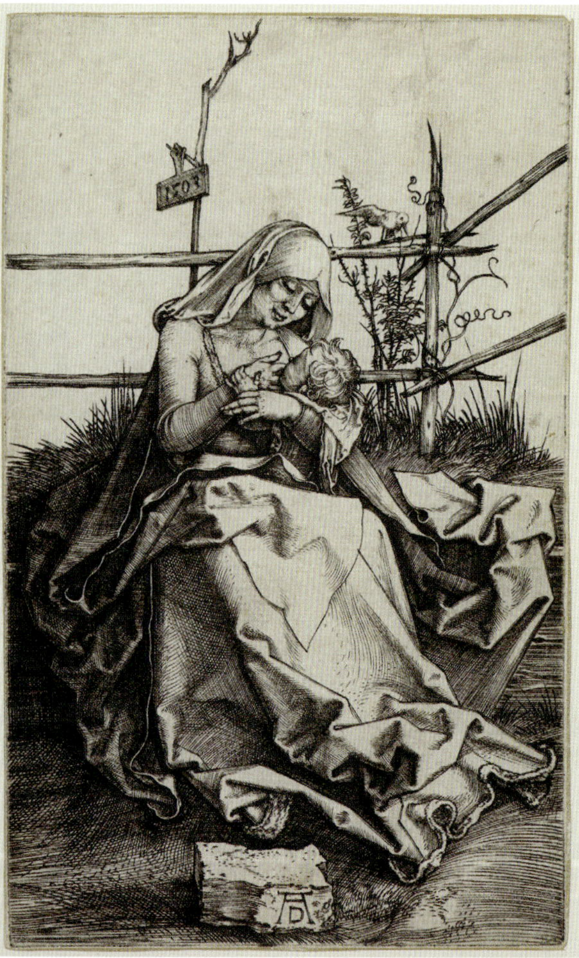

21
Albrecht Dürer
*The Embrace of Joachim and Anne at the
Golden Gate (Life of the Virgin),* 1504.

Woodcut, 302 x 213 mm
Schoch, Mende and Scherbaum, *Albrecht Dürer,* II,
232–4, 1 no. 69; B.VII.131.79: H.191

The Whitworth, The University of Manchester, P.3035.
Presented by George Thomas Clough in 1921.
© The Whitworth, The University of Manchester.
Photo: Michael Pollard.

> 22
Albrecht Dürer
The Birth of the Virgin (Life of the Virgin),
1503.

Woodcut, 294 x 205 mm
Schoch, Mende and Scherbaum, *Albrecht Dürer,* II,
235–7, no. 170; B.VII.131.80; H.192

Ashmolean Museum, University of Oxford,
WA1863.2451. Bequeathed by Francis Douce in 1834.
© Ashmolean Museum, University of Oxford.

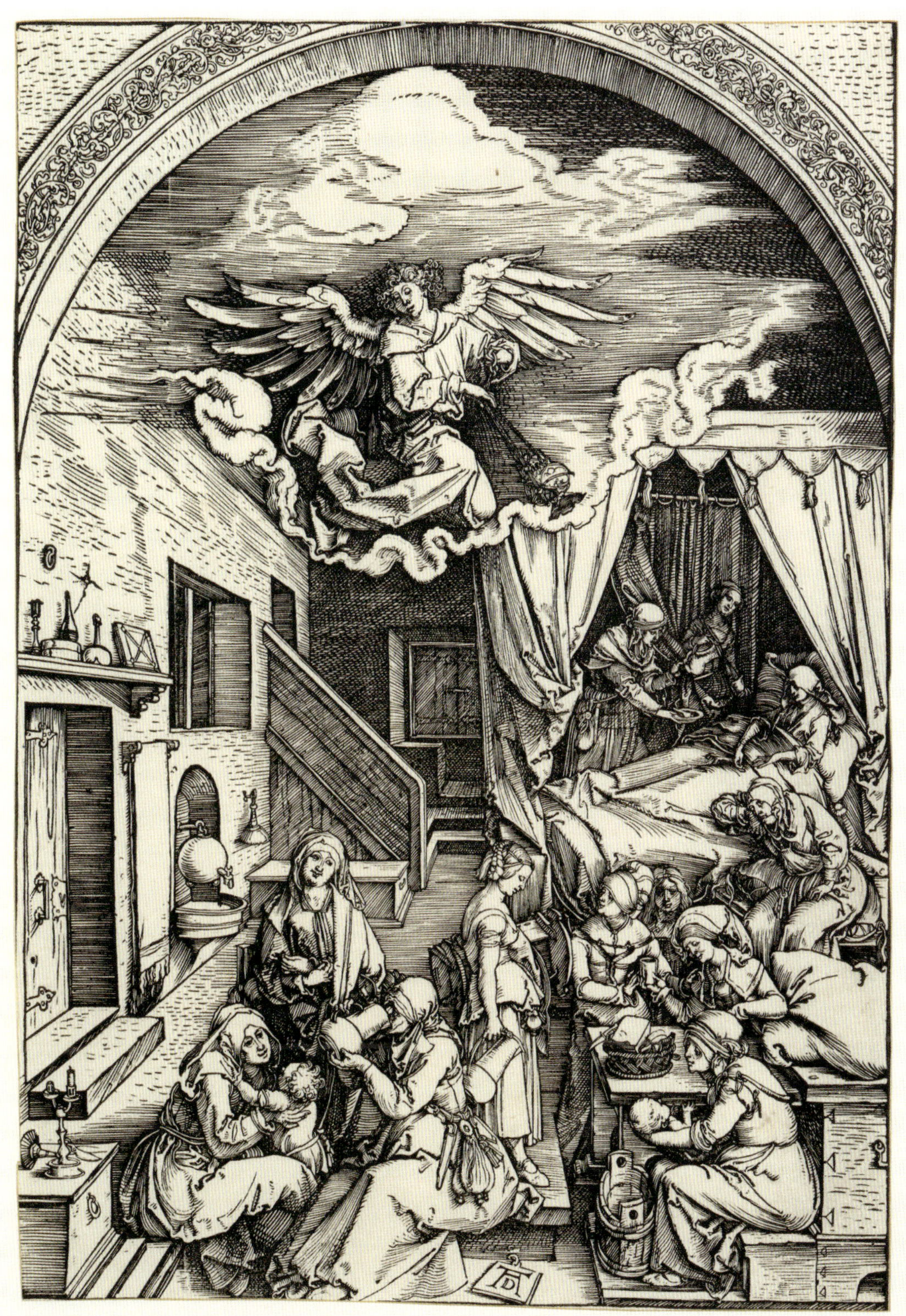

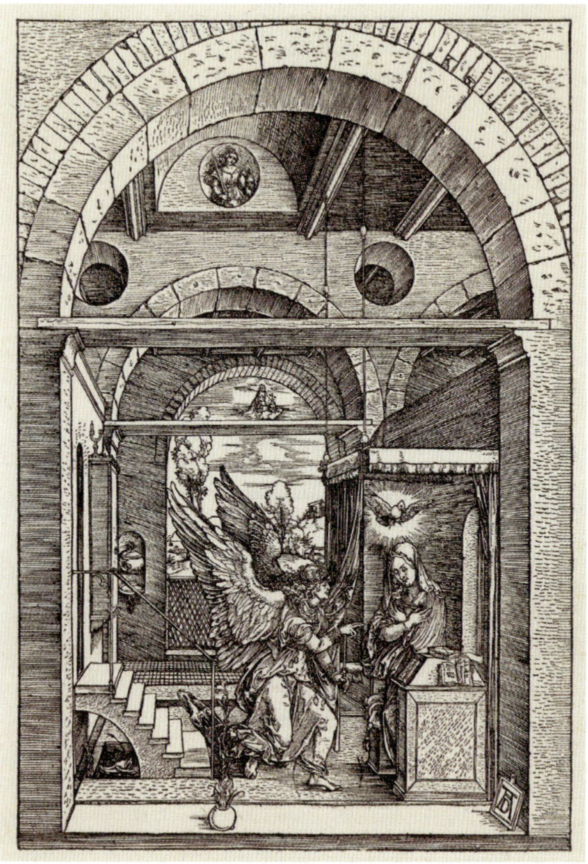

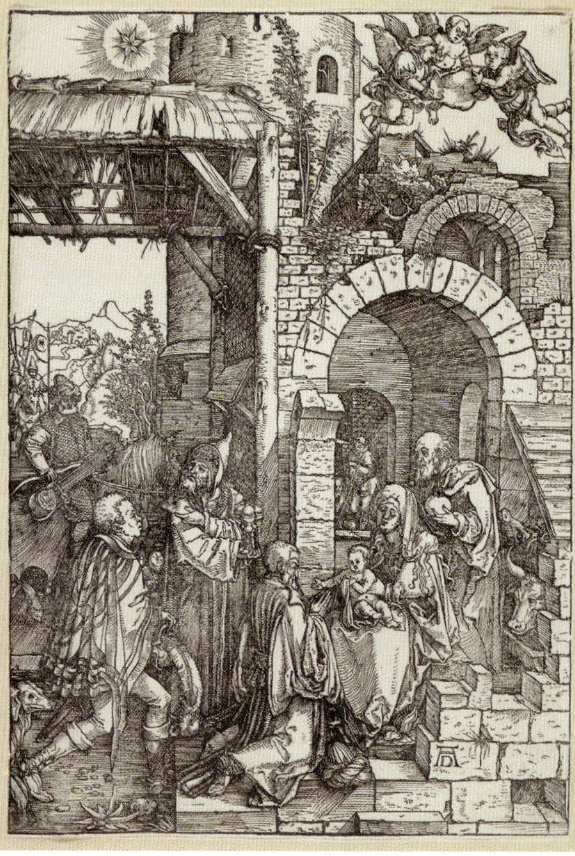

23
Albrecht Dürer
The Annunciation (*Life of the Virgin*), c. 1502–3.

Woodcut, 389 x 278 mm
Schoch, Mende and Scherbaum, *Albrecht Dürer*, II, 243–5, no. 173;
B.VII.132.83; H.195

The Whitworth, The University of Manchester, P.3036. Presented by
George Thomas Clough in 1921. © The Whitworth, The University of
Manchester. Photo: Michael Pollard.

24
Albrecht Dürer
The Adoration of the Magi (*Life of the Virgin*), c. 1503.

Woodcut, 301 x 212 mm
Schoch, Mende and Scherbaum, *Albrecht Dürer*, II, 254–6, no. 177;
B.VII.132.87; H.199

The Whitworth, The University of Manchester, P.3038. Presented by
George Thomas Clough in 1921. © The Whitworth, The University of
Manchester. Photo: Michael Pollard.

25
Albrecht Dürer
The Holy Family in Egypt (*Life of the Virgin*), c. 1502.

Woodcut, 302 x 209 mm
Schoch, Mende and Scherbaum, *Albrecht Dürer*, II, 262–5, no. 180;
B.VII.132.90; H.201

The Whitworth, The University of Manchester, P.3040. Presented by
George Thomas Clough in 1921. © The Whitworth, The University of
Manchester. Photo: Michael Pollard.

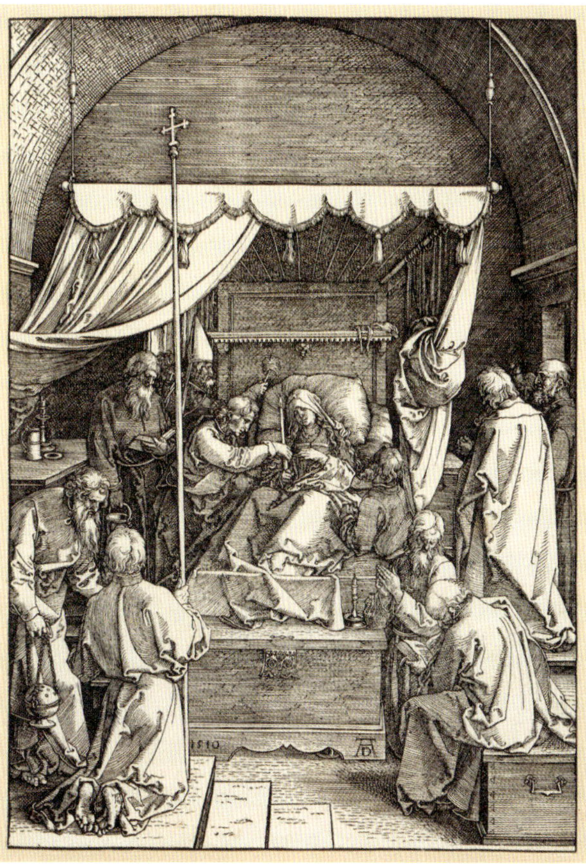

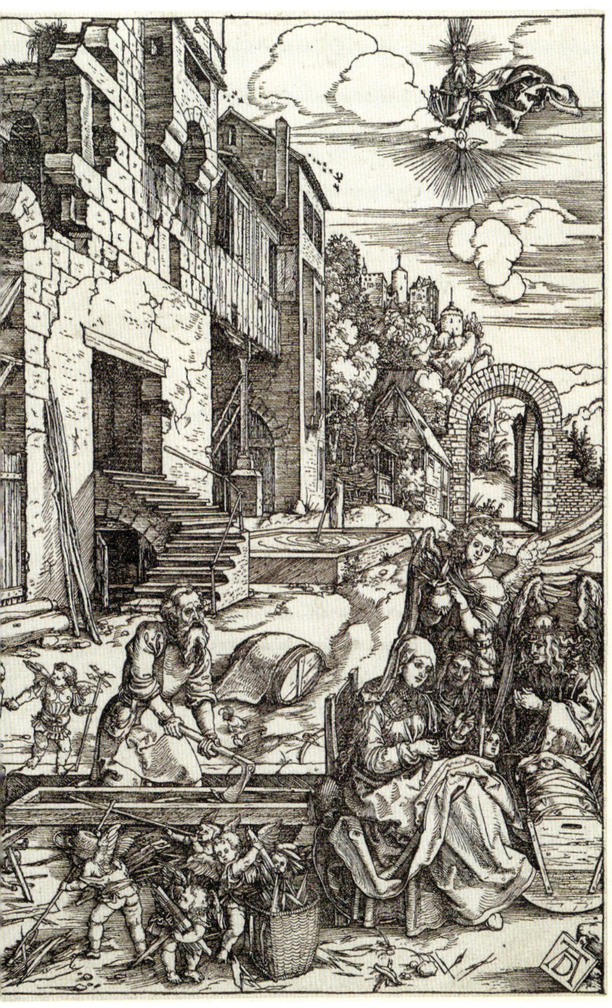

26
Albrecht Dürer
The Death of the Virgin (*Life of the Virgin*),
1510.

Woodcut, 294 x 209 mm
Schoch, Mende and Scherbaum, *Albrecht Dürer*, II,
171–3, no. 183; B.VII.132.90; H.205

Ashmolean Museum, University of Oxford,
WA1863.2468. Bequeathed by Francis Douce in 1834.
© Ashmolean Museum, University of Oxford.

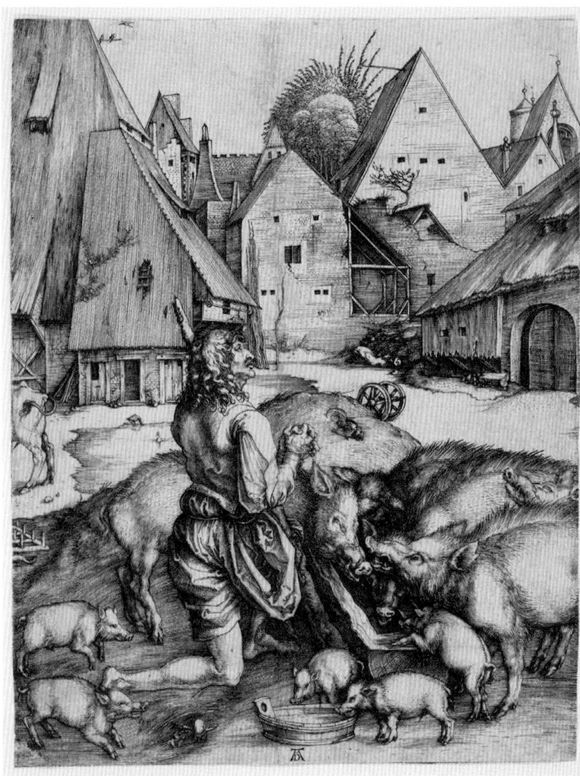

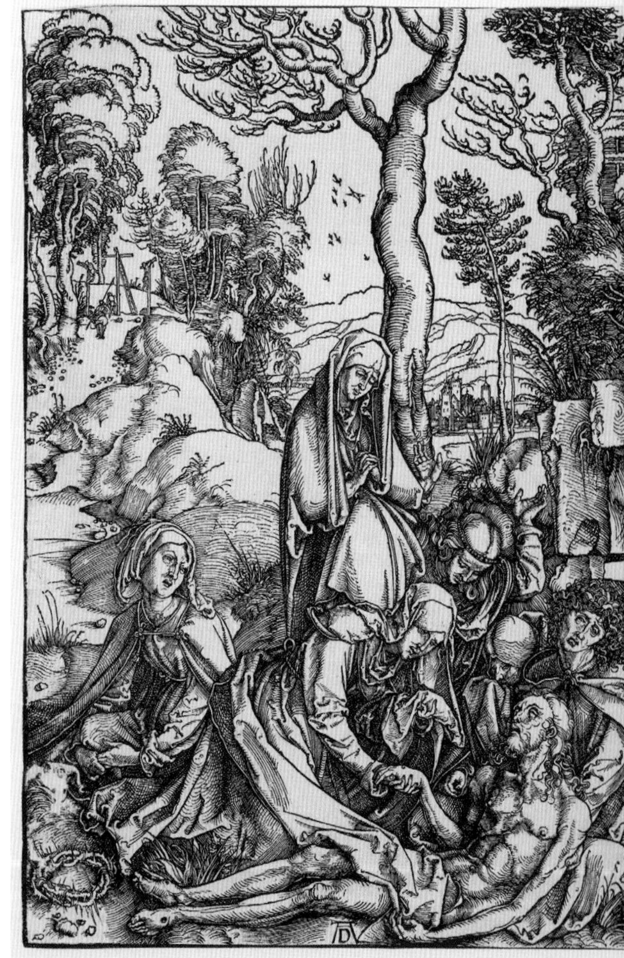

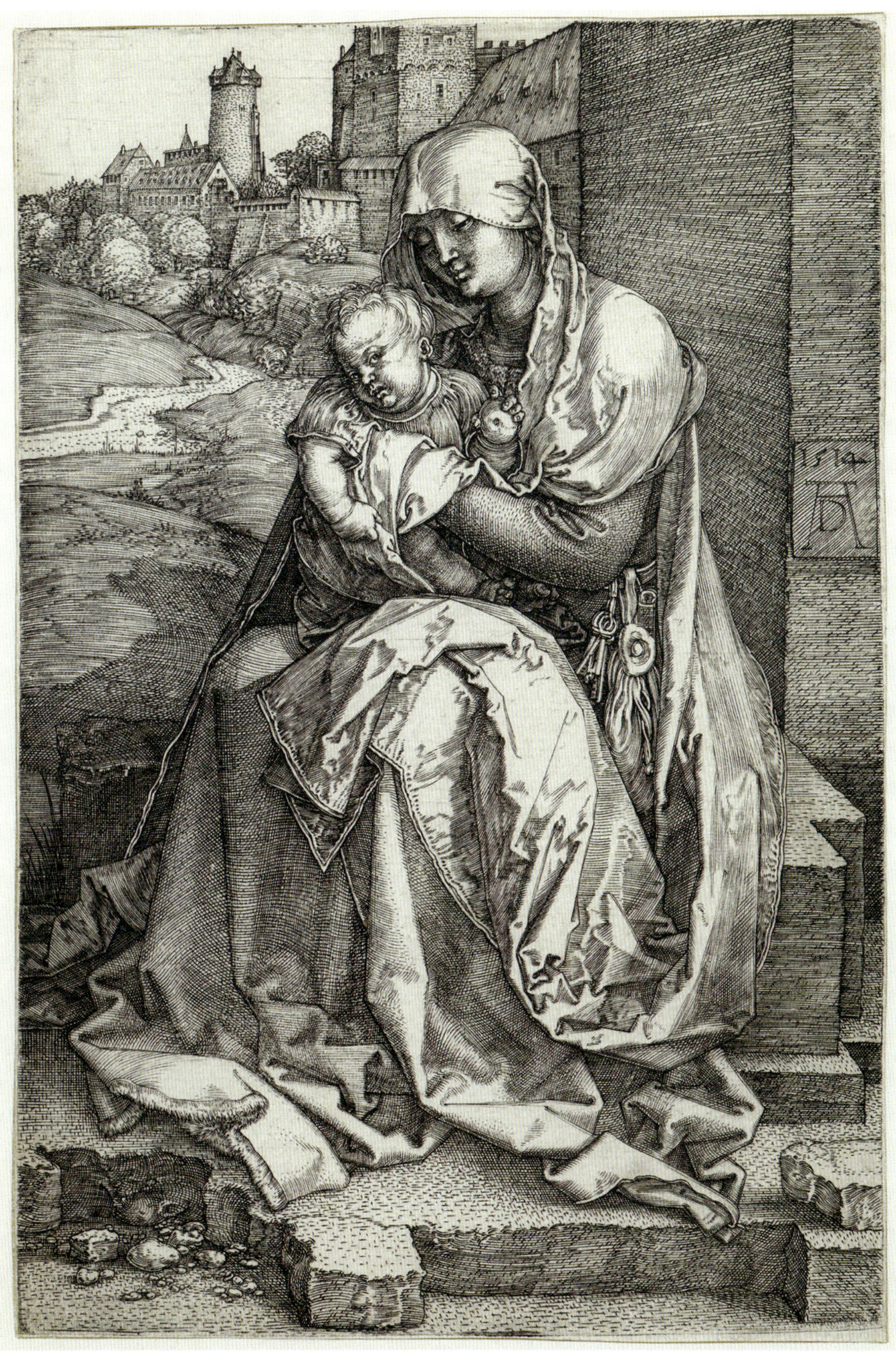

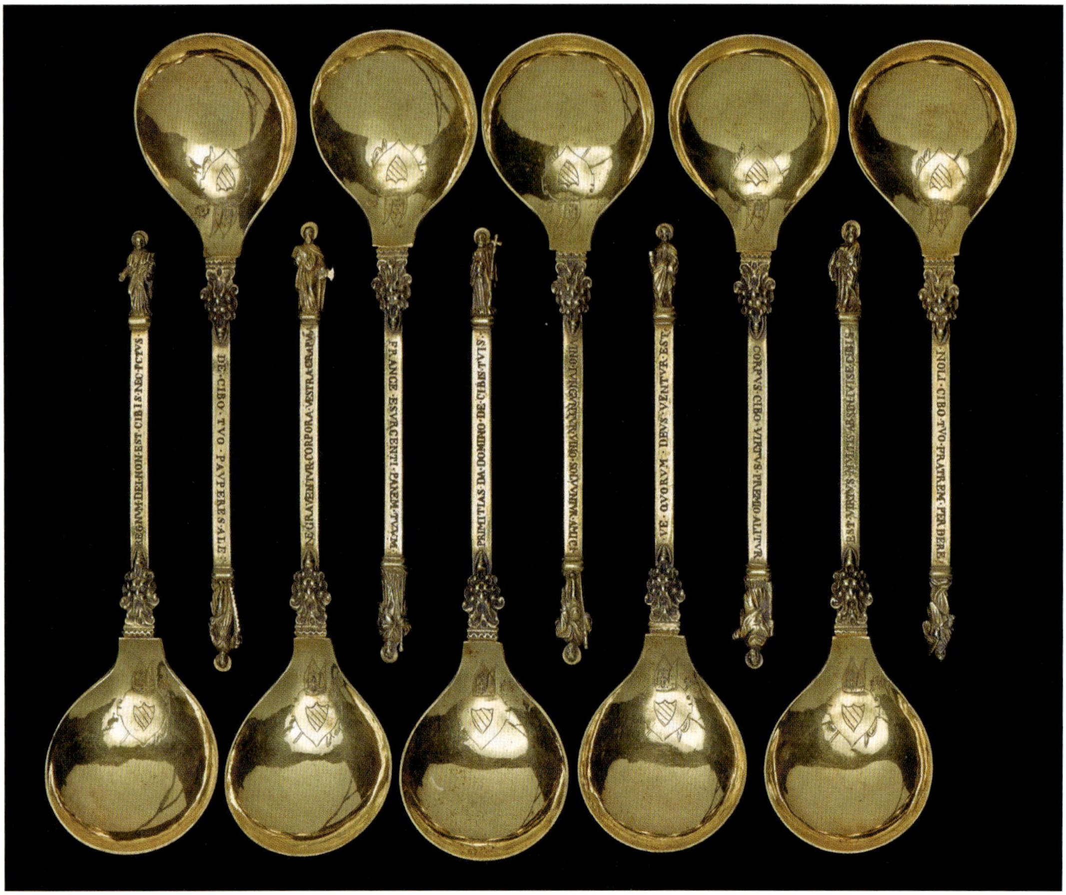

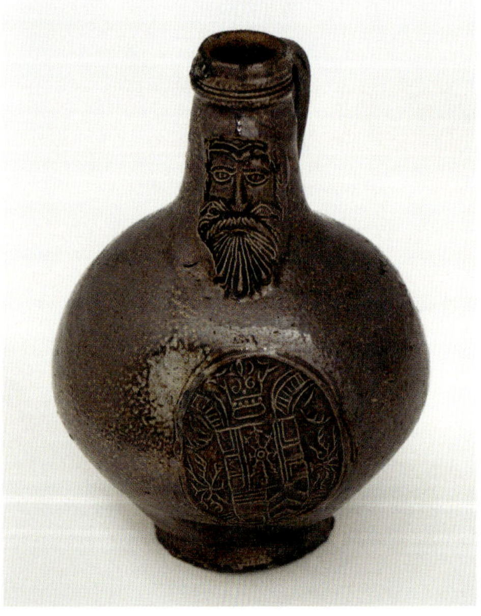

30
Unknown
Apostle Spoons, sixteenth century, German (Nuremberg).

Silver-gilt, 18.5 x 5.1 x 2.0 cm each

National Museums Scotland, A.1920.270; A.1920.271; A.1920.275; A.1920.280.
© Trustees of the National Museums Scotland.

31
Unknown
Bartmannkrug (Bellarmine Jug) with the Julich-Kleve-Berg Coat of Arms, c. 1625–50, German (Frechen).

Pottery with glossy brown salt glaze, 19.0 cm

Manchester Art Gallery, 1923.375. Bequeathed by Thomas Tylston Greg.
© Manchester Art Gallery. Photo: Michael Pollard.

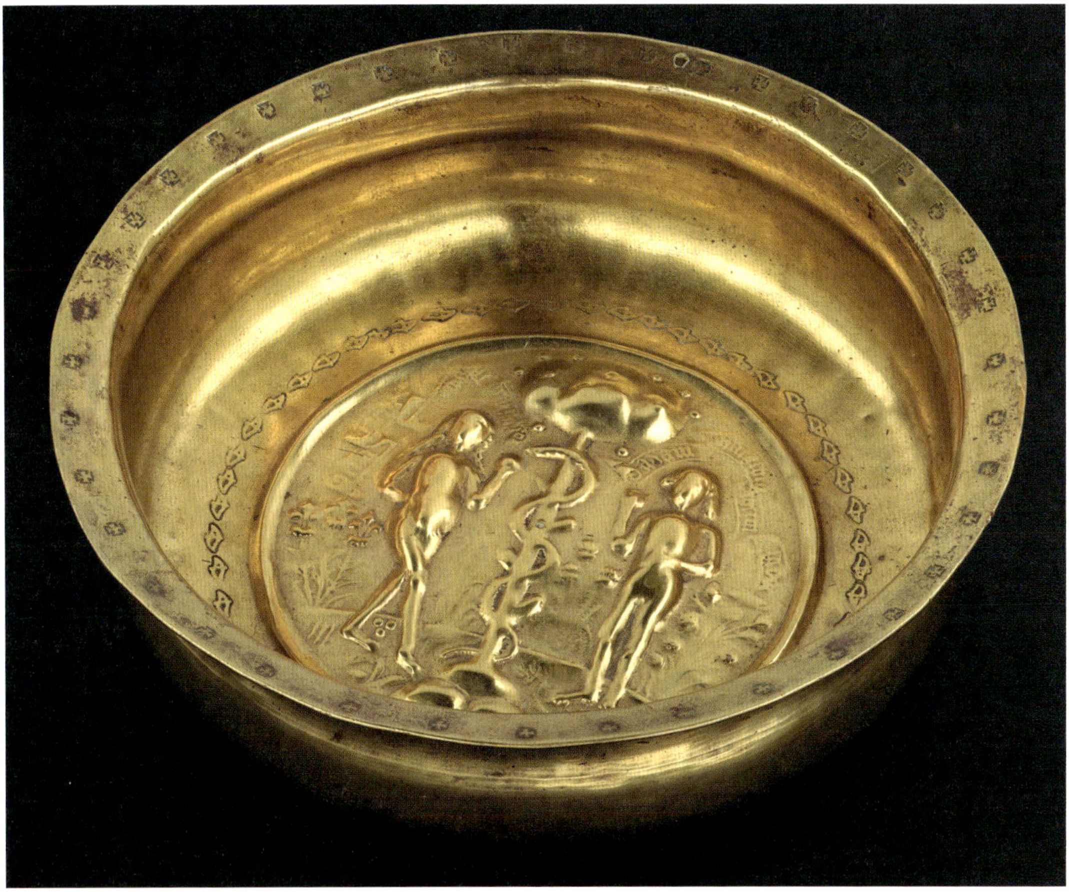

32
Unknown
Adam and Eve Bowl, c. 1500, German.

Brass, 6.8 x 25.5 (diameter) cm

National Museums Scotland, A.1924.420.
© Trustees of the National Museums Scotland.

33
Unknown
Bell, marked with HL monogram, arms of
a double headed eagle, the Crucifixion
with Saint John and the Virgin set
in a conventional Anthemion motif,
seventeenth century, German.

Bronze, 3.3 (diameter) x 2.8 cm

Manchester Art Gallery, 1922.1192.
Gift of Mrs Mary Greg. © Manchester Art Gallery.
Photo: Michael Pollard.

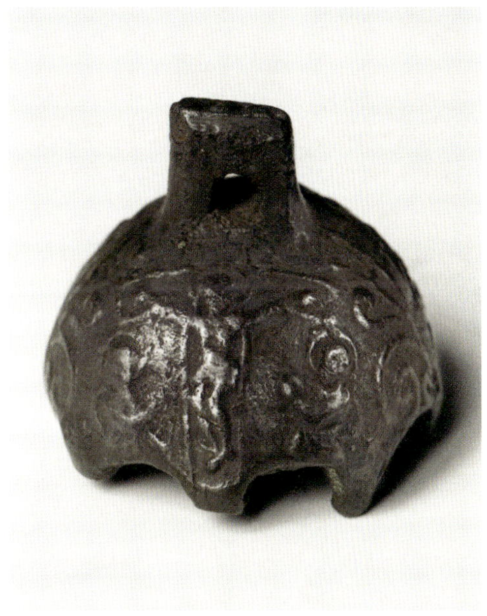

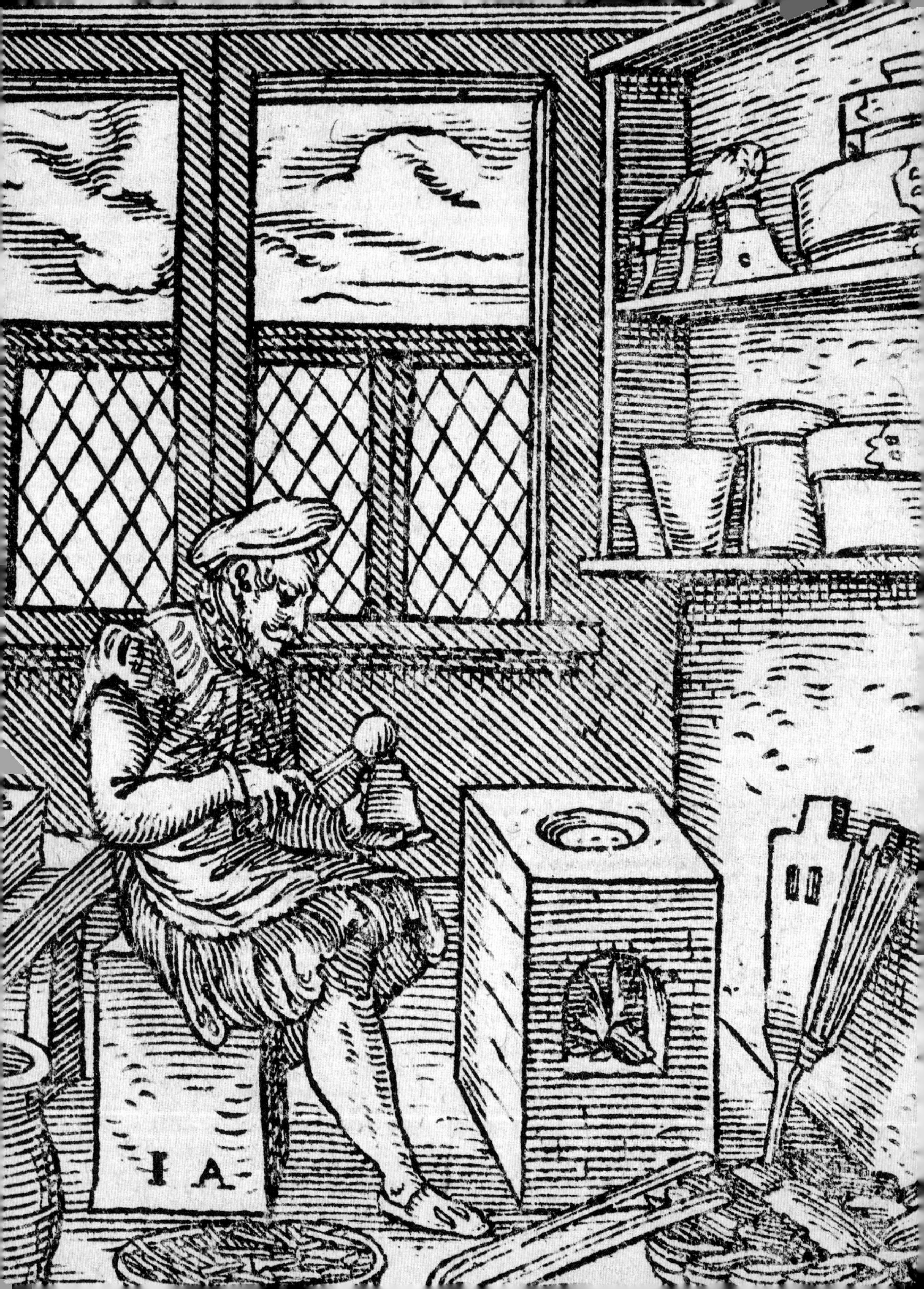

[13] The workshop

Stefan Hanß, Jennifer Spinks and Edward H. Wouk

Early modern artisans were skilled makers of objects, and their workshops were sites of astonishing technical and creative innovation. In the 'material Renaissance', a time of heightened appreciation for the intricate making of artefacts, the artisan's workshop was a space of acquiring, manufacturing and transforming materials and pushing established boundaries of what was considered achievable in the arts. In the workshop, the artisans' mind, body, knowledge, technology and materials merged into an interactive, productive assemblage that yielded new forms of material thinking and doing.[1] Albrecht Dürer himself had grown up in the household of his goldsmith father and trained in that craft. This experience is reflected, for example, in his *Nemesis* (cat. 34) engraving (see Jennifer Spinks' 'Objects in motion' in this volume). *Nemesis* – which builds on Dürer's earlier *Little Fortune* (cat. 36) – reveals Dürer's astounding skills as a printmaker working on a metal plate, while the figure of Nemesis holds an exquisite metal cup that reveals his eye for goldsmithing design. We also see Dürer experimenting with material aesthetics in his *Design for a Gothic Cup* (see Figure 4.2; cat. 35), one of several studies for drinking vessels that the artist produced around 1500. The drawing, which offers two possibilities for the cup's vegetal stem, was possibly intended as the basis for an actual object to be sold in his father's goldsmith's shop near Nuremberg's city hall.[2]

Renaissance Nuremberg attracted many skilled artisans, above all metalworkers who – along with the other 'sworn crafts' – performed under the oversight of the powerful Council rather than within a traditional, closed guild structure. Nuremberg artisans were sought-after for objects which included finely tuned measuring instruments, luxury clothing and armour,

and were regarded as amongst the best in Europe.[3] The *Ständebuch* by Jost Amman (1539–91), or 'Book of Trades' (1568), for example, shows a type-founder (*Schriftgießer*) hard at work in a typical setting and surrounded by specialist tools (cat. 37). Painting and sculpture were 'free arts', albeit under the hand of the Council, and Dürer's entrepreneurial approach worked well within this system. Humble as well as luxury items – Dürer's prints included – circulated through the city's extensive local sales and export markets, which were boosted by the annual religious and trade fair (*Heiltumsfest*).[4] Dürer's Nuremberg, in short, was a vibrant hub for the exchange of commodities and ideas.

Workshops set the stage for a vibrant climate of artisanal collaboration and competition, which in turn drove innovation. Even his early revolutionary *Apocalypse* cycle of c. 1498 (cat. 38–42) brims with objects of local manufacture. These ranged from candlesticks and vessels, to pikes, spears, and in the case of *Four Horsemen of the Apocalypse* (cat. 40), a contemporary crossbow similar to the one in this exhibition (cat. 43).

Dürer's artistic inventiveness, skill, intellectual range and social aspirations all fed his desire to elevate the status of the artist. This was encapsulated in his famous, if not entirely accurate, lament in a 1506 letter from Venice to his friend Willibald Pirckheimer (1470–1530): 'Here I'm a gentleman, at home "that scrounger".'[5] Demonstrating how artists were beginning to be regarded as a special class in Italy, Dürer draws a distinction with the situation in his home city. Alongside his wife, Agnes (1475–1539), Dürer ran a successful workshop aided by assistants and apprentices, balancing painting commissions with lucrative work as a printmaker. It was a space in which specialist tools for printmaking and expensive pigments for painting jostled with the daily material world of the household, and where the master set his apprentices and junior artists to work on skilled tasks but also fed, educated and provided a home for them.[6] A rare surviving woodblock of *Saint Veronica between Saints Peter and Paul* of 1510 (cat. 45), from Dürer's *Small Passion* cycle, comprising thirty-six woodcuts and a frontispiece published in 1511, allows us to see the translation of the artist's design into a carved printing surface. Specialist tools carefully cut away those parts of wood that were not to print, leaving a relief image composed of a network of lines. When inked and run through a press, such a woodblock could produce literally thousands of impressions including the one seen here (cat. 46).[7] As far as Dürer's engravings are concerned, however, fewer impressions could be pulled from a plate made of copper, which was run through a different type of press called an *intaglio* press and was under much greater pressure.[8] Dürer's etchings were produced in even smaller print runs, possibly because of the technical instabilities of the medium or because audiences were not yet prepared to appreciate its loose, drawing-like aesthetics.[9] Dürer treated the subject of the *sudarium*, the veil Veronica used to wipe the sweat from Christ's face, in all three of the printmaking techniques in which he worked, including the aforementioned woodcut, an engraving of 1513 (cat. 47) and an etching, *Sudarium Displayed by an Angel*, of 1516 (cat. 48). Scholars have observed the artist's interest in exploring the meaningful resonances between the subject of the image – a lasting impression made by contact between a cloth surface and Christ's face – and the technology of printmaking, in which paper is similarly impressed with an image (see Edward Wouk's 'Landscape with a Cannon' in this volume).

As Dürer discovered when seeking information about measurement and proportion from Jacobo de' Barbari (c. 1460/70–1516), knowledge could be jealously guarded. De' Barbari stayed in Nuremberg at the emperor's behest between 1500 and 1503, and one of the assistants in Dürer's workshop, Hans Suess von Kulmbach (c. 1485–1522), worked with him. Young Dürer carved out a space for himself as an artist in-between acclaimed names like de' Barbari and

Martin Schongauer (1440/53–91). But in a world where copying was common commercial practice and part of absorbing new techniques and forms of imagery, questions of creative ownership were complex. Dürer sought 'privileges' to protect his printed work and was reported to be infuriated when the Italian engraver Marcantonio Raimondi (1438–1534) replicated prints from his innovative *Small Passion* and from his *Life of the Virgin* cycle of twenty woodcuts, which Dürer had begun around 1500 (see the 'The home' in this volume). Comparing Dürer's woodcut *The Visitation* (cat. 55) and Marcantonio Raimondi's engraved 'copy' (cat. 56) reveals that the Italian printmaker not only replicated Dürer's composition but also his distinctive monogram, even as he translated the image from one print medium to another, introducing subtle but noticeable differences in the process. In his *Lives of the Artists*, Giorgio Vasari (1511–74) records the story, likely apocryphal, that Dürer lodged a grievance against Raimondi before the Venetian Senate, who apparently ruled that the Italian engraver could duplicate Dürer's prints, but that the famous 'AD' monogram was to be off limits.[10]

Dürer turned to writing to codify his status and expertise as artisan author, pass on knowledge to apprentices and secure his legacy. Dürer's *Treatise on Measurement* appeared in 1525, with one illustration depicting a workshop scene (cat. 57).[11] His *Four Books … on the Symmetry of the Parts of the Human Body*, or *Four Books on Human Proportion* (cat. 58) appeared posthumously in 1528 and was likewise later translated into Latin.[12] Both reflect his fascination with the application of geometry to the creation of harmonious and beautiful forms, from snail shells to the human body. In Dürer's understanding, these treatises were aimed at 'painters, sculptors in wood, stonemasons, likewise metal casters, goldsmiths, silk embroiderers, [and] potters', demonstrating that he continued to see himself as a member of a larger artisanal community.[13]

Material experimentation

The success of Dürer's printmaking ventures fed his urge to experiment with new techniques. One of those, we have seen, was etching, which at the time was widely used for decorating armour but not for prints. Dürer was among the first to explore its potentials for the graphic arts. Dürer's *Desperate Man* (cat. 49), sometimes considered his first etching though roughly contemporaneous with his *Christ on the Mount of Olives* (cat. 50) of 1515, already shows the artist joining the experimental technique with highly unusual, even inscrutable subject matter.[14] Other artists also experimented with the technique of etching, including Hans Burgkmair (1473–1531). His only attempt at etching, in *Venus, Mercury and Cupid* (cat. 51), reveals extensive areas of corrosion at the edges of an unusually playful scene in which Venus attempts to rouse Mercury with the knocked end of one of Cupid's arrows.[15] Yet, for Dürer, etching offered a wellspring of experiment, and by the time he completed *Landscape with a Cannon* in 1518 (cat. 52), he had already begun to test the limits of what was possible in this relatively new printmaking technique. This etching resides at the intersection between his interest in print and military technology, which he and members of his workshop explored in earlier woodcuts, including battle scene prints for the massive *Triumphal Arch of Emperor Maximilian* (cat. 53) and in the pages of his *Treatise on the Fortification of City, Castle and Places* (cat. 54), published posthumously (see Edward Wouk's 'Landscape with a Cannon' in this volume).

Dürer's artisanal creativity was also deeply enmeshed in the world of textiles. In 1481, when Dürer was ten years old, the Council declared Nuremberg residents to be obsessed with fashion 'novelties' (*Newikait*) such as new materials, special cuts, precious adornments, extravagant arrangements or foreign clothing.[16] Notwithstanding the authority's concerns about God's punishment of such vanity, Dürer's art was firmly anchored in what scholars have described as 'the cloth age'.[17] In the company of his humanist friends, Dürer took pride in owning a French and Hungarian-style cloak, and during his journey in the Netherlands, he was excited 'to have bought my wife a thin Dutch kerchief for the head'.[18] Further, Dürer had taken an active role in designing his own shoes, liaising with craftspeople to communicate his preferences (cat. 59–60).[19] 'This is how the shoe is to be cut out, and the decoration (*zird*) is to be stamped into the wet leather',

Dürer explained in the annotation to his drawing: 'The shoe is to have a strap and buckle. The sole of this shoe shall be absolutely straight and flat underneath'.[20] Similarly, the artist would have communicated with tailors, furriers, ribbon- or bonnet-makers, among others. Tools such as these early modern German scissors (cat. 63) enabled practitioners to work their materials with precision, transforming fabrics into objects of visual and haptic appeal.

Fabrics and bodies

In Renaissance Nuremberg, clothing was a visual act that stimulated the artist's imagination and practices. Textiles could inspire artists to generate new types of imagery and ways of working.[21] Portraiture in particular was a site of experimentation. Artists used sophisticated assemblages of hair, jewellery and clothing, such as furs or caps, to foreground materials and create the sense of character that amplified the presence of the sitter.[22] In the engraving of *Friedrich the Wise, the Elector of Saxony* (cat. 4), Dürer used the strokes of his burin to animate the curls of Friedrich's beard, the softness of fur and the folding of fabric, to enliven the presence of his esteemed sitter. In the engraving of Frederick the Wise (cat. 4), Dürer used his burin to animate the curls of the beard, the softness of the fur and the folding of the fabric, as a means of enlivening the presence of the Elector of Saxony, who had sent a 'boy' for training in Dürer's workshop as early as 1502.[23] Fabrics could be used to establish relationships, as well as to adorn bodies and decorate households, even furniture. The application of printing on sixteenth-century fabrics, like block printed fustians (cat. 64), encouraged Dürer's artisanal experimentation in rendering cloth through different techniques and by capturing the visual dynamism of textiles. Clothing materialised social status and global customs, topics of interest to Dürer who drew and compared the fabrics worn by Venetian and Nuremberg women. Embroidery could turn textiles into depictions of life, as seen for instance in the head and torso of Christ from a surviving fragment of fabric dated to the mid-sixteenth century (cat. 67). Dürer excelled in rendering the Saxon elector's extravagant cap-folding techniques, and he put considerable efforts into animating new cuts, clothing habits and material fineness in engraving. For example, in two depictions of Saint Christopher, *Saint Christopher* of 1511 (cat. 61) and *Saint Christopher Turned to the Left*, of 1521 (cat. 62), Dürer exploited the depiction of textiles to animate the pose of the saint in motion.

Renaissance textiles allowed Dürer to convey notions of movement that animated and lent emotions to figures.[24] Developing the characteristics of clothing empowered him to engage in visual storytelling. For instance, the striped, tight costume of the executioner in the *Martyrdom of Saint Catherine* (cat. 44) references the 'striped layman', widely debated among humanists as a middling-class character whose social ambitions led to the inappropriate transgression of boundaries. This liminal figure's status called attention to contemporary visual and emotional registers in Renaissance Nuremberg such as anxieties about social trespassing.[25] In his engravings, Dürer further pushed and deployed the innovative adornment potential of fabrics to explore the creative depth of the surface. The intricacy of lacework, finely woven fabrics and embroidered portraits called the artist's attention to material details; bobbin lacework in particular illustrated that ingenuity in making resulted from both dexterous movements of hands and masterful calculations of the mind (cat. 65). The use of metal threads by embroiderers would have attracted the eye, mind and hand of the goldsmith-trained artist to reflect on the potential of metals and textiles alike. Weaving textiles, then, was a line-centred form of material engagement: of thinking and working in grids (cat. 66). Since the Renaissance mind could associate intricately made knots and textiles with ingenuity (see Stefan Hanß's 'The nature of lines' in this volume), Dürer's woodcuts of intricate knots inspired by Leonardo da Vinci (1452–1519; cat. 68–70) and his depictions of refined textiles can be considered a pun on the artist's ingenuity in animating such material performances, visual appearances and emotional appeals through artisanal means. The artisan's workshop, in sum, was the space that forged the artist's creative role as a visual and material entrepreneur, spearheading the 'material Renaissance's' new forms of making and knowing.

Notes

1   Smith, 'Making as Knowing'; Smith, *Body of the Artisan*; Smith, *Lived Experience*.

2   Bartrum, *Dürer and his Legacy*, 130–1, no. 65. The drawing is closely related to Dürer's drawing *Six Goblets* now in the Sächsische Landesbibliothek – Staats – und Universitätsbibliothek, Dresden; see Strauss, *Complete Drawings*, 1499/6. The legend on that drawing reads 'morgen will ich ir mer machn' (tomorrow I shall make more of them). Dürer's father opened his shop in 1486, and it closed with his death in 1502.

3   Kahsnitz and Wixom, eds, *Gothic and Renaissance Art*, 11–20. See also Schinder, Keller and Schürer, *Zünftig!*

4   Maué, Eser, Hauschke and Stolzenberger, *Quasi Centrum Europæ*.

5   Ashcroft, *Albrecht Dürer*, I, 168.

6   This has been recreated in the Albrecht-Dürer-Haus in modern-day Nuremberg, on the site of Dürer's last house in the city.

7   The woodcuts were first published by Hieronymus Höltzel in Nuremberg in 1511 as part of a book with thirty-six images and Latin texts.

8   Griffiths, *The Print Before Photography*, 50–8.

9   Dackerman, 'Dürer's Etchings: Printed Drawings?'; Bartrum, *German Renaissance Prints*, 102.

10   Pon, *Raphael, Dürer and Marcantonio Raimondi*, 39–41, 58, 139–40. As Pon argues, this may be related to a 1512 legal ruling in Nuremberg.

11   Schoch, Mende and Scherbaum, *Albrecht Dürer*, III, 168–278, no. 274.

12   *Ibid.*, III, 319–474, no. 277.

13   Ashcroft, *Albrecht Dürer*, II, 868.

14   Parshall, 'Graphic Knowledge'; Dackerman, 'Dürer's Etchings', 45–6; Jenkins, Orenstein and Spira, eds, *Renaissance of Etching*, 46–9, no. 15.

15   Bartrum, *German Renaissance Prints*, 145; Wouk, *Imprinting the Imagination*, 18, no. 4 (entry by Naomi Chu).

16   Burgemeister, *Kleider*, 350; Zander-Seidel, *Textiler Hausrat*.

17   Lemire, *Global Trade*, 32.

18   Rupprich, *Nachlass*, I, 57, 162. For these texts, see also Ashcroft, *Albrecht Dürer*, I, 163, 569–70.

19   Beyer, 'Dürers Schuhe'.

20   Trans. Ashcroft, *Albrecht Dürer*, II, 822, no. 239, modified by Stefan Hanß.

21   Rublack, *Dressing Up*.

22   Hanß, 'Face-Work'; Zitzlsperger, *Dürers Pelz*.

23   Rupprich, *Nachlass*, I, 245. For this text, see also Ashcroft, *Albrecht Dürer*, I, 104–5.

24   This concept is indebted to Warburg, *Botticellis 'Geburt der Venus'*, 6, 8, 28.

25   Taape, 'Common Medicine'.

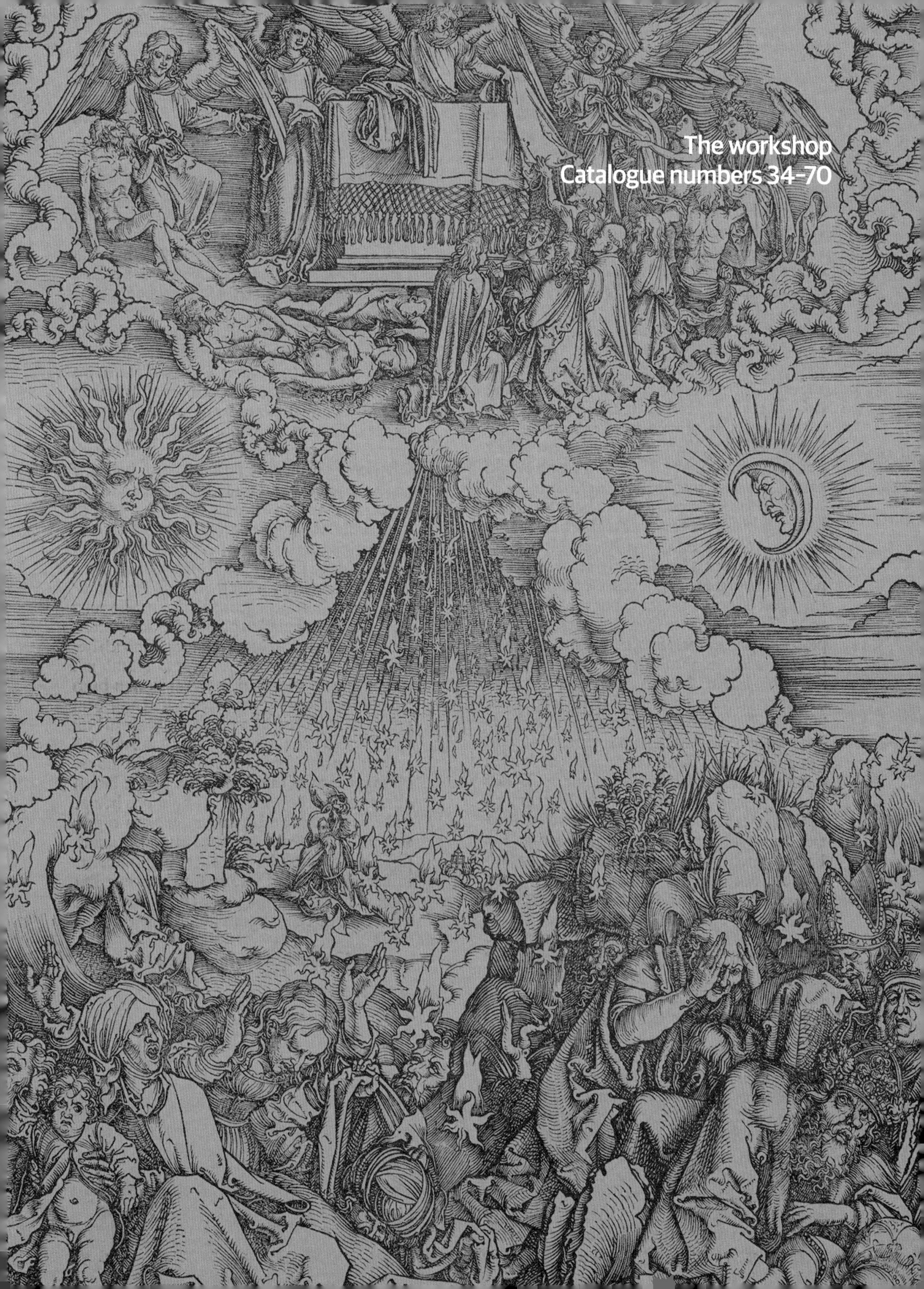
The workshop
Catalogue numbers 34–70

34
Albrecht Dürer
Nemesis (The Great Fortune), c. 1501.

Engraving, 331 x 231 mm
Schoch, Mende and Scherbaum, *Albrecht Dürer*, I,
95–9, no. 33; B.VII.91.77; H.72

The Whitworth, The University of Manchester, P.3019.
Presented by George Thomas Clough in 1921. © The
University of Manchester. Photo: Michael Pollard.

For illustration, see figure 4.1, p. 36.

35
Albrecht Dürer
Design for a Gothic Cup, c. 1495–1500.

Pen and brown ink, 256 x 166 mm
Strauss, *Complete Drawings*, 1499/7; Bartrum, *Dürer
and his Legacy*, 130–1, no. 65

London, The British Museum, SL,5218.78. Bequeathed
by Sir Hans Sloane.© The Trustees of the British Museum.

For illustration, see figure 4.2, p. 38.

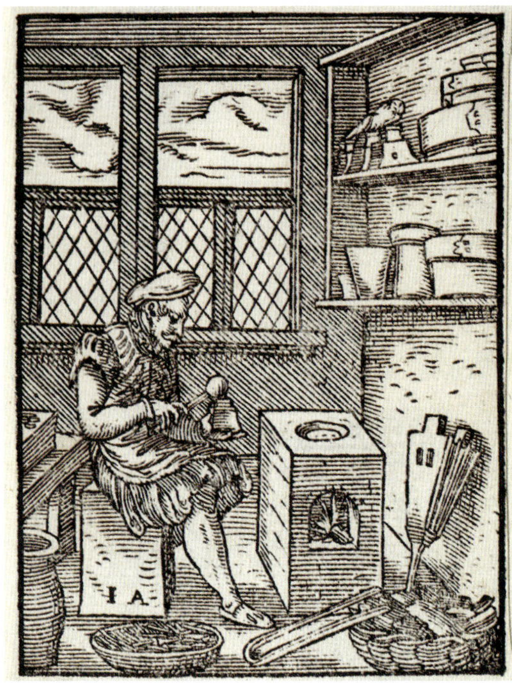

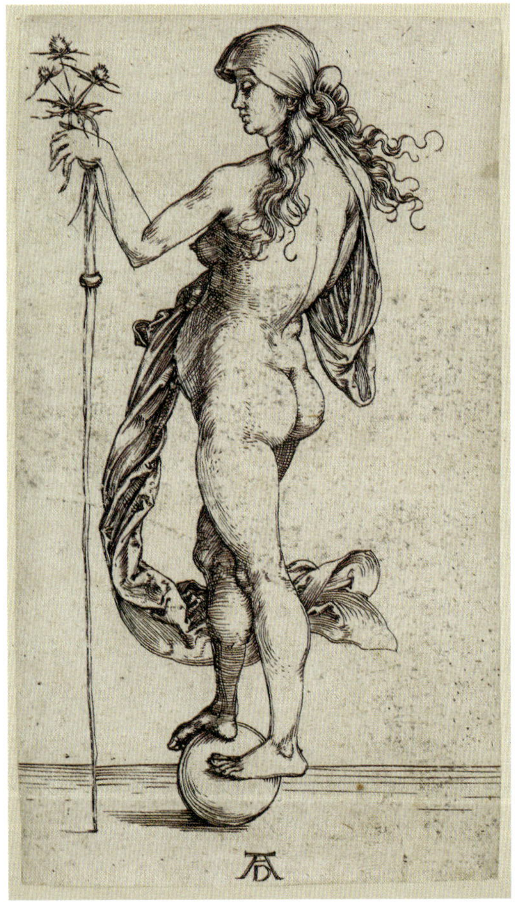

< 36
Albrecht Dürer
Fortune (The Little Fortune), 1496–8.

Engraving, 104 x 59 mm, trimmed
Schoch, Mende and Scherbaum, *Albrecht Dürer*, I, 36–7, no. 5;
B.VII.92.78; H.71

The University of Manchester, The Whitworth, P.5109.
Presented by the executors of Dr E. J. Sidebotham in 1929.
© The Whitworth, The University of Manchester. Photo: Michael Pollard.

^ 37
Jost Amman
The Type Founder (Fusor Literarius. Der Schriftgießer)
in *The Book of Trades (Ständebuch)*. Frankfurt:
Hans Sachs, 1568.

Woodcut, 126 x 63 mm

Manchester Art Gallery, 1967.106/8. © Manchester Art Gallery.
Photo: Michael Pollard.

> 38
Albrecht Dürer
Martyrdom of Saint John Evangelist (Apocalypse), 1511.

Woodcut, 384 x 281 mm, trimmed
Schoch, Mende and Scherbaum, *Albrecht Dürer*, II, 70–2, no. 112;
B.VII.127.61; H.164

The Whitworth, The University of Manchester, P.3058.
Presented by George Thomas Clough in 1921.
© The Whitworth, The University of Manchester. Photo: Michael Pollard.

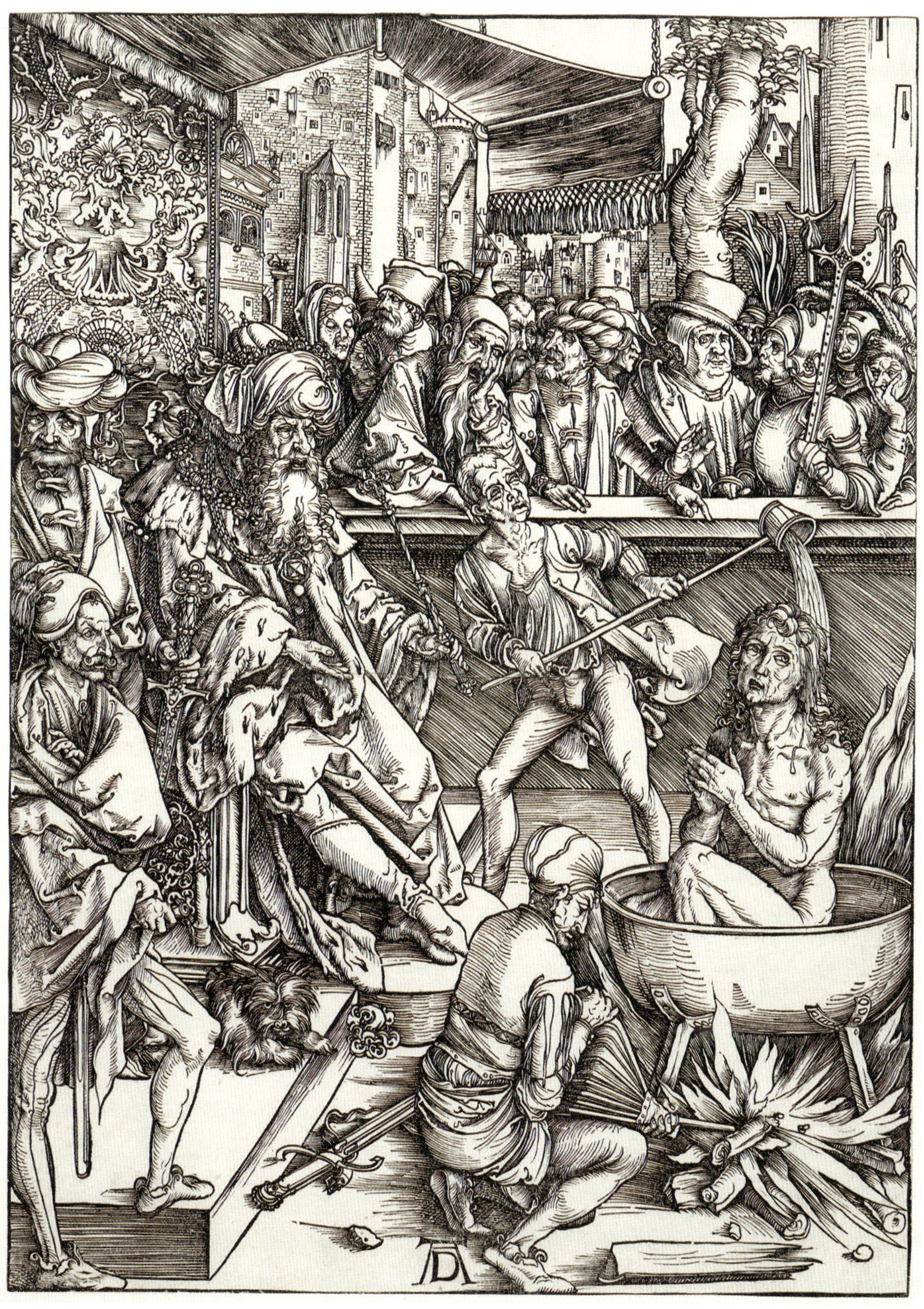

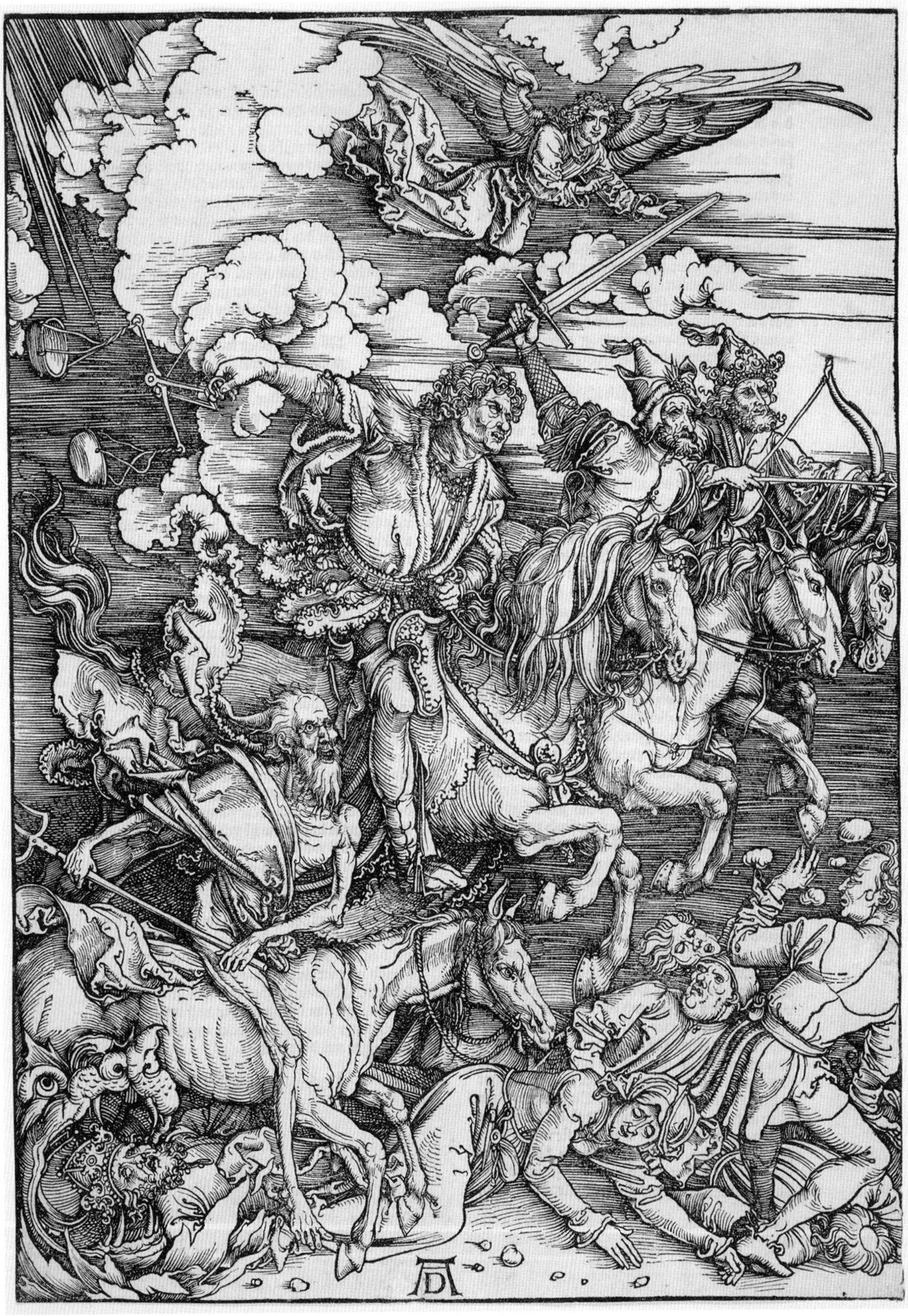

39
Albrecht Dürer
*Saint John's Vision of Christ
and the Seven Golden
Candlesticks* (*Apocalypse*),
1498.

Woodcut, 392 x 283 mm, trimmed
Schoch, Mende and Scherbaum,
Albrecht Dürer, II, 72–4, no. 113;
B.VII.127. 62; H.165

The Whitworth, The University of
Manchester, P.3059. Presented by
George Thomas Clough in 1921.
© The Whitworth, The University of
Manchester. Photo: Michael Pollard.

*For illustration, see fig. 6.2,
p. 66.*

< 40
Albrecht Dürer
*Four Horsemen of the
Apocalypse: Death, Famine,
War, and the Conqueror
(Apocalypse)*, 1498.

Woodcut, 393 x 281 mm, trimmed
Schoch, Mende and Scherbaum,
Albrecht Dürer, II, 76–9, no. 115;
B.VII.128.64; H.167

The Whitworth, The University of
Manchester, P.3061. Presented by
George Thomas Clough in 1921.
© The Whitworth, The University of
Manchester. Photo: Michael Pollard.

> 41
Albrecht Dürer
*Opening of the Fifth and
Sixth Seals (Apocalypse)*,
1498.

Woodcut, 390 x 282 mm, trimmed
Schoch, Mende and Scherbaum,
Albrecht Dürer, II, 79–81, no. 116;
B.VII.128.65; H.168

The Whitworth, The University of
Manchester, P.3062. Presented by
George Thomas Clough in 1921.
© The Whitworth, The University of
Manchester. Photo: Michael Pollard.

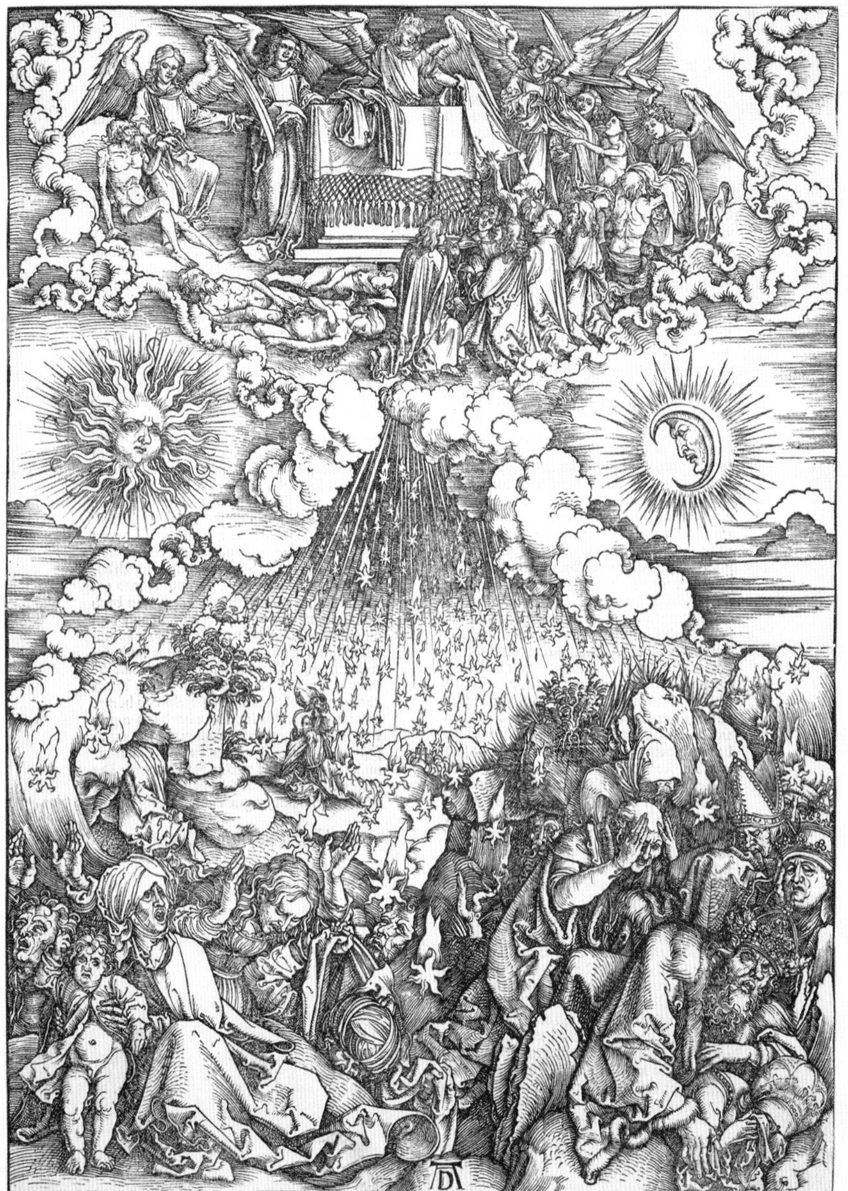

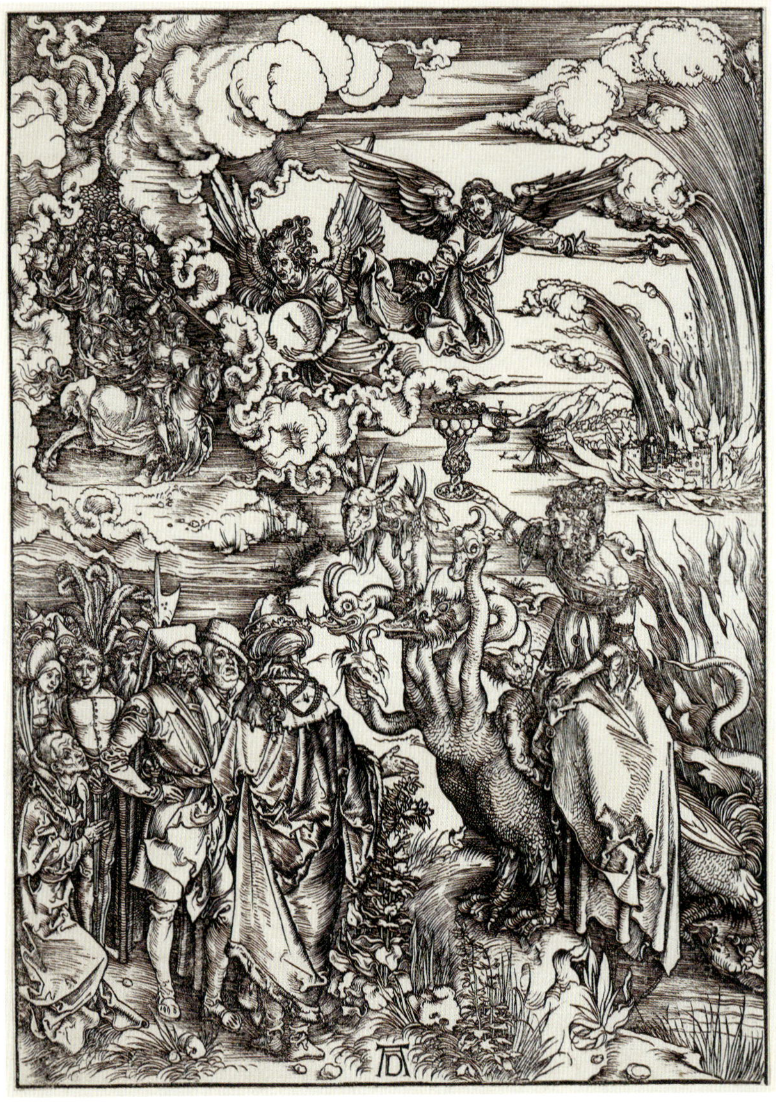

42
Albrecht Dürer
The Babylonian Whore
(*Apocalypse*), 1498.

Woodcut, 387 x 282 mm
Schoch, Mende and Scherbaum,
Albrecht Dürer, II, 101–3, no. 125;
B.VII.129.73; H.177

The Whitworth, The University of
Manchester, P.3070. Presented by
George Thomas Clough in 1921.
© The Whitworth, The University of
Manchester. Photo: Michael Pollard.

> 44
Albrecht Dürer
*Martyrdom of Saint
Catherine*, 1498.

Woodcut, 382 x 282 mm, trimmed
Schoch, Mende and Scherbaum,
Albrecht Dürer, II, 109–12, no. 128;
B.IIV.141.120; H.236

The Whitworth, The University of
Manchester, P.3051. Presented by
George Thomas Clough in 1921.
© The Whitworth, The University of
Manchester. Photo: Michael Pollard.

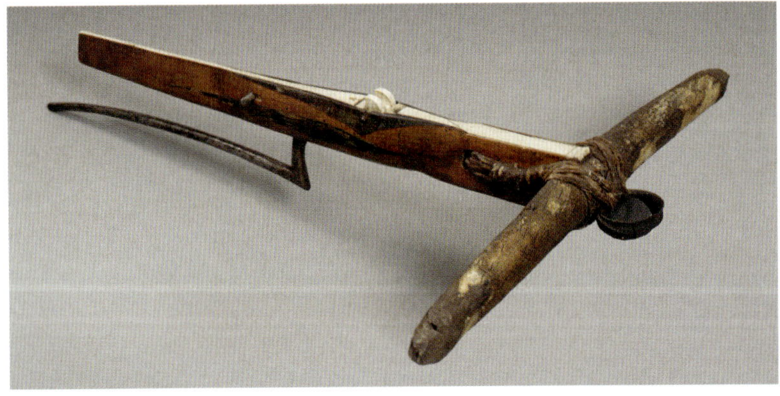

43
Unknown
Crossbow, c. 1500, German.

Birch, iron, ivory, sinew cord,
63.5 x 65.0 x 44.0 cm

Manchester Museum, The
University of Manchester, SA.12/1.
© Manchester Museum,
The University of Manchester.

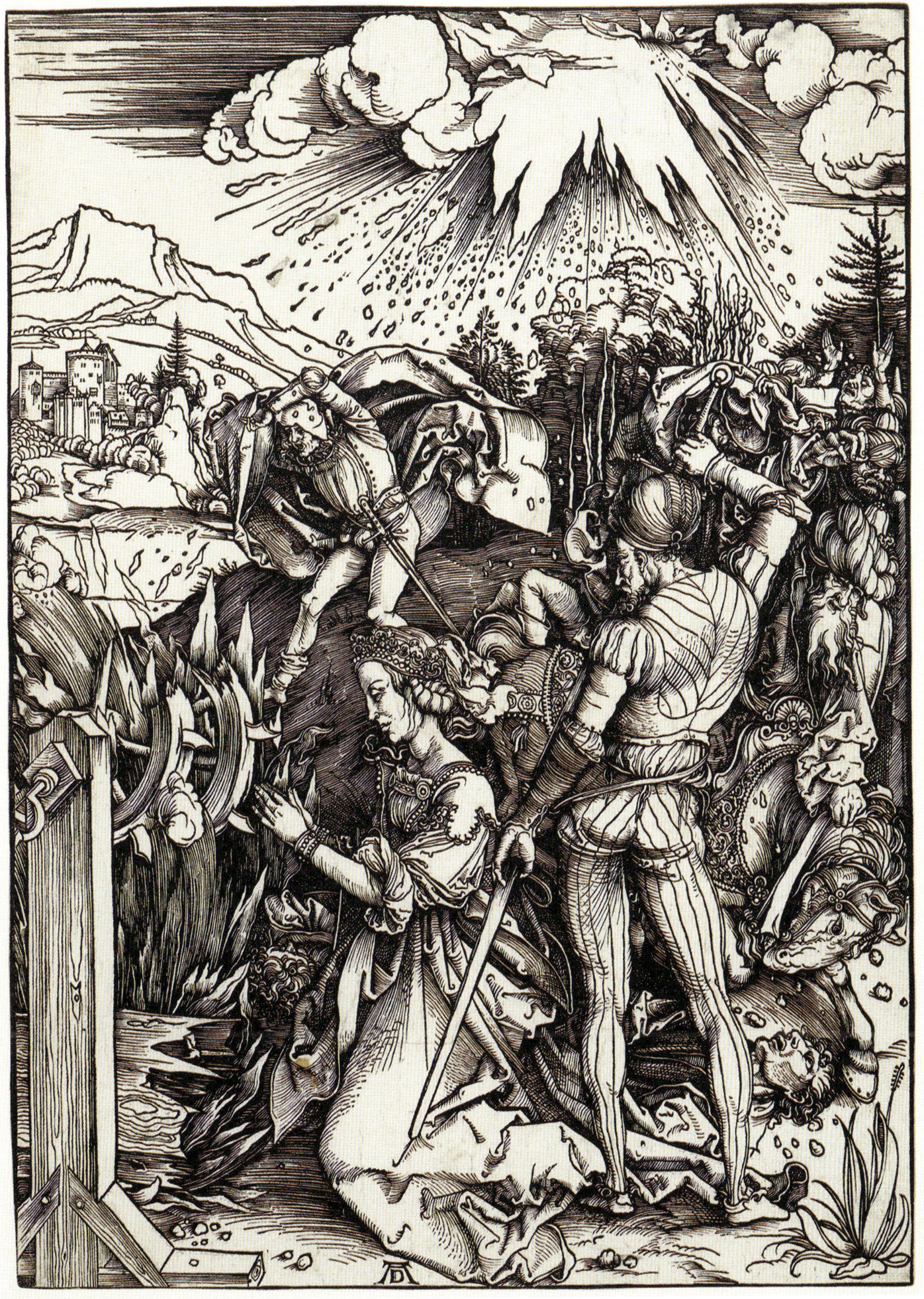

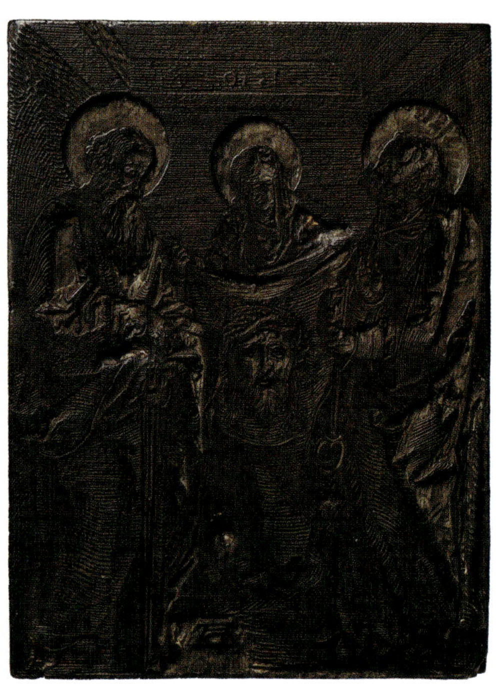

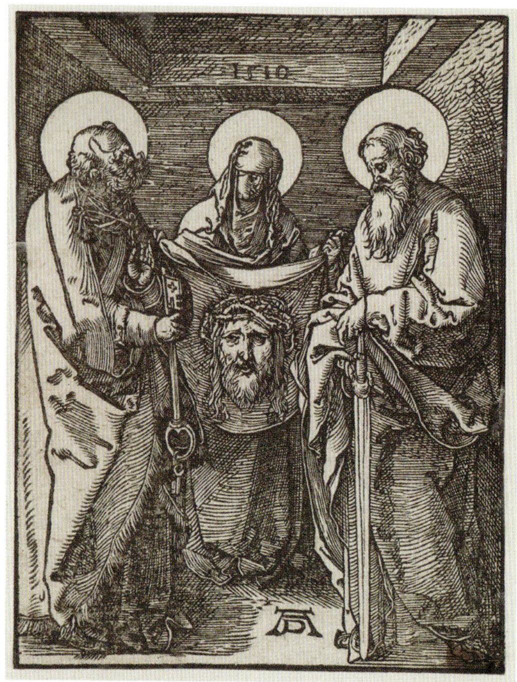

45
Albrecht Dürer
Woodblock of Saint Veronica between Saints Peter and Paul (The Small Passion), 1510.

Wood, probably pearwood, 12.9 x 9.8 x 2.5 cm
First edition published by Hieronymus Höltzel, Nuremberg, 1511.
Schoch, Mende and Scherbaum, *Albrecht Dürer*, II, 321–2, under no. 208

London, The British Museum, 1839,0608.3.38.
© The Trustees of the British Museum.

46
Albrecht Dürer
Saint Veronica between Saints Peter and Paul (The Small Passion), 1510.

Woodcut, 128 x 99 mm, trimmed
Schoch, Mende and Scherbaum, *Albrecht Dürer*, II, 321–2, no. 208;
B.VII.120.38; H.147

The Whitworth, The University of Manchester, P.4788. Bequeathed
by William Sharp Ogden in 1926. © The Whitworth, The University of
Manchester. Photo: Michael Pollard.

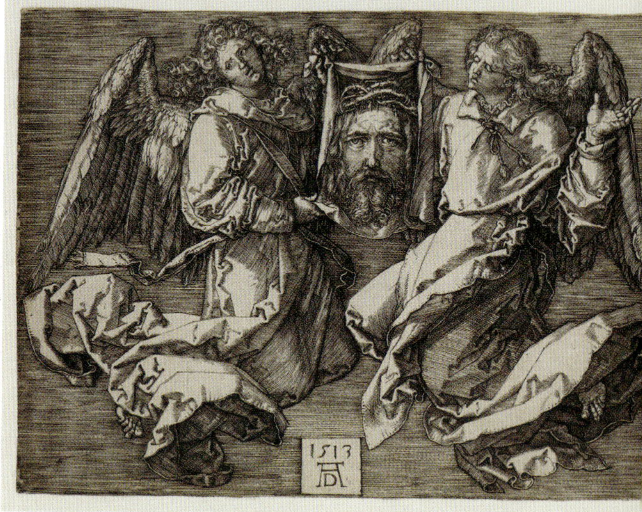

47
Albrecht Dürer
Sudarium Held by Two Angels, 1513.

Engraving, 101 x 129 mm
Schoch, Mende and Scherbaum, *Albrecht Dürer*, I, 164–5, no. 68;
B.VII.47.25; H.26

The Whitworth, The University of Manchester, P.3005. Presented by
George Thomas Clough in 1921. © The Whitworth, The University of
Manchester. Photo: Michael Pollard.

48
Albrecht Dürer
Sudarium Displayed by an Angel, 1516.

Etching, 181 x 133 mm
Schoch, Mende and Scherbaum,
Albrecht Dürer, I, 205–6, no. 82;
B.VII.47.26; H.27

The Whitworth, The University of
Manchester, P.3006. Presented by
George Thomas Clough in 1921.
© The Whitworth, The University of
Manchester. Photo: Michael Pollard.

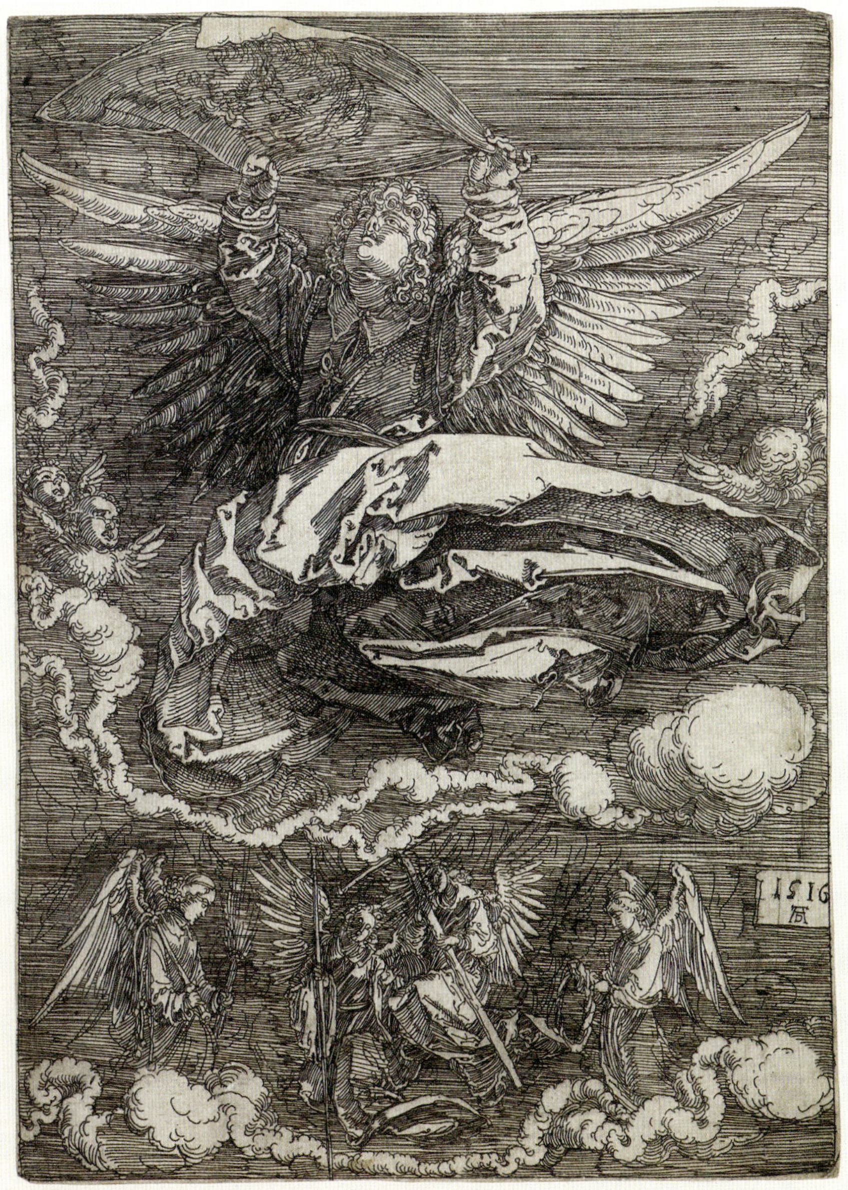

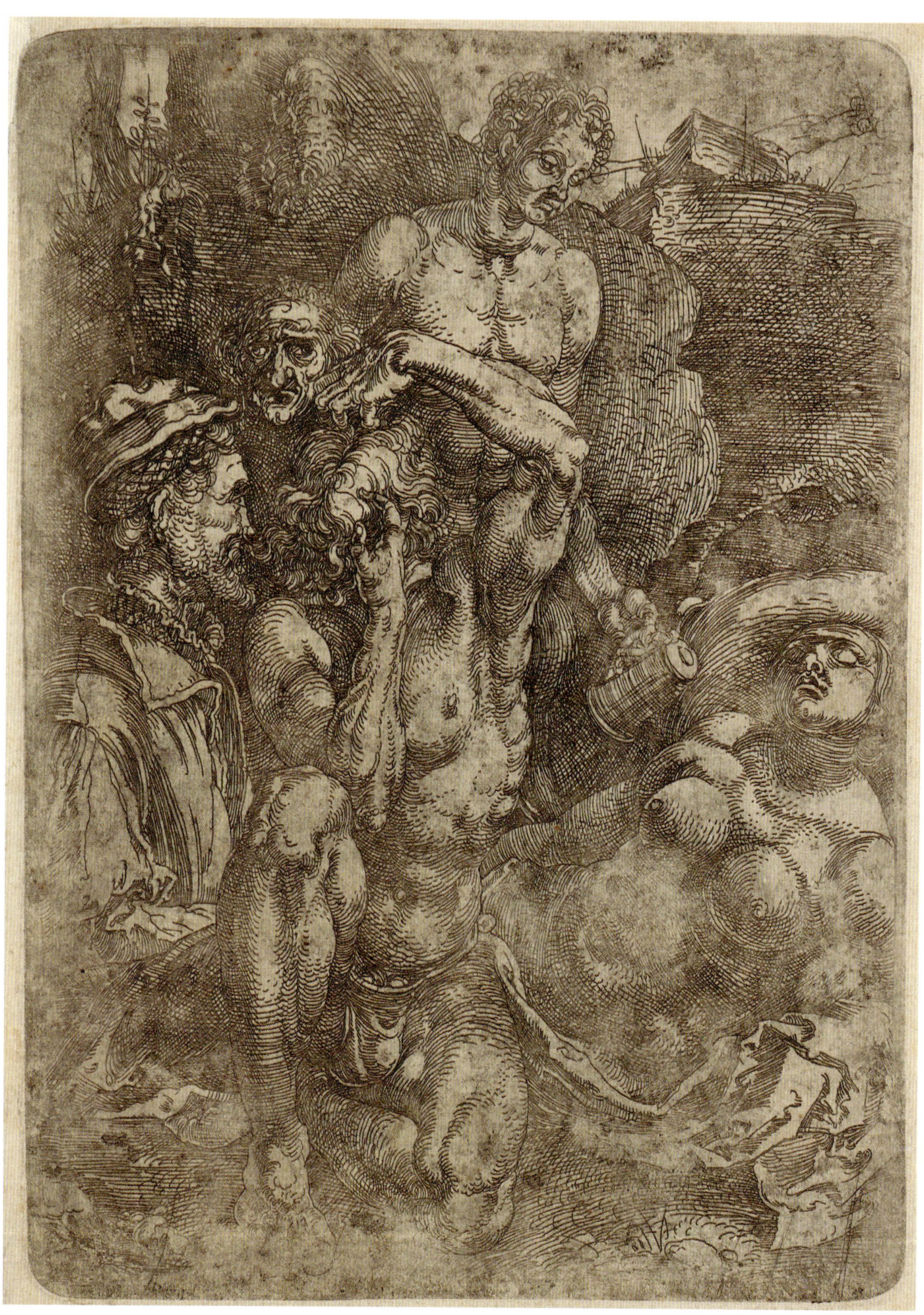

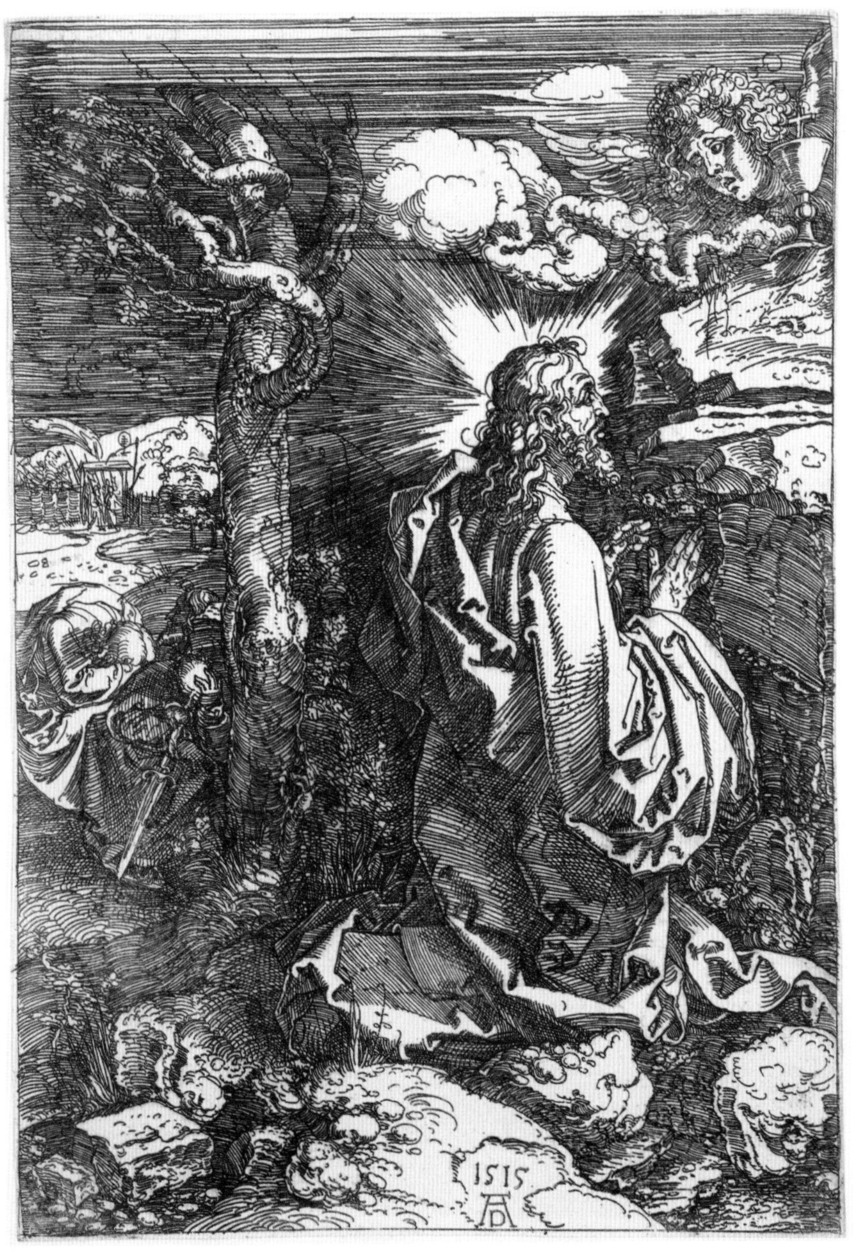

< 49
Albrecht Dürer
The Desperate Man, c. 1515–16.

Etching, 188 x 134 mm
Schoch, Mende and Scherbaum, *Albrecht Dürer*, I, 198–9, no. 79;
B.VII.84.70; H.95

The John Rylands Research Institute and Library, The University of
Manchester, Holtorp 9/1/29/1.© The University of Manchester.

50
Albrecht Dürer
Christ on the Mount of Olives (*Agony in the Garden*), 1515.

Etching, 220 x 154 mm
Schoch, Mende and Scherbaum, *Albrecht Dürer*, I, 200–2, no. 80;
B.VII.42.19; H.19

The Whitworth, The University of Manchester, P.3003. Presented by
George Thomas Clough in 1921. © The Whitworth, The University of
Manchester. Photo: Michael Pollard.

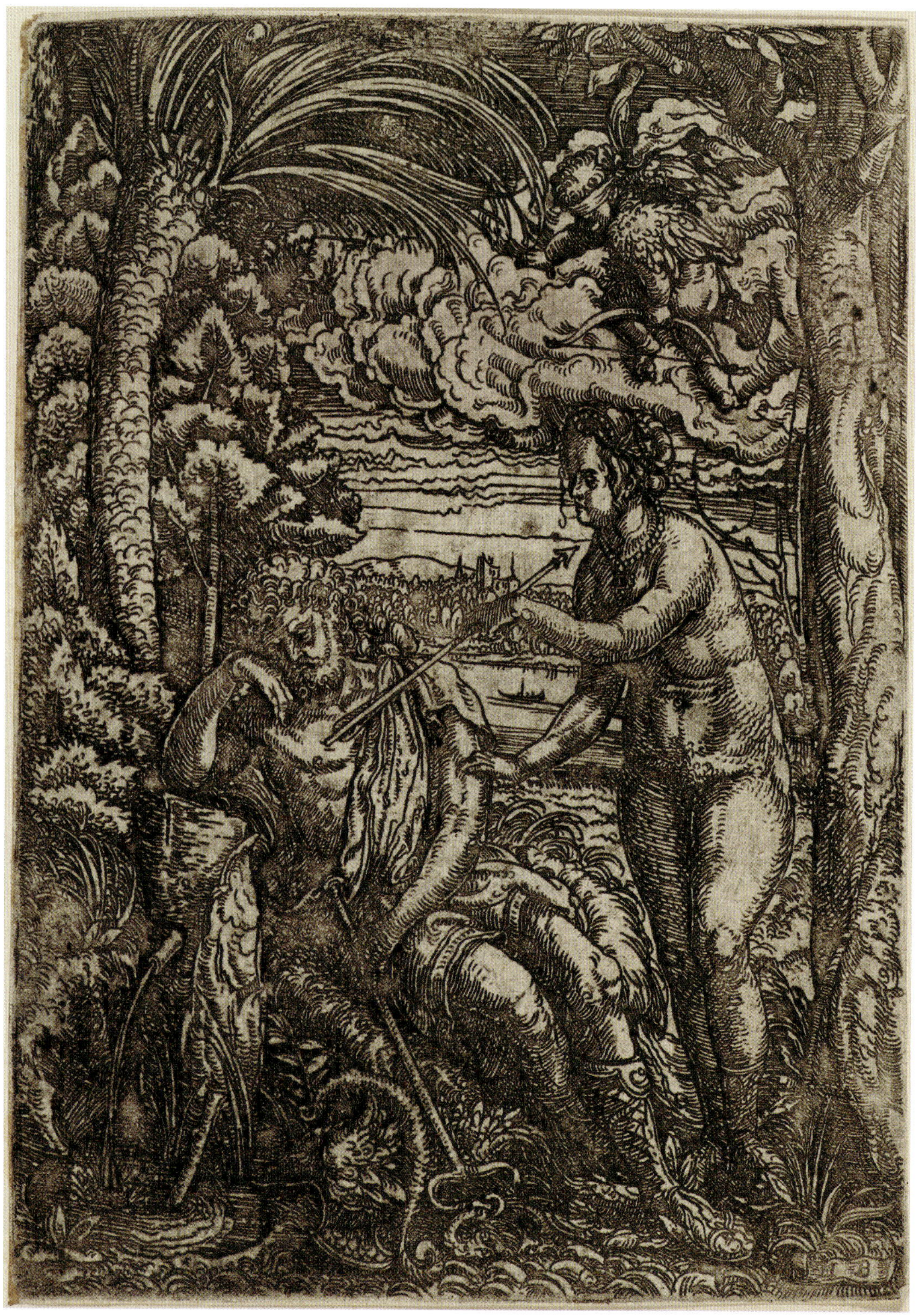

< 51

Hans Burgkmair
Venus, Mercury and Cupid, c. 1518–20.

Etching, 183 x 132 mm
B.VII.199.1; Hollstein German V.174.834.

The John Rylands Research Institute and Library,
The University of Manchester, Holtorp 9/1/6/1.
© The University of Manchester.

52
Albrecht Dürer
Landscape with a Cannon, 1518.

Etching, 217 x 236 mm, trimmed
Schoch, Mende and Scherbaum, *Albrecht Dürer*, I,
210–12, no. 85; B.VII.108.99; H.96

The Whitworth, The University of Manchester, P.3022.
Presented by George Thomas Clough in 1921.
© The Whitworth, The University of Manchester.
Photo: Michael Pollard.

For illustration, see figure 9.1, p. 100.

> 53

Attr. to Wolf Traut after Albrecht Dürer
*Page from the Triumphal Arch of Emperor
Maximilian Showing Maximilian Successful
in Battle Against France in 1492–1493*, 1515.

Woodcut, 230 x 154 mm
Schoch, Mende and Scherbaum, *Albrecht Dürer*, II,
399–404, no. 238.49; Schauerte, *Die Ehrenpforte*,
270–71, no. C 2, 12

The John Rylands Research Insitute and Library,
The University of Manchester, Holtorp 7/1/40/ 2.
© The University of Manchester.

54
Albrecht Dürer
*Medium Calibre Cannon and Lafette seen
from above* in *Treatise on Fortification,* lit.
*Several Lessons on the Fortification of City,
Castle and Places* (*Etliche underricht zu
befestigung der Stett, Schloß und Flecken*),
first edition published Nuremberg:
Hieronumus Andraea, 1527; this edition,
Paris: Chrestien Wechel, 1528.

Woodcut, 30 x 21 x 0.8 cm (book)
Schoch, Mende and Scherbaum, *Albrecht Dürer*, III, 316,
no. 276.21

Chetham's Library 0.9.49(3). © Chetham's Library.
Photo: Michael Pollard.

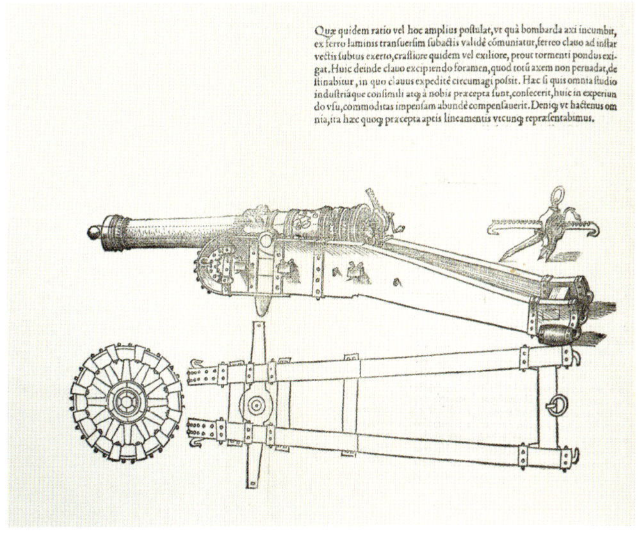

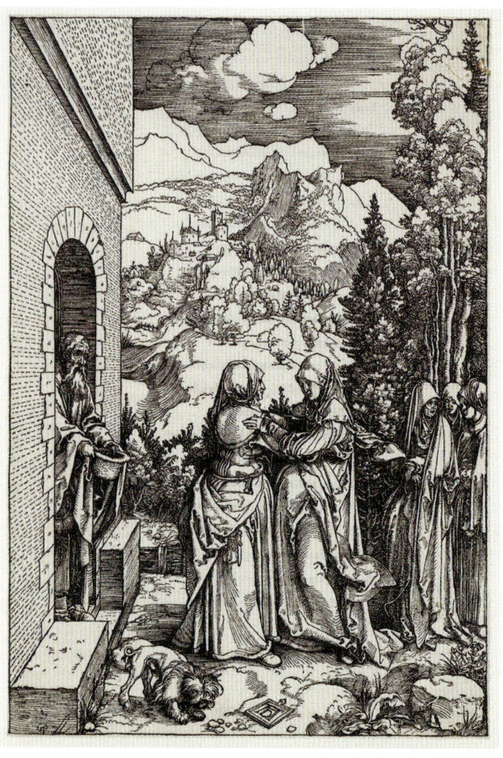

55

Albrecht Dürer

The Visitation (*Life of the Virgin*), c. 1503–4.

Woodcut, 304 x 211 mm
Schoch, Mende and Scherbaum,
Albrecht Dürer, II, 246–8, no. 174;
B.VII.312.84; H.196

The Whitworth, The University of
Manchester, P.3037. Presented by
George Thomas Clough in 1921.
© The Whitworth, The University of
Manchester. Photo: Michael Pollard.

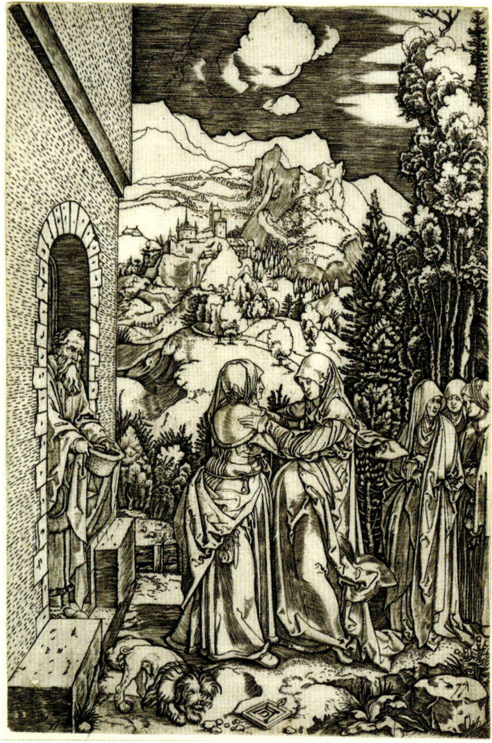

56

Marcantonio Raimondi after
Albrecht Dürer

The Visitation, c. 1506.

Engraving, 302 x 208 mm,
trimmed
B.XIV.406.628

The Whitworth, The University of
Manchester, P.3107. Presented by
George Thomas Clough in 1921.
© The Whitworth, The University of
Manchester. Photo: Michael Pollard.

> 57

Albrecht Dürer

*Draftsman Using of
an Optical Device to
Draw a Seated Man* in
Treatise on Measurement
(*Underweysung der
messung, mit dem zirckel
un[d] richtscheyt, in linien
ebnen unnd gantzen
corporen*).
Nuremberg: Hieronymus
Andreae, 1525.

Woodcut, 28 x 21.1 x 2.4 cm (book)
Schoch, Mende and Scherbaum,
Albrecht Dürer, III, 265–6,
no. 274.197

The John Rylands Research
Institute and Library, The University
of Manchester, Spencer 19439.
© The University of Manchester.

>> 58

Albrecht Dürer

*Frontal View of a Man, Right
Arm Extended Upward
and Left Leg Extended
Out, Inscribed in an Arc
Extending from the Umbilics*
in *Four Books on Human
Proportion* (*Clarissimi
pictoris et geometrae
de symmetria partium
humanorum corporum
libri quatuor ...*, lit. *Four
Books of the Most Famous
Painter and Geometer on
the Symmetry of the Parts
of the Human Body ...*), first
German edition published in
Nuremberg by Hieronymus
Andreae for Agnes Dürer,
1528; this edition, Paris:
Charles Perier, 1557.

Woodcut, 26.8 x 20.2 x 3.0 cm
(book)
Schoch, Mende and Scherbaum,
Albrecht Dürer, III, 384–5,
nos. 277.47, 277.48.

Chetham's Library, O.9.19(1).
© Chetham's Library.
Photo: Michael Pollard.

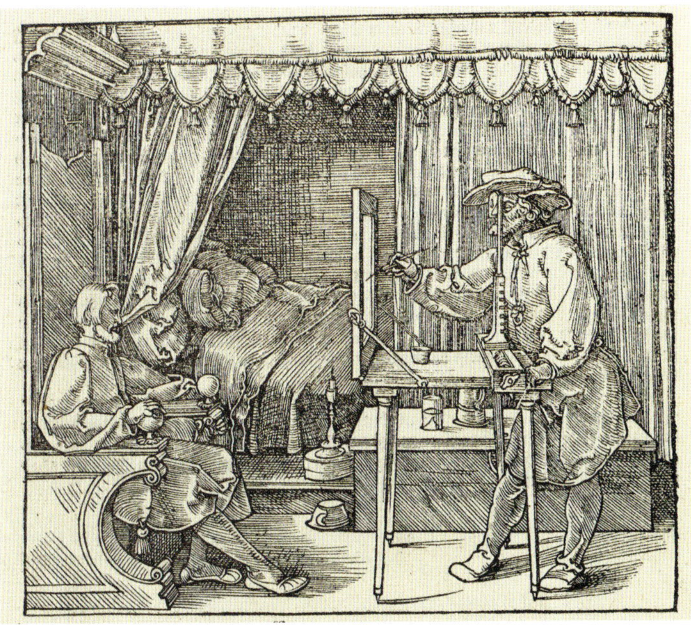

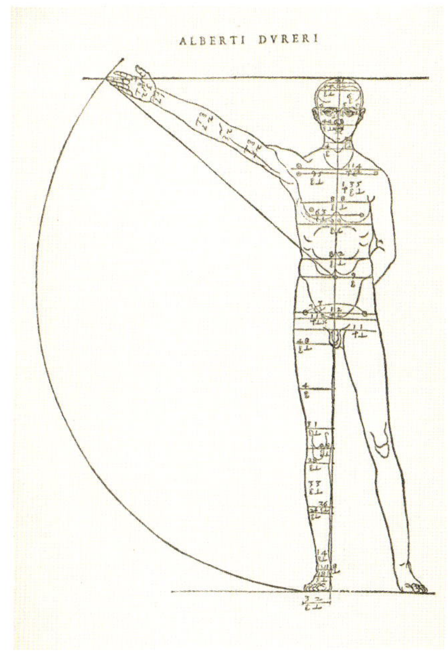

59
Albrecht Dürer
Design for a Shoe,
c. 1522–8.

Pen and black ink, 271 x 111 mm
Strauss, *Complete Drawings*,
1526/24; Rowlands, *Dürer*, 47,
no. 306; Ashcroft, *Albrecht Dürer*,
II, 822–4, no. 239

London, The British Museum,
SL,5218.200. Bequeathed by Sir
Hans Sloane. © The Trustees of the
British Museum.

60
Albrecht Dürer
*Design for the Sole of
a Shoe,* c. 1522–8.

Brush drawing in brown wash,
271 x 111 mm
Strauss, *Complete Drawings*,
1526/26; Rowlands, *Dürer*, 47, no. 307

London, The British Museum,
SL,5218.199. Bequeathed by Sir
Hans Sloane. © The Trustees of the
British Museum.

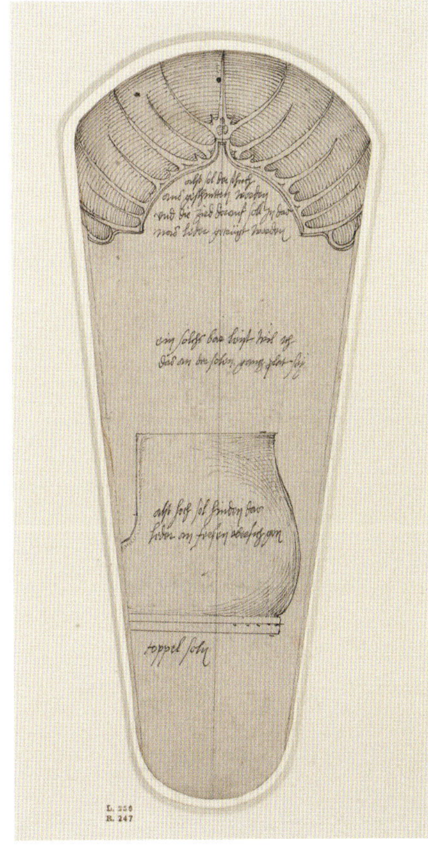

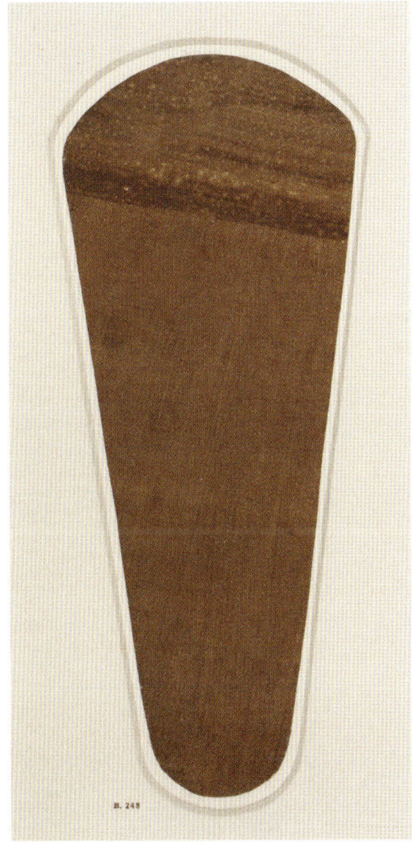

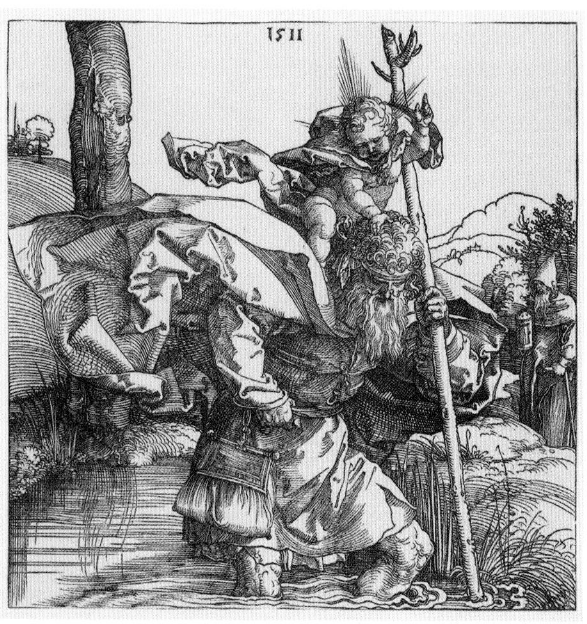

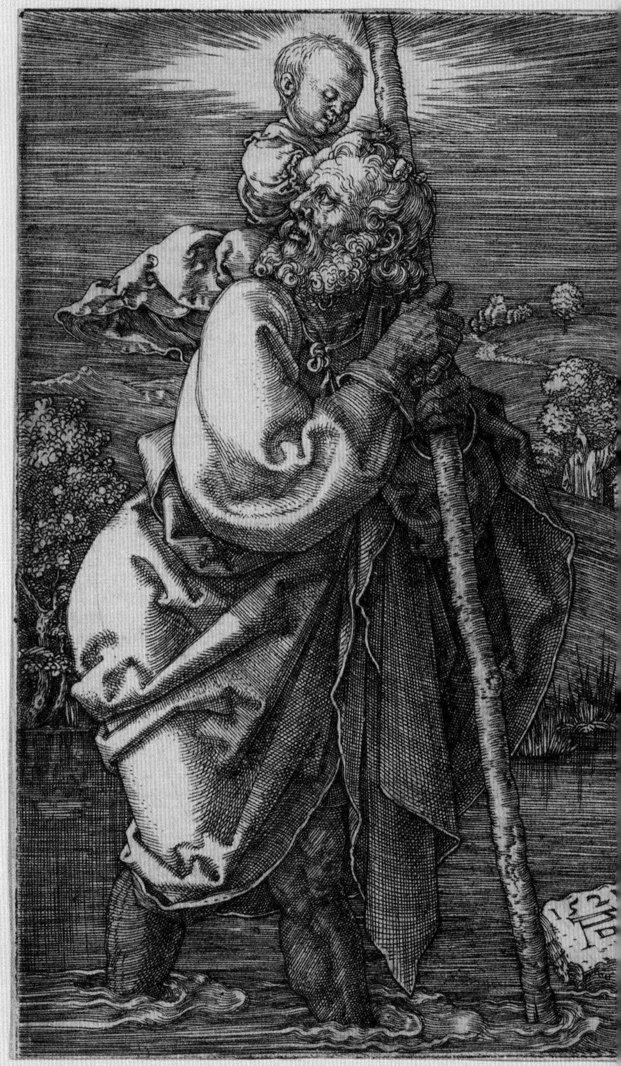

61
Albrecht Dürer
Saint Christopher, 1511.

Woodcut, 209 x 209 mm, trimmed
Schoch, Mende and Scherbaum, *Albrecht Dürer*, II,
357–9, no. 228; B.VII.136.103; H.223

The Whitworth, The University of Manchester, P.3047.
Presented by George Thomas Clough in 1921.
© The Whitworth, The University of Manchester.
Photo: Michael Pollard.

62
Albrecht Dürer
Saint Christopher Turned to the Left, 1521.

Engraving, 119 x 75 mm, trimmed
Schoch, Mende and Scherbaum, *Albrecht Dürer*, I,
228–9, no. 93; B.VII.68.51; H.53

The Whitworth, The University of Manchester, P.3012.
Presented by George Thomas Clough in 1921.
© The Whitworth, The University of Manchester.
Photo: Michael Pollard.

63
Unknown
Tailor's Scissors, sixteenth–
seventeenth century.

Iron, 13.4 x 8.1 x .5 cm

Museum of Medicine and Health,
Faculty of Biology, Medicine
and Health, the University of
Manchester, 2018.JK85. Presented
by Mr John Kirkup, FRCS.
© The Whitworth, The University of
Manchester. Photo: Michael Pollard.

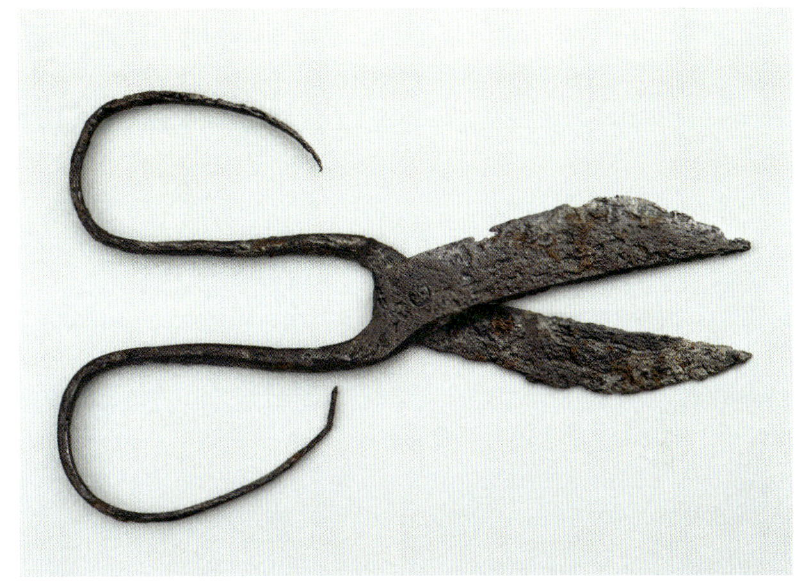

64
Unknown
*Fragment of Block Printed
Fustian*, sixteenth century,
German.

Linen warp and cotton weft, 44.6
x 24.2 cm

The Whitworth, The University of
Manchester, T.10843. Purchased
from Dr Hahn in 1961.
© The Whitworth, The University of
Manchester. Photo: Michael Pollard.

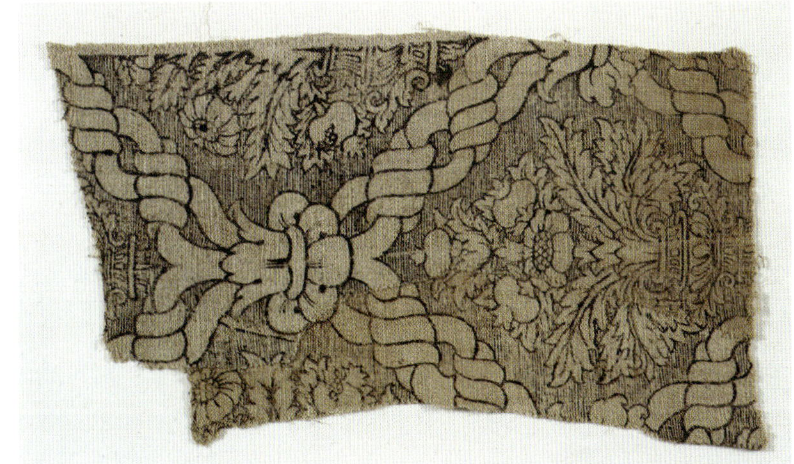

65
Unknown
Bobbin Lace Insertion, late
sixteenth century, German.

Linen, 2.2 x 16.3 cm

The Whitworth, The University of
Manchester, T.13461. Transferred
from Manchester College of
Art and Design in 1966 (Bock
Collection). © The Whitworth,
The University of Manchester.
Photo: Michael Pollard.

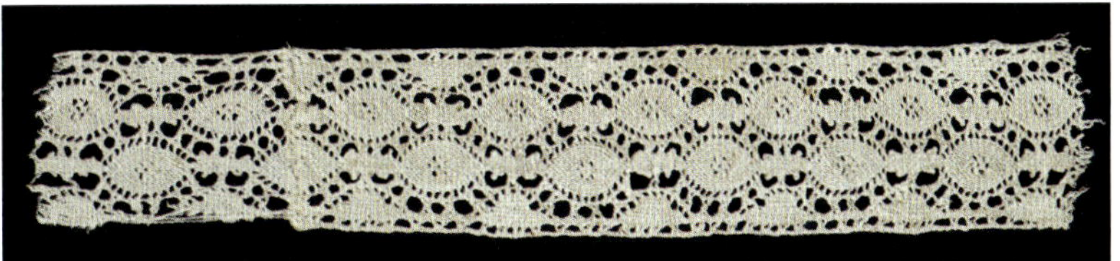

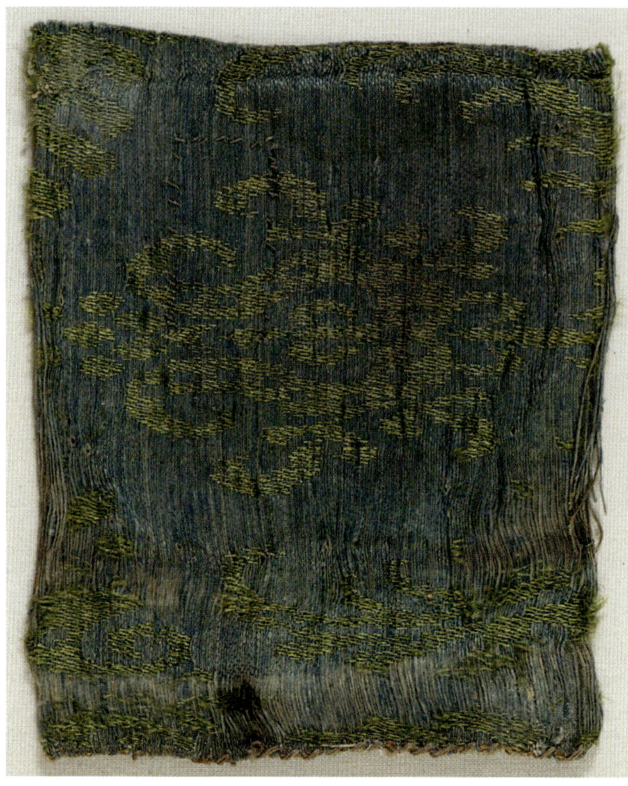

66
Unknown
Green-blue Silk-linen Fragment, late sixteenth or early seventeenth century, Italian.

Silk and linen, 11.5 x 13.8 cm

The Whitworth, The University of Manchester, T.12630. Transferred from Manchester College of Art and Design in 1966 (Bock Collection).
© The Whitworth, The University of Manchester. Photo: Michael Pollard.

67
Unknown
Fragment: Head and Torso of Christ, c. 1545–55, German.

Embroidery, 12.2 x 9 cm

The Whitworth, The University of Manchester, T.11382.1-8. Transferred from Manchester College of Art and Design in 1966 (Bock Collection).
© The Whitworth, The University of Manchester. Photo: Michael Pollard.

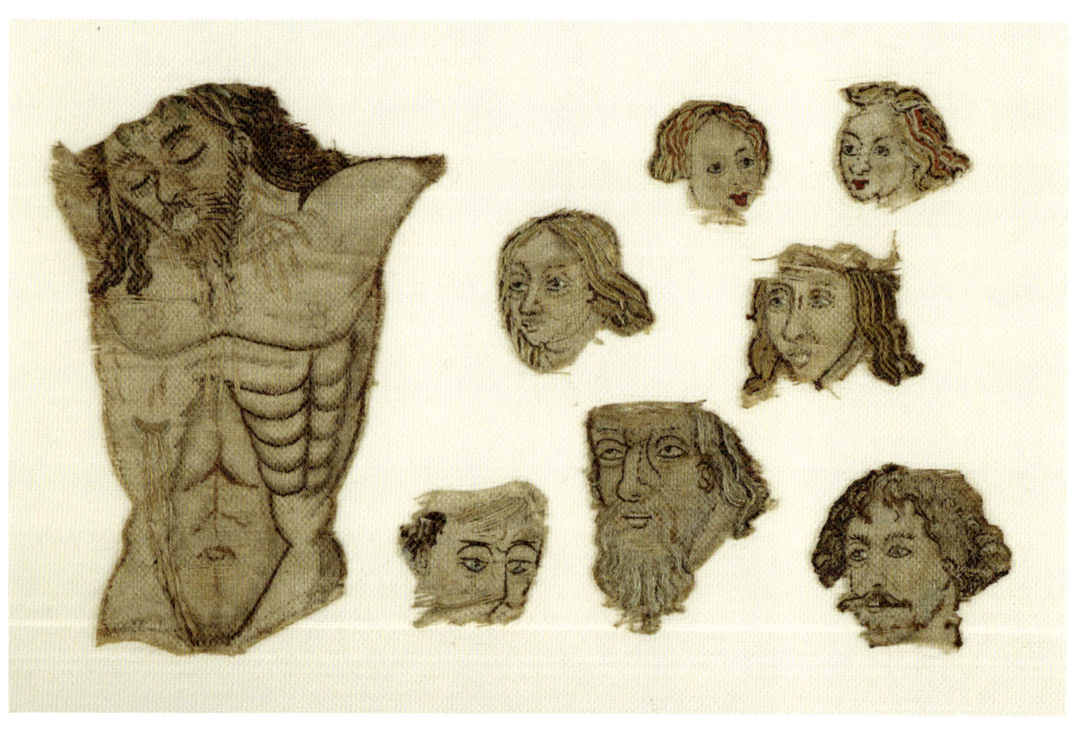

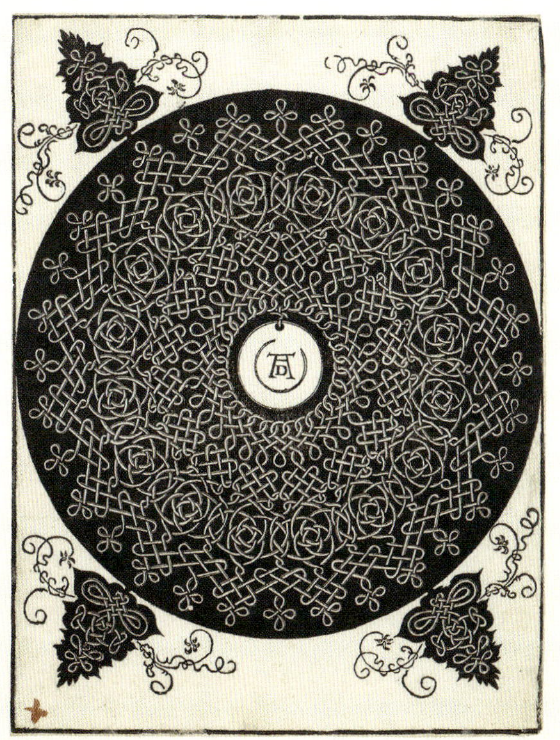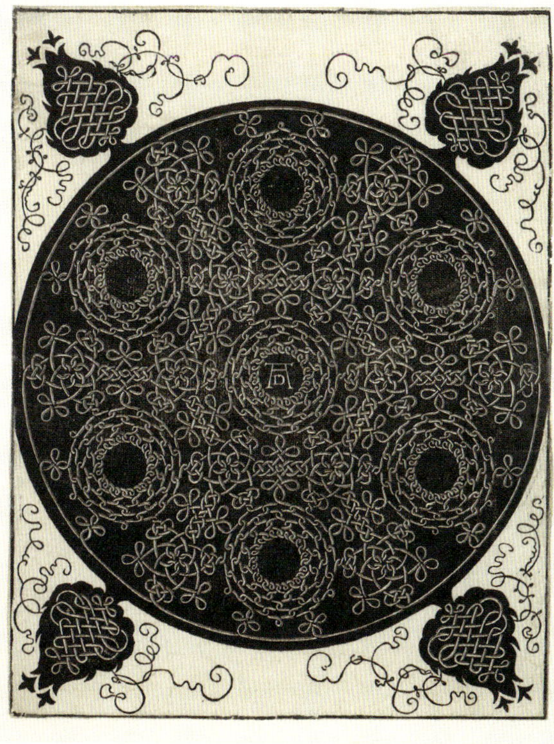

69
Albrecht Dürer
The Third Knot, c. 1506–8.

Woodcut, 276 x 210 mm
Schoch, Mende and Scherbaum, *Albrecht Dürer*, II, 152–3, no. 144.2;
B.VII.142.143; H.276

The Whitworth, The University of Manchester, P.3054. Presented by
George Thomas Clough in 1921. © The Whitworth, The University of
Manchester. Photo: Michael Pollard.

70
Albrecht Dürer
The Fourth Knot, c. 1506–8.

Woodcut, 270 x 210 mm, trimmed
Schoch, Mende and Scherbaum, *Albrecht Dürer*, II, 155, 157, no. 147.2;
B.VII.159.143; H.277

The Whitworth, The University of Manchester, P.3056. Presented by
George Thomas Clough in 1921. © The Whitworth, The University of
Manchester. Photo: Michael Pollard.

68
Albrecht Dürer
The Second Knot, c. 1506–8.

Woodcut, 271 x 210 mm, trimmed
Schoch, Mende and Scherbaum, *Albrecht Dürer*, II, 149, 151, no. 143.2;
B.VII.159.141; H.275

The Whitworth, The University of Manchester, P.3055. Presented by
George Thomas Clough in 1921. © The Whitworth, The University of
Manchester. Photo: Michael Pollard.

For illustration, see fig. 5.1, p. 50.

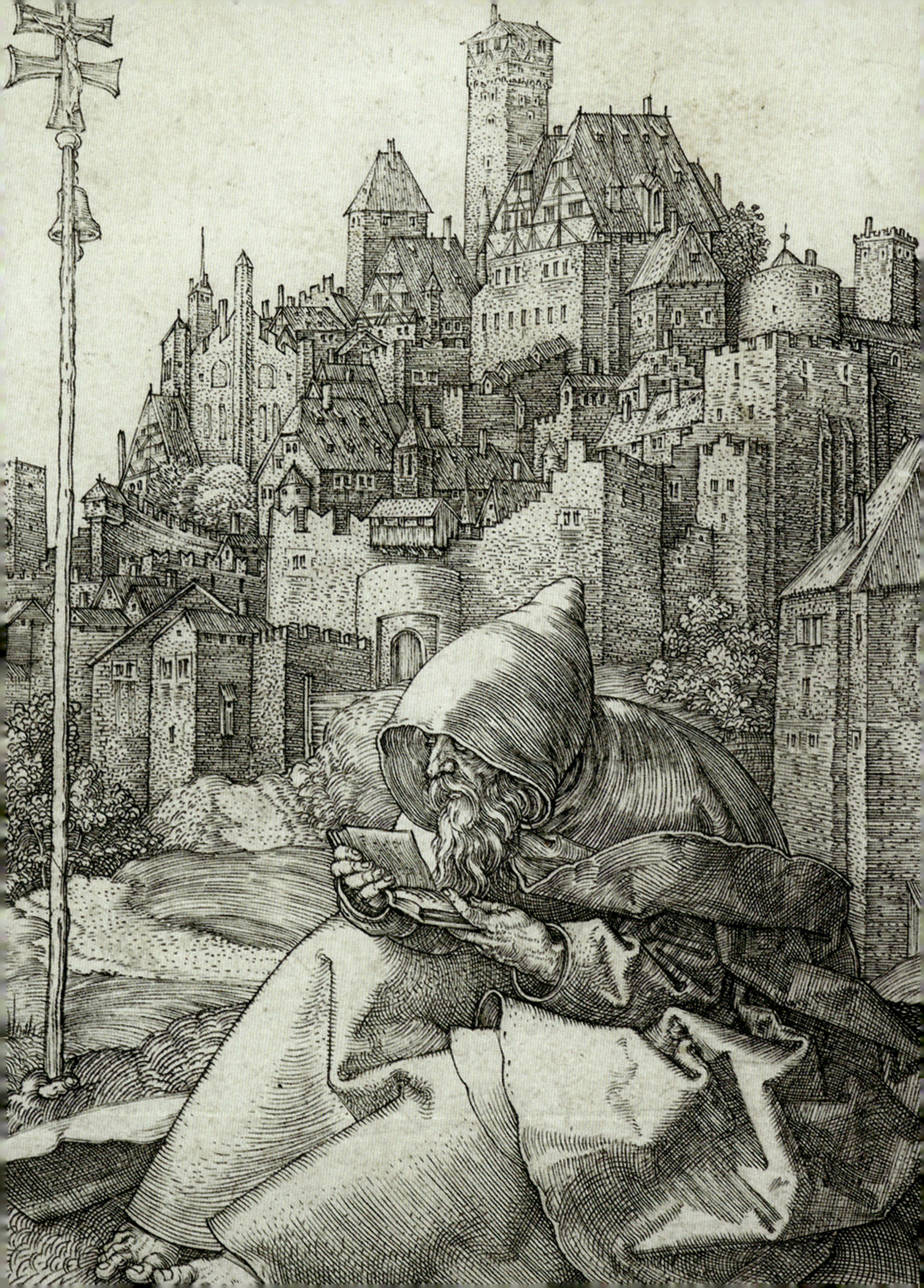

[14] The study

Edward H. Wouk and Dagmar Eichberger

Dürer's engraving with *Saint Jerome in his Study* (see Figure 8.1; cat. 73), epitomising the idea of knowledge, erudition and scholarly writing, is one of the most famous prints by the Nuremberg artist. As in Dürer's earlier woodcut *Saint Jerome in his Cell* of 1511 (cat. 72), Jerome (354–43), a bearded elderly man, sits at his table with an opened manuscript placed on the tilted writing desk in front of him. Jerome's attributes – the cardinal's hat, the crucifix, the skull and the lion – are distributed across the interior space to which the saint has withdrawn to work. Further objects – an hourglass, candlesticks, a letter rack and a rosary – embellish the scene.[1] While Dürer later showed the hermit Saint Anthony absorbed in study outdoors, seated before the walls of a town evocative of Nuremberg in his *Saint Anthony Before the Town* (cat. 103), *Saint Jerome in his Study* instead portrays the scholar saint engrossed in study within a German-style living room from the early sixteenth century. Wooden shelves, benches with cushions and large wooden beams create a warm and almost cosy atmosphere. Books in contemporary bindings, resembling the illustrated German translation of the *New Testament* of 1522 exhibited here (cat. 74), rest on the windowsill and bench, suggesting active use. The light filtering through the windowpanes made from bullseye glass throws abstract patterns on the thick walls.

The early modern scholar's study was the site where collections were kept and activated through handling, use, study, classification and exchange. Both in Italy and in Northern Europe, businessmen like Lorenzo de' Medici (1449–92),[2] rulers like King Charles V of France (1338–80)[3] and regents like Margaret of Austria had a small cabinet (*petit cabinet*, *retraite*) within their living quarters.[4] This space was used as a private retreat where these individuals could withdraw from their busy lives, either to read, write, pray or to ponder small-scale objects in their possession. Such cubicles were often attached to the bedroom in order to guarantee privacy, and they often did not measure more than three to four square metres. Ideally, they had a small window to allow working by daylight. As Dora Thornton has shown in her investigation of Italian studies, this custom was soon adopted by the urban elite and was also favoured by humanist scholars such as Erasmus of Rotterdam (c. 1466–1536) and others. This is the type of space that Dürer evokes in *Saint Jerome in his Study*.[5]

In these scholars' cabinets one could find all sorts of objects relevant to the respective function of the location: a table, a chair, books, writing utensils, mirrors and devices for measuring time. These include sand clocks, like the 'travelling' *Sandglass* of Nuremberg manufacture (cat. 81), which is distinguished by its relatively modest size, the brass tube protecting its two blown glass chambers and lack of decoration apart from the markings on its base comprising the holy name of Jesus (the initials IHS) and the symbol of its maker in the form of three nails.[6] Other timepieces were far more ornate, however. Here we see a gilded-brass mechanical clock to which a spring driven alarm has been added (cat. 85). The canister case of the clock is decorated with detailed engraving, including an image of a boy playing a lute. Alongside these timepieces, scholars also frequently collected astronomical instruments such as small globes and astrolabes, including this fine example from the Nuremberg instrument maker and goldsmith Georg Hartmann (1489–1564), who signed this work and dated it 1532 (cat. 82). Like astrolabes and many other objects of the scholar's study, sand clocks were a well-known Nuremberg product, forming part of its vibrant culture of instrument making (see Figure 7.3).[7] These instruments often included devotional imagery. For example, the cruciform ivory sundial (cat. 83) of 1541, also made by Georg Hartmann, bears carvings with the arms of Brandenburg, a scene of Moses and the Brazen Serpent from the Hebrew Bible, the *Deposition of Christ*, and the zodiac, as well as markings of the hour scale that the instrument measures. The late fifteenth-century ivory diptych sundial and compass included in this exhibition (cat. 84) is carved with a relief depicting Saint John the Baptist.[8] Such objects evoke the virtue of temperance alongside an awareness of the limits of human knowledge in the face of death and eternity. Ornate sand clocks notably appear in Dürer's two other so-called *Meisterstiche*, or master prints, *Melencolia I* (cat. 79) and *Knight, Death and the Devil* (cat. 75), which Dürer entitled *Reuter*, meaning *Horseman* or *Knight*.[9] The protagonist of the latter print, a figure based on a drawing of 1498, wears armour associated with a calvary unit of Emperor Maximilian I (1459–1513) established in that year.[10] It is not only the sandglass held by the monstrous figure before him that is of contemporary manufacture; the *sallet* or helmet also closely resembles the southern German example exhibited here (cat. 76), alongside a pike head (cat. 77), which is similar to the one appearing at the end of the pike held by this 'Knight of Christ'. Here, as in his *Small Horse* and *Large Horse*, both of 1505 (cat. 78), Dürer balanced his observation of nature with a close study of the antique sculptures he was able to see in Venice and with his intense interest in proportion.[11]

Humanism and the study

Dürer's prints reveal his intimate connection to a humanist community that provided him with subjects, collected his graphic work (often preserved in their studies), and promoted his art. Though resident in Nuremberg, these humanists were connected, through travel and exchange, to other centres of learning and creativity.[12] Dürer's *The Bath House* of c. 1496 (cat. 87), one of his finest large woodcuts, provides light-hearted insight into Nuremberg's humanist culture. It depicts a space of enjoyment, relaxation and conversation for men of different ages, while also revealing Dürer's skill in representing landscape and interiors and men

in various contrasting positions. Some scholars even contend that the nude men in this outdoor bath, enjoying drink, music and discussion, represent actual individuals in Dürer's circle.[13]

Later in his career, Dürer produced some of the most memorable printed portraits of luminaries in his humanist community, setting each behind a fictive plinth carved with their names and dedicatory texts. These include the *Portrait of Willibald Pirckheimer* (cat. 2), who amassed an important library of Greek and Latin books and played an important role in introducing Dürer to humanist culture, and the *Portrait of Philip Melanchthon* of 1526 (cat. 3), who was appointed professor of Greek at Wittenberg in 1518, became one of Luther's most ardent supporters, and held Dürer in high regard as an artist and intellectual. The inscription on the latter print states that Dürer was able to capture his likeness, but not his soul. Dürer depicted his first significant patron in *Friedrich the Wise, Elector of Saxony* (cat. 4). Friedrich (1463–1525) invited the Italian painter and printmaker Jacopo de' Barbari (c. 1460/70–1516) to his court. Dürer was familiar with de' Barbari's works, including *Pegasus* (cat. 92), and he credited de' Barbari with teaching him how to represent the body – a skill which is evident in his de' Barbari's *Judith with the Head of Holofernes* (cat. 91) and *Saint Sebastian* (cat. 90). Dürer had already represented the early Christian martyr in two engravings that were similarly focused on the suffering of the body shot through with arrows against a tree (cat. 88) and against a column (cat. 89). Yet by 1506 Dürer's views had shifted. He wrote to Willibald Pirckheimer (1470–1530) to confess that he had lost interest in the work of de' Barbari, possibly frustrated by the latter's refusal to share a treatise he had composed.[14]

Dürer actively engaged in visualising subjects related to science, wonder and astronomy. *The Monstrous Pig* of 1496 (cat. 93), often titled *The Monstrous Sow of Landser*, was primarily inspired by a widely discussed prodigious birth from a newsworthy story, reported that year in a broadside by Sebastian Brant (1457–1521) and generally associated with portents and prognostications. Dürer creates a beautiful image of the wonderous creature, as credible as the pig in

The Prodigal Son (cat. 27).[15] A similar transformation
is evident in Dürer's *Satyr Family* (cat. 94) – possibly
based on the ancient Roman author Lucian's
description of a lost ancient painting – which treats
these mythic creatures of the forest with unusual
sensitivity, offering a glimpse of their family life in a
dense sylvan setting. Dürer's skills were also called
upon to produce the first printed maps of the celestial
spheres (see *The Celestial Map – Northern Hemisphere*,
cat. 86), based on the writings of Johannes Stabius
(1468–1522), court historian and astronomer to Dürer's
patron, Maximilian I.[16] This woodcut updates earlier
drawn maps with recent discoveries that were likely
provided by the astronomer Conrad Heinfogel (d.
1507), although Dürer himself could observe the stars
from an observatory at his house in the Zisselgasse,
which previously belonged to the great astronomer
Regiomontanus (1436–76).[17]

These scholarly pursuits intersect with Dürer's interest
in nature, exemplified by his intense study of landscapes,
of animals – seen in his treatment of the stag, horse and
hunting dogs in *Saint Eustace* (cat. 104) – and of birds.
His interest in birds led him to study the bright green
coloured orange-winged Amazon (*Amazona amazonica*,
cat. 100), the blue-green *Coracias garrulus* (cat. 101) and
Coracias benghalensis indicus (cat. 102). The leading
humanist Peter Martyr (1457–1526) described such birds
as material novelties and declared that their never-seen
'very lively colours' were 'a joy to behold'. In 1520 Dürer
used the same terms of wonder and delight to describe
his experience of seeing 'New World' featherwork in
Brussels.[18] By that time, Dürer had long been captivated
by Amazonians and their association with the idea of
paradise-like abundance in the 'New World'. Dürer drew
the parrot centre stage in his *Madonna of the Animals*
(1503) and, one year later, the *Amazona amazonica*
featured prominently in his famous engraving of *Adam
and Eve*, dated 1504 (cat. 99). During his travels to the
Low Countries in 1520–21, Dürer gave this *Adam and
Eve* – alongside other works like *Melencolia I*, *Nemesis*,
the *Apocalypse*, the *Great Passion* and the *Small
Passion* – to the Portuguese imperial factor in Antwerp,
Rodrigo Fernandez d'Almada (active 1514–40). In
return, Agnes Dürer received 'a little green parakeet'.[19]
Later, during the same trip D'Almada presented

the artist with yet another parrot which was said to
originate from Malaca.[20]

Print collecting

Such specimens might find their way into *Kunst-* or
Wunderkammern, or cabinets of curiosity, which
developed in close dialogue with collections of
prints and printed books, many of which were richly
illustrated.[21] Early collectors like the Nuremberg
humanist, doctor and bibliophile Hartmann Schedel
(1440–1514), the author of the *Nuremberg Chronicle*
(cat. 1), pasted many of the prints he collected into
books, often to illustrate the text.[22] Soon, however,
print collections began to emerge as distinct entities,
though often still closely connected with books. For
example, Ferdinand Columbus (1488–1539), the son of
Christopher Columbus (1451–1506) who had joined his
father on his final transatlantic expedition, amassed an
important and well-documented collection of prints
at his home in Seville, which included many Dürer
impressions. He kept his prints within his library of
books.[23] Gabriele Vendramin of Venice (1484–1552),
whose collection Dürer may have seen during his
travels, acquired books, manuscripts, drawings,
paintings and sculptures as well as prints, which he
stored in his 'Camerino delle Antigaglie', placing some
woodcuts and engravings into albums.[24] Dürer's
friend Konrad Peutinger (1465–1547), collecting in
Nuremberg at roughly the same time, kept prints
loose and in books, although the exact contents of his
collection is unknown.[25]

What inspired these collectors to acquire prints, and
what sorts of prints did they acquire? Recent studies
have revealed a variety of functions and uses for prints
that ranged from aesthetic appreciation, religious
devotion, moral and pedagogical instruction, to the
exploration of scholarly pursuits including astronomy,
botany, natural philosophy, anatomy, magic and alchemy,
as well as history.[26] Dürer's vast graphic output touched
upon all these subjects. Although no inventory has
come down to us, Dürer was known to collect prints
himself. He was interested, for instance, in the work
of Andrea Mantegna (1431–1506), who had begun to
engrave subjects from classical mythology in the final

decades of the fifteenth century. Following advice he
would later give to aspiring artists keen to train their
hands, Dürer drew exacting copies of Mantegna's work,
all dated 1494, and possibly made during his first trip
to Italy.[27] These included a study of Mantegna's *Battle
of the Tritons and Sea Gods* (cat. 95), the right half of an
engraved frieze that may have inspired his own *Sea
Monster* (cat. 96), in which the abduction of the nymph
is transposed to an incongruous setting before a hill
dominated by Nuremberg's castle.[28] In addition to his
attention to Mantegna, Dürer also closely observed the
art of earlier German printmakers, particularly Martin
Schongauer (1440/53–91). Once thought to have been
Dürer's teacher, Schongauer produced fine engravings,
such as *The Annunciation* (cat. 97), which established
a precedent for northern European excellence in
printmaking and cultures of collecting.[29]

The previously mentioned diaries of Dürer's travels to
the Low Countries provide a rich account of how he
sold prints in great quantities and exchanged them for
other works of art or curiosities, which in turn became
part of his own collection. In addition, Dürer used his
prints to gain favour with potential patrons, such as
Margaret of Austria. He also gave prints as expressions
of friendship – for instance when presenting Erasmus
of Rotterdam with his engraved *Passion*. Through the
medium of prints, he established connections with
other artists, such as the court sculptor Conrat Meit
(1480–1551) and the painter and printmaker Lucas van
Leyden (1494–1533), represented in this exhibition by
his *Joseph with Potiphar's Wife* (cat. 98).[30] By these
means, he actively promoted his art and celebrity,
ensuring the prominence of his prints in collections
across Europe.

Dürer's prints evidence how, in the Renaissance, works
on paper became a driving force behind a range of
artistic and intellectual activities in the scholars' study
and were connected closely to practices of learning and
devotion. His woodcuts and engravings complemented
the role that had hitherto been played by illuminated
manuscripts and early printed books (*incunabula*), and
they soon commanded a privileged status as crucial
agents in the cultures of scientific inquiry, scholarly
investigation, artistic exchange and devotional practice.
The study was the locus of this transformation.

Notes

1 See Dagmar Eichberger's 'The material and the immaterial' in this volume.

2 Liebenwein, *Studiolo*, 30–55; Prinz and Kecks, *Das französische Schloss*, 142–8.

3 Minges, *Sammelwesen der frühen Neuzeit*, 19–22.

4 Eichberger, *Leben mit Kunst*, 109–115, 372–88.

5 Thornton, *The Scholar in his Study*, 77–98.

6 Hasselmeyer, 'Sanduhren aus Nürnberg', 70–1.

7 See Matthew Champion's 'Measure and the material world' in this volume.

8 Maué, Eser, Hauschke and Stolzenberger, *Quasi Centrum Europae*, 367–71.

9 As described in his account of his travels in the Netherlands; see Ashcroft, *Albrecht Dürer*, I, 567.

10 Strauss, *Complete Drawings*, 1495/48; Metzger, ed., *Albrecht Dürer*, 360, 461, no. 170.

11 Bartrum, *Dürer and his Legacy*, 186–7, no. 126, 229–30, no. 181; Mende, 'Bukephalos und Alexander der Große?'. See also Schoch, Mende and Scherbaum, *Albrecht Dürer*, I, 117–21, nos 42–3.

12 For a detailed study, see Schmid, *Dürer als Unternehmer*.

13 Schauerte, *Dürer und Celtis*, esp. 157–65.

14 Ashcroft, *Albrecht Dürer*, I, 89, 140–1. See also Luber, *Albrecht Dürer and the Venetian Renaissance*, 64.

15 Schoch, Mende and Scherbaum, *Albrecht Dürer*, I, 43–44. See further Spinks, *Monstrous Births*, 34–36, 39–40.

16 Dackerman, *Prints and the Pursuit of Knowledge*, 90–2, no. 16 (entry by Marisa Bandabach); Marr, 'Ingenuity in Nuremberg'.

17 Bartrum, *Dürer and his Legacy*, 194 no. 138; Dackerman, *Prints and the Pursuit of Knowledge*, 90–2, no. 16 (entry by Marisa Mandabach); see Matthew Champion's 'Measure and the material world' in this volume.

18 Hanß, 'New World Feathers'.

19 Ashcroft, *Albrecht Dürer*, I, 559.

20 *Ibid.*, 586.

21 See, among others, Parshall, 'Art and the Theater of Knowledge'.

22 Hernad, *Die Graphiksammlung*.

23 McDonald, *Print Collection*, 79–87; see also McDonald, 'The Physical life of the Print Collection', esp. 120–1.

24 Ravà, 'Il "Camerino delle antigaglie"'; Fortini Brown, *Private Lives*, 224–9.

25 Künast, 'Konrad Peutinger'.

26 See especially Dackerman, *Prints and the Pursuit of Knowledge*.

27 Vienna, Albertina; Strauss, *Complete Drawings* 1494/13; Bartrum, *Dürer and his Legacy*, 107–8, no. 37.

28 Bartrum, *Dürer and his Legacy*, 121, no. 53.

29 Hollstein German XLIX, 19, no. 3. Dürer's earliest biographer Johann Neudörfer (1497–1563) incorrectly described Schongauer as his teacher.

30 Hollstein German X, 20.

Background: Catalogue 92 (detail), see p. 192.

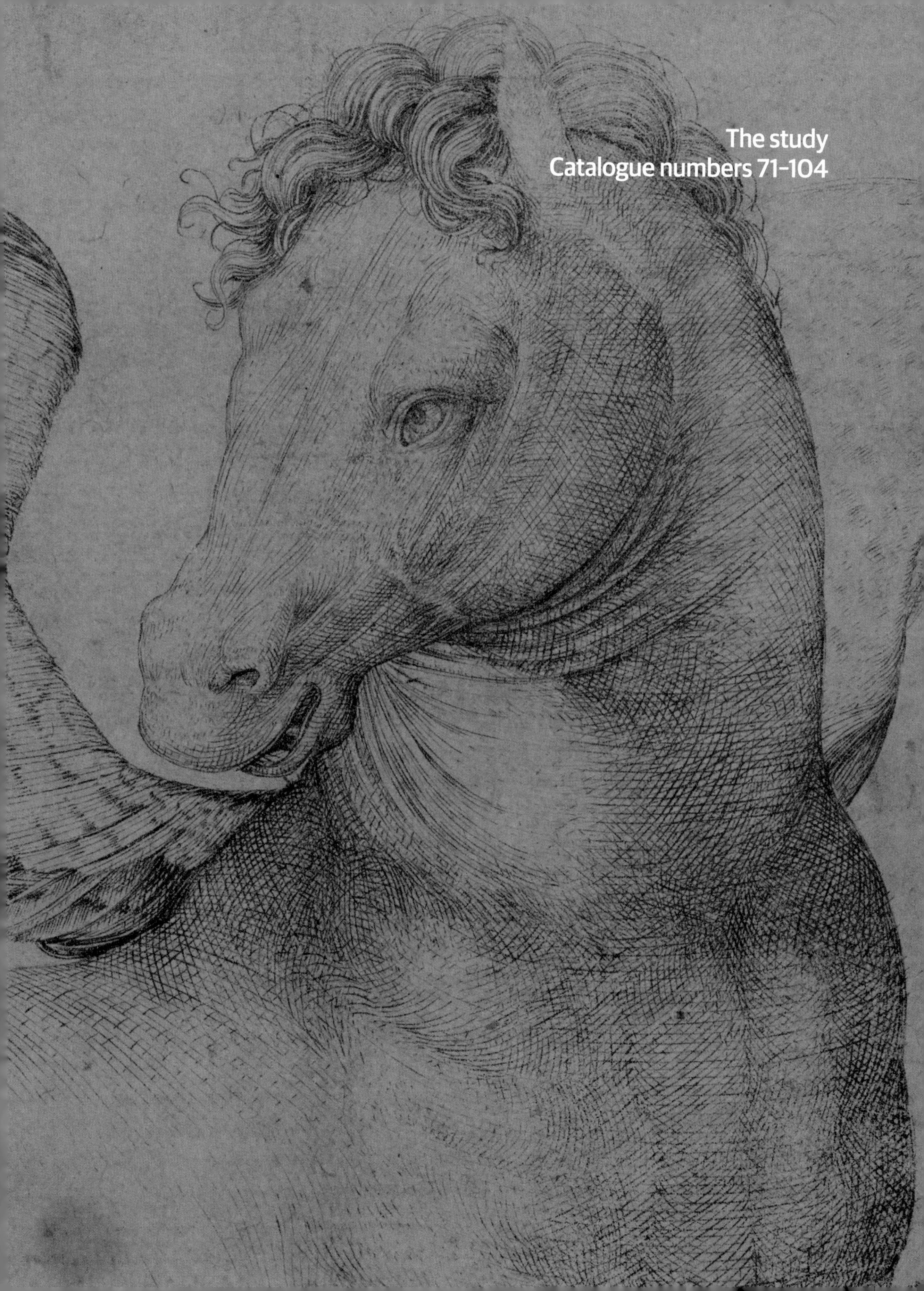
The study
Catalogue numbers 71–104

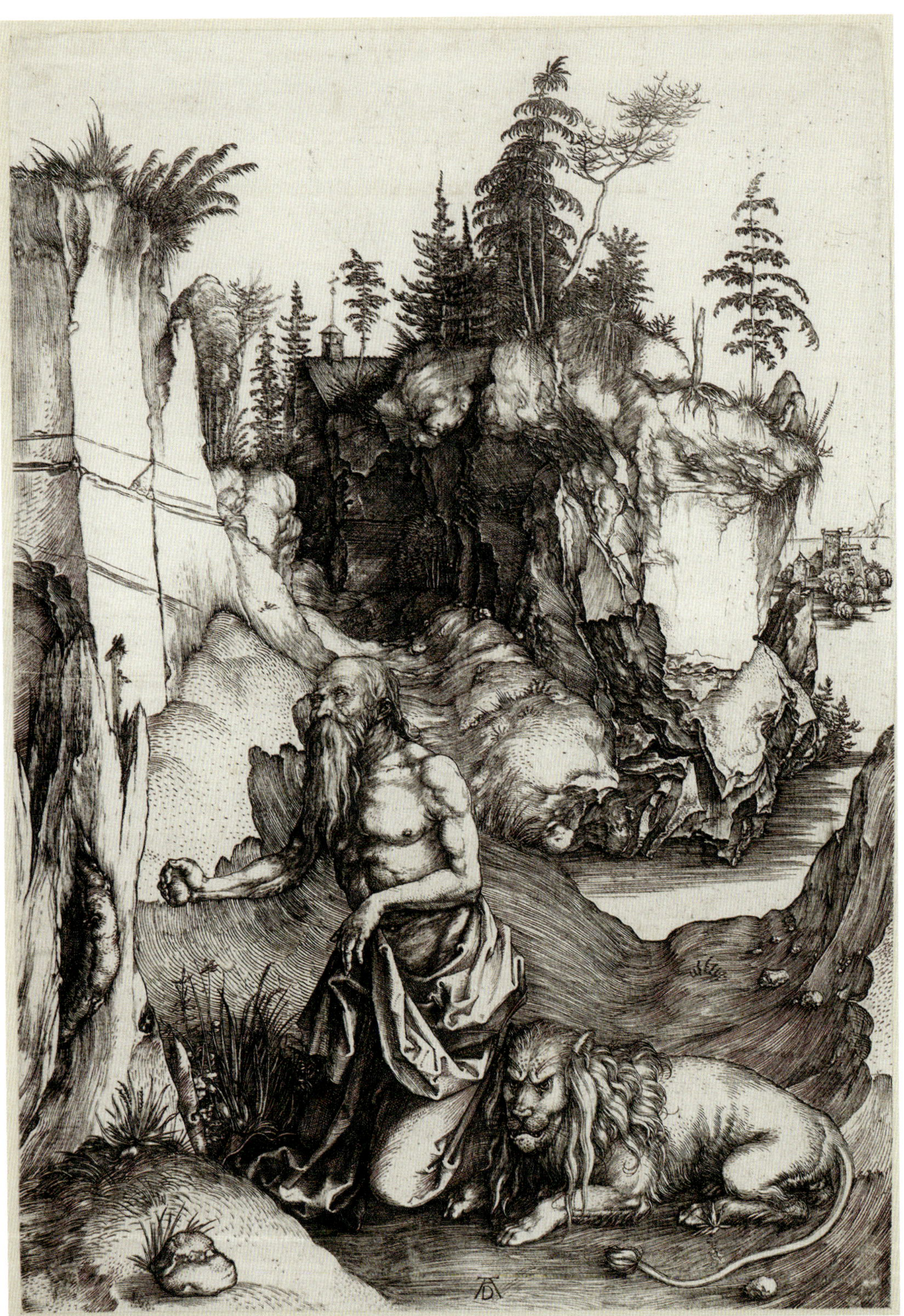

Albrecht Dürer
Saint Jerome Penitent in the Wilderness, 1496.

Engraving, 320 x 223 mm, trimmed
Schoch, Mende and Scherbaum,
Albrecht Dürer, I, 38–40, no. 6;
B.VII.77.61; H.57

The Whitworth, The University of
Manchester, P.5105. Bequeathed
by Dr E. J. Sidebotham in 1929.
© The Whitworth, The University of
Manchester. Photo: Michael Pollard.

72
Albrecht Dürer
Saint Jerome in his Cell, 1511.

Woodcut, 232 x 159 mm, trimmed
Schoch, Mende and Scherbaum,
Albrecht Dürer, II, 360–2, no. 229;
B.VII.139.114; H.228

The Whitworth, The University of
Manchester, P.3049. Presented by
George Thomas Clough in 1921.
© The Whitworth, The University of
Manchester. Photo: Michael Pollard.

*For illustration, see fig. 8.7
p. 95.*

73
Albrecht Dürer
*Saint Jerome in his Study
(Meisterstiche)*, 1514.

Engraving, 240 x 187 mm, trimmed
Schoch, Mende and Scherbaum,
Albrecht Dürer, I, 174–8, no. 70;
B.VII.76.60; H.59

The Whitworth, The University of
Manchester, P.3015. Presented by
George Thomas Clough in 1921.
© The Whitworth, The University of
Manchester. Photo: Michael Pollard.

*For illustration, see fig. 8.1,
p. 86.*

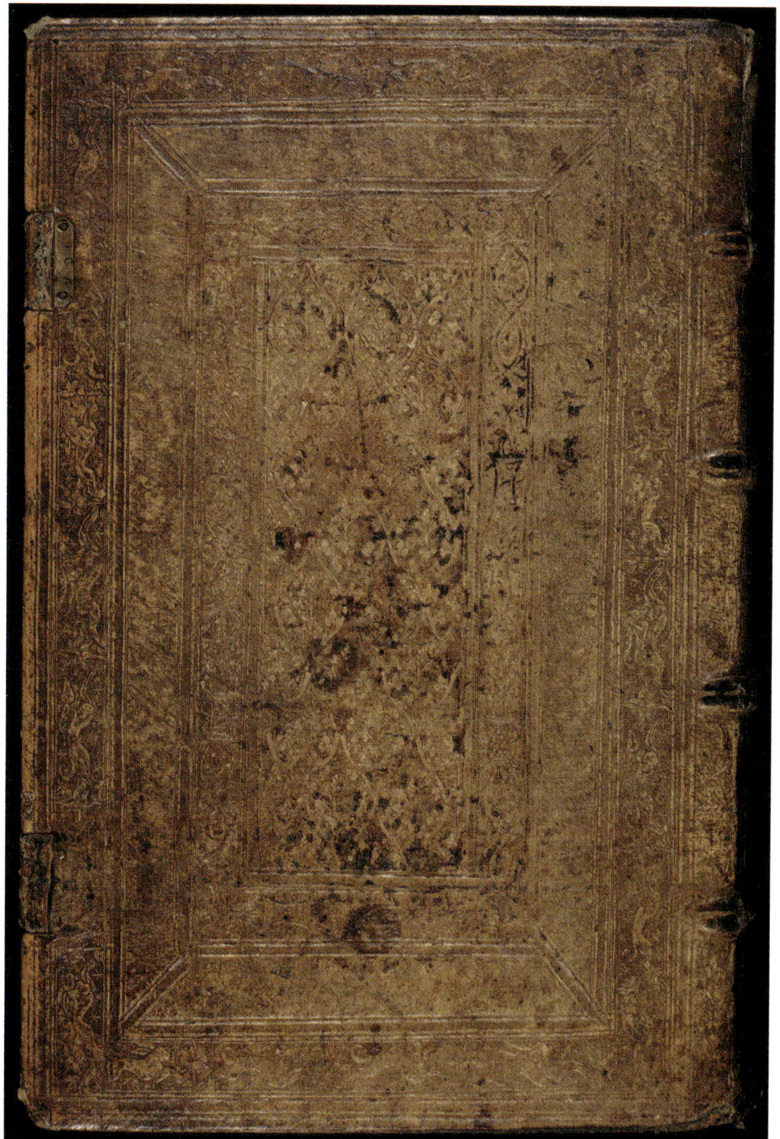

^ 74

*The New Testament in German (Das Newe Testament
Deutzsch Vuittemberg)*, translated by Martin Luther.
Wittenberg: Melchior Lotter, 1522.

With twenty-one woodcuts of the *Apocalypse* attributed to Lucas
Cranach the Elder, many adapted from Dürer's prints, 314 x 217 mm
Day, *Engravings and Woodcuts by Albrecht Dürer, 1471–1528*, 30–1, no. 86

The John Rylands Research Institute and Library, The University of
Manchester, R7621.2. © The University of Manchester.

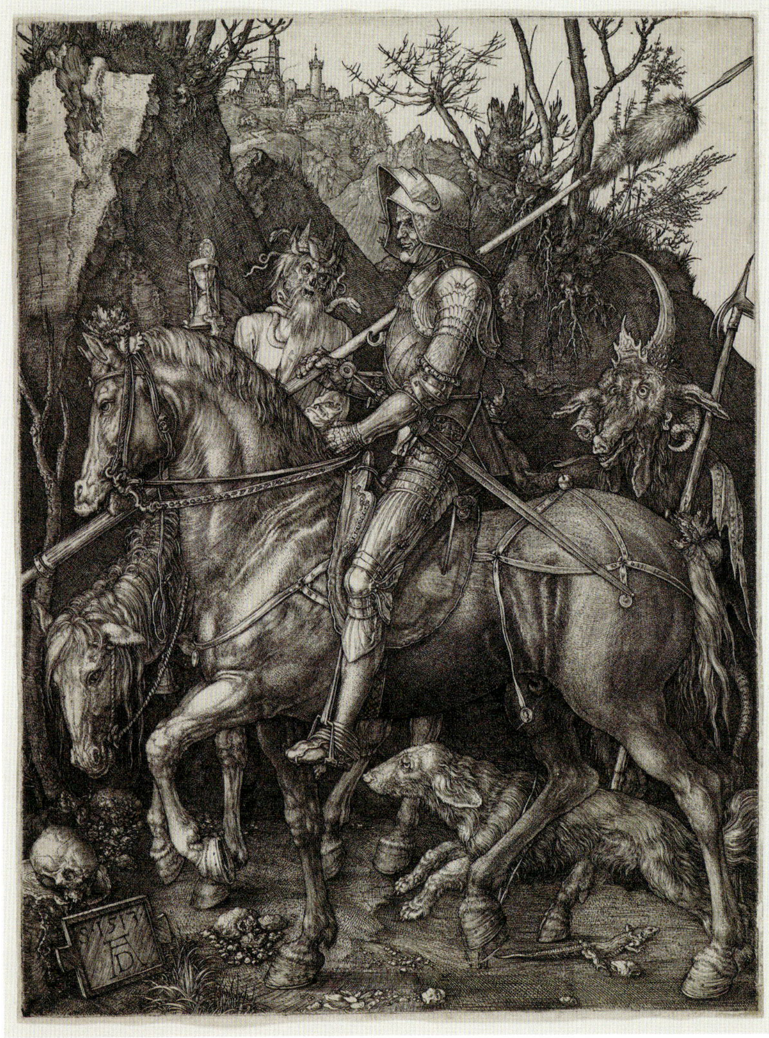

75
Albrecht Dürer
Knight, Death and the Devil
(*Meisterstiche*), 1513.

Engraving, 245 x 189 mm
Schoch, Mende and Scherbaum,
Albrecht Dürer, I, 169–73, no. 69;
B.VII.69.74; H.74

The Whitworth, The University of
Manchester, P.3021. Presented by
George Thomas Clough in 1921.
© The Whitworth, The University of
Manchester. Photo: Michael Pollard.

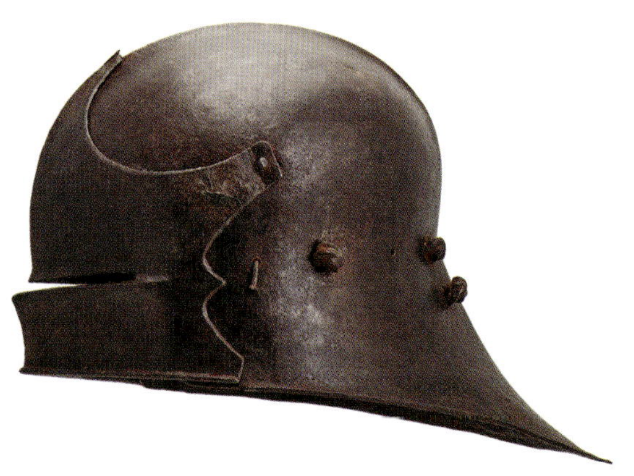

76
Unknown
*Sallet with Long Neck-
Guard*, c. 1480–90,
South German.

Ferrous metal, 24.0 x 23.5 x
39.5 cm

Royal Armouries, IV.427
© Royal Armouries.

77
Unknown
Pike Head, c. 1500, German.

Ferrous metal, 189.0 x 3.5 x 3.5 cm

Royal Armouries, VII.1480
© Royal Armouries.

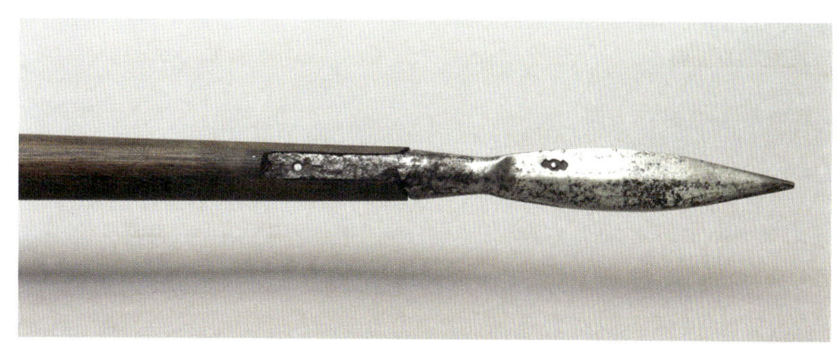

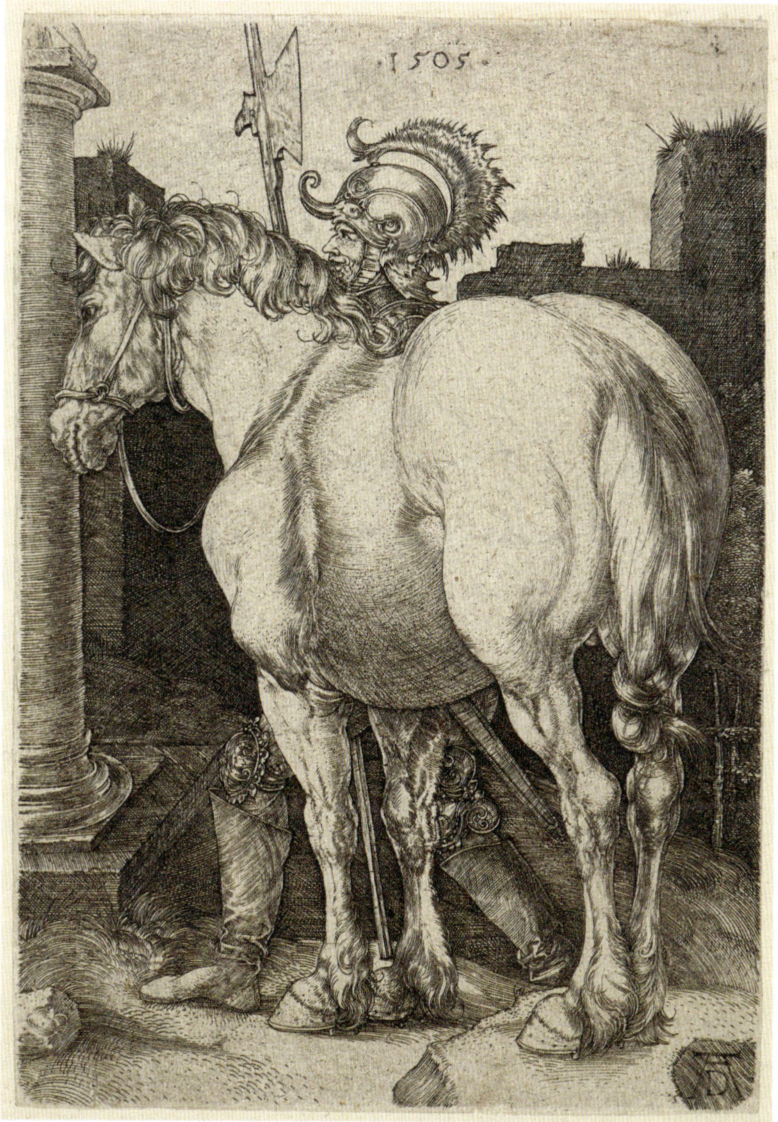

78
Albrecht Dürer
The Large Horse, 1505.

Engraving, 165 x 115 mm, trimmed
Schoch, Mende and Scherbaum,
Albrecht Dürer, I, 120–1, no. 43;
B.VII.106.97; H.94

The Whitworth, The University of
Manchester, P.4683. Gift of Dr J.
Barnes Burt. © The University of
Manchester. Photo: Michael Pollard.

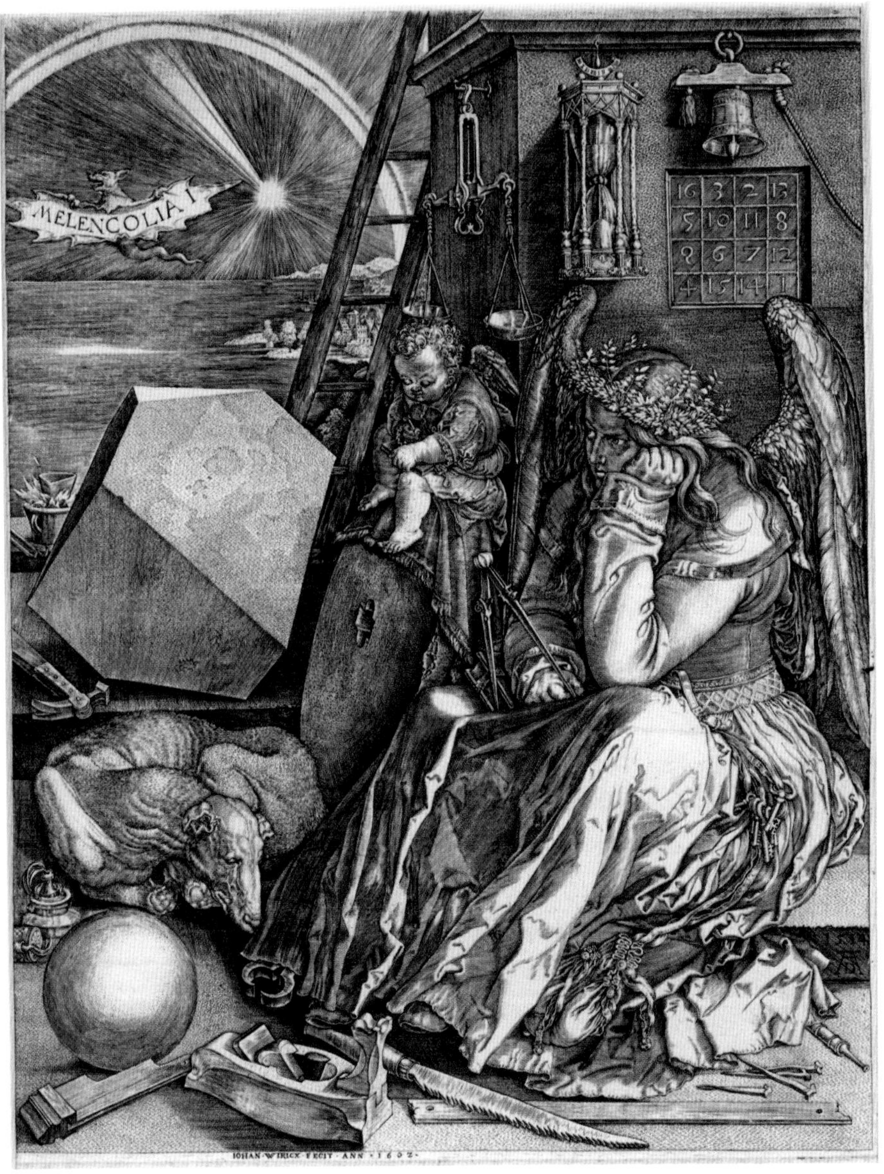

79
Albrecht Dürer
Melencolia I (Meisterstiche), 1514.

Engraving, 241 x 189 mm, trimmed
Schoch, Mende and Scherbaum, *Albrecht Dürer*, I,
179–84, no. 71; B.VII.87.74; H.75

The Whitworth, The University of Manchester, P.3018.
Presented by George Thomas Clough in 1921.
© The Whitworth, The University of Manchester.
Photo: Michael Pollard.

For illustration, see fig. 7.1, p. 74.

^ 80
Johannes Wierix after Albrecht Dürer
Melencolia I, 1602.

Engraving, 240 x 190 mm
Mauquoy-Hendrickx 1556; Hollstein Dutch and Flemish
LXVII.144.2000 (Hollstein Wierix 2000)

Ashmolean Museum, University of Oxford, WA1863.9095.
Bequeathed by Francis Douce in 1834.
© Ashmolean Museum, University of Oxford.

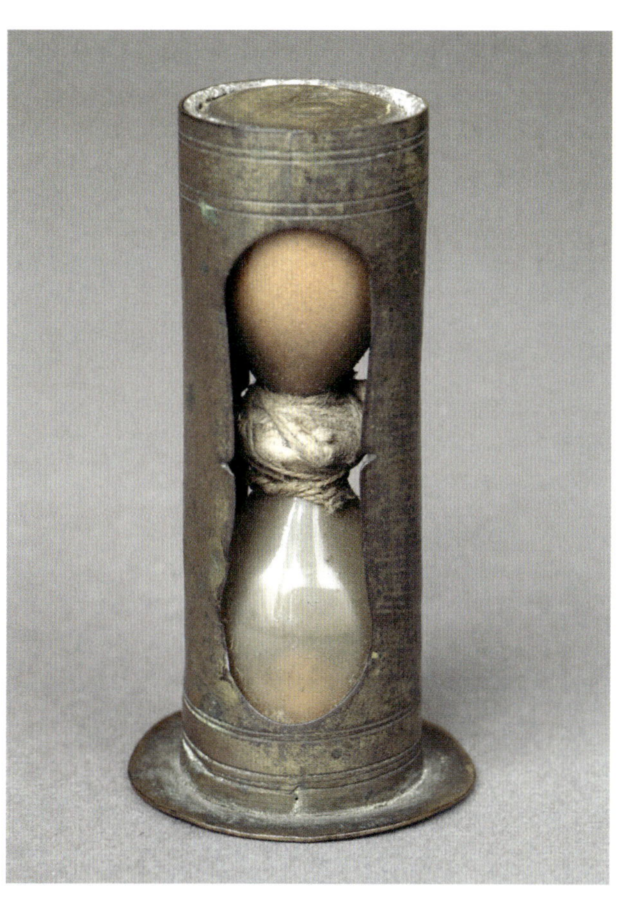

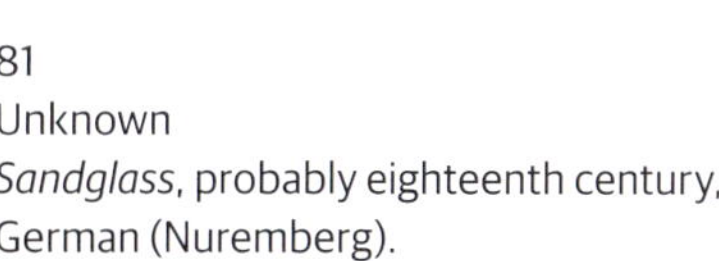

81
Unknown
Sandglass, probably eighteenth century,
German (Nuremberg).

Glass blown in two parts with brass frame, marked on the base with the
holy name of Jesus (IHS) and three nails, 6.7 x 3.5 (diameter) cm

Manchester Art Gallery, 1922.1194. Gift of Mrs Mary Greg.
© Manchester Art Gallery. Photo: Michael Pollard.

82
Georg Hartmann
Astrolabe, 1532, German (Nuremberg).

Brass, 0.7 x 14.0 (diameter) cm
Ward, *Instruments*, 115, no. 333.

London, The British Museum, 1871,1115.3. Presented by Sir Augustus
Wollaston Franks, 1871. © The Trustees of the British Museum.

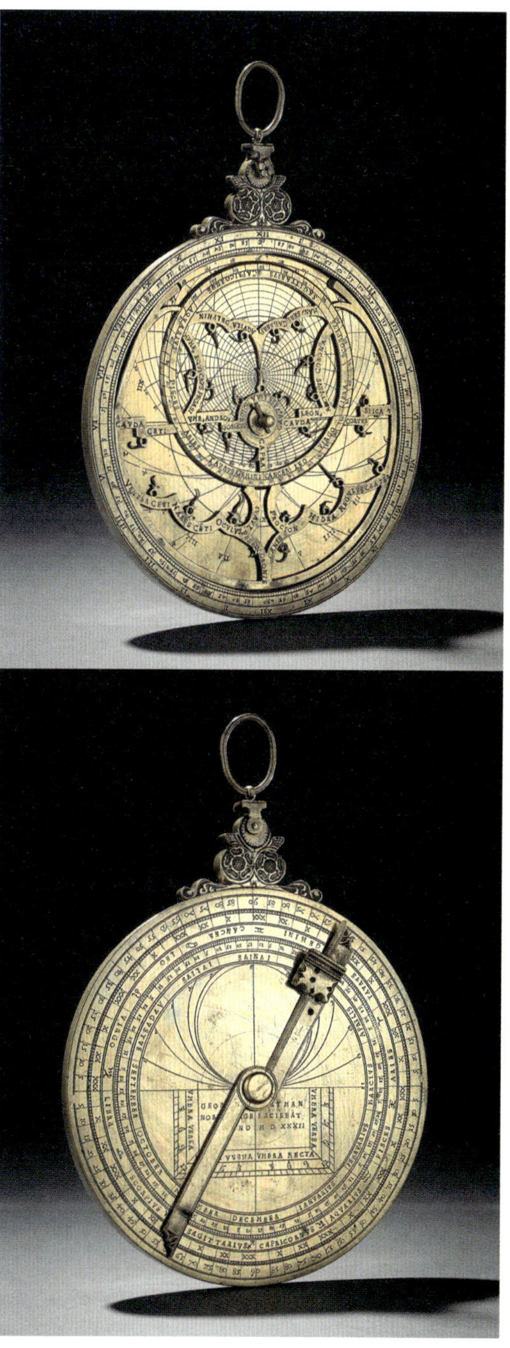

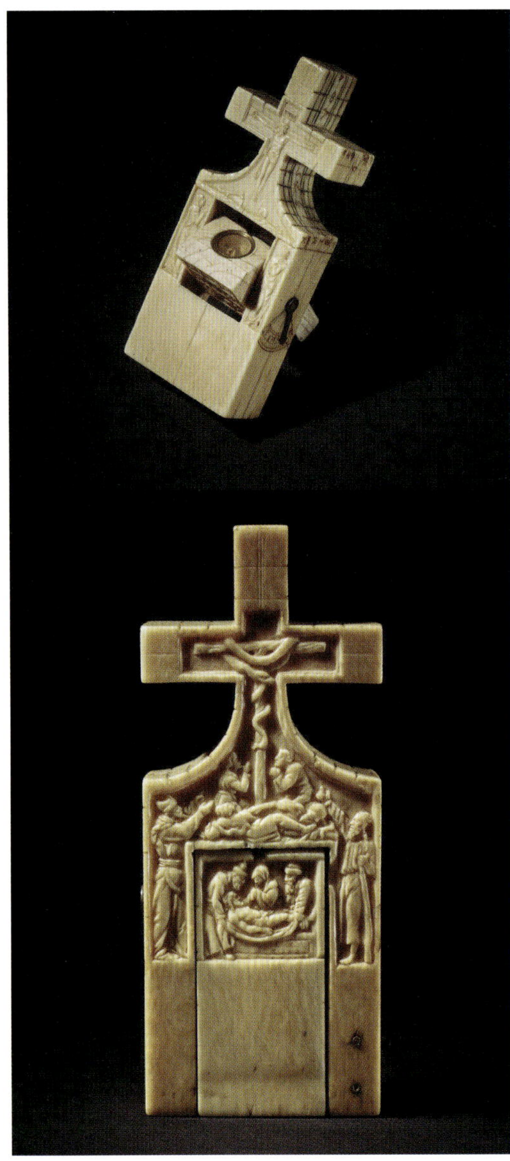

83
Georg Hartmann
Crucifix Sundial, 1541, German (Nuremberg).

Ivory, 9.6 x 3.9 x 1.7 cm , carved and engraved with the Crucifixion, the
arms of Brandenburg, the Brazen Serpent, and the Deposition.
Maué, Eser, Hauschke and Stolzenberger, *Quasi Centrum Europae,*
367–71.

London, The British Museum, 1894,0722.1.
© The Trustees of the British Museum.

84
Unknown
Diptych Sundial,
c. 1485–95, German (Nuremberg).

Ivory and copper alloy (brass?), 1.5 x 9.5 x 7.5 cm,
gnomon dial laid out for latitude of Nuremberg,
carved with relief of Saint John the Baptist.
Ward, *Scientific Instruments,* 35, no. 76.

London, The British Museum, 1877,0521.23.
Presented by Sir Augustus Wollaston Franks, 1877.
© The Trustees of the British Museum.

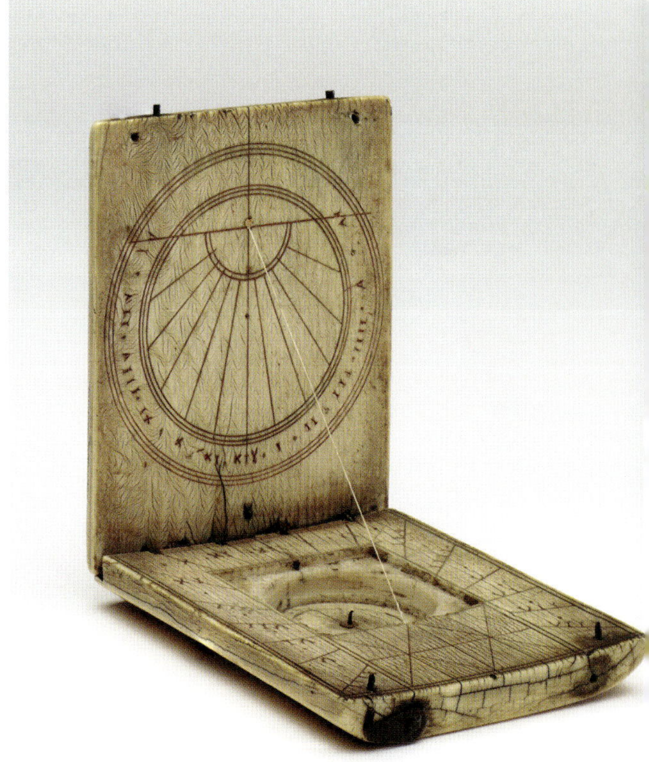

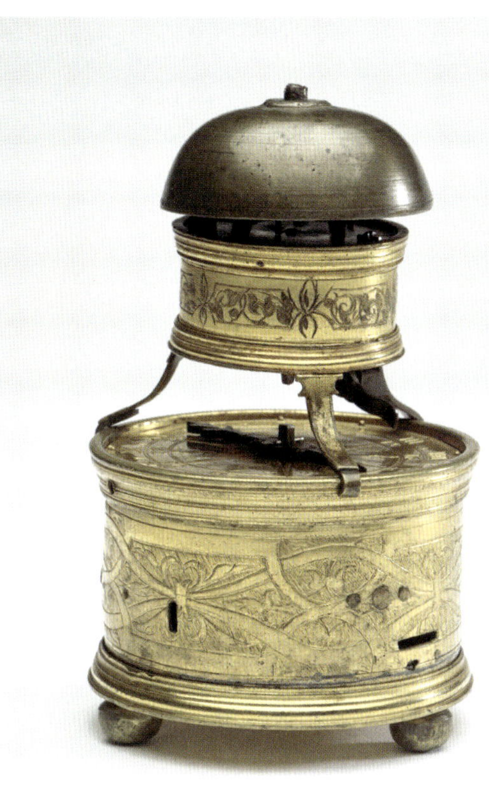

85
Unknown
Table Clock with Detachable Spring-Driven Alarm, Base Engraved with Young Boy Playing a Lute, c. 1535–45, German (Nuremberg?).

Engraved gilded brass case, 10.87 (height including alarm) x 7.28 cm (diameter).
Eser, *Die älteste Taschenuhr*, 218, no. M45

London, The British Museum, 1958,1006.2151. Donated by Gilbert Edgar. © The Trustees of the British Museum.

86
Albrecht Dürer, in collaboration with Johannes Stabius
The Celestial Map – Northern Hemisphere (Imagines coeli Septentrionales cum duodecim imaginibus zodiaci), 1515.

Woodcut, 455 x 430 mm
Schoch, Mende and Scherbaum, *Albrecht Dürer*, II, 430–4, no. 243; B.VII.161.151; H.260

London, The British Museum, 1895,0122.734. Donated by William Mitchell. © The Trustees of the British Museum.

For illustration, see figure 7.2, p. 77.

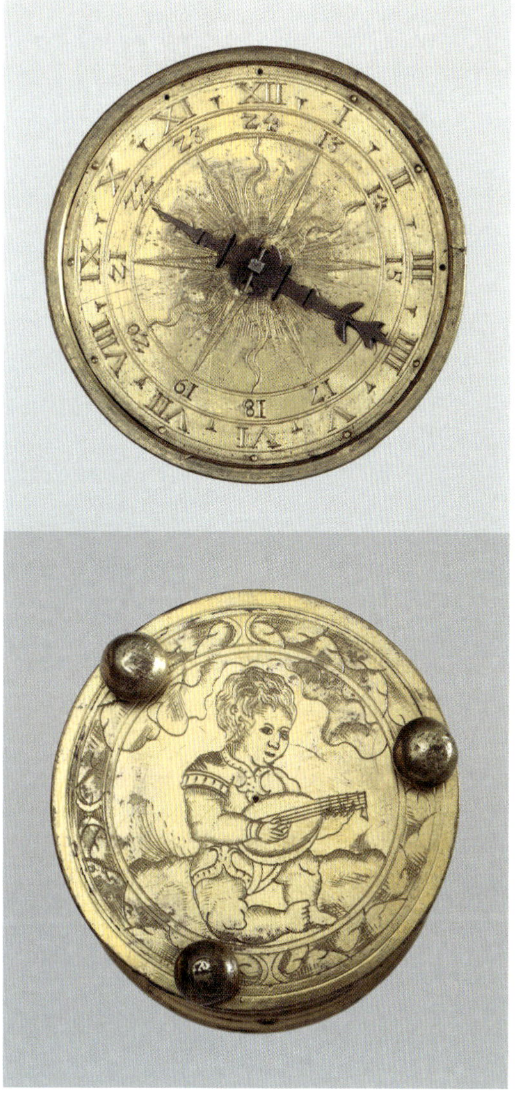

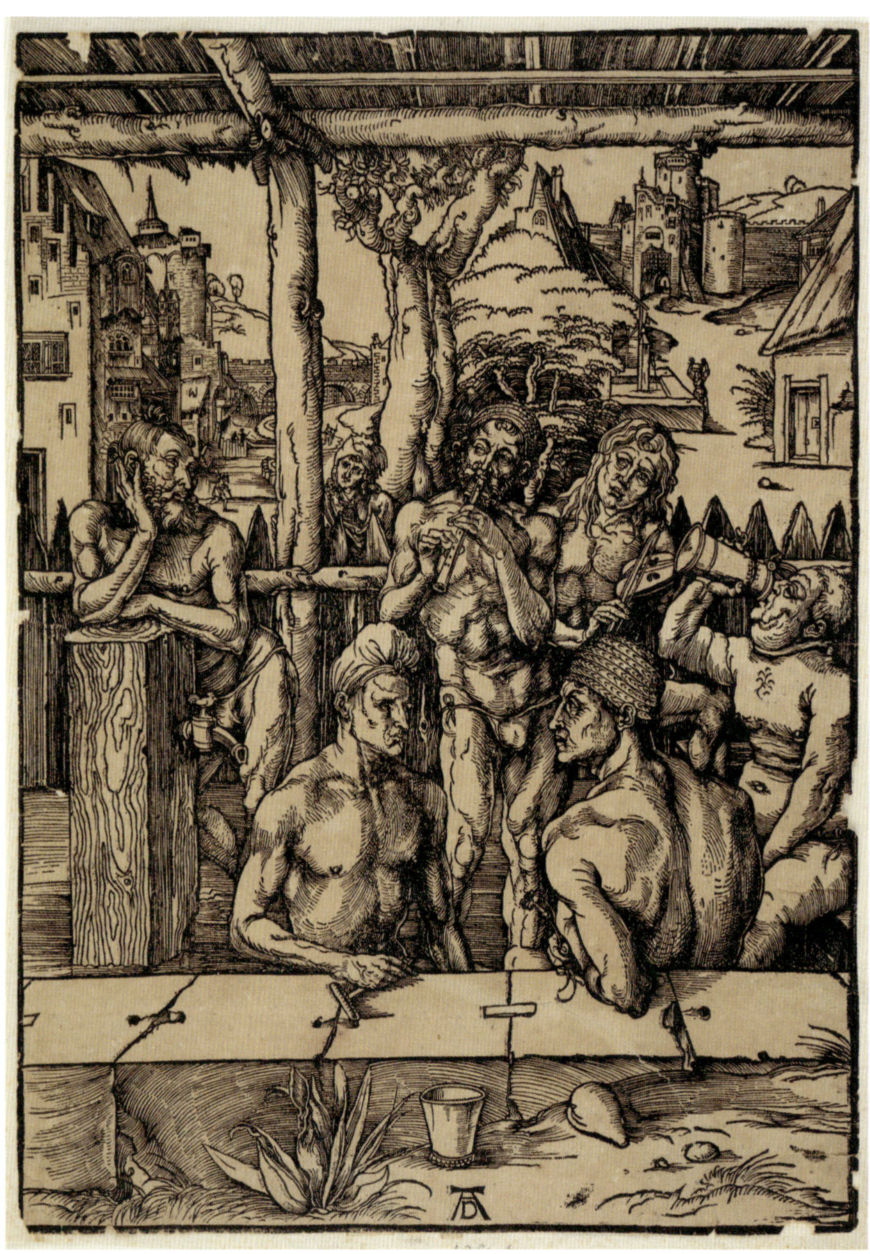

87
Albrecht Dürer
The Bath House, c. 1496–7.

Woodcut, 394 x 284 mm
Schoch, Mende and Scherbaum, *Albrecht Dürer*, II, 52–5, no. 107;
B.VII.144.128; H.266

Ashmolean Museum, University of Oxford, WA1863.2393.
Bequeathed by Francis Douce in 1834. © Ashmolean Museum,
University of Oxford.

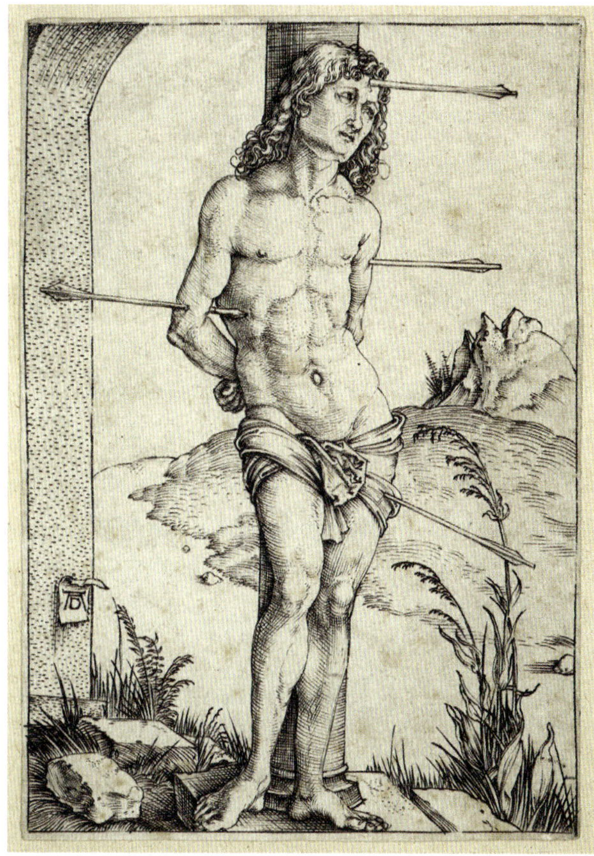

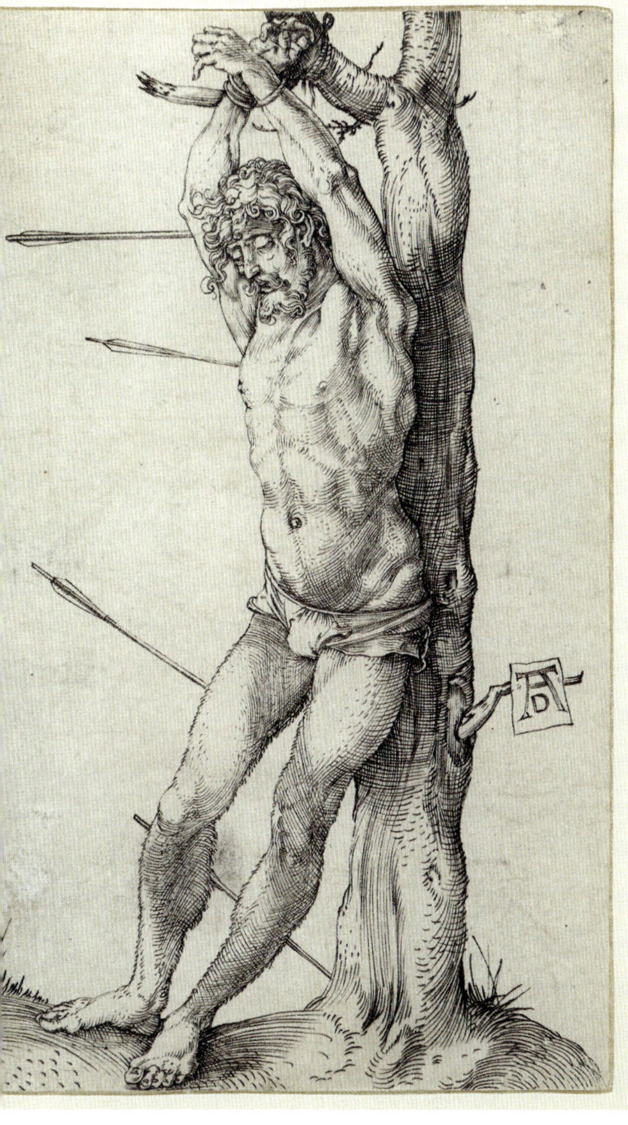

89
Albrecht Dürer
Saint Sebastian at the Column, c. 1498–9.

Engraving, 107 x 76 mm
Schoch, Mende and Scherbaum, *Albrecht Dürer*, I, 82–3,
no. 25; B.VII.72.56; H.61

The Whitworth, The University of Manchester, P.3013.
Presented by George Thomas Clough in 1921.
© The Whitworth, The University of Manchester.
Photo: Michael Pollard.

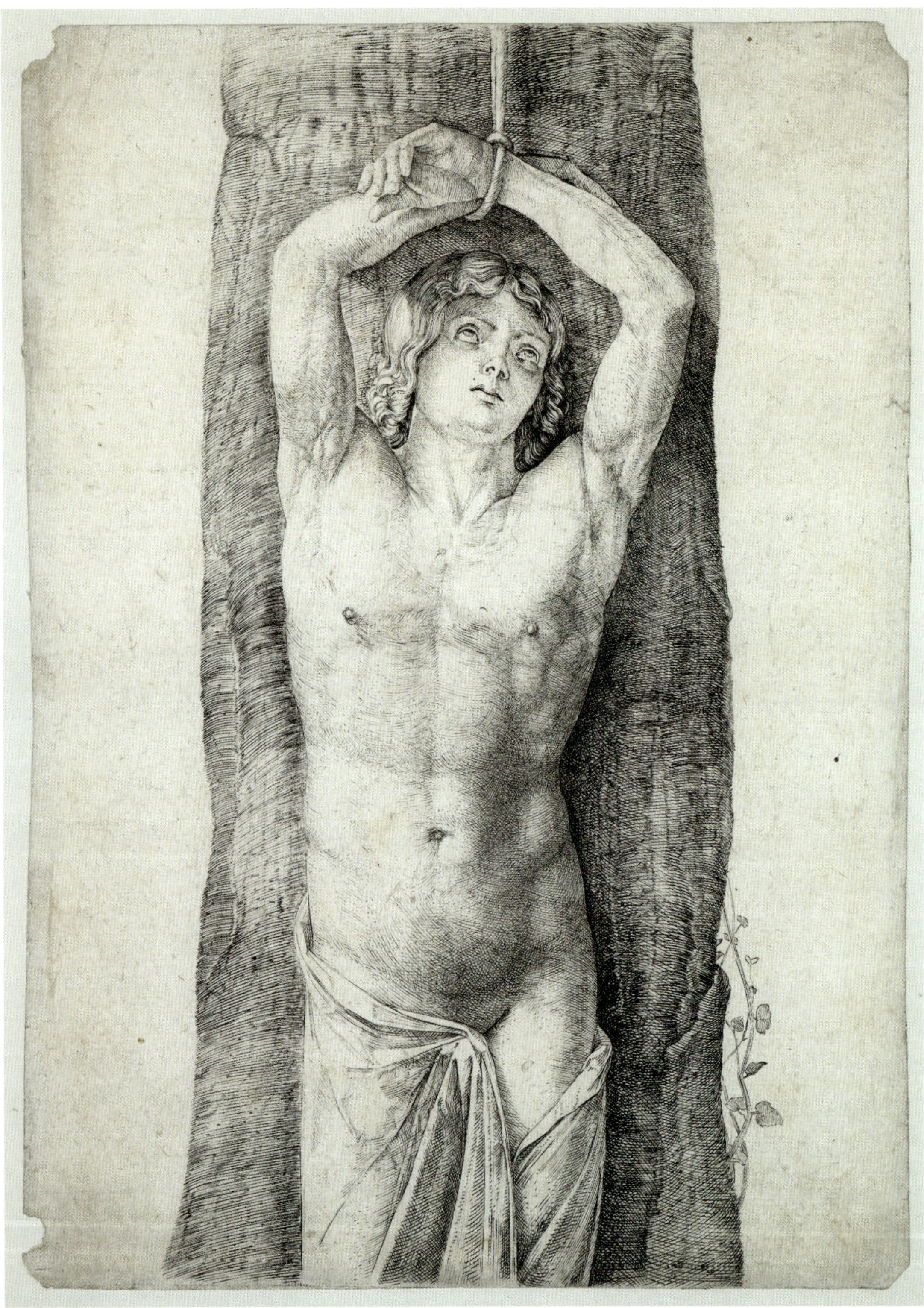

< 90

Jacopo de' Barbari
Saint Sebastian, c. 1510–12.

Engraving, 228 x 163 mm, trimmed
Hind, *Engraving*, V, 152, no. 9;
Ferrari, *Jacopo de' Barbari*, 145–6,
no. 29

The Whitworth, The University of
Manchester, P.5520. Presented by
Friends of the Whitworth in 1951.
© The Whitworth, The University of
Manchester. Photo: Michael Pollard.

91

Jacopo de' Barbari
*Judith with the Head of
Holofernes*, c. 1501–3.

Engraving, 288 x 163 mm, trimmed
B.VII.517.1; Hind, *Engraving*, V, no.
7; Ferrari, *Jacopo de' Barbari*, 118-8,
no. 7

The Whitworth, The University of
Manchester, P.3146. Presented by
George Thomas Clough in 1921.
© The Whitworth, The University of
Manchester. Photo: Michael Pollard.

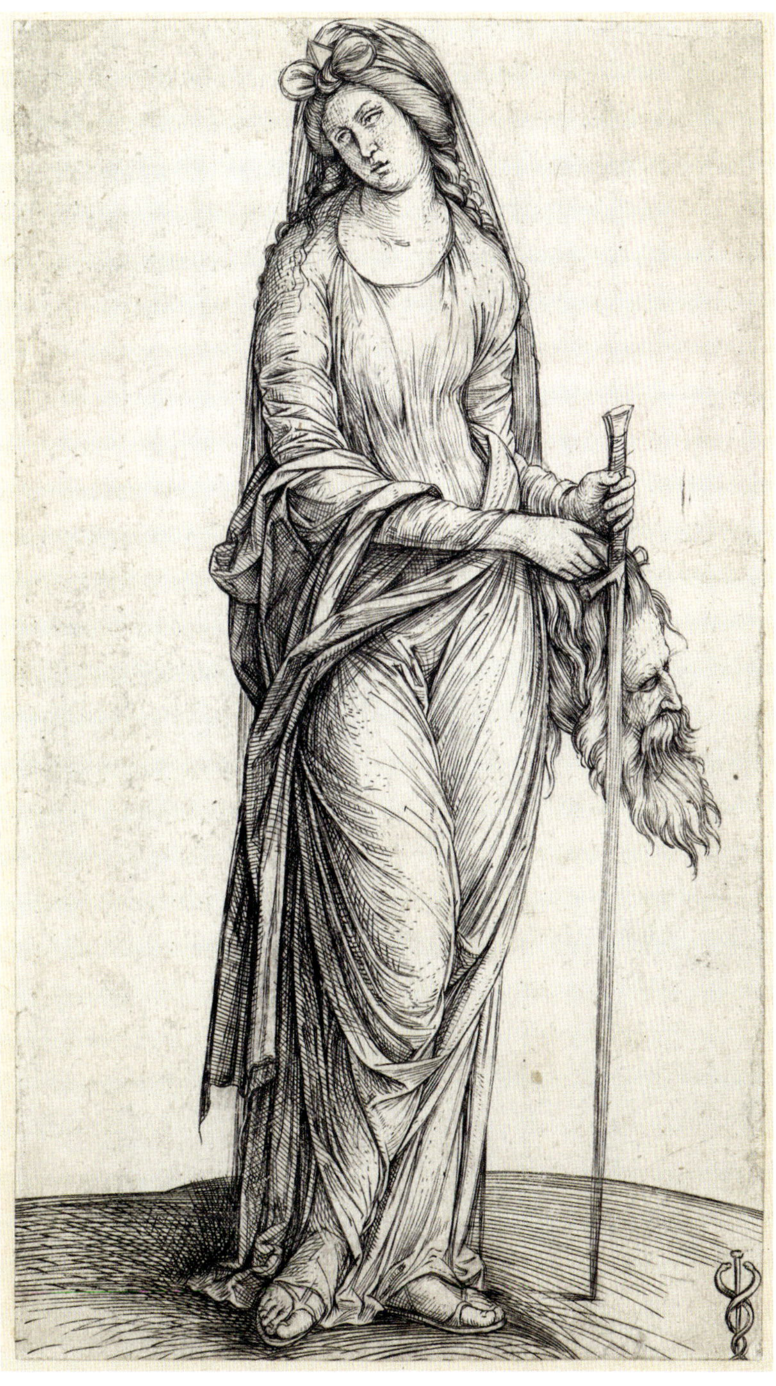

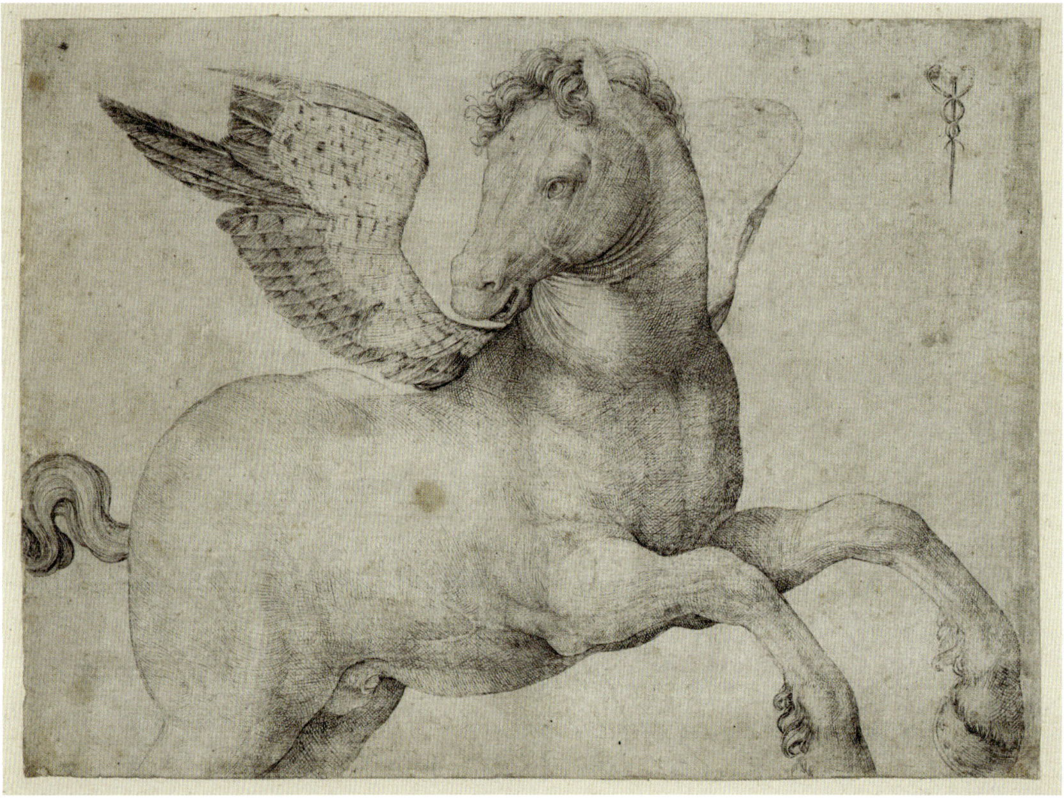

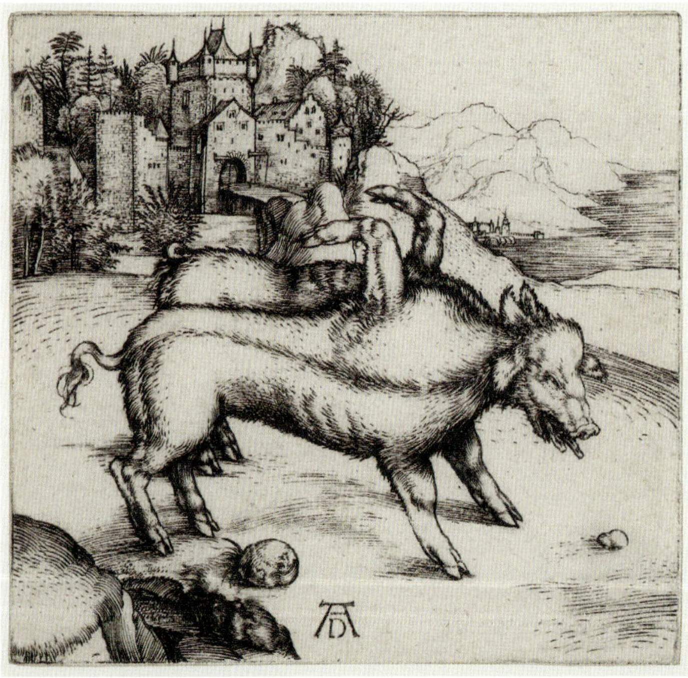

92
Jacopo de' Barbari
Pegasus, c. 1509–16.

Engraving, 150 x 205 mm, trimmed
Hind, *Engraving*, V, 157, no. 29; Ferrari,
Jacopo de' Barbari, 143–4, no. 27

The Whitworth, The University of
Manchester, P.3145. Presented by
George Thomas Clough in 1921.
© The Whitworth, The University of
Manchester. Photo: Michael Pollard.

93
Albrecht Dürer
*The Monstrous Pig (The
Monstrous Sow of Landser)*,
1496.

Engraving, 117 x 126 mm
Schoch, Mende and Scherbaum, *Albrecht
Dürer*, I, 43–4, no. 8; B.VII.105.95; H.82

The Whitworth, The University of
Manchester, P.3020. Presented by
George Thomas Clough in 1921.
© The Whitworth, The University of
Manchester. Photo: Michael Pollard.

94
Albrecht Dürer
Satyr Family, 1505.

Engraving, 126 x 71 mm, trimmed
Schoch, Mende and Scherbaum,
Albrecht Dürer, I, 122–224, no. 44;
B.VII.83.69; H.65

The Whitworth, The University of
Manchester, P.3016. Presented by
George Thomas Clough in 1921.
© The Whitworth, The University of
Manchester. Photo: Michael Pollard.

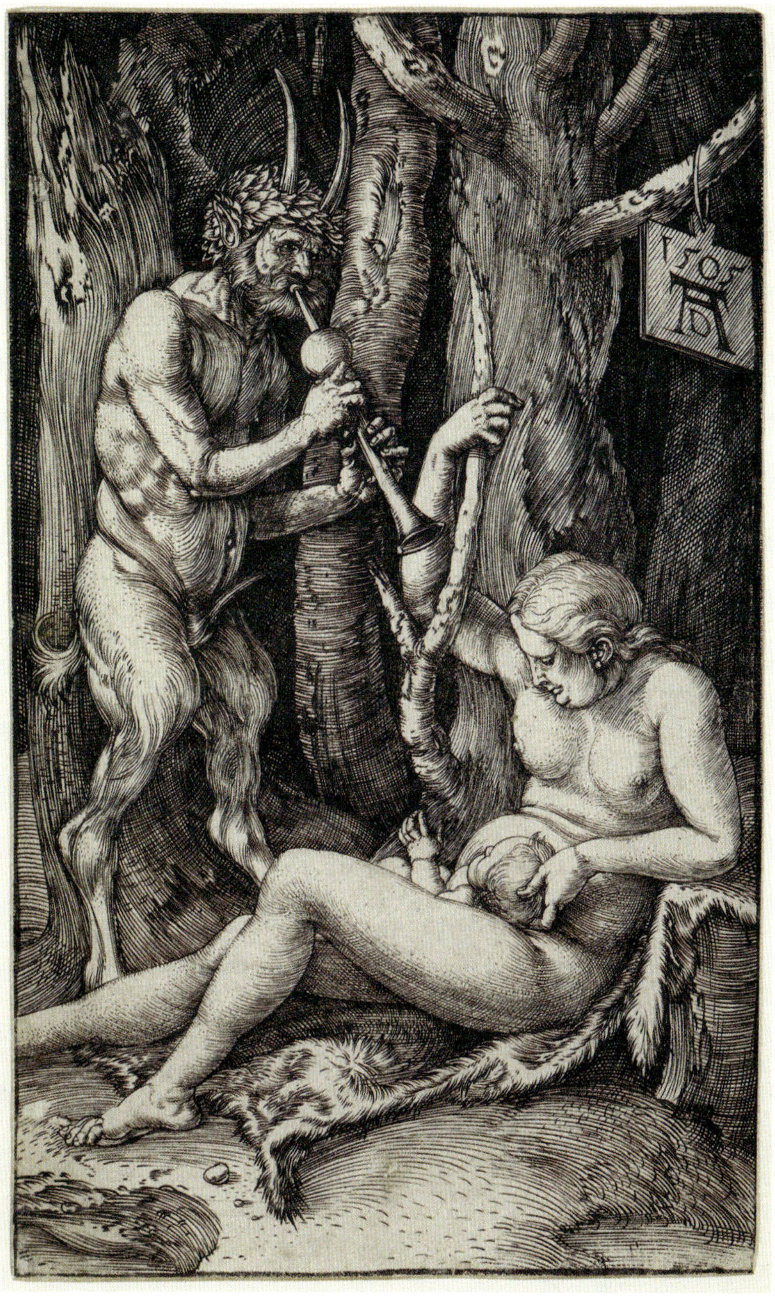

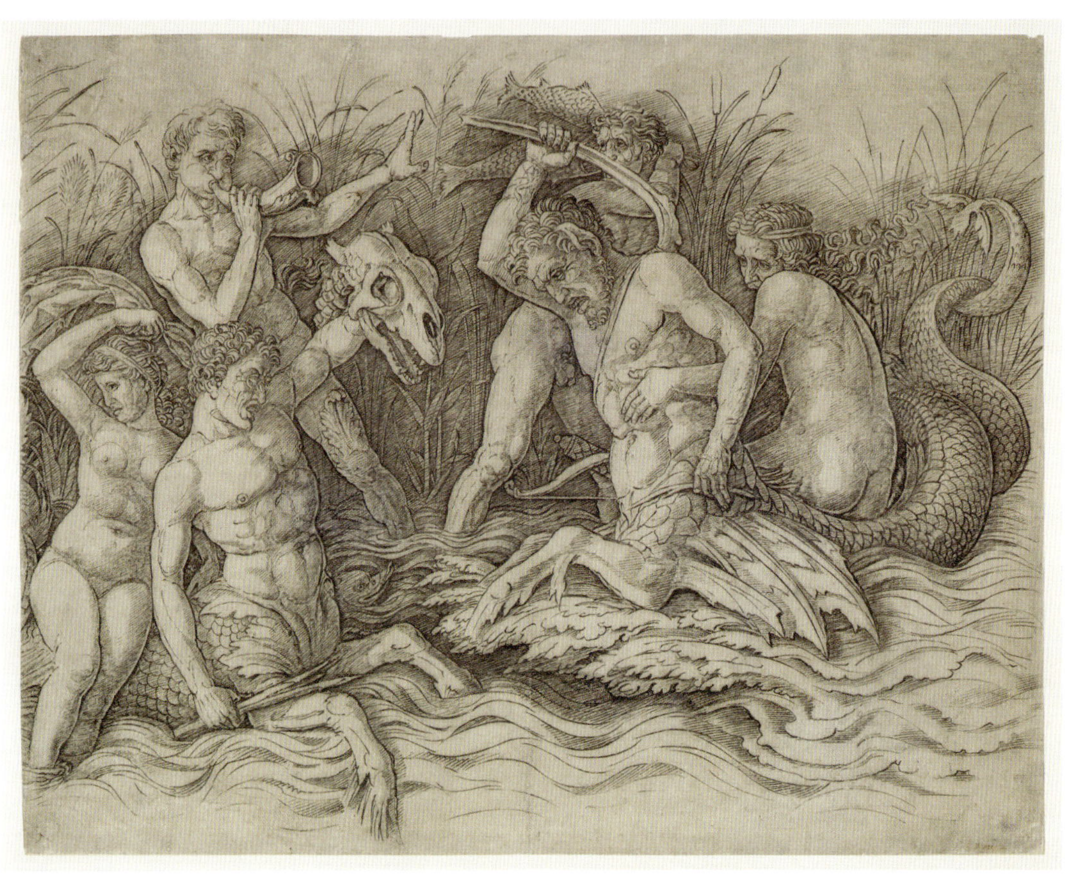

95

Andrea Mantegna
Battle of the Tritons and Sea Gods (right
portion of frieze), c. 1470–9.

Engraving, 298 x 392 mm, trimmed
B.XII.238.5; Hind, *Engraving*, V, 15, no. 6

The Whitworth, The University of Manchester, P.3121.
Presented by George Thomas Clough in 1921.
© The Whitworth, The University of Manchester.
Photo: Michael Pollard.

96
Albrecht Dürer
The Sea Monster, c. 1498–1501.

Engraving, 245 x 188 mm
Schoch, Mende and Scherbaum, *Albrecht Dürer,* I, 73–5,
no. 21; B.VII.84.71; H.66

The Whitworth, The University of Manchester, P.3017.
Presented by George Thomas Clough in 1921.
© The Whitworth, The University of Manchester.
Photo: Michael Pollard.

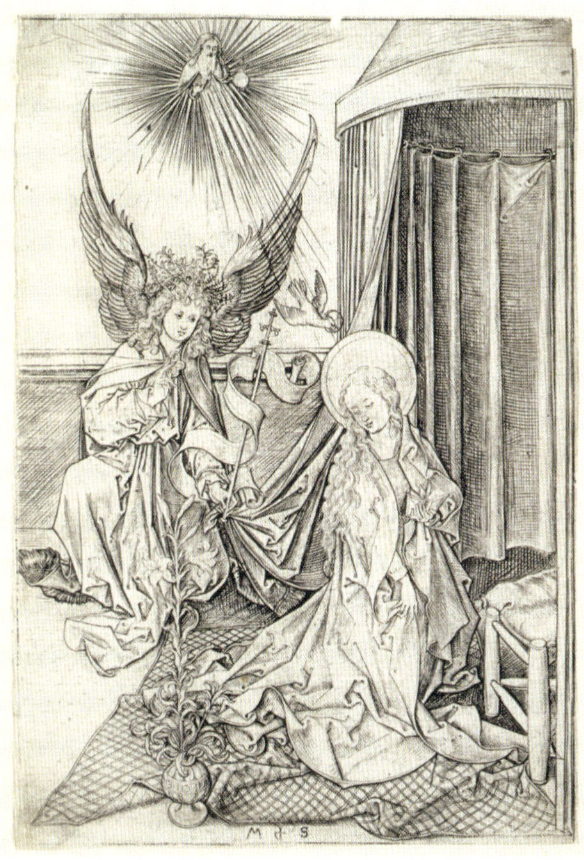

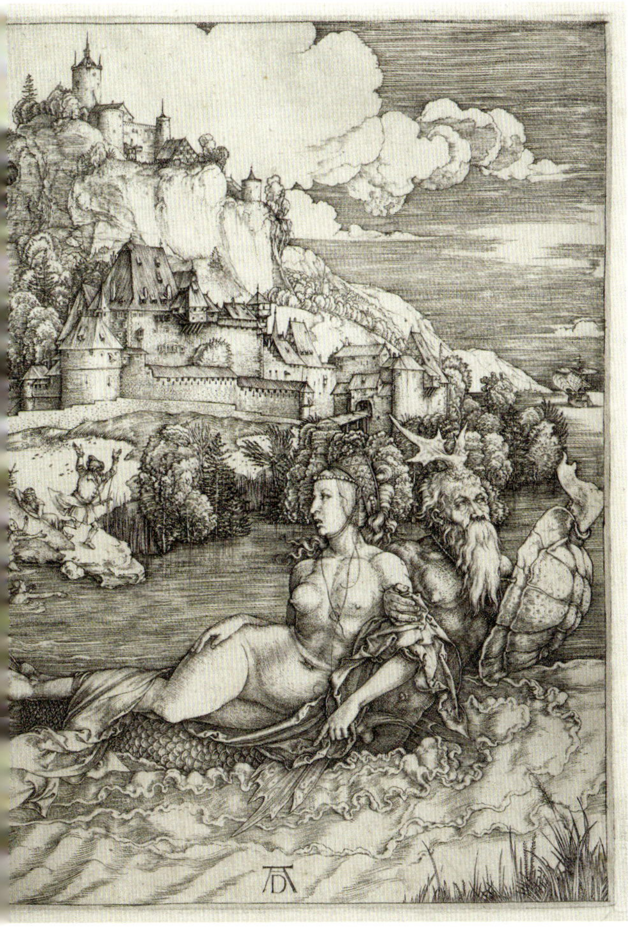

97
Martin Schongauer
The Annunciation, c. 1480.

Engraving, 161 x 101 mm, trimmed
Hollstein German XLIX.15.1

The Whitworth, The University of Manchester, P.3230.
Presented by George Thomas Clough in 1921.
© The Whitworth, The University of Manchester.
Photo: Michael Pollard.

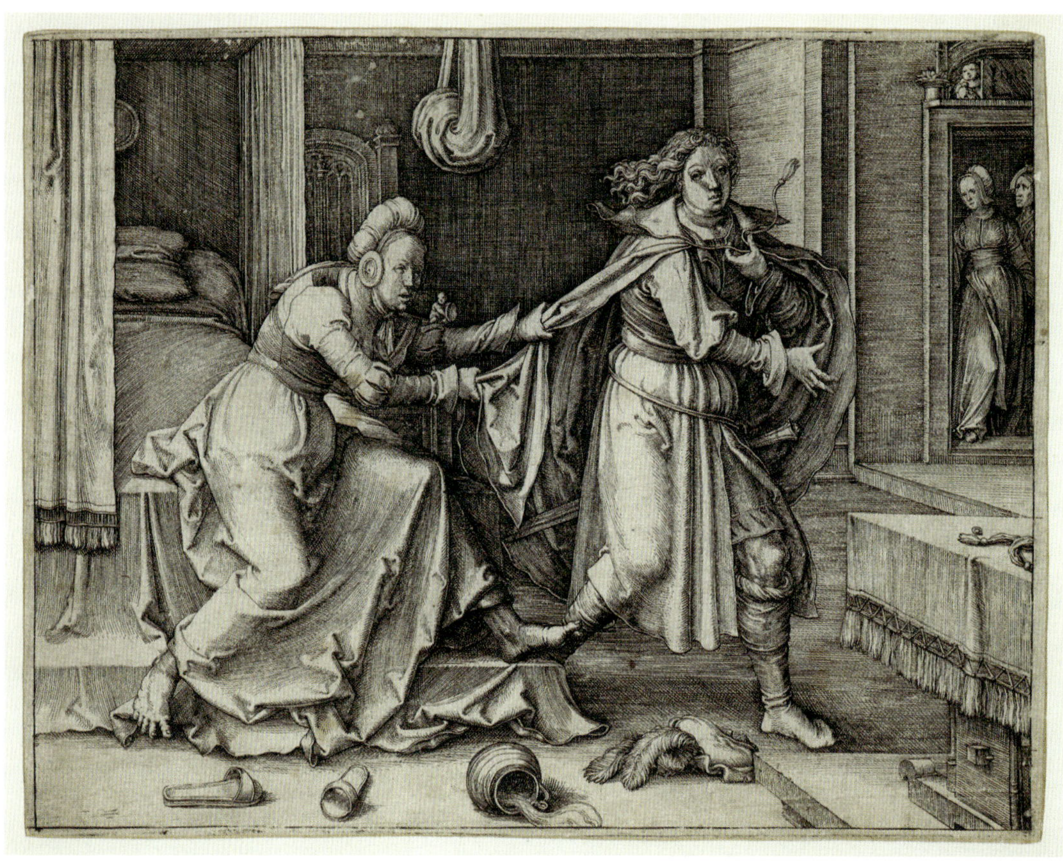

98
Lucas van Leyden
Joseph with Potiphar's Wife, 1512.

Engraving, 125 x 164 mm
Hollstein Dutch and Flemish X.71.20

The Whitworth, The University of Manchester, P.2000.227.
Bequeathed by William Sharp Ogden in 1926.
© The Whitworth, The University of Manchester.
Photo: Michael Pollard.

> 99
Albrecht Dürer
Adam and Eve, 1504.

Engraving, 264 x 191 mm
Schoch, Mende and Scherbaum, *Albrecht Dürer*, I, 110–3, no. 39;
B.VII.30.1; H.1

Ashmolean Museum, University of Oxford, WA.RS.STD.010
Bequeathed by Francis Douce in 1834.
© Ashmolean Museum, University of Oxford.

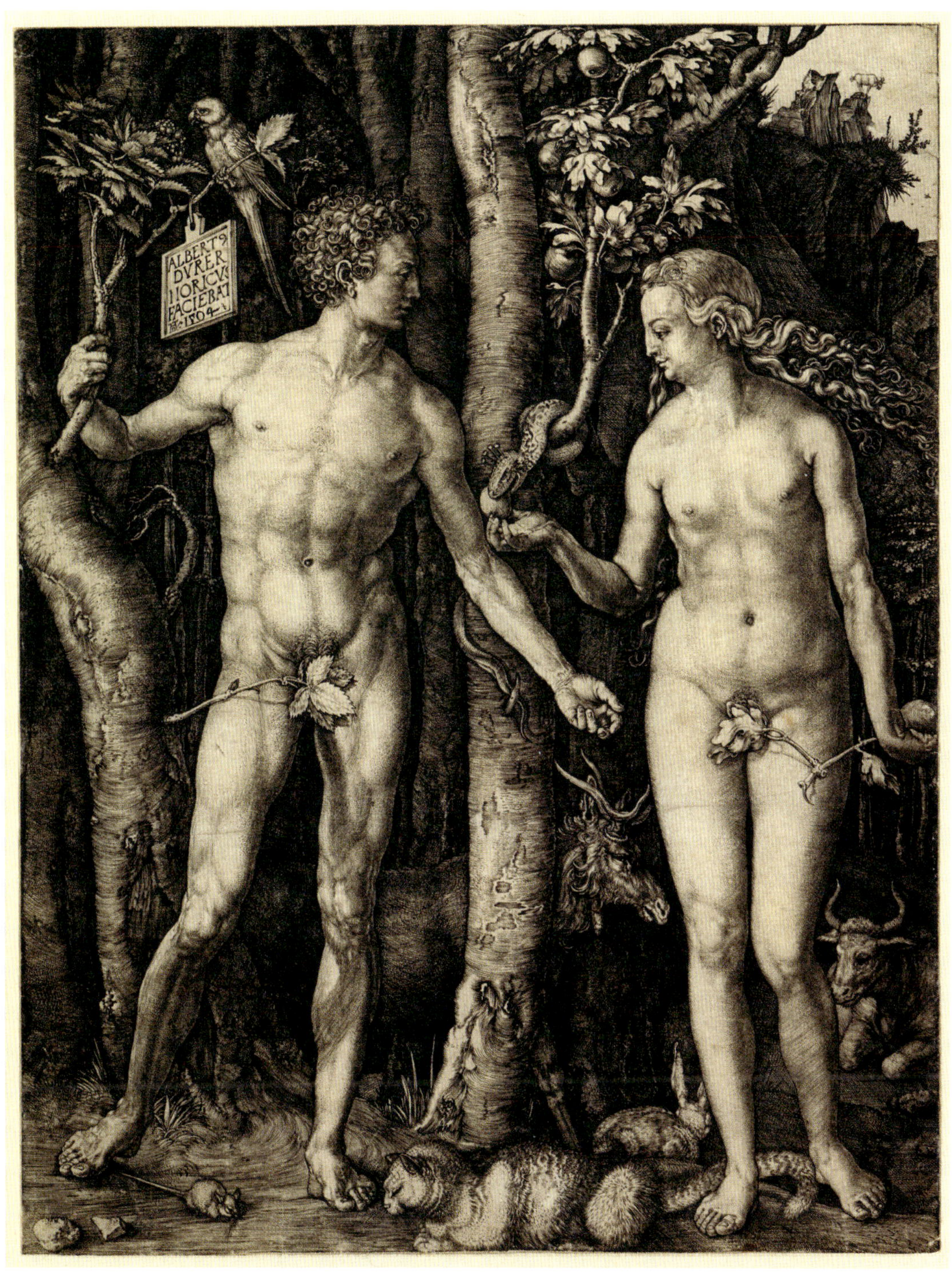

ALBERT9
DVRER
HORICV
FACIEBAT
1504

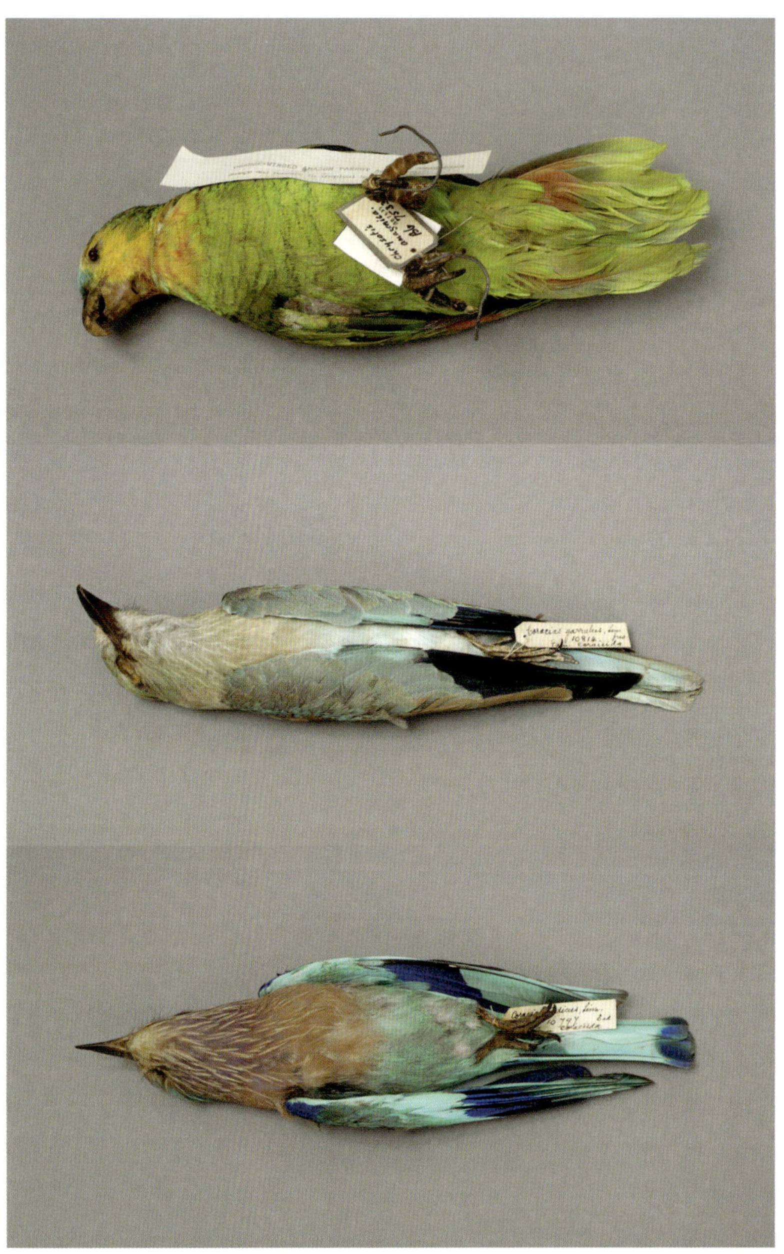

100

Amazona amazonica
(Orange-winged Parrot).

Mounted orange-winged parrot,
31.0 cm

Manchester Museum, James
Jennison & co. Bellevue Zoological
Gardens Donation, 1946, BB.7533.
© Manchester Museum,
The University of Manchester.
Photo: Michael Pollard.

101

Coracias garrulus
(European Roller).

Study Skin of European Roller,
28.0 cm

Manchester Museum, Henry
Dresser Collection, B.10814.
© Manchester Museum,
The University of Manchester.
Photo: Michael Pollard.

102

*Coracias
benghalensis indicus*
(Indian Roller).

Study Skin of an Indian Roller,
31.0 cm

Manchester Museum, Henry
Dresser Collection, B.10797.
© Manchester Museum,
The University of Manchester.
Photo: Michael Pollard.

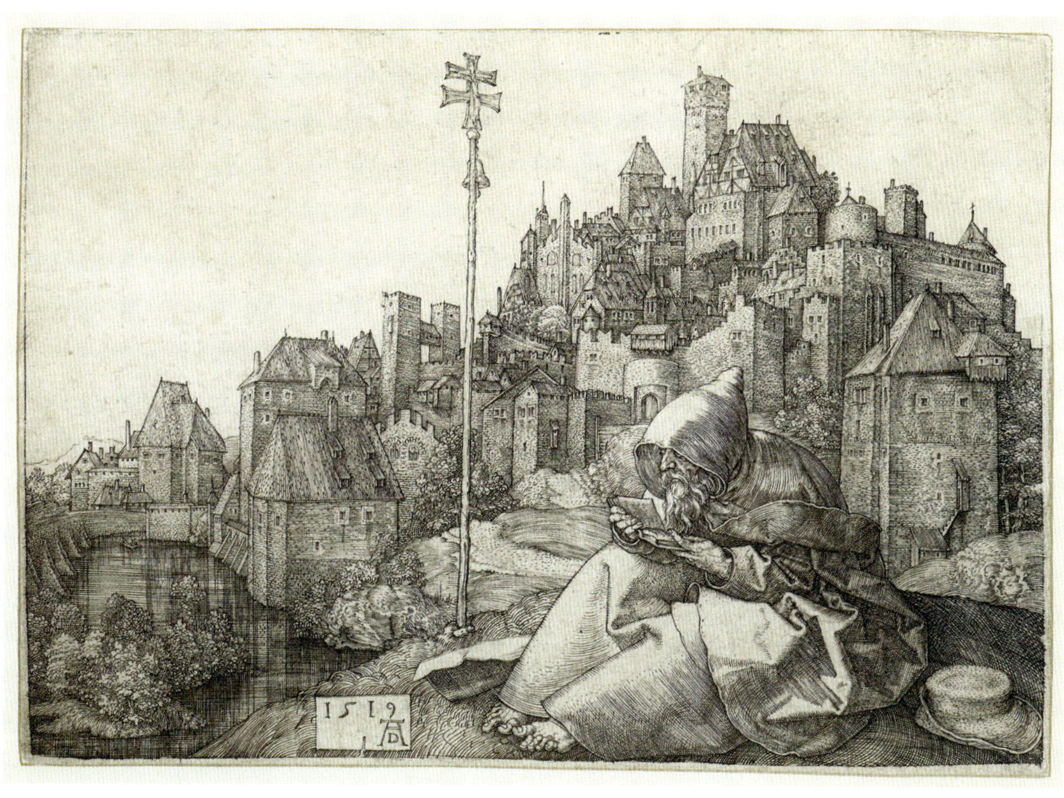

103

Albrecht Dürer
Saint Anthony Before the Town, 1519.

Engraving, 98 x 142 mm
Schoch, Mende and Scherbaum, *Albrecht Dürer*, I, 214–5, no. 87;
B.VII.74.58; H.51

The Whitworth, The University of Manchester, P.20596.
Purchased from J.O. Seed in 1964. © The Whitworth, The University
of Manchester. Photo: Michael Pollard.

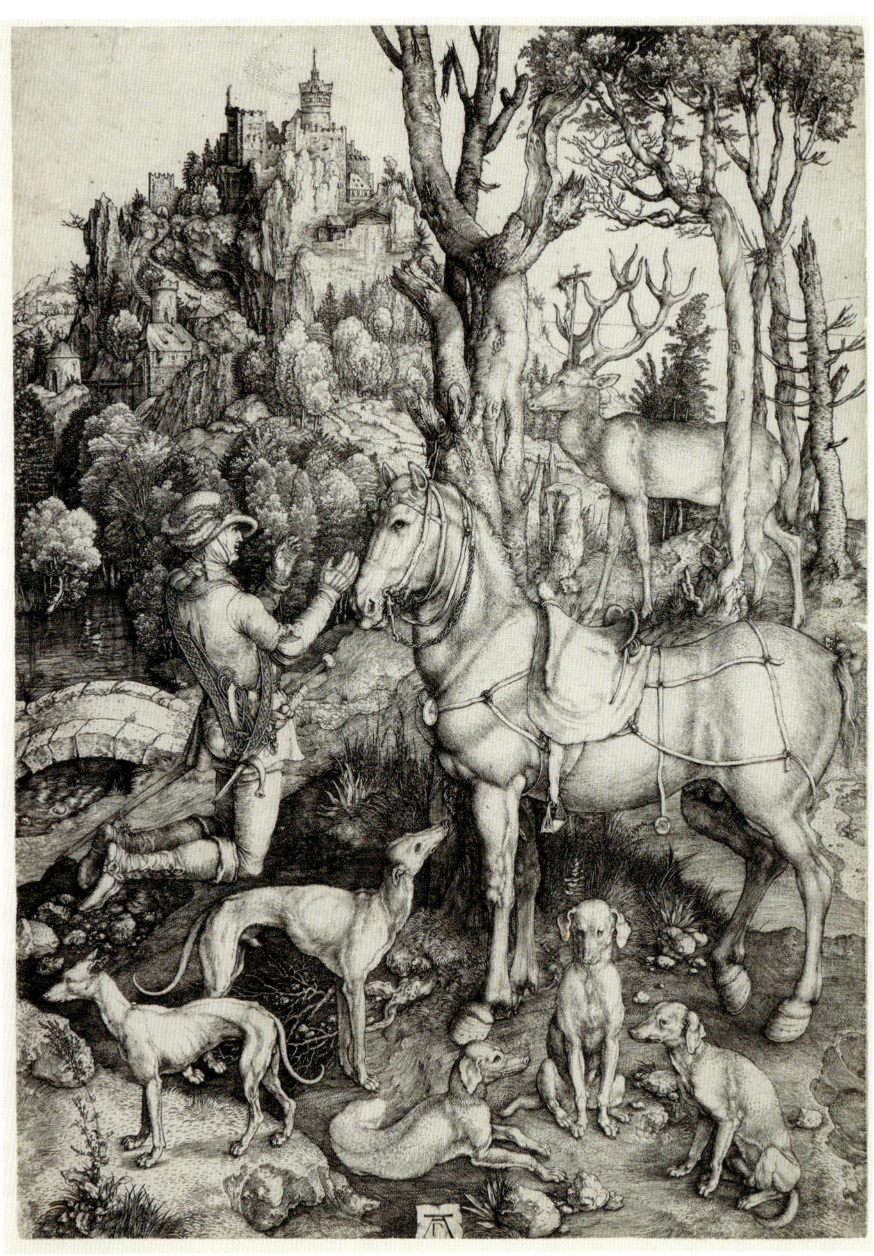

104

Albrecht Dürer
Saint Eustace, 1501–2.

Engraving, 355 x 261 mm, trimmed
Schoch, Mende and Scherbaum, *Albrecht Dürer*, I, 92–5, no. 33;
B.VII.73.57; H.60

The Whitworth, The University of Manchester, P.3014. Presented by
George Thomas Clough in 1921. © The Whitworth, The University of
Manchester. Photo: Michael Pollard.

Publications cited

Abbreviations

B.
Bartsch, Adam von. *Le Peintre-graveur.* 21 vols. Vienna: Degen, 1803–21.

H.
Hollstein German vol. VII, *Albrecht Dürer,* following the order of Meder, *Dürer-Katalog.*

Hollstein Dutch and Flemish
Hollstein, F. W. H. *Dutch and Flemish Engravings, Etchings, and Woodcuts, c. 1450–1700.* Amsterdam etc.: M. Hertzberger, 1949–2010.

Hollstein German
Hollstein, F. W. H. *German Engravings, Etchings and Woodcuts, c. 1400–1700.* Amsterdam etc.: M. Hertzberger and Sound and Vision, 1954–.

New Hollstein
Ger Luijten and Huigen Leeflang, general eds. *The New Hollstein: Dutch and Flemish Etchings, Engravings, and Woodcuts, 1540–1700.* Ouderkerk-aan-den-IJssel: Sound and Vision Interactive, 1993–.

New Hollstein German
Giulia Bartrum et al., general eds. *The New Hollstein: German Engravings, Etchings and Woodcuts, 1400–1700.* Ouderkerk-aan-den-IJssel: Sound and Vision Interactive, 1996–.

Bibliography

Adams, J. N. *The Latin Sexual Vocabulary.* London: Gerald Duckworth, 1982.

Agoston, Gábor. *Guns for the Sultan: Military Power and the Weapons Industry in the Ottoman Empire.* Cambridge: Cambridge University Press, 2005.

—. 'Ottoman Artillery and European Military Technology in the Fifteenth and Seventeenth Centuries'. *Acta Orientalia Academiae Scientiarum Hungaricae* 47.1/2 (1994), 15–48.

Aikema, Bernard *De Heilige Hieronymus in het studeervertrek of: Hoe Vlaams is Antonello da Messina?* Nijmegen: Nijmegen University Press, 2000.

Aikema, Bernard and Beverly Louise Brown, eds. *Renaissance Venice and the North: Crosscurrents in the Time of Bellin, Dürer, and Titian.* New York, NY: Rizzoli, 1999.

Ajmar-Wollheim, Marta, and Flora Dennis, eds. *At Home in Renaissance Italy.* London: V & A Publications, 2006.

Alberti, Alessia, ed. *Le finzioni del potere: l'Arco Trionfale di Albrecht Dürer per Massimiliano I d'Asburgo tra Milano e l'imperio.* Milan: Officina Libraria, 2019.

Andersen, Elizabeth, Henrike Lähnemann, and Anne Simon, eds. *A Companion to Mysticism and Devotion in Northern Germany in the Late Middle Ages.* Leiden: Brill, 2014.

Andrade, Tonio. *The Gunpowder Age: China, Military Innovation, and the Rise of the West in World History.* Princeton, NJ: Princeton University Press, 2016.

Andrews, Noam. 'Albrecht Dürer's Personal *Underweysung der Messung'. Word and Image,* 32.4 (2016), 409–29.

Anonymous, *The grete herbal whiche giveth parfyt knowledge and understanding of all manner of herbes [and] their gracious vertues.* London: Peter Treveris, 1526.

Anzelewsky, Fedja. 'Entwürfe Hans Burgkmairs für das Innsbrucker Grabmal Kaiser Maximilians'. *Berliner Museen* 19 (1969), 59–62.

Appuhn-Radtke, Sibylle. 'Fortuna Bifrons: Zu einem mittelalterlischen Bildtyp und dessen Nachleben in der Ikonographie Albrecht Dürers'. *Das Mittelalter* 1 (1996), 129–48.

Appuhn, Horst. *Der Triumphzug Maximilians I, 1516–1518.* Dortmund: Harenberg Kommunikation, 1979.

Aristotle. *The Metaphysics,* trans. Hugh Tredennick. 2 vols. Cambridge, MA: Harvard University Press, 1969–75.

Ashcroft, Jeffrey, ed. *Albrecht Dürer: Documentary Biography.* 2 vols. New Haven, CT: Yale University Press, 2017.

Barbera, Giocchino, ed. *Antonello da Messina. San Girolamo nello studio.* Messina: Museo regionale di Messina, 2006.

Bartrum, Giulia. *German Renaissance Prints in the British Museum, 1490–1550.* London: British Museum, 1995.

Bartrum, Giulia, ed. *Albrecht Dürer and his Legacy: The Graphic Work of a Renaissance Artist.* London: British Museum, 2002.

Bate, Heidi Eberhardt. *The Measures of Men: Virtue and the Arts in the Civic Imagery of Sixteenth-Century Nuremberg.* PhD thesis, University of California, 2000.

—. 'Portrait and Pageantry: New Idioms in the Interaction between City and Empire in Sixteenth-Century Nuremberg'. In Christopher Ocker, Michael Printy, Peter Starenko and Peter G. Wallace, eds, *Politics and Reformations: Communities, Polities, Nations and Empires: Essays in honour of Thomas A. Brady, Jr.* Leiden: Brill, 2007, 121–41.

Barlow, Thomas. *Albert Dürer: His Life and Work, being a Lecture delivered to the Print Collectors' Club on November 15th 1922.* London: The Print Collectors' Club, 1925.

—. *Woodcuts of Albrecht Dürer*. London: Penguin Books, 1948.

—. *Woodcuts and Engravings by Albert Dürer*. Cambridge: Cambridge University Press, 2011.

Baumbauer, Benno, Dagmar Hirschfelder and Manuel Teget-Welz, eds. *Michael Wolgemut. Mehr als Dürers Lehrer*. Regensburg: Schnell & Steiner, 2019.

Baxandall, Michael. *The Limewood Sculptors of Renaissance Germany*. New Haven, CT: Yale University Press, 1980.

Bayer, Andreas. 'Dürers Schuhe'. In Tina Asmussen, Eva Brugger, Maike Christadler, Anja Rathmann-Lutz, Anna Reimann, Carla Roth, Sarah-Maria Schober and Ina Serif, eds, *Materialized Histories. Eine Festschrift 2.0*. https://mhistories.hypotheses.org/3392

Bechtold, Arthur. 'Zu Dürers Radierung "Die große Kanone"'. In Georg Habich, ed., *Festschrift für Georg Habich zum 60. Geburtstag*. Munich: Kress and Hornung Vorm. Kuhn, 1928, 112–20.

Bedal, Konrad. 'Wohnen wie zu Dürers Zeiten: Stuben und Wohnräume im süddeutschen, insbesondere fränkischen Bürgerhaus des späten Mittelalters'. In G. Ulrich Grossmann and Franz Sonnenberger, eds, *Das Dürerhaus: Neue Ergebnisse der Forschung*. Nuremberg: Verlag des Germanischen Nationalmuseum, 2007, 27–60.

Belting, Hans. 'St. Jerome in Venice: Giovanni Bellini and the Dream of Solitary Life'. *I Tatti Studies* 17.1 (2014), 5–33.

Bernau, Anke. 'Figuring with Knots'. *Digital Philology: A Journal of Medieval Cultures* 10.1 (2021), 13–38.

Białostocki, Jan. *Dürer and his Critics 1500–1971: Chapters in the History of Ideas: Including a Collection of Texts*. Baden-Baden: Koerner, 1986.

Bindewald, Maik. 'An Undiscovered State of Albrecht Dürer's *Large Cannon*'. *Art in Print* 5.5 (2016), 6–7.

Boeheim, Wendelin. 'Die Zeugbücher des Kaisers Maximilian I'. *Jahrbuch der Kunsthistorichen Sammlungen des allerhöchsten Kaiserhauses* 13 (1892), 94–201.

—. 'Die Zeugbücher des Kaisers Maximilian II'. *Jahrbuch der Kunsthistorichen Sammlungen des allerhöchsten Kaiserhauses* 15 (1894), 295–391.

Böhme, Hartmut. *Albrecht Dürer Melencolia I. Im Labyrinth der Deutung*. Frankfurt a. M.: Fischer Taschenbuch, 1989.

Bond, Katherine. 'Mapping Culture in the Habsburg Empire: Fashioning a Costume Book in the Court of Charles V'. *Renaissance Quarterly* 71.2 (2018), 530–79.

Bott, Gerhard, ed. *Focus Behaim-Globus*. 2 vols. Nuremberg: Verlag des Germanischen Nationalmuseum, 1992.

Boudet, Jacques. *The Ancient Art of Warfare, vol. I, Antiquity, Middle Ages, Renaissance*. London: Barrie and Rockliff, 1966.

Brant, Sebastian. *Das Narrenschiff*. Paris: Johann Philippi de Cruzenach, 1498.

Brisman, Shira. 'Sternkraut: "The Word that Unlocks" Dürer's Self-Portrait of 1493'. In Hess and Eser, eds, *The Early Dürer*, 194–207.

—. *Albrecht Dürer and the Epistolary Mode of Address*. Chicago, IL: University of Chicago Press, 2017.

—. 'The Image that Wants to be Read: An Invitation for Interpretation in a Drawing by Albrecht Dürer'. *Word & Image* 29.3 (2013), 273–303.

—. 'A Matter of Choice: Printed Design Proposals and the Nature of Selection, 1470–1610'. *Renaissance Quarterly* 71.1 (2018), 114–64.

The British and Foreign Anti-Slavery Society. *The Anti-Slavery Reporter*, 11.7 (1 July 1863).

Brown, Ramona and Anja Grebe. 'Albrecht Dürer von Nörmergk. Zur Frage von Dürers Basler Holzschnitten'. In Ulrich Großmann und Franz Sonnenburger, eds, *Das Dürer-Haus. Neue Ergebnisse der Forschung zur Dürer Werkstatt*. Nuremberg: Germanisches Nationalmuseum, 2006, 121–40.

Brundin, Abigail, Deborah Howard and Mary Laven. *The Sacred Home in Renaissance Italy*. Oxford: Oxford University Press, 2018.

Bubenik, Andrea. 'The Shape of Things to Come: Dürer's Polyhedron'. In Andrea Bubenik, ed., *The Persistence of Melancholia in Arts and Culture*. London: Routledge, 2019, 68–93.

Büchert, Gesa. 'Die mechanische Herstellung von Glasspiegeln im Landgebiet der Reichsstadt Nürnberg'. *Mitteilungen des Vereins für Geschichte der Stadt Nürnberg* 85 (1998), 51–140.

Buck, Stephanie, and Stephanie Porras. *The Young Dürer: Drawing the Figure*. London: Paul Holberton, 2013.

Burgemeister, Melanie. *Kleider – Kultur – Ordnung: Kulturelle Ordnungssysteme in Kleiderordnungen aus Nürnberg, Regensburg und Landshut zwischen 1470 und 1485*. Münster: Waxmann, 2019.

Bynum, Caroline Walker. *Christian Materiality: An Essay on Religion in Late Medieval Europe*. New York, NY: Zone, 2011.

—. *Wonderful Blood: Theology and Practice in Late Medieval Northern Germany and Beyond*. Philadelphia, PA: University of Pennsylvania Press, 2007.

Cain, Andrew, ed. *Jerome of Stridon, his Life. Writings and Legacy*. Farnham: Ashgate, 2009.

Carboni, Stefano. 'Moments of Vision: Venice and the Islamic World, 828–1797'. In Stefano Carboni, ed., *Venice and the Islamic World, 828–1797*. New Haven, CT: Yale University Press, 2007, 12–32.

Cardano, Gerolamo. *De Sapientiae (…)*. Nuremberg: Petreius, 1543.

—. *De Svbtilitate (…)*. Nuremberg: Petreius, 1550.

Cavallo, Sandra. *Healthy Living in Late Renaissance Italy*. Oxford: Oxford University Press, 2013.

City of Manchester Art Galleries. *Albrecht Dürer Woodcuts and Engravings Lent by Sir Thomas D. Barlow, K. B. E. 21 October to 1 December 1935*. Manchester: City of Manchester Art Galleries, 1935.

Champion, Matthew S. *The Fullness of Time: Temporalities of the Fifteenth-Century Low Countries*. Chicago, IL: University of Chicago Press, 2017.

—. 'Pointing to a Deeper Now: Time, Sound, Touch and the Devotional Present in Fifteenth-Century Northern Europe'. In Armin Bergmeier and Andrew Griebeler, eds, *Time and Presence in Art: Moments of Encounter (200–1600 CE)*. Berlin: De Gruyter, 2022, 113–34.

—. '"To See beyond the Moment is Delightful": Devout Chronologies of the Late Medieval Low Countries'. *Viator* 49.3 (2018), 119–221.

Clifton, James. 'Adriaen Huybrechts, the Wierix Brothers, and Confessional Politics in the Netherlands'. *Nederlands Kunsthistorisch Jaarboek* 52 (2001), 104–25.

Clough, G. T. *Catalogue of the Clough Collection of Early German, Flemish, and Italian Engravings and Woodcuts Presented in 1921 by G. T. Clough, Esq.* Manchester: The Manchester Whitworth Institute Art Galleries, 1924.

Cole, Michael and Madeleine Viljoen, eds. *The Early Modern Painter-Etcher.* University Park, PA: The Pennsylvania State University Press, 2006.

Coole, P. G., C. B. Drover, P. A. Sabine and C. Tyler. 'Sand-Glass "Sand": Historical, Analytical and Practical'. *Journal of Antiquarian Horology* 3.3 (1960), 62–72.

Cooper, Donal. 'Devotion'. In Ajmar-Wollheim and Dennis, eds, *At Home in Renaissance Italy*, 190-203.

Corry, Maya, Deborah Howard, and Mary Laven, eds. *Madonnas and Miracles: The Holy Home in Renaissance Italy.* London: Philip Wilson, 2017.

Costello, Eileen E. 'Knot(s) made by Human Hands: Copying, Invention, and Intellect in the Work of Leonardo da Vinci and Albrecht Dürer'. *Athanor* 23 (2005), 25–33.

Cox, Leonard B. *The National Gallery of Victoria 1861 to 1968: A Search for a Collection.* Melbourne: The National Gallery of Victoria, 1970.

Cuneo, Pia F. 'The Artist, His Horse, a Print and its Audience: Producing and Viewing the Ideal in Dürer's *Knight, Death and the Devil* (1513)'. In Silver and Smith, eds, *The Essential Dürer*, 115–29.

Currie, Christina, Luc Sterk and Jacques Toussaint, eds. *Saint Jérôme dans un paysage par Henri met Bles et Lambert van Noort.* Namur: Société Archéologie de Namur, 2005.

Dackerman, Susan. 'Dürer's Etchings: Printed Drawings?'. In Cole and Viljoen, *The Early Modern Painter-Etcher*, 37–51.

—. *Prints and the Pursuit of Knowledge in Early Modern Europe.* New Haven, CT: Yale University Press, 2011.

Damm, Roland, Yasmin Doosry and Alexandra Scheld. *Der Venedig-Plan von 1500: Restaurierung eines Reisenholzschnitts im Germanischen Nationalmuseum.* Nuremberg: Verlag des Germanischen Nationalmuseums, 2012.

Day, Peter. *Engravings and Woodcuts by Albrecht Dürer, 1471-1528, 22 October to 22 December 1971.* Manchester: Whitworth Art Gallery, 1971.

De Voragine, Jacobus. *The Golden Legend*, trans. William Caxton. London: William Caxton, 1483.

Dodwell, C. R. *The Whitworth Art Gallery: The First Hundred Years.* Manchester: The Whitworth Art Gallery, University of Manchester, 1988.

Dohrn-van Rossum, Gerhard. *History of the Hour: Clocks and Modern Temporal Orders*, trans. Thomas Dunlap. Chicago, IL: Chicago University Press, 1996.

Downes, Stephanie, Sally Holloway and Sarah Randles, eds. *Feeling Things: Objects and Emotions through History.* Oxford: Oxford University Press, 2018.

'Dürer Prints: Sir Thomas Barlow's Collection'. *The Manchester Guardian*, 21 October 1935.

Dreßler, Fridolin. 'Nürnbergisch-fränkische Landschaften bei Albrecht Dürer'. *Mitteilungen des Vereins für Geschichte der Stadt Nürnberg* 50 (1960), 258–70.

Dürer, Albrecht. *Underweysung der messung mit dem zirckel un richt scheyt.* Nuremberg: Hieronymus Andreae, 1525.

Dupré, Sven, ed. *Perspective as Practice: Renaissance Cultures of Optics.* Turnhout: Brepols, 2019.

Egg, Erich. *Die Hofkirche in Innsbruck: Das Grabdenkmal Kaisers Maximilian I. und die Silverne Kapelle.* Innsbruck: Tyrolia-Verlag, 1974.

Egmond, Florike. *Eye for Detail: Images of Plants and Animals in Art and Science, 1500-1630.* London: Reaktion Books, 2017.

Eichberger, Dagmar. *Leben mit Kunst, Wirken durch Kunst. Hofkunst und Sammelwesen unter Margarete von Österreich, Regentin der Niederlande.* Turnhout: Brepols, 2002.

—. 'Naturalia and artefacta: Dürer's Nature Drawings and Early Collecting'. In Eichberger and Zika, eds, *Dürer and his Culture*, 13–37.

—. 'Visualizing the Seven Sorrows of the Virgin: Early Woodcuts and Engravings in the Context of Netherlandish Confraternities'. In Emily S. Thelen, ed., *The Seven Sorrows Confraternity of Brussels: Drama, Ceremony, and Art Patronage (16th-17th Centuries).* Turnhout: Brepols, 2015, 113–45.

Eichberger, Dagmar and Charles Zika, eds. *Dürer and his Culture.* Cambridge: Cambridge University Press, 1998.

Enenkel, Karl A. E. and Walter Melion, eds. *Meditatio – Refashioning the Self: Theory and Practice in Late Medieval and Early Modern Intellectual Culture.* Leiden: Brill, 2011.

'Engravings by Duerer: Manchester Exhibition Value of Private Collecting'. The *Manchester Guardian.* 22 October 1935.

Erasmus, Desiderius. *La vie de saint Jérôme*, trans. André Godin. Turnhout: Brepols, 2013.

Eser, Thomas. *Die älteste Taschenuhr der Welt? Der Henlein-Uhrenstreit.* Nuremberg: Germanisches Nationalmuseum, 2014.

—. 'Dürer's Self-Portraits and Self-Documentation'. In Hess and Eser, eds, *The Early Dürer*, 261–70.

Eser, Thomas and Anja Grebe, eds. *Heilige und Hasen: Bücherschätze der Dürerzeit.* Nuremberg: Verlag des Germanischen Nationalmuseums, 2008.

Faietti, Marzia and Gerhard Wolf, eds. *The Power of Line.* Munich: Hirmer, 2015.

Ferrari, Simone. *Jacopo de' Barbari: Un protagonista del Rinascimento tra Venezia e Dürer.* Milan: Mondadori, 2006.

Feulner, Karoline. 'Tradition and Innovation: Dürer's Goldsmith Training as a Foundation for his Printing Activity'. In Sander, ed., *Albrecht Dürer: His Art in Context*, 2013, 22–25.

Fleischmann, Peter, ed. *Norenberc – Nürnberg 1050 bis 1806. Eine Ausstellung des Staatarchivs Nürnberg zur Geschichte der Reichsstadt, Kaiserburg Nürnberg, 16. September – 12. November 2000.* Munich: Staatlichen Archive Bayerns, 2000.

Fleisher, Alexandra and Zhenia Fleisher. 'The Fragrance of Biblical Mandrake'. *Economic Botany* 48.3 (1994), 243–51.

Flötner, Peter. *Das Kvnstbvch des Peter Flötner: Zeichners, Bildhauers und Formschneiders von Nürnberg gestorben im Jahre fünfzehn hunder sechs und vierzig: enthält vierzig Blätter mit allerlei Zierrat für Malerei eingelegte tauschierte und geätzte Arbeit.* Berlin: Schvster, 1882 [1549].

Foister, Susan and Peter van den Brink, eds. *Dürer's Journeys: Travels of a Renaissance Artist.* London: National Gallery, 2021.

Fortini Brown, Patricia. *Venetian Narrative Painting in the Age of Carpaccio*. New Haven, CT: Yale University Press, 1988.

—. 'Carpaccio's Augustine in His Study: A Portrait within a Portrait'. In Joseph C. Schanubelt, ed., *Augustine in Iconography: History and Legend*. Frankfurt, Vienna and Paris: Lang, 1999, 507–47.

—. *Private Lives in Renaissance Venice: Art, Architecture, and the Family*. New Haven, CT: Yale University Press, 2004.

Franz, Rosemarie. *Der Kachelofen: Entstehung und kunstgeschichtliche Entwicklung vom Mittelalter bis zum Ausgang des Klassizismus*. Graz: Universitätsverlag, 1981.

Friedmann, Herbert. *A Bestiary for Saint Jerome. Animal Symbolism in European Religious Art*. Washington DC: Smithsonian Institution Press, 1980.

Fuchs, Leonhart. *New Kreüterbu[o]ch*. Basel: Isengrin, 1543.

Fürst, Alfons, ed. *Hieronymus. Askese und Wissenschaft in der Spätantike*. Freiburg, Basel and Vienna: Herder, 2016.

Gaab, Hans. *Die Sterne über Nürnberg: Albrecht Dürer und seine Himmelskarten von 1515*. Petersberg: Michael Imhof Verlag, 2015.

Gabbarelli, Jamie. *Sharing Images: Renaissance Prints into Maiolica and Bronze*. Washington DC: National Gallery of Art, 2017.

Gaimster, David. 'Material Culture, Archaeology and Defining Modernity: Case Studies in Ceramic Research'. In Gerritsen and Riello, eds, *Writing Material Culture History*. 56–66.

Gaimster, David and Roberta Gilchrist, eds. *The Archaeology of the Reformation 1480–1580*. London: Routledge, 2017.

Gamber, Ortwin. 'Der Turnierharnisch zur Zeit König Maximilians I. und das *Thunsche Skizzenbuch*'. *Jahrbuch der Kunsthistorischen Sammlungen in Wien* 53.1 (1957), 33–70.

Garzelli, Annarosa. 'Sulla fortuna del 'Gerolamo' mediceo del van Eyck nell'arte fiorentina del Quattrocento'. In *Scritti di Storia dell'arte in onore di Roberto Salvini*. Florence: Sansoni, 1984, 347–53.

Geddes, Leslie. *Watermarks: Leonardo da Vinci and the Mastery of Nature*. Princeton, NJ: Princeton University Press, 2020.

Gemeinhardt, Peter. *Antonius, der erste Mönch: Leben, Lehre, Askese*. Munich: Beck, 2013.

Gerritsen, Anne and Giorgio Riello, eds. *The Global Lives of Things: The Material Culture of Connections in the Early Modern World*. London: Routledge, 2016.

—. *Writing Material Culture History*. London: Bloomsbury, 2021.

Giehlow, Karl. 'Dürers Stich, "Melencolia I" und der maximilianische Humanistenkreis'. *Mitteilungen der* Gesellschaft *für vervielfältigende Kunst* 26. 2 (1903), 29–41.

Gill, Meredith J. 'Reformations: The Painted Interiors of Augustine and Jerome'. In Karla Pollmann and Meredith Gill, eds. *Augustine beyond the Book: Intermediality, Transmediality, and Reception*. Leiden and Boston Brill, 2012, 60–94.

Gombrich, Ernst H. *The Sense of Order: A Study in the Psychology of Decorative Art*. Oxford: Phaidon, 1979.

Gormans, Andreas, and Thomas Lentes, eds. *Das Bild der Erscheinung: die Gregorsmesse im Mittelalter*. Berlin: Reimer, 2007.

Gouk, Penelope. *The Ivory Sundials of Nuremberg, 1500–1700*. Cambridge: Whipple Museum for the History of Science, 1988.

Griffiths, Antony. *The Print Before Photography: An Introduction to European Printmaking 1550–1820*. London: British Museum, 2016.

Griggs, Robert. 'Studies on Dürer's Diary of His Journey to the Netherlands: The Distribution of the "Melencolia I"'. *Zeitschrift für Kunstgeschichte* 49.3 (1986), 398–409.

Guérout, Max. 'Sixteenth-century French Naval Guns'. In Carlo Beltrame and Renato Gianni Ridella, eds, *Ships and Guns: The Sea Ordinance in Venice and Europe between the 15th and the 17th Centuries*. Havertown, PA: Oxbow Books, 2011, 124–31.

Gulden, Sebastian. 'An Ideal Neighbourhood: The Physical Environment of the Early Dürer as a Space of Experience'. In Hess and Eser, eds, *The Early Dürer*, 29–38.

—. 'Dürer's Neighborhood ("Map of the Neighborhood")'. In Hess and Eser, eds, *The Early Dürer*, 596–603.

—. 'Nuremberg's Elites: Dürer's Models and Commissioners'. In Hess and Eser, eds, *The Early Dürer*, 286–95.

Haag, Sabine, Alfried Wieczorek, Matthias Pfaffenbicher and Hans-Jürgen Buderer, eds. *Kaiser Maximilian I. Der letzte Ritter und das höfische Turnier*. Regensburg: Schnell and Steiner, 2014.

Hahn, Cynthia. *The Reliquary Effect: Enshrining the Sacred Object*. London: Reaktion, 2017.

Hale, John Rigby. *Artists and Warfare in the Renaissance*. New Haven, CT: Yale University Press, 1990.

Hall, Edwin. 'Cardinal Albergati, St. Jerome and the Detroit Van Eyck'. *The Art Quarterly* 31.1 (1968), 2–34.

—. 'More About the Detroit Van Eyck: The Astrolabe, The Congress of Arras and Cardinal Albergati'. *The Art Quarterly* 34 (1971), 180–201.

Hallenkamp-Lumpe, Julia. *Studien zur Ofenkeramik des 12. bis 17. Jahrhunderts anhand von Bodenfunden aus Westfalen-Lippe*. Mainz: Zabern, 2006.

Hamburger, Jeffrey. *The Visual and the Visionary: Art and Female Spirituality in Late Medieval Germany*. New York, NY: Zone Books, 1998.

Hanß, Stefan. 'Digital Microscopy and Early Modern Embroidery'. In Gerritsen and Riello, eds, *Writing Material Culture History*, 214–21.

—. 'The Fetish of Accuracy: Perspectives on Early Modern Time(s)'. *Past & Present* 243 (2019), 267–84.

—. 'Face-Work: Making Hair Matter in Sixteenth-Century Central Europe'. *Gender and History* 33. 2 (2021), 314–45.

—. 'Making Featherwork in Early Modern Europe'. In Susanne Burghartz, Lucas Burkart, Christine Göttler and Ulinka Rublack, eds, *Materialized Identities in Early Modern Culture, 1450–1750: Objects, Affects, Effects*. Amsterdam: Amsterdam University Press, 2021, 137–85.

—. 'New World Feathers and the Matter of Early Modern Ingenuity: Digital Microscopes, Period Hands, and Period Eyes'. In Oosterhoff, López and Marr, eds, *Ingenuity in the Making: Materials and Technique in Early Modern Europe*, 189–202.

Harvey, Karen, ed. *History and Material Culture: A Student's Guide to Approaching Alternative Sources*. London: Routledge, 2017.

Hasselmeyer, Lothar. 'Sanduhren aus Nürnberg'. *Deutsche Gesellschaft für Chronometrie* 51 (2012), 51–82.

Hauschke, Sven. 'Globen und wissenschaftliche Instrumente: Die europäischen Höfe als Kunden Nürnberger Mathematiker'. In Maué, Eser, Hauschke and Stolzenberger, *Quasi Centrum Europae*, 365–89.

Hayum, Andrée. 'Dürer's Portrait of Erasmus and the Ars Typographorum'. *Renaissance Quarterly* 38.4 (1985), 650–87.

Heal, Bridget. *The Cult of the Virgin Mary in Early Modern Germany: Protestant and Catholic Piety, 1500–1648*. Cambridge: Cambridge University Press, 2014.

Hecht, Christian. 'Der Hl. Hieronymus im 16. Jahrhundert. Theologische Aspekte seines Bildes in der frühen Neuzeit'. In Meighörner and Thum, *Hieronymus in der Wildernis*, 20–27.

Heege, Eva Roth. *Ofenkeramik und Kachelofen: Typologie, Terminologie und Rekonstruktion*. Basel: Schweizerischer Burgenverein, 2012.

Heikamp, Detlef. 'Dürers Entwürfe für Geweihleuchter'. *Zeitschrift für Kunstgeschichte* 23.1 (1960), 42–55.

Helms, Mary. *Ulysses' Sail: An Ethnographic Odyssey of Power, Knowledge, and Geographical Distance*. Princeton, NJ: Princeton University Press, 1988.

Hernad, Béatrice. *Die Graphiksammlung des Humanisten Hartmann Schedel*. Munich: Prestel, 1990.

Heuer, Christopher. 'Evaporating Dürer'. *Grey Room* 85 (2021), 40–69.

Hess, Daniel, Dagmar Hirschfelder and Katja von Baum, eds. *Die Gemälde des Spätmittelalters im Germanischen Nationalmuseum*. Regensburg: Schnell & Steiner, 2019.

Hess, Daniel, and Thomas Eser, eds. *The Early Dürer*. Nuremberg: Verlag des Germanischen Nationalmuseums / Thames and Hudson, 2002.

Hind, Arthur M. *Early Italian Engraving: A Critical Catalogue*. 7 vols. London: Bernard Quaritch, 1938–48.

Hoff, Ursula. 'The Thomas D. Barlow Collection of Dürer's Engravings and Woodcuts'. *Annual Bulletin of the National Gallery of Victoria* 1 (1959), 15–20.

—. 'Thomas Barlow, Dürer Collector'. In Irena Zdanowicz, ed., *Albrecht Dürer in the Collection of the National Gallery of Victoria*. Melbourne: The National Gallery of Victoria, 1996, 83–85.

Holmes, M. R. 'The so-called "Bellarmine" Mask on Imported Rhenish Stoneware'. *The Antiquaries Journal* 31.3–4 (1951), 173–9.

'Housing a Famous Collection: Whitworth Gallery Print Room Two Years' Work Cases Made and Painted by the Staff'. The *Manchester Guardian*, 11 March 1927, 13.

Hutchinson, Jane Campbell. *Albrecht Dürer: A Biography*. Princeton, NJ: Princeton University Press, 1990.

Inglis, Alison and John Poynter. 'Desirable Things, The Private Collection of Alfred Felton'. *Art Journal of the National Gallery of Victoria* 44 (2014).

Ingold, Tim. *The Life of Lines*. London: Routledge, 2015.

Jeep, John M., ed. *Medieval Germany: An Encyclopaedia*. Abingdon: Routledge, 2019.

Jenkins, Catherine, Nadine Orenstein and Freyda Spira, eds. *The Renaissance of Etching*. New York, NY: Metropolitan Museum of Art, 2019.

Johnston, Sky Michael. 'Printing the Weather: Knowledge, Nature and Popular Culture in Two Sixteenth-Century German Weather Books'. *Renaissance Quarterly* 73.2 (2020), 391–440.

Jolly, Penny Howell. 'Antonello da Messina's "Saint Jerome in his Study": A Disguised Portrait?', *Burlington Magazine* 128 (1982), 26–9.

—. 'Antonello da Messina's Saint Jerome in His Study: An Iconographic Analysis'. *The Art Bulletin* 65.2 (1983), 238–53.

Kahsnitz, Rainer, and William D. Wixom, eds. *Gothic and Renaissance Art in Nuremberg, 1300–1550*. Munich: Prestel-Verlag; New York, NY: Metropolitan Museum of Art, 1986.

Kammel, Frank Matthias. 'Kaiser Sigismund und die Reichstadt Nürnberg: Künsthistorische Zeugnisse der Beziehung und des Nachruhms'. In Imre Takács, ed., *Sigismundus Rex et Imperator: Kunst und Kultur zur Zeit Sigismunds von Luxemburg 1387–1437*. Mainz: Philipp von Zabern, 2006, 480–6.

Kauffman, Hans. 'Dürers "Nemesis"'. In *Tymbos für Wilhelm Ahlmann: Ein Gedenkbuch*. Berlin: De Gruyter, 1951, 135–59.

Keen, Ralph. 'Johannes Cochlaeus: An Introduction to his Life and Work'. In Johannes Cochlaeus, *Brevis Germaniae descriptio*, ed. and trans. Karl Langosch. Darmstadt: Wissenschaftliche Buchgesellschaft, 1976.

Kemp, Martin. *The Science of Art: Optical Themes in Western Art from Brunelleschi to Seurat*. New Haven, CT: Yale University Press, 1990.

Kempis, Thomas à. *De imitatione Christi*. Nuremberg: Anton Koberger, 1492.

—. *The Imitation of Christ: Four Books*, trans. William Benham. London: J. C. Nimmo, 1886.

Kessler, Herbert L. *Seeing Medieval Art*. Peterborough, Ontario: Broadview Press, 2004.

—. 'Face and Firmament: Dürer's *An Angel with the Sudarium* and the Limit of Vision'. In Christopher Frommel and Gerhard Wolf, eds. *L'immagine di Christo*. Vatican City: Biblioteca Apostolica Vaticana, 2006, 143–65.

—. 'Veronica's Textile'. In Debra Taylor Cashion, Henry Luttikhuizen and Ashley D. West, eds. *The Primacy of the Image in Northern European Art, 1400–1700: Essays in Honor of Larry Silver*. Leiden: Brill, 2017, 125–37.

Keunecke, Hans-Otto. 'Friedrich Peypus (1485–1535): Zu Leben und Werk des Nürnberger Buchdruckers und Buchhändlers'. *Mitteilungen des Vereins für Geschichte der Stadt Nürnberg* 72 (1985), 1–65.

Kiening, Christian. 'Mediating the Passion in Time and Space'. In Christian Kienig and Martina Stercken, eds., *Temporality and Mediality in Late Medieval and Early Modern Culture*. Turnhout: Brepols, 2018, 115–46.

Kim, David. 'Gentile in Red'. *I Tatti Studies in the Italian Renaissance* 18.1 (2015), 157–92.

Klee, Paul. 'Schöpferische Konfession'. In Paul Klee, *Kunst-Lehre: Aufsätze, Vorträge, Rezensionen und Beiträge zur bildnerischen Formlehre*. Leipzig: Reclam, 1987, 60–6.

Klibanksy, Raymond, Erwin Panowsky and Fritz Saxl. *Saturn and Melancholy: Studies in the History of Natural Philosophy. Religion, and Art*. Montreal and Kingston: McGill-Queen's University Press, 2019.

Koerner, Joseph Leo. *The Moment of Self-Portraiture in German Renaissance Art*. Chicago, IL: University of Chicago Press, 1993.

—. 'Dürer in Motion'. In Foister and van den Brink, eds, *Dürer's Journeys*, 43–57.

—. 'The Fortune of Dürer's "Nemesis"'. In Walter Haug and Burghart Wachinger, eds, *Fortuna*. Berlin: De Gruyter, 2018, 239–94.

Kohlhaussen, Heinrich. *Nürnberger Goldschmiedekunst des Mittelalters und der Dürerzeit, 1240 bis 1540*. Berlin: Deutscher Verlag für Kunstwissenschaft, 1968.

Koreny, Fritz. *Albrecht Dürer und die Tier- und Pflanzenstudien der Renaissance*. Munich: Prestel, 1985.

Koslofsky, Craig. 'The Kiss of Peace in the German Reformation'. In Karen Harvey, ed., *The Kiss in History*. Manchester: Manchester University Press, 2005, 12–32.

Krause, Stefan. 'Die ritterspiel als ritter Freydalb hat gethon aus retterlichem grnute'. In Sabine Haug, Alfried Wieczorek, Matthias Pfaffenbicher and Hans-Jürgen Buderer, eds, *Kaiser Maximilian I. Der letzte Ritter und das höfische Turnier*. Regensburg: Schnell and Steiner, 2014, 173–86.

—. *Freydal. Medieval Games: The Book of Tournaments of Emperor Maximilian I*. Cologne: Taschen, 2019.

Kress, Berthold. *Divine Diagrams: The Manuscripts and Drawings of Paul Lautensack (1477/78–1558)*. Leiden: Brill, 2014.

Kuder, Ulrich, ed. *Des Menschen Gemüt ist wandelbar. Druckgraphik der Dürer-Zeit*. Kiel: Kunsthalle, 2004.

Kuder, Ulrich. *Dürers 'Hieronymus im Gehäus', der Heilige im Licht*. Hamburg: Kovač, 2013.

Künast, Hans-Jörg. 'Die Graphiksammlung des Augsburger Stadtschreibers Konrad Peutinger'. In John Roger Pass, ed., *Augsburg, die Bilderfabrik Europas. Essays zur Augsburger Druckgraphik der Frühen Neuzeit*. Augsburg: Wißner-Verlag, 2001, 11–19, 123–4.

Künzle, Pius. *Heinrich Seuses Horologium Sapientiae*. Freiburg: Universitätsverlag Freiburg-Schweiz, 1977.

Lanckorańska, Maria. 'Die zeitgeschichtliche Komponente in Dürers Kupferstich "Nemesis"'. *Gutenberg-Jahrbuch* 53 (1978), 286–96.

Landau, David and Peter Parshall. *The Renaissance Print, 1470–1550*. New Haven, CT: Yale University Press, 1994.

Lange-Krach, Heidrun. *Das Gebetbuch Kaiser Maximilians I: meisterhafte Zeichnungen der deutschen Renaissance*. Lucerne: Quaternio Verlag, 2017.

Lange-Krach, Heidrun, ed. *Maximilian I. (1459–1519): Kaiser, Ritter, Bürger zu Augsburg*. Augsburg: Maximilianmuseum, 2019.

—. *Stiften gehen! Wie man aus Not eine Tugend macht*. Regensburg: Verlag Schnell und Steiner, 2021.

Lassnig, Ewald. 'Dürers *Melencolia-I* und die Erkenntnistheorie bei Ulrich Pinder: Versuch einer Interpretation aus einer naheliegenden Quelle'. *Wiener Jahrbuch für Kunstgeschichte* 57.1 (2019), 51–96.

Leahy, Cathy, Jennifer Spinks and Charles Zika, eds. *The Four Horsemen: Apocalypse, Death and Disaster*. Melbourne: National Gallery of Victoria, 2012.

Lemire, Beverly. *Global Trade and the Transformation of Consumer Cultures: The Material World Remade, c. 1500–1820*. Cambridge: Cambridge University Press, 2018.

Lentes, Thomas. 'Verum Corpus und Vera Imago. Kalkulierte Bildbeziehung in der Gregorsmesse'. In Andreas Gormans and Thomas Lentes, eds, *Das Bild der Erscheinung: die Gregorsmesse im Mittelalter*. Berlin: Reimer, 2007, 13–36.

Levy, Michael, and Charles Reginald Dodwell. *Essays on Dürer*. Manchester: Manchester University Press, 1973.

Lichtert, Katrien, and Alexandra Van Dongen. *De Blik van Dürer. Albrecht Dürers reis door de Nederlanden (1520–1521)*. Veurne: Hannibal, 2021.

Liebenwein, Wolfgang. *Studiolo. Zur Entstehung eines Raumtyps und seiner Entwicklung*. Berlin: Mann, 1977.

'Love Apples'. *The Medieval Garden Enclosed. The Metropolitan Museum of Art*. 19 April 2012. https://blog.metmuseum.org/cloistersgardens/2012/04/19/love-apples/ [accessed 21 March 2022].

Luber, Katherine. *Albrecht Dürer and the Venetian Renaissance*. Cambridge: Cambridge University Press, 2005.

Luther, Martin. *Annotierungen zu den Werken des Hieronymus*, ed. Martin Brecht. Weimar and Vienna: Böhlau, 2000.

Mack, Rosamund. *Bazaar to Piazza: Islamic Trade and Italian Art, 1300–1600*. Berkeley, CA: University of California Press, 2002.

Maclehose, William F. 'Captivating Thoughts: Nocturnal Pollution, Imagination and the Sleeping Mind in the Twelfth and Thirteenth Centuries'. *Journal of Medieval History* 46.1 (2020), 98–131.

Madersbacher, Lukas and Erwin Pokorny, eds. *Maximilianus: Die Kunst des Kaisers*. Berlin and Munich: Deutscher Kunstverlag, 2019.

Marincola, D. Michele and Lucretia Kargerè. *The Conservation of Medieval Polychrome Wood Sculpture: History, Theory, Practice*. Los Angeles, CA: The Getty Conservation Institute, 2020.

Marr, Alexander. 'Ingenuity in Nuremberg: Dürer and Stabius's Instrument Prints'. *The Art Bulletin* 100.3 (2018), 48–79.

Marr, Alexander, Raphaële Garrod, José Ramón Marcaida López and Richard J. Oosterhoff. *Logodaedalus: Word Histories of Ingenuity in Early Modern Europe*. Pittsburgh, PA: University of Pittsburgh Press, 2018.

Maué, Hermann, Thomas Eser, Sven Hauschke and Jana Stolzenberger. *Quasi Centrum Europæ: Europa kauft in Nürnberg 1400–1800*. Nuremberg: Germanisches Nationalmuseum, 2002.

Mauquoy-Hendrickx, Marie. *Les estampes des Wierix conserves au Cabinet des Estampes de la Bibliothèque royale Albert [ler]*. 3 vols. Brussels: Bibliothèque royale Albert [ler], 1982–83.

McColl, Donald A. 'Agony in the Garden: Dürer's "Crisis of the Image"'. In Silver and Smith, eds, *The Essential Dürer*, 166–84.

McDonald, Mark. *Ferdinand Columbus: Renaissance Collector (1488–1539)*. London: British Museum, 2005.

—. 'The Physical Life of the Print Collection and Ferdinand's Universal Library'. In Mark Macdonald, ed., *The Print Collection of Ferdinand Columbus (1488–1539): A Renaissance Collector in Sevilla*, 2 vols. London: British Museum, 2004.

Meder, Joseph. *Dürer-Katalog: ein Handbuch über Albrecht Dürers Stiche, Radierungen, Holzschnitte, deren Zustände, Ausgaben und Wasserzeichen*. Vienna: Gilhofer & Rauschburg, 1932.

Meier, Esther. *Die Gregorsmesse: Funktionen eines spätmittelalterlichen Bildtypus*. Cologne: Böhlau, 2006.

Meighörner, Wolfgang and Agnes Thum, eds. *Cranach natürlich. Hieronymus in der Wildernis*. Innsbruck: Haymon, 2018.

Melion, Walter. 'Hendrick Goltzius's Project of Reproductive Engraving'. *Art History* 13.4 (1990), 458–87.

Mende, Matthias. 'Bukephalos und Alexander der Große? zur inhaltlichen Deutung von Albrecht Dürers Kupferstich "Das kleine Pferd" (B. 96)'. In Bodo Brinkmann and Hartmut Krohm, eds, *Aus Albrect Dürers Welt, Festschrift für Fedja Anzelewsky*. Turnhout: Brepols, 2001, 69–75.

—. 'Hieronymus im Gehäus'. In Schoch, Mende and Scherbaum, eds, *Albrecht Dürer*, I, 174–8.

Mende, Ursula. *Die Mittelalterlichen Bronzen im Germanischen Nationalmuseum: Bestandskatalog*. Nürnberg: Germanisches Nationalmuseum, 2013.

Merback, Mitchell B. *Perfection's Therapy: An Essay on Albrecht Dürer's Melencolia I*. New York, NY: Zone, 2017.

—. *The Thief, the Cross and the Wheel: Pain and the Spectacle of Punishment in Medieval and Renaissance Europe*. Chicago, IL: The University of Chicago Press, 1999.

Metzger, Christof. *Daniel Hopfer: ein Augsburger Meister der Renaissance. Eisenradierungen, Holzschnitte, Zeichnungen, Waffenätzungen*. Munich: Staatliche Graphische Sammlung, Deutscher Kunstverlag, 2009.

—. 'The Iron Age: The Beginnings of Etching about 1500'. In Jenkins, Orenstein and Spira, eds, *The Renaissance of Etching*, 25–31.

Metzger, Christof, ed. *Albrecht Dürer*. Vienna: Albertina / Munich: Prestel, 2019.

Meurer, Suzanne. 'Translating the Hand into Print: Johan Neudörffer's Etched Writing Manual.' *Renaissance Quarterly* 75.2 (2022), 403–58.

Mezquita Mesa, Teresa. 'El Códice de Trajes de la Biblioteca Nacional de España'. *Goya: revista de Arte* 346 (2014), 16–41.

Michel, Eva and Maria Luise Sternrath, eds. *Emperor Maximilian I and the Age of Dürer*. Vienna: Albertina / Munich: Prestel, 2012.

Miller, Gregory. *The Turks and Islam in Reformation Germany*. New York, NY: Routledge, 2021.

Minges, Klaus. *Das Sammlungswesen der frühen Neuzeit. Kriterien der Ordnung und Spezialisierung*, Münster: LIT, 1998.

Mitius, Otto. 'Die Landschaft auf Dürers Eisenradierung *Die große Kanone* vom Jahre 1518'. *Mitteilungen aus dem germanischen Nationalmuseum* (1911), 141–9.

Morrall, Andrew. 'Domestic Decoration and the Bible'. In Kevin Killeen, Helen Smith and Rachel Judith Willie, eds, *The Oxford Handbook of the Bible in Early Modern England, c.1530–1700*. Oxford: Oxford University Press, 2018, 577–97.

Morris, David. 'The Clough Collection of Prints at the Whitworth Institute'. *Bulletin of The John Rylands Library* 92.2 (2016), 168–85.

Mossman, Stephen. *Rulman Merswin and the Knights Hospitaller: Literary Spirituality and Urban Religion in Medieval Germany*. Unpublished monograph.

Müller, Matthias, et al., eds. *Apelles am Fürstenhof. Facetten der Hofkunst um 1500 im Alten Reich*. Coburg: Kunstsammlungen der Veste Coburg / Berlin: Lukas, 2010.

Muller, Heinrich. *Albrecht Dürer: Waffen und Rüstungen*. Mainz: Zabern, 2002.

Mummenhoff, Erich. 'Die Anbringung des Viertelschlagwerks an der Turmuhr bei St. Sebald'. *Mitteilungen des Vereins für Geschichte der Stadt Nürnberg* 7 (1888), 271–2.

Murphy, Hannah. *A New Order of Medicine: The Rise of Physicians in Reformation Nuremberg*. Pittsburgh, PA: University of Pittsburgh Press, 2019.

—. 'From Scribal Marks to Calligraphic Signatures? Print, Scribe, and Script in Early Modern European Writing Manuals'. In Christopher D. Bahl and Stefan Hanß, eds, *Scribal Practice and the Global Cultures of Colophons, 1400–1800*. Basingstoke: Palgrave Macmillan, 2022, 155–75.

Murphy, Amanda, Herbert L. Kessler, Marco Petoletti, Eamon Duffy, and Guido Milanese, eds. *The European Fortune of the Roman Veronica in the Middle Ages*. Turnhout: Brepols, 2017.

Nagel, Alexander and Christopher S. Wood. *Anachronic Renaissance*. New York, NY: Zone, 2010.

Nebelsick, Louis D., and Tomoko Emmerling. '"Finding Luther": Towards an Archaeology of the Reformer and the Earliest Reformation'. *Church History* 86.4 (2017), 1155–207.

Necipoglu, Gülru. 'Süleyman the Magnificent and the Representation of Power in the Context of Ottoman-Habsburg-Papal Rivalry'. *The Art Bulletin* 71.3 (1989), 401–27.

Nickel, Helmut. 'Arms and Armor from the Permanent Collection'. *Metropolitan Museum of Art Bulletin* 49.1 (1991), 1–67.

Norman, Alexander. 'Albrecht Dürer: Armour and Weapons'. *Apollo* 94.113 (1971), 36–9.

Oakes, S. P. 'A New Proposal for Dürer's Drawing of "a house in Venice"'. *Apollo* 155.481 (2002), 3–10.

Oberhammer, Vinzenz. *Die Bronzestandbilder des Maximiliangrabmales in der Hofkirche zu Innsbruck*. Innsbruck: Tyrolia-Verlag, 1935.

O'Malley, Michelle and Evelyn Welch. *The Material Renaissance*. Manchester: Manchester University Press, 2007.

Oosterhoff, Richard J. and José Ramón Marcaida López, eds. *Ingenuity in the Making: Matter and Technique in Early Modern Europe*. Pittsburgh, PA: University of Pittsburgh Press, 2021.

Ose, Ieva. *Stove Tile Ceramics of the Turaida Castle, 16th–18th Century. The Catalogue*. Riga: Turaidas muzejrezervāts., Latvijas vēstures institūta apgāds, 2013.

Panofsky, Erwin. '"Nebulae in Pariete"; Notes on Erasmus' Eulogy on Dürer'. *Journal of the Warburg and Courtauld Institutes* 14.1/2 (1951), 34–41.

—. *Life and Art of Albrecht Dürer.* (1st edn., 1955) Princeton, NJ: Princeton University Press, 2005.

—. '"Virgo & Victrix": A Note on Dürer's *Nemesis*'. In Carl Zigrosser, ed., *Prints.* London: Peter Owen, 1962, 13–38.

Panofsky, Erwin, and Fritz Saxl. *Dürers Melencolia I: Eine quellen- und typengeschichtliche Untersuchung.* Leipzig: Teubner, 1923.

Parshall, Peter. 'Art and the Theater of Knowledge: The Origins of Print Collecting in Northern Europe'. *Harvard University Art Museums Bulletin* 2.3 (1994), 7–36.

—. 'Graphic Knowledge: Albrecht Dürer and the Imagination'. *Art Bulletin* 95.3 (2013), 392–410.

Passarge, Walter. *Das deutsche Vesperbild im Mittelalter.* Cologne: F. J. Marcan, 1924.

Pease, Arthus Stanley. 'Medical Allusions in the Works of St. Jerome'. *Harvard Studies in Classical Philology* 18 (1914), 73–86.

Pettegree, Andrew. *The Book in the Renaissance.* New Haven, CT: Yale University Press, 2010.

Petz, Hans. 'Urkundliche Nachrichten über den literarischen Nachlass Regiomontans und B. Walthers 1478–1522'. *Mitteilungen des Vereins für Geschichte der Stadt Nürnberg* 7 (1888), 237–62.

Pfaffenbichler, Matthias. 'Maximilian I. und das höfische Turnier'. In Sabine Haag, Alfried Wieczorek, Matthias Pfaffenbicher and Hans-Jürgen Buderer, eds, *Kaiser Maximilian I. Der letzte Ritter und das höfische Turnier.* Regensburg: Schnell and Steiner, 2014, 129–65.

Pilkington, Margaret. 'Letter to the Editor: Sir Thomas Barlow'. The *Guardian*, 27 November 1964, 8.

Pilz, Kurt. 'Der Goldschmied Albrecht Dürer d. Ä.: Ein Beitrag zur Identifikation seiner Arbeiten und der Bildnisse, die ihn darstellen'. *Mitteilungen des Vereins für die Geschichte der Stadt Nürnberg* 72 (1985), 67–74.

Plutarch. *Plutarchvs Chaeronevs: De compescenda Ira (...)*, trans. Willibald Pirckheimer. Nuremberg: Peypus, 1523.

—. *Moralia*, vol. 6, trans. William C. Helmbold. Cambridge, MA: Harvard University Press, 1939.

Poliziano, Angelo. *Silvæ*, trans. and ed. Charles Fantazzi. Cambridge, MA: I Tatti Library, 2004.

Pollak, Martha. *Cities at War in Early Modern Europe.* Cambridge: Cambridge University Press, 2010.

Pon, Lisa. *Raphael, Dürer, and Marcantonio Raimondi: Copying and the Italian Renaissance Print.* New Haven, CT: University Press, 2004.

Pope, Stephanie. 'Powder for Hourglasses'. In Pamela H. Smith et al., eds, *Secrets of Craft and Nature in Renaissance France: A Digital Critical Edition and English Translation of BnF Ms. Fr. 640.* New York, NY: Making and Knowing Project, 2015. https://edition640.makingandknowing.org/#/essays/ann_021_sp_15.

Preising, Dagmar, Ulrike Villwock and Christine Vogt. *Albrecht Dürer: Apelles des Schwarz-Weiss.* Aachen: Suermondt-Ludwig-Museum, 2005.

Price, David Hotchkiss. *Albrecht Dürer's Renaissance: Humanism, Reformation, and the Art of Faith.* Ann Arbor, MI: University of Michigan Press, 2003.

Prinz, Wolfram and Roland G. Kecks. *Das französische Schloss der Renaissance. Form und Bedeutung der Architektur, ihre geschichtlichen und gesellschaftlichen Grundlagen*, 2nd edn. Berlin: Mann, 1994.

Proctor, Caroline. 'Between Medicine and Morals: Sex in the Regimens of Maino de Manieri'. In April Harper and Caroline Proctor, eds, *Medieval Sexuality: A Casebook.* London: Routledge, 2007, 113–31.

Puppi, Lionello. 'Antonello da Messina. Esercizio di Lettura di un ritratto "nascosto"'. In Barbera, Giocchino, ed., *Antonello da Messina. San Girolamo nello studio.* Messina: Museo regionale di Messina, 2006, 21–30.

Radway, Robyn. *In the Name of Saint George: Ivory Saddles from the Fifteenth Century.* Honors thesis, University of Central Florida, 2009.

Ravà, Aldo. 'Il "Camerino delle antigaglie" di Gabirele Vendramin'. *Nuovo Arcivio Veneto* n.s. 39 (1920), 155–81.

Rebenich, Stefan. *Jerome.* London: Routledge, 2002.

Remond, Jaya. 'Distributing Dürer in the Netherlands: Gifts, Prints, and the Mediation of Fame in the Early Sixteenth Century'. In Grażyna Jurkowlaniec, Ika Matyjaszkiewicz and Zuzanna Sarnecka, eds, *The Agency of Things in Early Modern Art.* New York: Routledge, 2018, 117–26.

Rice, Eugene F. *Saint Jerome in the Renaissance.* Baltimore, MD: John Hopkins University Press, 1988.

Richter, Leonhard G. *Dürer-Code. Albrecht Dürers entschlüsselte Meisterstiche.* Dettelbach: Röll, 2014.

—. 'Hieronymus im Gehäus. Ein metaphysischer Zugang zu Albrecht Dürer'. *Perspektiven der Philosophie* 38 (2012), 125–49.

Ridderbos, Herman N. B. *Saint and Symbol, Images of Saint Jerome in Early Italian Art.* Groningen: Bouma, 1984.

Riese, Adam. *Rechnung auff der Linien (...).* Nuremberg: Peypus, 1527.

Roberts, Lissa, Simon Schaffer and Peter Dear, eds. *The Mindful Hand: Inquiry and Invention from the Late Renaissance to Early Industrialisation.* Amsterdam: Koninklijke Nederlandse Akad. van Wetenschappen, 2007.

Robison, Andrew, ed. *Albrecht Dürer: Master Drawings, Watercolors and Prints from the Albertina.* Washington DC: National Gallery, 2013.

Rodini, Elizabeth. 'Describing Narrative in Gentile Bellini's *Procession in Piazza San Marco*'. *Art History* 21 (1998), 26–44.

Rooney, David. *About Time: A History of Civilization in Twelve Clocks.* London: Viking, 2021.

Rowlands, John. *The Graphic Work of Albrecht Dürer.* London: British Museum, 1971.

Rowlands, John and Giulia Bartrum. *The Age of Dürer and Holbein: German Drawings 1400-1550.* London: British Museum, 1988.

Rublack, Ulinka. 'Fluxes: The Early Modern Body and the Emotions'. *History Workshop Journal* 53 (2002), 1-16.

—. *Dressing Up: Cultural Identity in Renaissance Europe*. Oxford: Oxford University Press, 2010.

—. 'Matter in the Material Renaissance'. *Past & Present* 219.1 (2013), 41-85.

Rublack, Ulinka and Maria Hayward, eds. *The First Book of Fashion: The Book of Clothes of Matthäus and Veit Konrad Schwarz of Augsburg*. London: Bloomsbury, 2015.

Rücker, Elisabeth. *Hartmann Schedels Weltchronik. Das größte Buchunternehmung der Dürer-Zeit*. Munich: Prestel, 1988.

Rudy, Kathryn M. 'Kissing Images, Unfurling Rolls, Measuring Wounds, Sewing Badges and Carrying Talismans: Considering Some Harley Manuscripts through the Physical Rituals they Reveal'. *Electronic British Library Journal* (2011), 1-56.

—. *Rubrics, Images and Indulgences in Late Medieval Netherlandish Manuscripts*. Leiden: Brill, 2017.

Rupprich, Hans. 'Dürer, Albrecht der Ältere'. In *Neue Deutsche Biographie*, vol. 4. Berlin: Duncker & Humblot, 1959, 163-4.

Rupprich, Hans, ed. *Dürer: Schriftlicher Nachlass*. 3 vols. Berlin: Deutscher Verein für Kunstwissenschaft, 1956-69.

Russell, Gordon. 'Sir Thomas [Tommy] Dalmahoy Barlow 1883-1964'. In *Oxford Dictionary of National Biography*. Oxford: Oxford University Press, 2004.

Russo, Daniel. *Saint Jérôme en Italie, étude iconographique et de spiritualité (XIIIe – Xve siècle)*. Paris: La Découverte, 1987.

Rylff, Walther H. *Lustgarten der Gesundheit (...)*. Frankfurt: Egenolff, 1546.

Sakuma, Hironobu. *Die Nürnberger Tuchmacher, Weber, Färber und Bereiter vom 14. bis 17. Jahrhundert*. Nuremberg: Stadtarchiv Nürnberg, 1993.

Sander, Jochen, ed. *Albrecht Dürer: His Art in Context*. Frankfurt: Städel Museum / Prestel, 2013.

Sarti, Raffaella. *Europe at Home: Family and Material Culture, 1500-1800*. New Haven, CT: Yale University Press, 2002.

Scaliger, Julius C. *De Subtilitate (...)*. Frankfurt a. M.: Wechel, 1582.

Schauerte, Thomas. 'Annäherung an ein Phantom. Maximilians I. Grabmal im Kontext europäischer Traditionen'. In Heinz Noflatscher, Michael Chisholm, and Bertram Schnerb, eds, *Maximilian I. (1459-1519). Wahrnehmung-Übersetzungen-Gender*. Innsbruck: Innsbrucker Historische Studien, 2011, 373-400.

—. *Die Ehrenpforte für Kaiser Maximilian I.* Munich: Deutscher Kunstverlag, 2001.

—. *Dürer als Zeitzeuge der Reformation: neuer Geist und neuer Glaube*. Nuremberg: Museen der Stadt Nürnberg, 2017.

Schedel, Hartmann. *Das Buch der Chroniken [Weltchronik]*. Nuremberg: Anton Koberger, 1493.

Scheichl, Andrea. 'Who Was (or Were) Jörg Kölderer'. In Michel and Sternrath, eds, *Emperor Maximilian I and the Age of Dürer*, 80-9, 170-1.

Scheicher, Elisabeth. 'Kaiser Maximilian plant sein Grabmal'. *Jahrbuch des Kunsthistorischen Museums Wien* 1 (1999), 81-117.

Schier, Volker and Corine Schleif, 'Seeing and Singing, Touching and Tasting the Holy Lance: The Power and Politics of Embodied Religious Experiences in Nuremberg 1424-1524'. In Nicolas Bell, Claus Clüver and Nils Holger Petersen, eds, *Signs of Change: Transformations of Christian Traditions and their Representation in the Arts, 1000–2000*. Amsterdam; New York, NY: Rodopi, 2004, 401-26.

Schiller, Gertrud. *Iconography of Christian Art*, trans. Janet Seligman. 2 vols. London: Lund Humphries, 1972.

Schindler, Thomas. 'Tempus Fugit – Sanduhren als Relikte des Handwerks'. *KulturGut – Aus der Forschung des Germanischen Nationalmuseums* 27 (2010), 5-7.

Schindler, Thomas, Anke Keller and Ralf Schürer. *Zünftig! geheimnisvolles Handwerk 1500–1800*. Nuremberg: Verlag des Germanischen Nationalmuseums, 2013.

Schmidt, Suzanne Karr. 'Making Time and Space: Collecting Early Modern Printed Instruments'. In Schmidt and Wouk, eds, *Prints in Translation*, 114-35.

—. *Interactive and Sculptural Printmaking in the Renaissance*. Leiden: Brill, 2018.

Schmidt, Suzanne Karr and Edward H. Wouk, eds. *Prints in translation, 1450-1750: Image, Materiality, Space*. London: Routledge, 2017

Schmid, Wolfgang. *Dürer als Unternehmer. Kunst, Humanismus und Ökonomie in Nürnberg um 1500*. Trier: Porta Alba, 2003.

Schnelbögl, Julia. 'Die Reichskleinodien in Nurnberg, 1424-1523'. *Mitteilungen des Vereins for Geschichte der Stadt Nurnberg* 51 (1962), 78-159.

Schoch, Rainer, Matthias Mende, and Anna Scherbaum. *Albrecht Dürer: Das druckgraphische Werk*. 3 vols. Munich: Prestel, 2004.

Schröder, Eberhard. *Dürer, Kunst und Geometrie: Dürers künstlerisches Schaffen aus der Sicht seiner 'Underweysung'*. Basel: Birkhäuser Verlag, 1980.

Schuler, Carol M. 'The Seven Sorrows of the Virgin: Popular Culture and Cultic Imagery in Pre-Reformation Europe'. *Simiolus: Netherlands Quarterly for the History of Art* 21 (1992), 5-28.

Scribner, Bob. 'Ways of Seeing in the Age of Dürer'. In Eichberger and Zika, eds, *Dürer and his Culture*, 93-117, 221-28.

Seipel, Wilfried, ed. *Werke für die Ewigkeit: Kaiser Maximilian I. und Ferdinand von Tirol*. Vienna: Kunsthistorisches Museum, 2002.

Senensis, Barnardinus. *Ein allerhailsamste Warnung von der falschen Liebe dieser Werlt*. Nuremberg: Peter Wagner. 1489.

Siebenhüner, Kim. *Die Spur der Juwelen: Materielle Kultur und transkontinentale Verbindungen zwischen Indien und Europa in der Frühen Neuzeit*. Cologne: Böhlau, 2018.

Silver, Larry. 'Shining Armor: Maximilian I as Holy Roman Emperor'. *Art Institute of Chicago Museum Studies* 12 (1986), 8-29.

—. 'Germanic Patriotism in the Age of Dürer'. In Eichberger and Zika, eds, *Dürer and his Culture*, 38-68, 216-20.

—. *Marketing Maximilian: The Visual Ideology of a Holy Roman Emperor*. Princeton, NJ: Princeton University Press, 2008.

—. 'The "*Papierkaiser*": Burgkmair, Augsburg, and the Image of the Emperor'. In Michel and Sternrath, eds, *Emperor Maximilian I and the Age of Dürer*, 91-9.

Silver, Larry and Michael Cole, 'Fluid Boundaries: Formations of the Painter-Etcher'. In Cole and Viljoen, eds, *The Early Modern Painter-Etcher*, 5–35.

Silver, Larry and Jeffrey Chipps Smith, eds. *The Essential Dürer*. Philadelphia, PA: University of Pennsylvania Press, 2010.

Simons, Patricia. *The Sex of Men in Premodern Europe: A Cultural History*. Cambridge: Cambridge University Press, 2011.

Simons, Patricia and Charles Zika, 'The Visual Arts'. In Andrew Lynch and Susan Broomhall, eds, *A Cultural History of the Emotions in the Late Medieval, Reformation, and Renaissance Age*. London: Bloomsbury, 2019, 85–106.

'Sir Thomas Barlow'. The *Guardian*, 24 November 1964, 5.

Smith, Charlotte Colding. *Images of Islam, 1453–1600: Turks in Germany and Central Europe*. London: Routledge, 2014.

Smith, Jeffrey Chipps. *Nuremberg, A Renaissance City, 1500–1618*. Austin, TX: University of Texas Press, 1983.

—. 'Nuremberg and the Topographies of Expectation'. *Journal of the Northern Renaissance* 1 (2009). https://northernrenaissance.org.

—. 'Dürer and Sculpture'. In Silver and Smith, eds, *The Essential Dürer*, 74–98.

—. 'The 2010 Josephine Waters Bennett Lecture: Albrecht Dürer as Collector'. *Renaissance Quarterly* 64.1 (2011), 1–49.

—. *Dürer*. London: Phaidon, 2012.

—. *Albrecht Dürer and the Embodiment of Genius: Decorating Museums in the Nineteenth Century*. University Park, PA: Penn State University Press, 2020.

Smith, Pamela H. *The Body of the Artisan: Art and Experience in the Scientific Revolution*. Chicago, IL: University of Chicago Press, 2004.

—. *From Lived Experience to the Written Word: Reconstructing Practical Knowledge in the Early Modern World*. Chicago, IL: University of Chicago Press, 2022.

—. 'Making as Knowing: Craft as Natural Philosophy'. In Pamela H. Smith, Amy R. W. Meyers and Harold J. Cook, eds, *Ways of Making and Knowing: The Material Culture of Empirical Knowledge*. New York, NY: Bard Graduate Center, 2017, 17–47.

—. 'In a Sixteenth-Century Goldsmith's Workshop'. In Roberts, Schaffer and Dear, eds, *The Mindful Hand*, 33–58.

Smith, Pamela H., and Tonny Beentjes. 'Nature and Art, Making and Knowing: Reconstructing Sixteenth-Century Life-Casting Techniques'. *Renaissance Quarterly* 63.1 (2010), 128–79.

Sohm, Philip L. 'Dürer's "Melencolia I": The Limits of Knowledge'. *Studies in the History of Art* 9 (1980), 13–32.

Speakman Sutch, Susie and Anne-Laure van Bruaene. 'The Seven Sorrows of the Virgin Mary: Devotional Communication and Politics in the Burgundian Habsburg Low Countries, c. 1490–1520'. *Journal of Ecclesiastical History* 61 (2010), 252–78.

Spinks, Jennifer. *Monstrous Births and Visual Culture in Sixteenth-Century Germany*. London: Pickering & Chatto, 2009.

—. 'The Southern Indian "Devil in Calicut" in Early Modern Northern Europe: Images, Texts and Objects in Motion'. *Journal of Early Modern History* 18.1–2 (2014), 15–48.

Spira, Freyda. '"Wie man schrifft vn Gemalde auf stäheline eysene Waffen etzen soll": Daniel Hopfer und die geätzte Dekoration von Rüstungen'. In Christof Metzger, ed., *Daniel Hopfer: ein Augsburger Meister der Renaissance*. Munich: Staatliche Graphische Sammlung, 2009, 68–85.

—. 'Between Paper and Sword: Daniel Hofer and the Translation of Etching in Renaissance Augsburg'. In Schmidt and Wouk, eds, *Prints in Translation*, 59–73.

Stielau, Allison. 'Intent and Independence: Late Fifteenth-Century Object Engravings'. In Jeffrey Chipps Smith, ed., *Visual Acuity and the Arts of Communication in Early Modern Germany*. Farnham: Ashgate, 2014, 22–42.

Stoichiță, Victor I. *Über einige telepathische Dispositive: Vittore Carpaccios Gemäldezyklus in der Scuola degli Schiavoni in Venedig*. Munich: Zentralinstitut für Kunstgeschichte, 2016.

Strauss, Gerald. *Nuremberg in the Sixteenth Century: City Politics and Life between Middle Ages and Modern Times*. Bloomington, IN: Indiana University Press, 1976.

Strauss, Konrad. *Die Kachelkunst des 15. bis 17. Jahrhunderts in europäischen Ländern, III. Teil*. Munich: Heydenreich, 1983.

Strauss, Walter. *The Complete Engravings, Etchings and Drypoints of Albrecht Dürer*. New York, NY: Dover Publications, 1972.

—. *The Book of Hours of the Emperor Maximilian the First*. New York, NY: Abaris Books, 1974.

—. *The Complete Drawings of Albrecht Dürer*, 6 vols. New York, NY: Abaris Books, 1974.

Strauss, Walter, ed. *Albrecht Dürer, The Painter's Manual*. New York, NY: Abaris Books, 1977.

Strieder, Peter. *Dürer*, third edition. Königstein im Taunus: Verlagsbuchhandlung KG, 2012.

—. *Tafelmalerei in Nürnberg, 1350–1550*. Königstein im Taunus: K. Robert, 1993.

Strieder, Peter, Gisela Goldberg, Joseph Harnest, and Matthias Mende. *Dürer*. Augsburg: Bechtermünz, 1996.

Stumpel, Jeroen. 'Dürer and Death: On the Iconography of "Knight, Death and the Devil"'. *Simiolus: Netherlands Quarterly for the History of Art* 34.2 (2009/2010), 75–88.

—. 'Luther in Dürer's Journal: On the *Lutherklage*, its Authorship and Persecution in Antwerp'. In Foister and van den Brink, eds, *Dürer's Journeys*, 229–39.

Sullivan, Margaret. 'Alter Apelles: Dürer's 1500 Self-Portrait'. *Renaissance Quarterly* 68.4 (2015), 1161–91.

Taape, Tillmann. 'Common Medicine for the Common Man: Picturing the "Striped Layman" in Early Vernacular Print'. *Renaissance Quarterly* 74.1 (2021), 1–58.

Tacke, Andreas. 'Albrecht als Heiliger Hieronymus, damit "der Barbar überall dem Gelehrten weiche"'. In Andreas Tacke, ed., *Der Kardinal: Albrecht von Brandenburg – Renaissancefürst und Mäzen*. Regensburg: Schnell + Steiner, 2006, 116–29.

—. 'Nicht nur der Löwe hinkte. Interpretationsversuch zu Cranachs "Albrecht als Hieronymus"- Gemälden'. In Wolfgang Meighörner and Agnes Thum, eds, *Cranach natürlich. Hieronymus in der Wildernis*. Innsbruck: Haymon, 2018, 108–17.

Talbot, Charles, ed. *Dürer in America*. Washington DC: National Gallery, 1971.

Talbot, Charles, 'Dürer and the High Art of Printmaking'. In Silver and Smith, eds, *The Essential Dürer*, 33–61.

Tebbe, Karin, Ursula Timann and Thomas Eser, eds. *Nürnberger Goldschmiedekunst 1541–1868*, 2 vols. Nuremberg: Verlag des Germanischen Nationalmuseums, 2007.

Tebbe, Karin. 'Nürnberger Goldschmiedekunst – Formtypen und stilistische Entwicklung'. In Tebbe, Timann and Eser, eds, *Nürnberger Goldschmiedekunst*, 165–95.

Teget-Welz, Manuel. *Ingeniosus Magister. Der Augsburger Bildhauer Gregor Erhart.* Petersberg: Michael Imhof Verlag, 2021.

Teja-Bach, Friedrich. *Struktur und Erscheinung: Untersuchungen zu Dürers graphischer Kunst.* Berlin: Mann, 1996.

Terjanian, Pierre. 'Princely Armor in the Age of Dürer: A Renaissance Masterpiece in the Philadelphia Museum of Art'. *Philadelphia Museum of Art Bulletin* 5 (2011), 1–54.

—. 'The Currency of Power: The Central Place of Armor in the Ambitions and Life of Maximilian I'. In Terjanian, ed., *The Last Knight*, 17–37.

Terjanian, Pierre, ed. *The Last Knight: The Art, Armor, and Ambition of Maximilian I.* New York, NY: Metropolitan Museum of Art, 2019.

Thausing, Moriz. *Albrecht Dürer, His Life and Works*, 2 vols, trans. Frederick Alexis Eaton. London: J. Murray, 1882.

Thimann, Michael. 'Erinnerung an das Fremde: Jean Jacques Boissards Trachtenbuch für Johann Jakob Fugger: Zu Provenienz und Zuschreibung der Bildhandschrift Cod. Oct. 193 in der Herzogin Anna Amalia Bibliothek in Weimar'. *Marburger Jahrbuch für Kunstwissenschaft* 32 (2005), 117–48.

Thompson, Jeremy. 'The Solar History of Acedia in the Latin Middle Ages and its Intersection with Melancholy in Henry Suso'. *History of European Ideas* 47 (2021), 850–70.

Thornton, Dora. *The Scholar in his Study. Ownership and Experience in Renaissance Italy.* New Haven, CT: Yale University Press, 1997.

Tlusty, B. Ann. *Bacchus and Civic Order: The Culture of Drink in Early Modern Germany.* Charlottesville, VA: University of Virginia Press, 2001.

Trexler, Richard C. *The Journey of the Magi: Meanings in History of a Christian Story.* Princeton, NJ: Princeton University Press, 1997.

Tricot, Xavier. *Van Patinir tot Ribera. De heilige Hiëronymus in woord en beeld.* Antwerp: VZW Museum Nicolaas Rockox, 2014.

van den Brink, Peter, ed. *Dürer war Hier: eine Reise wird Legende.* Aachen: Michael Imhof Verlag, 2021.

Vasari, Giorgio. *The Lives of the Most Excellent Painters, Sculptors, and Architects*, 2 vols., ed. Philip Jacks, trans. Gaston du C. De Vere. New York: Modern Library, 2006.

Vasari, Giorgio. *Le vite de' più eccellenti pittori, scultori ed architettori*, 9 vols, ed. Gaetano Milanesi. Florence: G. C. Sansoni, 1906.

Vavra, Elisabeth. 'Bildmotiv und Frauenmystik – Funktion und Rezeption'. In Peter Dinzelbacher and Dieter R. Bauer, eds, *Frauenmystik im Mittelalter*. Ostfildern: Schwabenverlag, 1985, 201–30.

Veil, Helmut. *Künstler, Kriege und Kanonen Eine kulturhistorische Analyse von Dürers 'Landschaft mit Kanone'.* Frankfurt am Main: Humanities Online. 2021.

Vogt, Christine. *Das druckgraphische Bild nach Vorlagen Albrecht Dürers (1471–1528). zum Phänomen der graphischen Kopie (Reproduktion) zu Lebzeiten Dürers nördlich der Alpen.* Munich: Deutscher Kunstverlag, 2008.

Walcher von Molthein, Alfred. 'Arbeiten der Nürnberger Hafnerfamilie'. *Kunst und Kunsthandwerk* 8 (1905), 134–42.

Warburg, Aby. *Sandro Botticellis 'Geburt der Venus' und 'Frühling': Eine Untersuchung über die Vorstellung von der Antike in der italienischen Renaissance.* Hamburg and Leipzig: Voss, 1893.

Ward, F. A. B. *A Catalogue of European Scientific Instruments in the Department of Medieval and Later Antiquities of the British Museum.* London: British Museum Publications, 1981.

Warncke, Carsten-Peter. *Die ornamentale Groteske in Deutschland, 1500–1625.* 2 vols. Berlin: Spiess, 1979.

Watson, Gilbert. *Theriac and Mithridatium. A Study in Therapeutics.* London: Wellcome Medical Library, 1966.

Weiss, Roberto. 'Jan van Eyck's "Albergati" Portrait', *Burlington Magazine* 97, 626 (1955), 145–7.

Welch, Evelyn. *Shopping in the Renaissance: Consumer Cultures in Italy 1400–1600.* New Haven, CT: Yale University Press, 2005.

Wenderhorst, Alfred. 'Nuremberg, the Imperial City: From its Beginnings to the End of its Glory'. In Kahsnitz and Wixom, eds, *Gothic and Renaissance Art in Nuremberg*, 11–26.

West, Ashley. 'Albrecht Dürer, Hans Burgkmair and the Practice of Early Etching'. *Print Quarterly* 30.4 (2013), 379–95.

Westermann, Ekkehard. 'Das "Journal" der Nürnberger Handelsgesellschaft Hans Walther, Wolfgang Berger und Nikolaus Finch von 1512/13'. *Mitteilungen des Vereins für Geschichte der Stadt Nürnberg* 58 (1971), 116–20.

The Whitworth Art Gallery: The First Hundred Years. Manchester: Whitworth Art Gallery, 1989.

Wickram, Georg. 'Rollwagenbüchlin (1555)'. In Hans-Gert Roloff, ed., *Georg Wickram: Sämtliche Werke.* Berlin: De Gruyter, 1967–73.

Wiener, Claudia, Anna Scherbaum and Georg Drescher, eds. *Dürers Marienleben - Andachtsliteratur als Künstlerbuch: eine Ausstellung der Bibliothek Otto Schäfer zu einem Buchprojekt des Nürnberger Humanismus.* Schweinfurt: Bibliothek Otto Schäfer, 2005.

Wilckens, Leonie von. 'Ein Modelbuch von 1517 aus dem Nürnberger Clarenkloster'. *Anzeiger des Germanischen Nationalmuseums* (1967), 27–9.

—. *Die textilien Künste: Von der Spätantike bis um 1500.* Munich: C. H. Beck, 1991.

Willers, Johannes. 'Bemerkungen zu Albrecht Dürers Interesse an Waffen, Kriegstechniken und Festungsbau'. *Anzeiger des Germanischen Nationalmuseums* (1976), 72–6.

Williams, A. R. 'The Metallographic Examination of a Burgkmair Etching Plate in the British Museum'. *Historical Metallurgy: Journal of the Historical Metallurgical Society* 8.2 (1974), 92–4.

Williams, Robert. *Art, Theory and Culture in Sixteenth-Century Italy: From Techne to Metatechne.* Cambridge: Cambridge University Press, 1997.

Wilson, Adrian, *The Making of the Nuremberg Chronicle*. Amsterdam: Nico Israel, 1977.

Wood, Christopher. *Albrecht Altdorfer and the Origins of Landscape*. Chicago, IL: University of Chicago Press, 1993.

—. 'Maximilian I as Archeologist'. *Renaissance Quarterly* 58.4 (2005), 1128–74.

Wood, Christopher, ed. *The Vienna School Reader: Politics and Art Historical Method in the 1930s*. New York, NY: Zone Books, 2003.

Wouk, Edward H., ed. *Imprinting the Imagination: Northern Renaissance Prints from the Holtorp Collection*. Manchester: The John Rylands Library, 2014.

—. *Marcantonio Raimondi, Raphael and the Image Multiplied*. Manchester: Manchester University Press, 2016.

Wouk, Edward H. 'Toward an Anthropology of Print'. In Schmidt and Wouk, eds, *Prints in Translation*, 1–18.

Zander-Seidel, Jutta. *Textiler Hausrat: Kleidung und Haustextilien in Nürnberg von 1500–1650*. Munich: Deutscher Kunstverlag, 1990.

Zdanowicz, Irena, ed. *Albrecht Dürer in the Collection of the National Gallery of Victoria*. Melbourne: National Gallery of Victoria, 1994.

Zika, Charles. 'Nuremberg: The City and its Culture in the Early Sixteenth Century'. In Zdanowicz, ed., *Albrecht Dürer in the Collection of the National Gallery of Victoria*, 28–44.

—. 'Dürer's Witch, Riding Women and Moral Order'. In Eichberger and Zika, eds, *Dürer and His Culture*, 118–40.

—. *The Appearance of Witchcraft: Print and Visual Culture in Sixteenth-Century Europe*. London: Routledge, 2007.

Zinner, Ernst. *Regiomontanus: His Life and Work*, trans. Ezra Brown. Amsterdam: North-Holland, 1990.

Zitzlsperger, Philipp. *Dürers Pelz und das Recht im Bild: Kleiderkunde als Methode der Kunstgeschichte*. Berlin: Akademie Verlage, 2008.

Zuidervaart, Huib J., and Marlise Rijks. '"Most rare workmen": Optical Practitioners in Early Seventeenth-Century Delft'. *The British Journal for the History of Science* 48.1 (2015), 53–85.

Index